Lecture Notes in Business Information Processing 85

Christian Huemer
Thomas Setzer (Eds.)

E-Commerce and Web Technologies

12th International Conference, EC-Web 2011
Toulouse, France, August 30 - September 1, 2011
Proceedings

Springer

Volume Editors

Christian Huemer
Vienna University of Technology
Institute of Software Technology and Interactive Systems
Business Informatics Group (BIG)
Favoritenstr. 9 - 11 / 188-3
1040 Vienna, Austria
E-mail: huemer@big.tuwien.ac.at

Thomas Setzer
Technical University Munich
Institute of Computer Science
Decision Sciences and Systems (DSS)
Boltzmannstr. 3
85748 Garching, Germany
E-mail: setzer@in.tum.de

ISSN 1865-1348 e-ISSN 1865-1356
ISBN 978-3-642-23013-4 e-ISBN 978-3-642-23014-1
DOI 10.1007/978-3-642-23014-1
Springer Heidelberg Dordrecht London New York

Library of Congress Control Number: 2011933559

ACM Computing Classification (1998): J.1, K.4.4, I.2.11, H.3.5, H.4

Typesetting: Camera-ready by author, data conversion by Scientific Publishing Services, Chennai, India

Printed on acid-free paper

Springer is part of Springer Science+Business Media (www.springer.com)

Message from the General Chairs

We welcome you to the proceedings of the 12th International Conference on Electronic Commerce and Web Technologies—EC-Web 2011—which took place at IRIT, Paul Sabatier University in Toulouse, France from August 29 to September 2, 2011.

EC-Web 2011 provided a platform for researchers and practitioners interested in the theory and practice of e-commerce and Web technologies. In order to address a broad range of topics we invited paper submissions in a number of tracks, each dedicated to a special area in e-commerce. The Recommender Systems Track called for papers on new trends and challenges to support both customers and providers in making better business decisions. The Agent-Based E-Commerce Track sought for trends and concerns on computer systems that are capable of autonomous actions in order to meet their design objectives. The Business Services and Process Management Track put its focus on the alignment of business and IT allowing smoother business operations and business processes. The Semantic E-Business Track was centered around managing knowledge for the coordination of E-business processes through the systematic application of Semantic Web technologies. Finally, the E-Business Architectures Track looked for approaches leveraging Web technologies to implement mission-critical e-business systems.

This year's EC-Web conference joined the success of the previous joint conferences. We were happy to see that our community was still active in sharing their research on future trends in e-commerce and Web technologies. This fact is underpinned by the 60 submissions from authors of 21 countries to the various tracks of the conference. Each submission received at least three review reports from Program Committee members, whereby the reviews were based on four criteria—originality, quality, relevance, and presentation—which resulted in a recommendation of each reviewer. Based on these recommendations the Track Chairs selected 25 papers for publication and presentation at EC-Web 2011. Accordingly, the acceptance rate of EC-Web 2011 was about 41%.

Similar to past conferences, presentations on innovative research results and contributions on a broad range of topics in e-commerce and Web technologies were sought. These presentations were organized in eight sessions:

- Semantic Services
- Business Processes and Services
- Context-Aware Recommender Systems
- Collaborative Filtering and Preference Learning
- Social Recommender Systems
- Innovative Strategies for Preference Elicitation and Profiling
- Intelligent Agents and E-Negotiation Systems
- Agent Interaction and Trust Management

A scientific conference always depends on the volunteer efforts of a large number of individuals. We are grateful that many dedicated persons were willing to join our team. Our special thanks go to our Track Chairs Marco de Gemmis, Birgit Hofreiter, Jörg Leukel, Fernando Lopes, and Pasquale Lops who nominated a prestigious Program Committee with members from all over the globe. We are grateful to the members of this Program Committee who devoted a considerable amount of their time in reviewing the submissions to EC-Web 2011.

We were privileged to work together with highly motivated people to arrange the conference and to publish these proceedings. We appreciate all the tireless support by the Publicity Chair Christian Pichler for announcing our conference on various lists. Special thanks go to Amin Anjomshoaa who was always of great help in managing the conference submission system. Last, but not least, we want to express our thanks to Gabriela Wagner who dedicated hours and hours in making EC-Web 2011 a success. Not only was she always of great help in solving organizational matters, but she also maintained the EC-Web 2011 Website and was responsible for the compilation of all the papers in the proceedings.

We hope that you will find these proceedings a valuable source of information on E-Commerce and Web technologies.

June 2011

Christian Huemer
Thomas Setzer

Organization

General Co-chairs

Christian Huemer	Vienna University of Technology, Austria
Thomas Setzer	Technische Universität München, Germany

Track Chairs

Track: E-Business Architectures

Christian Huemer	Vienna University of Technology, Austria

Track: Semantic E-Business

Jörg Leukel	University of Hohenheim, Germany

Track: Business Services and Process Management

Birgit Hofreiter	University of Liechtenstein, Liechtenstein

Track: Recommender Systems

Marco de Gemmis	University of Bari "Aldo Moro", Italy
Pasquale Lops	University of Bari "Aldo Moro", Italy

Track: Agent-Based E-Commerce

Fernando Lopes	National Research Institute, Portugal

Publicity Chair

Christian Pichler	Research Studios Austria

Program Committee

Track: E-Business Architectures

Brian Blake	University of Notre Dame, USA
Kuo-Ming Chao	University of Coventry, UK
Ernesto Damiani	Universitá degli Studi di Milano, Italy
Clemens van Dinther	Karlsruhe Institute of Technology, Germany
Patrick Hung	University of Ontario, Canada
Christian Markl	TU Munich, Germany
Szabolcs Rozsnyai	IBM Research

Michael Strommer	Research Studios Austria
Andreas Wombacher	University of Twente, The Netherlands
Jih-Shyr Yih	IBM Research, USA
Marco Zapletal	TU Vienna, Austria

Track: Semantic E-Business

Maria Laura Caliusco	Universidad Tecnológica Nacional, Argentina
Jen-Yao Chung	IBM Thomas J. Watson Research Center, USA
Diogo R. Ferreira	IST - Technical University of Lisbon, Portugal
Agata Filipowska	Poznan University of Economics, Poland
Jingzhi Guo	University of Macau, Macau
Andre Ludwig	University of Leipzig, Germany
Alex Norta	University of Helsinki, Finland
Jun Shen	University of Wollongong, Australia
Yan Tang	VUB STARLab, Belgium

Track: Business Services and Process Management

Francesco Buccafurri	University of Reggio Calabria, Italy
Cinzia Cappiello	University of Milan, Italy
Sven Casteleyn	Universidad Politécnica de Valencia, Spain
Marco Commuzzi	Technical University Eindhoven, The Netherlands
Florian Daniel	University of Trento, Italy
Paolo Giorgini	University of Trento, Italy
Chang Heng	Huawei Technologies Co. Ltd., P.R. China
Philipp Liegl	TU Vienna, Austria
Heiko Ludwig	IBM Research, USA
Uwe Zdun	University of Vienna, Austria
Christian Zirpins	University of Karlsruhe, Germany

Track: Recommender Systems

Sarabjot Singh Anand	University of Warwick, UK
Liliana Ardissono	University of Turin, Italy
Giuliano Armano	University of Cagliari, Italy
Pierpaolo Basile	University of Bari "Aldo Moro", Italy
Bettina Berendt	KU Leuven, Belgium
Shlomo Berkovsky	CSIRO, Australia
Robin Burke	De Paul University, USA
Ivan Cantador	Universidad Autónoma de Madrid, Spain
Pablo Castells	Universidad Autónoma de Madrid, Spain
Federica Cena	University of Turin, Italy
Antonina Dattolo	University of Udine, Italy

Ernesto William De Luca	DAI-Labor, Germany
Alexander Felfernig	University Klagenfurt, Austria
Michele Gorgoglione	Polytechnic of Bari, Italy
Leo Iaquinta	University of Bari "Aldo Moro", Italy
Dietmar Jannach	Dortmund University of Technology, Germany
Robert Jäschke	University of Kassel, Germany
Alípio Mário Jorge	University of Porto, Portugal
Alfred Kobsa	University of California, Irvine, USA
Stuart E. Middleton	University of Southampton, UK
Bamshad Mobasher	De Paul University, USA
Cosimo Palmisano	Ecce Customer, Italy
Umberto Panniello	Polytechnic of Bari, Italy
Roberto Pirrone	University of Palermo, Italy
Azzurra Ragone	Polytechnic of Bari, Italy
Francesco Ricci	Free University of Bozen-Bolzano, Italy
Giovanni Semeraro	University of Bari "Aldo Moro", Italy
Carlo Tasso	University of Udine, Italy
Eloisa Vargiu	University of Cagliari, Italy
Markus Zanker	University of Klagenfurt, Germany

Track: Agent-Based E-Commerce

Luis Botelho	Lisbon University Institute (ISCTE), Portugal
Alberto Fernández	University Rey Juan Carlos, Spain
Helder Manuel Ferreira Coelho	Instituto das Ciências da Complexidade, Portugal
Nicola Gatti	Politecnico di Milano, Italy
Massimiliano Giacomin	University of Brescia, Italy
Koen Hindriks	Delft University of Technology, The Netherlands
Souhila Kaci	Artois University, France
Paulo Leitão	Polytechnic Institute of Bragança, Portugal
Miguel Ángel López Carmona	University of Alcalá de Henares, Spain
Paulo Novais	University of Minho, Portugal
Nir Oren	University of Aberdeen, UK
Alexander Pokahr	University of Hamburg, Germany
Alberto Sardinha	Technical University of Lisbon, Portugal
Murat Sensoy	University of Aberdeen, UK
Paolo Torroni	University of Bologna, Italy
Laurent Vercouter	Graduate School of engineering, Saint-Étienne, France
Dongmo Zhang	University of Western Sydney, Australia

Table of Contents

Intelligent Agents and E-Negotiation Systems

Collaborative Filtering and Preference Learning

Social Recommender Systems

Agent Interaction and Trust Management

Innovative Strategies for Preference Elicitation and Profiling

A Conversational Approach to Semantic Web Service Selection

Friederike Klan and Birgitta König-Ries

Institute of Computer Science, Friedrich-Schiller-University Jena
{friederike.klan,birgitta.koenig-ries}@informatik.uni-jena.de

Abstract. Service consumers typically have no clear goal in mind when looking for service functionality and are not able to formulate their service needs in a formal or semi-formal language. We approach those issues by proposing a mechanism that implements semantic service selection as an incremental and interactive process alternating phases of intermediate service recommendation and requirements refinement by critiquing the presented alternatives. It thus facilitates the incremental construction of service requirements and their specification at an informal level. Our evaluation results demonstrate the effectiveness and efficiency of the proposed approach in an e-commerce domain.

Keywords: semantic web service selection, incremental, interactive.

1 Introduction

Semantic Web Services (SWSs) are an active area of research and are at the focus of numerous EU funded research projects . However, up to now virtually no real-world applications that use this technology are available [1]. This is particularly bad, since SWS technology and its advanced semantic description and discovery mechanisms have the potential to significantly improve existing retrieval-based applications such as required in e-commerce or web search. While Web Services (WSs) were originally envisioned for B2B applications, early on first ideas to also use them in B2C settings were developed [2, 3]. However, at this stage there are some serious barriers to the realization of this vision. In current SWS research, the focus is on the support of application developers and service providers. The end-users, i.e. service consumers, who require assistance in expressing their service needs and support in the subsequent process of service selection, are only marginally addressed. Hence, though SWS approaches provide adequate means to semantically describe service capabilities and in particular service needs, they require the user to do this at a formal, logic-based level that is not appropriate for many service consumers, e.g. in an e-commerce setting. Basic tools that support the task of requirements specification exist, but mainly address WS developers. Virtually, no end-user support for specifying service requirements is available. Moreover, existing approaches to SWS selection typically assume that service consumers have a clear goal in mind when looking for service functionality. However, as research results from behavioral decision

C. Huemer and T. Setzer (Eds.): EC-Web 2011, LNBIP 85, pp. 1–12, 2011.

theory indicate [4], this is often not true. Particularly, in service domains that are complex and unfamiliar, consumers have no clear-cut requirements and preferences. People rather construct them instantaneously when facing choices to be made [4]. Current SWS solutions do not account for those facts.

In this paper, we approach the addressed issues. We propose a mechanism that implements service selection as an incremental and interactive process with the service consumer. Inspired by conversational recommender systems [5] and example critiquing [6], it alternates phases of intermediate service recommendation and requirements refinement by critiquing the presented alternatives. It thus facilitates the incremental construction of service requirements. Moreover, it enables the user to specify his requirements at an informal level, either directly via a graphical representation of the requirements or indirectly by critiquing available service offers. Finally, the proposed solution considers the system's uncertainty that arises from incomplete and inaccurate knowledge about the user's true service requirements. We will show that by leveraging this information, the system is able to effectively direct and focus the requirements elicitation and specification process. As already argued, these are key requirements for the realization of SWS-based end-user applications. Our evaluation results will demonstrate the effectiveness and efficiency of the proposed approach in an e-commerce domain.

The remainder of the paper is structured as follows. As a basis for the further discussion, Sect. 3 briefly introduces the semantic service description language DSD [7] that underlies our approach. Sect. 4 constitutes the main part of the paper. It provides a detailed description of our approach to incremental and interactive service selection. After that, we present our evaluation results (Sect. 5), briefly comment on existing approaches and conclude with (Sect. 6).

2 Basic Idea

We suggest a solution that implements service selection as an iterative and interactive process that alternates phases of intermediate service recommendation and requirements refinement. During that process, the user incrementally develops his service requirements and preferences and finally makes a selection decision. To effectively support him in that tasks, the system maintains an internal model of the consumer's requirements, which we call *request model.* Uncertainty about the service consumer's true requirements is explicitly represented within this model. During the refinement process the request model is continuously updated to accurately reflect the systems's growing knowledge about the user's service requirements and preferences. Starting with a request model constructed from the user's initially specified service needs, the system determines the set of service alternatives that fit to these requirements. The service alternatives are determined by transforming the internal request model into a semantic service request that reflects the requirements specified in the model, but also the system's uncertainty about this model. We will demonstrate that standard matchmaking with a minor extension can be applied to retrieve matching service results sorted by their expected overall preference value. The user may then critique

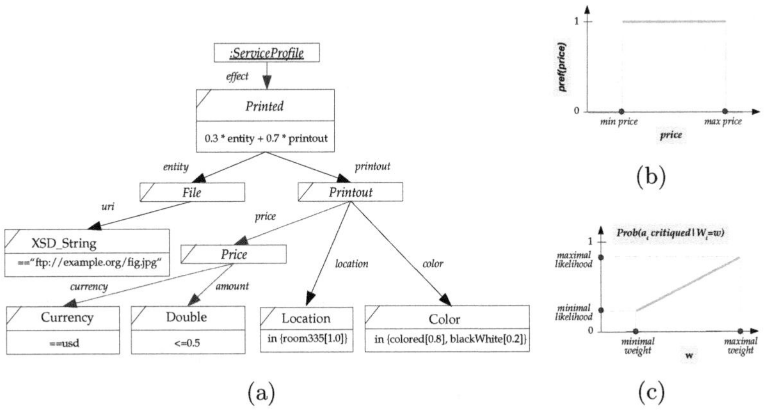

Fig. 1. DSD service request (a), preference function (b), linear likelihood function (c)

the presented service alternatives and thereby indicate desirable service characteristics. He can also specify new service requirements by directly modifying the internal request model via a graphical representation (not described in this paper). This will allow him to correct the system if necessary, will help him to become aware of his requirements and will enable him to actively develop them. All user interactions trigger appropriate model changes. Once modifications to the request model have been made, the user may decide to see service results fitting to the updated requirements. The process continues until the user finds an appropriate service among the presented alternatives or until he decides to stop without making a selection.

3 Diane Service Description

As a basis for the further discussion, we introduce the semantic service description language DSD (DIANE Service Description) [7] and its mechanisms for automatic semantic service matchmaking that underlie our approach. Similarly to other semantic service description approaches, DSD is ontology-based and describes the functionality a service provides as well as the functionality required by a service consumer by means of the precondition(s) and the possible effect(s) of a service execution. For instance, in the service request in Fig. 1(a), the desired effect is that something is printed after service execution. A single effect corresponds to a particular service instance that can be executed. While service offer descriptions describe the individual service instances that are offered by a service provider, e.g. possible printing jobs offered by a printer, service request descriptions declaratively characterize service instances that are acceptable for a consumer. In the service request in Fig. 1(a), acceptable instances are printing jobs that print the file located at "ftp://example.org/fig.jpg", that cost at most 0.5$ and where the printout is either colored or black-and-white and located at room 335.

As can be seen in the example, DSD utilizes a specific mechanism to declaratively and hierarchically characterize (acceptable) service effects. Service effects are described by means of their attributes, such as price or color. Each attribute has an ontological type and may be constrained by direct conditions on its values and by conditions on its subattributes. For instance, the attribute printout is constrained by a condition on its subattribute location, which indicates that only printouts located at room 335 are acceptable. The direct condition <= 0.5 on the price amount in Fig. 1(a) indicates that only prices lower than 0.5$ are acceptable. Attribute conditions induce a tree-like and more and more fine-grained characterization of acceptable service effects, where possible attributes as well as their required type are defined in an ontology. A DSD request does not only specify which service effects are acceptable, but also indicates to which degree they are acceptable. In this context, direct conditions specify a preference value from $[0, 1]$ for each considered attribute value (the default is 1.0 (totally acceptable)). DSD also allows for the specification of connecting strategies that indicate how the preference values of a certain attribute's subattributes shall be combined (see e.g. the effect-attribute in Fig. 1(a)).

4 Incremental and Interactive Service Selection

Request Model. We propose a request model that builds on DSD request descriptions (Sect. 3). In particular, it inherits its tree structure with the typed service attributes as its nodes. This will later on allow us to use the DIANE matchmaker to compare the user's (uncertain) requirements with the offered service functionality. The request model supports three types of direct conditions on attribute values: range conditions, in- and not-in-conditions[1]. A range condition defines a range of acceptable values for a certain attribute, e.g. a range of acceptable prices, and a preference function that assigns a preference value to each possible value of this attribute. The preference function is parameterized with the minimum and the maximum value of the range. We do not make any assumptions about the type of this preference function. However, it should appropriately model the user's preferences. Fig. 1(b) shows a simple example of a preference function for the attribute price. In-conditions allow the user to specify attribute values that are acceptable for him as well as a preference value for each of those values, e.g. 0.8 for colored printouts. At this time, the request model implementation supports only weighted sum as a connecting strategy. Though DSD descriptions are well suited for modeling service requirements and preferences, they are not capable of representing uncertainty associated with the model. To compensate for that, we propose the following extension that allows to represent uncertainty about direct conditions and connecting strategies. We do not model uncertainty about the structure of a request. Uncertainty about range conditions is modeled by probability distributions $prob_{Min}(x)$ and $prob_{Max}(x)$, which provide the likelihood of attribute value x being the minimum/maximum of the range. In-conditions are modeled as a set of probabilities $\{Prob_{in}(x)\}$ over possible values x of an attribute, where the probability $Prob_{in}(x)$ provides the likelihood of attribute value x being

[1] Not considered in this paper.

acceptable for the user. The preference values $\{pref(x)|Prob_{in}(x) \neq 0\}$ for acceptable attribute values are user-provided. We do not consider uncertainty about a user's preference for a certain attribute value. Analogously, we cope with uncertainty related to connecting strategies. While their type is fixed to weighted sum, the parameters of the strategy, i.e. the weights are unknown. Uncertainty about those parameters is modeled by probability distributions $prob_{W_1}, \ldots, prob_{W_n}$, where $prob_{W_i}$ is a probability distribution over the possible weights of attribute a_i. Weights are absolute and taken from $[0, 1]$. The probability $prob_{W_i}(w)$ provides the likelihood of the weight for attribute a_i being w.

Uncertain Matchmaking. To understand how uncertain matchmaking based on the request model can take place, we first have to look at how certain, i.e. standard DSD service requests, are matched against available service offers. In the DIANE matchmaker [7], the comparison of the effect(s) described in the request and those described in the offer descriptions is recursive and proceeds as follows. Starting from the effect attribute of the request, the matchmaker checks in each step, whether the service effect(s) described in the offer fulfill(s) the conditions in the request. Proceeding to the leaves of the request results in a preference value for each of those attributes. In a final pass, those values are aggregated to an overall preference value ($\in [0, 1]$) for each offered service instance, i.e. to a preference value for the effect attribute a of the request. This value is recursively defined as the product of the matching degree $M_{type}(a)$ between the type of a and that of its corresponding offer attribute (the attribute lying on the same path), by the user's preference $Pref_{dc}(a)$ for the offered attribute values (specified in the direct conditions) and the aggregated preference value $Pref_{sub}(a)$ for the attribute's subattributes. The latter is determined by the connecting strategy specified for the attribute, i.e. a weighted sum of the subattributes' preference values.

The requirements specified in the request model are uncertain. In particular, there is uncertainty about the user's preference for the offered attribute values as well as uncertainty about the importance of attributes, i.e. the weights of the connecting strategies. Hence, uncertain matchmaking can only deliver an expected preference value for each offered service instance. We will show that only minor changes to the matchmaker are required to implement this. Using well-known properties of expected values, it can be easily shown that the expected aggregated preference value $\mathbb{E}(Pref_{sub}(a))$ of an attribute a's subattributes w.r.t. a given offer o, i.e. the expected weighted sum of its subattribute's preference values, is given by

$$\mathbb{E}(Pref_{sub}(a)) = \mathbb{E}\left(\frac{\sum_{i=1}^{n}(W_i \cdot Pref(a_i))}{\sum_{j=1}^{n} W_j}\right) = \sum_{i=1}^{n}\left(\frac{1}{\sum\limits_{j=1, j\neq i}^{n} \frac{\mathbb{E}(W_j)}{\mathbb{E}(W_i)} + 1} \cdot \mathbb{E}(Pref(a_i))\right),$$

where $\mathbb{E}(W_i)$ is the expected weight of subattribute a_i and $\mathbb{E}(Pref(a_i))$ its expected preference value. Hence, assuming that the matchmaker is provided with the expected preference values for the offered attribute values (needed to compute $Pref_{dc}(a)$), it will return the expected preference value of the request model, when receiving a request whose attribute weights w_i' are defined by $1/\sum_{j=1,j\neq i}^{n}\frac{\mathbb{E}(W_j)}{\mathbb{E}(W_i)}+1$ as input. This is convenient, since we achieve the desired matchmaking functionality by simply transforming the request model into a standard DSD request. We do not have to make any changes to the matchmaker's implementation. Unfortunately, the expected preference values for the offered attribute values cannot always be pre-computed. Provided that a direct condition has been specified for a given attribute, the expected preference value $\mathbb{E}(Pref(x))$ for an offered attribute value x is given by $Prob_{in}(x)\cdot pref(x)$. Consequently, it is sufficient to provide those expected values for all attribute values that are specified in an in-condition to the matchmaker. The expected preference value $\mathbb{E}(Pref(x))$ of an element x, when given a range condition with the distributions $prob_{Min}$ and $prob_{Max}$ and a preference function *pref(x)* as depicted in Fig. 1(b) is given by

$$\mathbb{E}(Pref(x)) = Prob_{(Min<x)\wedge(Max\geq x)} = \int_{z=0}^{x} prob_{Min}(z)dz\cdot(1-\int_{z=0}^{x} prob_{Max}(z)dz).$$

Since we cannot pre-calculate this value for all attribute values that might potentially appear in an offer, we have to supply the matchmaker with a routine that computes this preference value to implement this. Summarizing, we can state that matching uncertain service requirements as specified in the request model can be implemented by generating a standard DSD service request with the properties detailed above and matching it with a slightly modified version of the standard matchmaker.

Adjusting the Service Results. Once the service offers, that match to the requirements that are specified in the request model, have been retrieved, the list of those offers sorted by their expected overall preference value is presented to the user (Fig. 2 left). This result table includes a column for each service attribute that is specified within the request model. The cells of a column show either the value of the corresponding attribute as specified in the depicted offer or the type of the attribute, if no value has been specified. Columns can be hidden and sorted to facilitate decision making. Besides viewing these service offers, the user may indicate desirable service characteristics based on the presented alternatives. The system supports three ways of doing this: (1) by adding a not yet specified attribute to the request model, (2) by refining, i.e. subtyping, an attribute's type and (3) by critiquing one of the listed service offers. To support the first two interaction opportunities, the system suggests the user a list of service attributes and attribute types that are specified in the matching service offers, but have not yet been included into the request model (Fig. 2 right). The suggested attributes are restricted to those that can be directly added as a subattribute to one of the service attributes that are already part of the request model. As soon as the user selects an attribute or a type, the request model is updated accordingly, matching offers are retrieved and presented to the user. In addition to these interaction opportunities, the user may select a service from

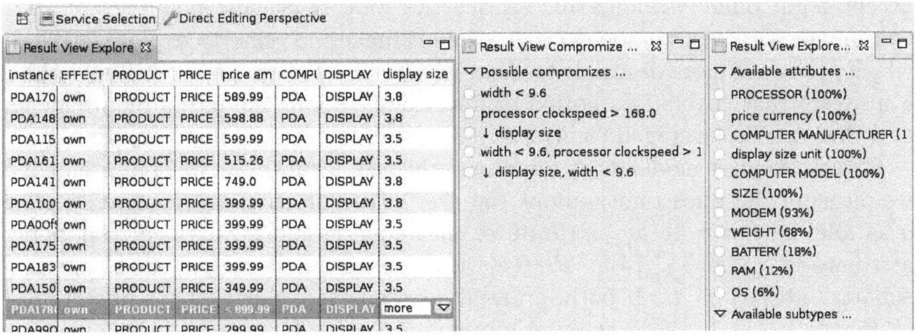

Fig. 2. Result view

the presented list of offers that fits reasonably well to his requirements. He may then indicate desirable service properties relative to this offer. For example, the user might indicate that the offer is fine, but too expensive (Fig. 2 left). This can be done by simply clicking on the referenced attribute value. Based on the indicated property and the properties of the available service alternatives that fulfill this requirement, the system produces a list of trade-off alternatives on other service aspects that the user has to accept when insisting on the indicated requirement. For example the system might indicate that the user has to accept a lower display size when critiquing on the price of a computer offer (Fig. 2 middle). After viewing the existing trade-off alternatives, the user can either decide to abandon his requirement, specify an additional requirement on the same service offer or he indicates that he is willing to accept one of the presented trade-off alternatives by clicking it. While the second option will lead to another set of trade-off alternatives that are produced by taking both requirements of the user into account, the third option will result in a model update reflecting the information provided by the user. In this context, trade-offs do not necessarily refer to service aspects that have been already considered in the request model, but may also refer to service attributes that have not yet been specified by the user. In this case, the value of the compromised attribute is depicted within the trade-off alternative. The presented feature encourages the user to make compromises where necessary and helps him in identifying yet unconsidered, but important service aspects. Presenting details on the implementation of this feature is out of the scope of this paper.

To effectively reduce uncertainty about the user's service requirements, we propose to direct and focus the process of requirements elicitation by suggesting those interaction opportunities to the user that have a high potential to increase the system's knowledge about the consumer's service requirements, i.e. his preferences for the available offers. Thereby, knowledge acquisition should concentrate on those aspects of the user's requirements that are relevant in light of the available service options and in light of the user's known requirements. Consider for example a flight booking scenario. If all available services offer food during the flight, then there is no need to know whether the user would also accept flight offers without this service. As well, if price is not relevant to a consumer's service selection decision, then it makes no sense to explore in detail which prices are more desirable for this user. In this paragraph, we will introduce a measure that covers this notion of uncertainty about the user's requirements and that can be leveraged to identify promising interaction opportunities.

Given a request model, that represents the user's known service requirements, we measure the uncertainty about the user's true preference for a service offer o as follows. Let a be an attribute of the request model, a' its corresponding attribute in o and $\sum_{i=1}^{n} W_i \cdot \mathit{Pref}(a_i)$ the connecting strategy defined over a's subattributes a_1 to a_n. If both, a and a' are specified, the system's uncertainty $U(\mathit{Pref}(a)) \in [0,1]$ about the user's preference value for o w.r.t. a is defined as the product of $M_{type}(a)$ and

$$U(\mathit{Pref}_{dc}(a)) \cdot U(\mathit{Pref}_{sub}(a)) \oplus \mathbb{E}(\mathit{Pref}_{dc}(a)) \cdot U(\mathit{Pref}_{sub}(a)) \oplus \mathbb{E}(\mathit{Pref}_{sub}(a)) \cdot U(\mathit{Pref}_{dc}(a)),$$

where $a \oplus b = a + b - a \cdot b$ and a higher value indicates higher uncertainty[2]. The intuition behind this definition is that the uncertainty about the user's preference value w.r.t. the attribute a is high, if and only if $M_{type}(a)$ is high and we either do not know much about both, $\mathit{Pref}_{dc}(a)$ and $\mathit{Pref}_{sub}(a)$, (first term), we are quite sure that the preference $\mathit{Pref}_{dc}(a)$ is high, but we do not know much about $\mathit{Pref}_{sub}(a)$ (second term) or we are quite sure that $\mathit{Pref}_{sub}(a)$ is high, but we do not know much about $\mathit{Pref}_{dc}(a)$ (third term). In case just a' is specified, we define $U(\mathit{Pref}(a)) = 1$. The uncertainty $U(\mathit{Pref}_{sub}(a))$ about the aggregated preference value for a's subattributes w.r.t. o is recursively defined by

$$U(\mathit{Pref}_{sub}(a)) = U(S_1) \cdot U(S_{2n}) \oplus \overline{\mathbb{E}(S_1)} \cdot U(S_{2n}) \oplus \overline{\mathbb{E}(S_{2n})} \cdot U(S_1),$$

where $S_i := W_i \cdot \mathit{Pref}(a_i)$, $S_{jn} := \sum_{i=j}^{n} W_i \cdot \mathit{Pref}(a_i)$ and $\mathbb{E}(S_{jn})$ and $\mathbb{E}(S_i)$ are the corresponding expected values. This means that the system's uncertainty about the aggregated preference value for a's subattributes is high, if either, the uncertainty about all the subattributes' preference values and weights is high (first term), the uncertainty about the preference values and weights of the subattributes a_2 to a_n is high and we are quite sure that S_1 is low (second term) or the uncertainty about the preference value and weight of subattribute a_1 is high and we are quite sure that S_{2n} is low (third term). The uncertainty $U(S_i)$ about the value of the product $W_i \cdot \mathit{Pref}(a_i)$ is similarly defined by

$$U(S_i) = U(W_i) \cdot U(\mathit{Pref}(a_i)) \oplus \mathbb{E}(W_i) \cdot U(\mathit{Pref}(a_i)) \oplus U(W_i) \cdot \mathbb{E}(\mathit{Pref}(a_i)).$$

The uncertainty $U(W_i)$ about the weight W_i is defined to be the Shanon entropy of the probability distribution $prob_{W_i}$ normalized to the interval $[0,1]$. Thanks to the tree-structure of DSD service offers and the request model, we can determine the system's uncertainty about the user's true preference for the service offer o w.r.t. the given request model by recursively computing $U(a)$ for the effect attribute a of o. Based on the proposed measure, we can determine those interaction opportunities, i.e. those subtypes, subattributes and trade-off alternatives, that, when

[2] We omit details about the definition of $U(\mathit{Pref}_{dc}(a))$.

selected, have the highest potential to reduce the system's uncertainty about the consumer's preferences for the offered services, and offer them to the user.

Model Update. Since the implementation of structural updates to the request model, e.g. when adding an attribute, is straight forward, we focus on the update of the probability distributions maintained within the model. We start with the weight distributions. Upon the addition of an attribute to the request model, a corresponding uniform probability distribution for its weight is created. This probability distribution is affected by two types of interactions, namely, either because the user directly adjusted the weight of the attribute via the graphical representation of the request model or because the user chose a compromise after critiquing one of the listed service offers. In both cases, a Bayesian update on the affected weight distributions is performed. The updated distribution is given by $prob_{W_i}(w|interaction) = c \cdot Prob(interaction|W_i{=}w) \cdot prob_{W_i}(w)$, where $prob_{W_i}(w)$ is the distribution before the update, $Prob(interaction|W_i{=}w)$ is the likelihood function indicating the likelihood of observing the interaction when the attribute's true weight is w and c is a normalizing constant. If a compromise was chosen by the user, the weight distributions of the critiqued and compromised attributes are adjusted. Weight distributions for attributes that have not yet been considered in the request model are created. In case of the critiqued attributes, we use a linear likelihood function increasing with the true weight w (see Fig. 1(c)). The intuition behind that is, that it is more likely that the user will critique an attribute, if it is important, i.e. it has a high weight. In case of the compromised attributes, we use the same update distribution, but reflected at its expected value. This is, because it is less likely that the user will compromise an attribute, if it is important, i.e. it has a high weight. Since the overall weight of an attribute is determined by the weights of all its parent attributes in the request model, we also adjust the weights of those attributes in a similar fashion. However, we reduce the impact of the update by decreasing *maxProb* the higher we get in the request model tree. We omit details on the direct model update via the graphical representation. The distributions related to range conditions are updated either when the user adjusts the minimum or maximum of the range via the graphical representation of the request model or when the user selected a compromise. In the latter case, the critiqued as well as the compromised attributes' range distributions are adjusted as indicated by the critiques and the chosen compromises. We omit details on this as well as on the update of the probabilities related to (not-)in-conditions.

5 Evaluation

In the evaluation, we wanted to find out, whether users that are not familiar with WSs and SWS descriptions were able to formulate their service needs by using our system, whether they were able to find the service functionality they desire and whether they felt supported in that task. To have a realistic set of services, we used information about computer items extracted from Amazon.com to generate semantic descriptions of services selling computer items.

We performed a preliminary evaluation with 5 test users. None of them was familiar with WSs. The test setting was inspired by [8]. Users were first asked to think about the type of service they would like to use. They were allowed to choose from 8 categories. Participants were then provided with a questionnaire containing questions related to their background and their initial service requirements. After a 5 minutes introduction into our system, the users were asked to use the tool to select the service offer that best suits to their requirements from a collection of 50 services. To make the choice more difficult, all offers presented to the user were taken from the selected service category. The users started with an empty request model, i.e. no specified attributes. Once a user made his final selection, he was asked to complete a second questionnaire comprising of questions about his (updated) service requirements, his confidence in the specified requirements and the selected service and questions related to the usefulness of the provided tool. To verify the suitability of the service that was selected by the user, we provided him with a list of all service offers and their properties. The participant was then asked to look through this list and check whether there is an offer other than the selected that fits better to his requirements. During the test, the user's interactions with the tool as well as the state of the internal request model was logged. Questions in the questionnaires were formulated as statements, where the users had to indicate their level of agreement on a scale from 1 (strongly disagree) to 5 (strongly agree). The presented evaluation results refer to the mean of the judgments for each question that have been provided by the users (indicated in brackets).

The test users indicated that the tool proposed in this paper was easy to use (3.8) and that they felt guided by it (4.0). They even preferred it over the e-commerce platforms they typically use (4.0). A comparison of the initial requirements specified by the participants and those they provided after having chosen a service offer by using the tool shows that the proposed system succeeded in stimulating the test users to develop and specify their requirements. In average, 8 attributes where specified by the users. The critiquing tool was averagely used 2.6 times per user. After having made their final choice, the test users had specified requirements on averagely 0.8 service aspects, they did not consider before. All of the participants changed the relative importance of their requirements and 80% changed their preferences related to the values of the considered service aspects. However, we were also interested in whether the participants did not just specify requirements, but also in whether they actually had the feeling that they learned more about their requirements and whether they felt confident about them. Moreover, we wanted to find out whether the test users actually made a good selection or whether they were just convinced of having made a good selection. As it turned out, the respondents indicated that they learned more about their requirements by using the tool (4.0) and felt confident about them (4.2). To evaluate the quality of the selection made by the participants, we compared the requirements they indicated after using the tool with those covered by the final request model maintained by the system. We also recorded the number of test users that switched to another service offer after having seen all available offers and their properties. As a result of our evaluation, we found that the conformance between the user specified requirements and those modeled by our system was high. In all cases, the internal request model covered all service aspects that were important to the user. Also the conformance between the relative importance of those aspects as indicated by the test person and that documented in the model, was high (at most one aspect's rank differed by one position). However, we found that 40% of the participants switched to a slightly different offer after having seen the complete list of available service offers. As it turned out, the reason for this was, that the finally selected offer was in fact better with respect to most of the service aspects that were important to the user, but did not provide information about some of them. As a result, the matchmaker did not mark those offers as match and hence did not present them to the user. However, it seems that this restriction is to strict and that consumers are willing to accept the risk that is associated with a selection that is based on incomplete information. Finally, we were interested in the amount of time that the test participants spent to select an offer via our tool. As it turned out, the users averagely required about 17 minutes to make a final selection. The respondents indicated that this amount of time was acceptable for them (4.2). These preliminary results show that the tool effectively supports potential service consumers in making a well-founded selection, even if they are unfamiliar with the concept of WSs and WS descriptions. For the future, we plan a follow-up study in another service domain and with more participants.

6 Related Approaches and Conclusion

Typically, approaches to SWS selection assume that application providers create generic request templates, that cover frequent service needs in a certain application domain at design time [9]. Since consumer requirements are various, even for a single application domain, it is unlikely, that a predefined template exists that can be instantiated to build a service request that accurately describes the user's service needs. Moreover, template-based approaches do not enable potential service consumers to develop their requirements. However, a number of approaches that provide advanced assistance with the specification and refinement of service requirements have been suggested. Colucci et al. [2] propose a visual interface for assisted and incremental refinement of OWL-based service requests. Though their approach provides advanced user support for service selection, it neither considers uncertainty about consumer requirements nor accounts for consumer preferences. Moreover, the process of requirements refinement is not directed to promising directions and does not encourage service consumers to make compromises between service aspects. With MobiXpl, Noppens et al. [3] propose a mobile user interface for personalized semantic service discovery, that facilitates the specification of service requirements as a set of preferences over service aspects and utilizes ontology-based preference relaxation techniques to avoid empty result sets. Unfortunately, the proposed solution implements a single shot approach, where preferences cannot be refined after viewing the matching results. Balke et al. [10] propose an approach that accounts for the fact that consumer requests might be incomplete. As a solution they suggest to automatically rewrite and expand service requests to retrieve additional services that might potentially fit to the user's needs. However, the user is not involved in that process and thus cannot actively construct his requirements.

The ideas of letting users critique presented alternatives and encouraging them to make compromises by clustering available alternatives by common trade-off properties, that have been presented in this paper, are not new and have been previously proposed in the area of recommender systems [11, 8]. Our work is inspired by those approaches, but largely differs from them. In particular, our system supports the user in the critiquing process by providing him with immediate feedback about the consequences of his critiquing wishes. This is in contrast to the solution of [8], where users can specify self-initiated critiques, which directly lead to model changes and of which they do not know whether they are reasonable in light of the available offers. Moreover, our solution allows to identify yet unconsidered, but important service aspects by selecting suggested compromises. A major difference to the mentioned solutions is that, by explicitly modeling the system's uncertainty about the consumers requirements, our system is able to effectively direct and focus the requirements elicitation process into promising directions. Finally, our approach enables the user to correct the requirements model maintained by the system by providing an intuitive graphical representation of the internal model. The mentioned approaches do not offer this opportunity and hence do not allow for model adjustments, if necessary.

References

1. Bachlechner, D., Fink, K.: Semantic web service research: Current challenges and proximate achievements. Intl. J. of Comp. Sci. and App. 5(3b), 117–140 (2008)
2. Colucci, S., Noia, T.D., Sciascio, E.D., Donini, F.M., Ragone, A., Rizzi, R.: A semantic-based fully visual application for matchmaking and query refinement in b2c e-marketplaces. In: Harper, R., Rauterberg, M., Combetto, M. (eds.) ICEC 2006. LNCS, vol. 4161, pp. 174–184. Springer, Heidelberg (2006)
3. Noppens, O., Luther, M., Liebig, T., Wagner, M., Paolucci, M.: Ontology-supported preference handling for mobile music selection. In: Workshop on Advances in Preference Handling (2006)
4. Payne, J.W., Bettman, J.R., Johnson, E.J.: The adaptive decision maker. Cambridge University Press, Cambridge (1993)
5. Smyth, B.: Case-based recommendation. The Adaptive Web, 342–376 (2007)
6. Burke, R.D., Hammond, K.J., Young, B.C.: The findme approach to assisted browsing. IEEE Expert 12, 32–40 (1997)
7. Küster, U., König-Ries, B., Klein, M., Stern, M.: Diane - a matchmaking-centered framework for automated service discovery, composition, binding and invocation. In: WWW (2007)
8. Chen, L., Pu, P.: Hybrid critiquing-based recommender systems. In: IUI (2007)
9. Agre, G.: INFRAWEBS designer – A graphical tool for designing semantic web services. In: Euzenat, J., Domingue, J. (eds.) AIMSA 2006. LNCS (LNAI), vol. 4183, pp. 275–289. Springer, Heidelberg (2006)
10. Balke, W.-T., Wagner, M.: Towards personalized selection of web services. In: WWW (2003)
11. Reilly, J., McCarthy, K., McGinty, L., Smyth, B.: Dynamic critiquing. In: Funk, P., González Calero, P.A. (eds.) ECCBR 2004. LNCS (LNAI), vol. 3155, pp. 763–777. Springer, Heidelberg (2004)

DS^3I - A Dynamic Semantically Enhanced Service Selection Infrastructure

Christoph Fritsch[1], Peter Bednar[2], and Günther Pernul[1,*]

[1] Department of Information Systems
University of Regensburg
93053 Regensburg, Germany
{christoph.fritsch,guenther.pernul}@wiwi.uni-regensburg.de
http://www-ifs.uni-regensburg.de

[2] Centre for Information Technologies
Technical University of Kosice
04200 Košice, Slovakia
peter.bednar@tuke.sk
http://www.ekf.tuke.sk

Abstract. Service-oriented computing (SOC), lately often in combination with business process modeling (BPM), is becoming reality in current enterprise systems. At the same time, process models do no longer only span different departments but more and more frequently multiple organizations. Current BPM approaches focus on syntactic specification of work flow structures and necessitate static service allocation during modeling time. Dynamic service allocation at runtime based on the semantics of service descriptions, however, allows for much more flexibility. This paper presents DS^3I as a concept and implementation for semantically enhanced dynamic service selection. DS^3I and its semantic middleware components are based upon an ESB and semantic annotations of services and allows for one-step service selection at runtime of a process.

Keywords: Dynamic Service Selection, Semantic Mediation, Global Service Infrastructures.

1 Introduction and Motivation

Today's companies are facing strong challenges in the markets. More and more companies are realizing that they can no longer operate as fully self-contained actors but have to advance their ways of doing business. They begin to reconsider their business structures and aim for flexible cross company business network structures to perform future business with anybody, anywhere, anytime[18]. Two major trends accompany this development: (1) *Process Modeling*, i.e. the investigation and structured graphical presentation of business processes (2) *Service Composition*, i.e. chaining and automated execution of services. Combined both

* The research leading to these results received funding from the European Community's Seventh Framework Programme under grant agreement no. 217098.

C. Huemer and T. Setzer (Eds.): EC-Web 2011, LNBIP 85, pp. 13–24, 2011.

technologies allow for automatic execution and control of business processes. The common approach to obtain such a executable process model is to first break down the overall process into single tasks, then assign appropriate electronic self-contained services and finally map their inputs and outputs. The allocation of services to tasks is static. The resulting executable process model together with references to all external services is then deployed to a work flow engine (WFE).

Consider for example an online shop that receives orders via a web application and passes order processing over to a WFE that executes BPEL processes. Order processing presumes communication with partner services for example for credit card verification or payment processing. Even if this kind of service is available from various providers, outage time or failures of the external services cause interruption of the overall order processing due to static assignment of partner links in the BPEL process. Thus service allocation at process modeling time brings along undesirable limitations: (1) It is susceptible to failures due to unavailable external services. Overall process execution fails if a single partner link is not available. (2) Newly published services cannot be considered in the process model without altering and redeploying it. Process modeling as the basis of controlled execution is essential but the trend towards intra- and inter-organizational service orientation necessitates more flexibility. Appropriate services have to be allocated at the latest possible point in time, i.e. at runtime of the process.

In this paper we present DS^{3}I as an approach for dynamic service selection and mediation as it is developed as part of the SPIKE project[1]. Using DS^{3}I process models do no longer (necessarily) establish static links between tasks and service instances but are rather built against generic service interfaces. Behind these facades, semantically enhanced dynamic service selection and allocation is performed. We particularly focus on non-intrusive dynamic service allocation, on the semantic description and resolving of services and the semantic and non-semantic mediation. DS^{3}I strives for suitability for legacy applications as 'real services' are just evolving in many organizations whereas thousands of legacy applications prove aptitude in everyday life.

The remainder of the paper is organized as follows: First we provide provides related work in Section 2. Section 3 summarizes the conceptual model before Sections 4 and 5 present the proposal in detail on the architectural level and implementation details of a prototype system, respectively. Finally, Section 6 draws conclusions and identifies current and future work.

2 Related Work

Schmidt et al. [16] noticed already back in 2005 that "SOA holds out the promise that services can be discovered [...] and bound together to form new and exciting, or simply more efficient applications". They developed two generic patterns: (1) The protocol switch pattern and (2) the service transformation pattern. Both

[1] `http://www.spike-project.eu`

allow for discovering suitable target services dynamically. However, as these patterns have not yet been broadly implemented, service discovery is still carried out before a client is developed or the business process is modeled and deployed. Most related and decisive approaches for dynamic service selection are presented below and improvements by semantic annotations are presented in section 2.3.

2.1 Degrees of Freedom

Both Alonso et al. [1] and Chang et al. [4] provide comprehensive classification schemes which uncover the main challenges. In combination both approaches cover the essential degrees of freedom for dynamic service selection approaches. Alonso et al. [1] distinguish between four concepts: (1) *Static Binding* is the concept current process modeling approaches , i.e. static allocation of services at modeling time. (2) *Dynamic Binding by Reference* depends on a variable defined in the process which contains a reference to the chosen service instance. (3) *Dynamic Binding by Lookup* employs service repositories to retrieve predefined services at runtime. Finally, (4) *Dynamic Operation Selection* in the authors grasp is a rather special case that deals with selecting different operations of the same service.

This classification focuses on service selection as part of the overall process and does not consider unequal responsibilities for modeling and service allocation and/or the need to modify service allocation criteria without modifying the process. Nevertheless, they realize the necessity to separate between process modeling and service allocation time. Chang et al. [4] provide a different classification of dynamic composition. They classify along the axes "decision time", i.e. the moment the decision is made , "target service visibility", i.e. if the set of service candidates is fixed or time-varying, and "provision of adaption method", i.e. if the target service can adopt to given service requests.

2.2 Dynamic Service Selection

Content-based routing (CBR) in Enterprise Service Buses (ESB) as mentioned by [15] and others is the most mature approach. Based on a service request messages' contents a component decides to which service instance a request is forwarded. DRESR [2] by Bai et al. introduces the idea of abstract routing paths (ARPs), where each service is identified by an URI and an abstract service name. An ARP is composed of abstract service names and is therefore not bound to particular service instances. To obtain concrete service instances, a central routing manager component selects a service instance from the pool of candidates for the given task. The Dynamic Wire Tap (DWT) approach by Wu et al. [20] builds upon the well-known EAI patterns Wire Tap, Enricher, Recipient List and Aggregator [8]. A service discovery engine retrieves a list of service candidates and forwards the request to the DWT component which in turn routes the request forward to one of the service candidates. CBR and DRESR, however, do not offer real dynamic service selection as the potential target services together with routing rules have to be statically defined beforehand and DWT depicts a rather cloudy low-level concept and demands for quite some adoptions.

Other approaches consider BPEL as a starting point: WS Binder [5] by Di Penta et al. binds tasks to proxy objects instead of service instances. During a pre-execution binding the proxy objects are initialized with service instances resulting in a quasi-static service allocation. VRESCo by [14] and [12] introduces an aspect-oriented extension for BPEL environments for monitoring and replacing partner links. While WS Binder does not consider transformation/mediation, VRESCo at least considers static, non-semantic transformation rules. It does, however, neither distinguish between abstract and concrete service interfaces nor does it harness semantic meta-data therefore potentially resulting in a big amount of complex static transformation rules.

The concept of Dynamic Composition Handlers (DCHs) by Chang et al.[3] builds upon an ESB and clearly separates between service interfaces specified in the process and realized interfaces. It does, however, only consider a BPEL-engine as service client. The ESB-based ProBus approach by Mietzner et al. [13] is a concept for policy-driven dynamic service selection. In contrast to other work, this approach mainly focuses on the definition of selection criteria. Following the ProBus idea, service requesters define their preferences in form of non-functional properties expressed as WS-Policy statements and the services are described by WSResourceProperties. ProBus matches the service requester's policy against resource properties of known services to obtain a service candidate.

2.3 Semantic Technologies

Improvements in the field of dynamic service selection gained from semantic technologies can be divided into two blocks: (1) Semantically annotated services and process models and (2) semantically supported mediation and resolving.

Semantically enhanced business process modeling and semantic ESB is in focus of several research initiatives, e.g. the Object Management Group or EU-fundend R&D projects such as STASIS or the SUPER project. Several rather mature but only scarcely used concepts exist. The *Resource Description Framework (RDF)* has primarily been designed as a meta-data data model for all kinds of (web) resources has become a standard semantic model for data interchange. *OWL-S* offers an ontology of services and aims at making semantic description, discovery and execution of services possible. The *Web Service Modeling Ontology (WSMO)* emerged as a result of several EU-funded research projects. Its main concepts are ontologies, web services, (service) goals and mediators. Finally, Semantic Annotations for WSDL and XML Schema *(SAWSDL)* forms a simple extension layer on top of WSDL that lets components specify their semantics.

Semantic process and service annotation alone does only provide the foundations for semantically enhanced dynamic service selection. As can be seen from the previous section, a number of authors pay attention to non-semantic dynamic service selection but only sporadically complete and comprehensive semantic approaches are published. Karastoyanova et al. [9] proposed a reference architecture for semantic business process management where they clearly distinguish between a process modeling and runtime environment. The reference architecture has later been implemented as an semantic service bus [10]. Fujii and

Suda [7] present another comprehensive framework for semantics-based dynamic service composition. The framework does neither embrace an prototype nor does it build upon an modeled processes and an ESB as infrastructure component. It considers user context information for service composition and allows users to formulate a request for an particular type of application in natural language.

3 Conceptual Model

The conceptual model of DS^3I is sketched in Fig. 1(b). The essential goal is dynamic service selection in a minimum-invasive way. The switch from static to dynamic service allocation shall not necessitate any modifications. Neither service requester, be it a stand-alone client application or a WFE, nor individual service instances shall be required to be modified. Instead, infrastructure components allow for dynamic service allocations.

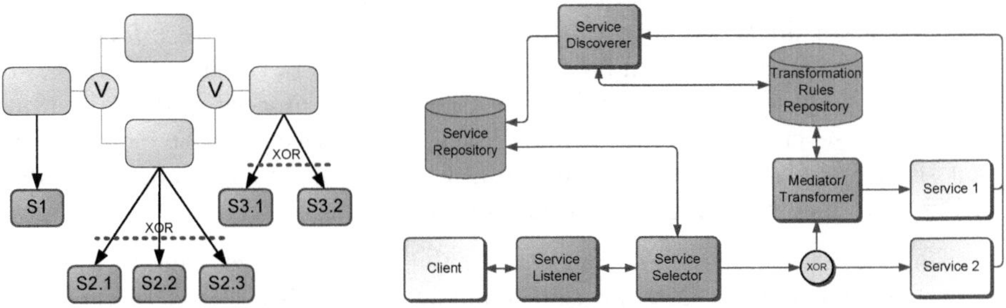

(a) Static Service Allocation (b) Service Selection and Mediation Scheme

Fig. 1. Static vs. Dynamic Service Allocation

Consequently, the conceptual model in Fig. 1(b) consists of two different types of components: (1) The white shaded actors depict unmodified parties that request or provide a given service. (2) The bluish shaded components depict components that facilitate the semantically supported dynamic service selection approach. These components are shielded by the infrastructure and are therefore neither visible for client nor service provider.

Details on components' functionality and implementation are illustrated in sections 4 and 5 so only a short overview is presented here: The *Service Listener* acts as a virtualized interface for a given type of service. We assume that service request messages are dispatched to these virtual services instead of concrete ones. Based on the request message and further selection criteria and non-functional properties, the *Service Selector* picks an appropriate service instance from the Service Repository. The *Service Repository* is charged with information and descriptions of available services via the *Service Discoverer* which in turn provides means for service providers to announce their services. As different services that provide the same functionality may vary in their interfaces and message format, the *Mediator/Transformer* mediates between clients' request messages and the

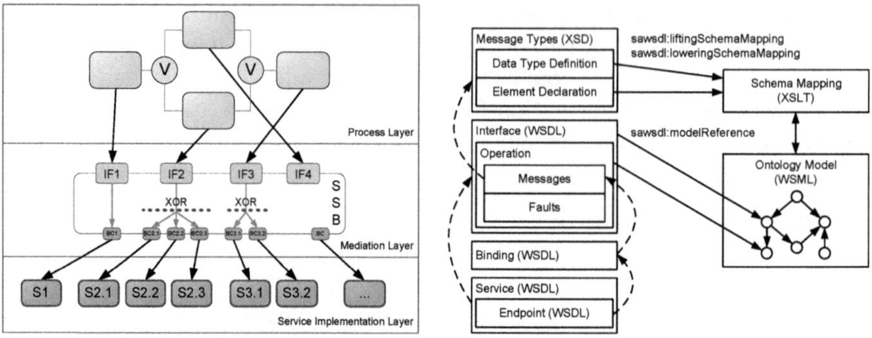

(a) 3-layered Operating Mode (b) Semantic Annotation of Services

Fig. 2. Operation Mode and Semantic Annotations

request messages expected by the selected service instance. It retrieves applicable transformation rules from the *Transformation Rules Repository* and transforms messages accordingly. We intentionally designed a comprehensive *infrastructure.* This way service selection can be delegated completely to the infrastructure, ensuring clear separation between different roles such as process modelers, service providers or service users. Applying the conceptual service selection model to current service binding concepts results in a 3-layered operating mode illustrated in Fig. 2(a). The three layers are organized as follows:

- The *Process Layer* focuses on modeling the business process and its stepwise refinement. Furthermore, process deployment to a WFE as well as execution monitoring is conducted at this layer. Different tasks of executable processes are linked to virtual service interfaces provided by DS^3I.
- The *Mediation Layer* forms the core of DS^3I. It provides generic interfaces (IF1 through IF4 in Fig. 2(a)) against which the process is linked and holds links (BC1 through BC4 in Fig. 2(a)) to all available service instances that form the pool of service candidates. As a result, the mediation layer mediates between virtualized service interfaces and concrete service instances.
- Actors on the *Service Implementation Layer* implement inquired functionality in form of services. Each service instance realizes an interface which is described and registered with DS^3I.
- A *Management Layer* is orthogonal to the other layers and therefore not displayed in Fig. 2(a). At this layer the service instances are announced to the mediation layer and the criteria and non-functional properties that determine the service selection procedure are defined.

4 Architecture

The overall architecture resulting from this conceptual model is depicted in Fig. 3. It consists of a service requester, several interchangeable service candidates and an extended enterprise service bus as a semantically supported dynamic service selection infrastructure.

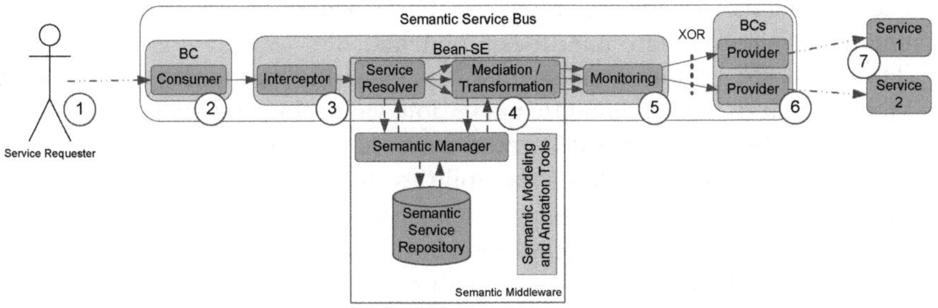

Fig. 3. DS^{3}I Architecture Overview

4.1 ESB - A Means to an End

DS^{3}I builds upon standards ESB capabilities. An ESB acts as an intermediary between service requesters and service instances and shall provide diverse messaging, routing and mediation capabilities [11,15] as defined in the Java Business Integration (JBI) standard [17]. A JBI compliant ESB consists of three components DS^{3}I is built upon:

- *Binding components (BCs)* allow connecting external services via various communication protocols and transforming data to a normalized form. Using existing BCs we employ the JBI-standard to interlink DS^{3}I not only with web services but with diverse kinds of legacy applications which were only seldom designed to be linked together.
- *Normalized Message Router (NMR)* forms the central messaging and routing backbone of the ESB, and therefore the backbone where service selection components are hooked in.
- *Service Engines (SEs)* provide business logic for integration of services (i.e. orchestration, data transformation, etc.). All semantic-enabled components are implemented as JBI SEs.

4.2 Components and Capabilities

DS^{3}I can be broken down into basically five different technical building blocks. The semantic middleware, in turn, is composed of several more modules as depicted in the black-bordered box in Fig. 3.

- The *Service Requester (1)* can be any stand-alone client or WFE that invokes services. For the time being we assume service requesters to communicate via SOAP with DS^{3}I. There is no need for the service requester to be changed in terms of additional functionality before it can benefit from the dynamic service selection infrastructure.
- *DS^{3}I* acts as the communication and messaging infrastructure. It provides both message sinks and sources for service requesters and service providers which is why JBI BCs reside at both ends: On the client side one for each exposed virtualized service interface (2), on the service candidate side one for

each connected service candidate (6). Furthermore, it serves as the runtime engine for the semantic middle components.
- The *Semantic Middleware (4)* consists of run-time components for ontologies storage, maintenance, semantic mediation, validation and querying/reasoning over semantically described data on services and messages. In combination, these components provide all capabilities depicted in Fig. 1(b). It consists of service resolving components, which actually select an appropriate service instances for a given virtualized interface based on semantic annotations of services and their interfaces. In a subsequent step, mediation components transform request and response messages into an adequate format for the selected service instance, again based on semantic interface descriptions. Both components employ the semantic manager, which shields all semantic mediation and reasoning related capabilities. The semantic manger in turn resorts to the semantic repository where all required information is stored.
- Functionality and interfaces of *Service Candidates* need to be semantically annotated. This is supported by *Semantic Modeling and Annotation Tools* for knowledge engineers and annotators at service provider side. Design tools are available as a set of Eclipse plug-ins and allow for visual modeling of ontology elements together with semantic annotations of WSDL files.
- Individual *service candidates* are realized by any kind of service implementation which is supported by a JBI BC. Hence, DS^{3}I is not restricted to SOAP-based webservices but can interlink with a broader set of service implementations. Merely, the provided functionality and their inputs and outputs have to be annotated semantically via previously mentioned tools.

The architecture involves two more auxiliary components: The *Message Interceptor (3)* allows for easily enabling or disabling the semantic middleware. Here a client-sided BC can easily be configured and statically be bound to a fixed service instance to circumvent the semantic middleware in case of need. The *Monitoring Component (5)* aims at collecting non-functional properties for each interaction with a service instance. Resulting data may provide a basis for both service evaluation and monitoring as well as for future service selection decisions.

5 Implementation

To evaluate the conceptual model and the DS^{3}I architecture we implemented and tested the individual components prototypically within the SPIKE project.

5.1 Implementation Considerations

As semantic framework we chose WSMO-Lite for handling ontologies and semantically enriched data. In particular, the implementation is based on the following components and frameworks:

- The *SPIKE API* for in-memory representation of the ontology elements (ontologies, concepts, instances, relations and axioms) is based on the wsmo4j library. Besides the ontology API, wsmo4j provides facilities for ontology validation and parsing/serialization from and to various formats.

- The main functionality of the *Framework for RDF persistence* is the mapping of top ontology elements into the RDF model. SPIKE RDF persistence is based on the ORDI framework, which allows integrating various data sources and provides a common RDF API for accessing underlying data.
- *RDF storage.* SPIKE ontologies are physically stored as RDF data using the Sesame repository. The current SPIKE configuration uses SwiftOWLIM extended by the TRREE inference engine as physical storage.
- For *infrastructure components* (external service interfaces, runtime environment for service selection and mediation components) the JBI-compliant ESB Apache ServiceMix and its various BCs and SEs are employed. For the implementation of virtualized service interfaces as well as for the links to external services the Apache CXF BC is used. As runtime environment for the sementic middleware the ServiceMix Bean SE is used which allows deploying Java classes into the ESB. Semantic (and non-semantic) dynamic service selection components are thus implemented as plain Java beans.
- *Semantic Annotation of Services* is implemented using the SAWSDL specification as shown in Fig. 2(b). SAWSDL extensions take two forms:
  1. Model references (`sawsdl:modelReference` attribute) which point to semantic concepts by URIs. Model references can be applied to WSDL elements (i.e. interface or operation) to specify the function of the service or XML scheme elements and describe the meaning of the input/output data.
  2. Schema mappings (`sawsdl:liftingSchemaMapping` and `sawsdl:loweringSchemaMapping` attributes) specify data transformations (usually defined with XSLT) between messages in normalized XML format (as used by the ESB) and the associated semantic model. The schema mappings are used for semantic data mediation. An automated semantic mediator can first lift data in one XML format to instances in the shared ontology and then again lower it to another XML format using the lifting annotation from the first format's schema and the lowering annotation from the second schema.

5.2 Semantic Resolving and Mediation

Preconditions. Semantic annotations of services are used to overcome the ambiguities during service discovery related to the description of services at the syntactic level only. For service composition, we adopt a semi-automatic approach where the business processes are modeled manually as BPEL processes. BPEL processes refer to abstract partner links, the virtualized service interfaces. The abstract partner links have to be resolved to concrete service instances during process execution. The process of resolving can be automatic and is based on semantic matching of descriptions of abstract partner links and service candidates provided by potentially several service providers.

In order to overcome data heterogeneity (i.e. when data expected by the abstract partner link has a different format than data defined for the selected service instance), DS^{3}I supports semantic data mediation. Matching of service candidates is based on two types of semantic annotations assigned to the abstract partner link using the `modelReference` SA-WSDL attribute: (1) SKOS ontology [19] for specification of classification schemes of categories. (2) Domain specific semantic types of input/output messages specified for the requested operation.

During matching both types can be combined arbitrarily and the hierarchical organization of categories and subclass/superclass relations of input/output types can be recursively expanded during reasoning. For semantic mediation, we adopt two approaches. The first approach is based on standard XSLT where ontologies are used as the common data vocabulary. This approach requires XSLT transformations for lifting and lowering of instances and is well supported by existing SEs. In the second approach incoming XML data is transformed to instances using a generic lifting scheme. Input instances are then transformed using semantic mappings into output instances which in turn are transformed to XML data again using the generic lowering scheme.

Operation Sequence. The whole procedure for business process execution in DS^{3}I consists of the following steps:

1. A business process definition is deployed to the BPEL SE. BPEL process invokes of abstract partner links are sent to the service resolving component.
2. The Service Resolver calls the Semantic Manager for discovery of services capable to provide outputs as specified for the abstract partner link. If there are more service candidates, a target service is selected for invocation according to predefined properties.
3. In case of unequal data formats specified for the abstract partner link and the target service, the message is forwarded to the Mediator, otherwise it is forwarded directly through the JBI BC to the selected service instance.

During mediation, the message is processed as follows: (1) Input data from the message exchange is transformed using the lifting schema specified for the abstract partner link. The result is a set of semantic instances. (2) Since the domain ontology specified for the partner link can be different to the ontology specified for the resolved service, instances are optionally transformed from the source ontology to the target ontology using semantic axioms and transformation rules (instance-to-instance transformation). (3) Instances are transformed back to normalized messages using the lowering schema specified for the resolved service.

In summary, data is first transformed using the lifting schema of the resolved service and then transformed back to normalized messages using the lowering schema specified for the partner link.

6 Conclusions and Future Work

In this paper we have introduced DS^{3}I for semantically enhanced dynamic service selection and mediation. DS^{3}I allows for one-step service selection without any negotiation phase between clients and service providers. DS^{3}I and its semantic middleware components are based upon an ESB and employ semantic annotations of services. Semantic descriptions are furthermore applied to find appropriate service candidates and mediate between unequal interfaces and data formats. Except for more detailed service descriptions, DS^{3}I does not necessitate any changes at client or service side.

Employing DS^{3}I, appropriate service candidates can be discovered and assigned at run-time This way process modelers and developers are no longer required to statically allocate service instances already at modeling time of a business process or implementation time of a stand-alone client application and service instances published at a later date can still be considered. Process modeling gains much more flexibility and a clear separation between process modelers or client application developers and business operation personnel can be accomplished. The former ones can focus on functional and business-process requirements while issues of service selection and mediation are delegated to business operation personnel and infrastructure components. We presented a detailed problem breakdown together with related work in this area. The core area of this work, however, is the DS^{3}I conceptual model, the overall architecture of the semantically enhanced dynamic service selection infrastructure and details on the prototypical implementation.

While our work yielded a suitable prototype for semantically supported dynamic service selection and mediation, future work is divided into two areas of research. (1) Requirements definition for the service selection phase along with performance penalties due to the gained flexibility have to be investigated in detail. (2) Dynamic service selection presupposes dynamic security enforcement and despite dynamic allocation of services, access control and accountability have to be ensured. We already developed a proposal [6] which is being elaborated and tested. Finally, as service selection criteria may vary depending on the sender of the initial message, both previously mentioned fields of research need to be reintegrated to allow for extracting service selection criteria from predefined configurations and user profiles.

References

1. Alonso, G., Casati, F., Kuno, H., Machiraju, V.: Web S: Concepts, Architectures and Applications. Springer, Berlin (2004)
2. Bai, X., Xie, J., Chen, B., Xiao, S.: DRESR: Dynamic Routing in Enterprise Service Bus. In: Proc. of the IEEE International Conference on e-Business Engineering (ICEBE 2007), pp. 528–531 (2007)
3. Chang, S.H., Bae, J.S., Jeon, W.Y., La Jung, H., Kim, S.D.: A Practical Framework for Dynamic Composition on Enterprise Service Bus. In: IEEE International Conference on Services Computing, pp. 713–714 (2007)
4. Chang, S.H., La, H.J., Bae, J.S., Jeon, W.Y., Kim, S.D.: Design of a Dynamic Composition Handler for ESB-based Services. In: Proc. of the IEEE International Conference on e-Business Engineering (ICEBE 2007), pp. 287–294 (2007)
5. Penta, M.D., Esposito, R., Villani, M.L., Codato, R., Colombo, M., Nitto, E.D.: WS Binder: A Framework to Enable Dynamic Binding of Composite Web Services. In: Proc. of the 2006 International Workshop on Service-oriented Software Engineering (SOSE 2006), pp. 74–80 (2006)

6. Fritsch, C., Pernul, G.: Security for Dynamic Service-Oriented eCollaboration - Architectural Alternatives and Proposed Solution. In: Proc. of the 7th International Conference on Trust, Privacy & Security in Digital Business (TrustBus 2010), pp. 214–226 (2010)
7. Fujii, K., Suda, T.: Semantics-based context-aware dynamic Service Composition. ACM Transactions on Autonomous and Adaptive Systems (TAAS) 4(2), 1–31 (2009)
8. Hohpe, G., Woolf, B., Brown, K.: Enterprise integration patterns: Designing, building, and deploying messaging solutions. Addison-Wesley, Boston (2008)
9. Karastoyanova, D., van Lessenand Frank Leymann, T., Ma, Z., Nitzsche, J., Wetzstein, B., Bhiri, S., Hauswirth, M., Zaremba, M.: A Reference Architecture for Semantic Business Process Management Systems. In: Multikonferenz Wirtschaftsinformatik (2008)
10. Karastoyanova, D., Wetzstein, B., van Lessen, T., Wutke, D., Nitzsche, J., Leymann, F.: Semantic Service Bus: Architecture and Implementation of a Next Generation Middleware. In: Proc. of the 2nd International ICDE Workshop on Service Engineering (SEIW 2007), pp. 347–354 (2007)
11. Leymann, F.: The (Service) Bus: Services Penetrate Everyday Life. In: Benatallah, B., Casati, F., Traverso, P. (eds.) ICSOC 2005. LNCS, vol. 3826, pp. 12–20. Springer, Heidelberg (2005)
12. Michlmayr, A., Rosenberg, F., Leitner, P., Dustdar, S.: End-to-End Support for QoS-Aware Service Selection, Binding, and Mediation in VRESCo. IEEE Transactions on Services Computing 3/2010, 193–205 (2010)
13. Mietzner, R., van Lessen, T., Wiese, A., Wieland, M., Karastoyanova, D., Leymann, F.: Virtualizing Services and Resources with ProBus: The WS-Policy-Aware Service and Resource Bus. In: Proc. of the 7th International Conference on Web Services, ICWS 2009, pp. 617–624 (2009)
14. Moser, O., Rosenberg, F., Dustdar, S.: Non-intrusive monitoring and service adaptation for ws-bpel. In: Proc. of the 17th Int. Conference on World Wide Web, WWW 2008, pp. 815–824. ACM, New York (2008)
15. Papazoglou, M.P., van den Heuvel, W.-J.: Service oriented Architectures: Approaches, Technologies and Research Issues. The VLDB Journal 16(3), 389–415 (2007)
16. Schmidt, M.-T., Hutchison, B., Lambros, P., Phippen, R.: The Enterprise Service Bus: Making Service-oriented Architecture Real. IBM Systems Journal 44(4), 781–797 (2005)
17. Ten-Hove, R., Walker, P.: Java Business Integration (JBI) 1.0. Java Specification Request 208 (2005)
18. van Heck, E., Vervest, P.: Smart Business Networks: How the Network Wins. Communications of the ACM 50(6), 28–37 (2007)
19. W3C. SKOS Simple Knowledge Organization System Reference. W3C Recommendation (2009)
20. Wu, B., Liu, S., Wu, L.: Dynamic Reliable Service Routing in Enterprise Service Bus. In: Proc. of the 2008 IEEE Asia-Pacific Services Computing Conference (APSCC 2008), pp. 349–354 (2008)

A Design Pattern to Decouple Data from Markup

Balwinder Sodhi and T.V. Prabhakar

Department of Computer Science and Engineering
IIT Kanpur, UP India 208016
{sodhi,tvp}@cse.iitk.ac.in

Abstract. Modern web applications have steadily increased in richness and complexity, and they put significant demands on system resources such as server CPU, memory and most importantly the network bandwidth. When seen at Internet scale, a tiny wastage in a resource can translate into a huge loss. For instance, we will show that youtube.com homepage can potentially save up to 4500 GB worth of bandwidth every day! It is, therefore, important for the application designers to: 1) identify what opportunities exist for improvement and 2) ensure that computing resources are efficiently utilized.

We present the results of an extensive investigation of how the *useful information* is distributed across various HTML tags and their attributes inside the served HTML pages taken from a large number of dynamic public websites. Our findings show that the *useful information* is often restricted to only a handful of the tags and attributes. We systematically explore the efficiency differences between various classes of frameworks that are used for developing modern web applications. Leveraging our findings, we propose a technique which decouples the view's markup and data thus allowing them to travel separately and only *on demand.* This improves the web application efficiency; for instance our experiments show that this approach increased the throughput by a factor of about 7.

1 Introduction

With the web browser increasingly becoming the powerful and popular platform for delivering business applications and services, the need to identify the opportunities that may exist for improving various aspects of the web applications design, therefore, becomes important. Typically, web applications are accessed via a browser that interacts with the application server via HTTP to fetch HTML content to be displayed in the browser. On the application server side, the web application may be serving just the static HTML pages; or, as in majority of the business web sites, it could be serving the dynamic content. Dynamic content is often created by combining *data* with the *templates* on the server. The *data* part is what we'll call the *useful information.* Often the *useful information* is the directly visible content on a web page in response to a specific query submitted by the user. For instance, on a shopping website's product catalogue page the

C. Huemer and T. Setzer (Eds.): EC-Web 2011, LNBIP 85, pp. 25–38, 2011.

information about each displayed product item is the useful information. The *template* is serving mainly as the presentation vehicle.

The problem with most dynamic web applications is that they often serve the final render-ready HTML to the browser. This is wasteful in terms of network bandwidth consumed, server side CPU and memory consumption etc.

Processing flow in most dynamic web application development frameworks follows these high level steps:

- Query the data from some data store like a relational database engine.
- Load and parse the template for the response page to be served. Often this results in some sort of object graph to be created to represent the page in memory.
- Go over the parsed page template and fill into it the data that was fetched from data store.
- Marshall the data-hyderated template as HTML and send it out as the response.

Clearly, all of this needs to happen on the application server and consumes server CPU and memory. We are interested in improving the situation. We examine how *useful information* is distributed inside HTML page elements in order to get insight into what changes in the content from one request to another for a given page. We make use of the empirical data that we derive from our experiments on large number of web applications to propose mechanisms which could result in better utilization of the computing resources.

Rest of this paper is organized as: section 2 describes our methodology that we followed to investigate the HTML pages and discuss the findings. In section 3 we provide relevant background on the working of popular web application frameworks. Section 4 we describe the proposed approach and discuss the experimentation results.

2 Investigation Methodology and Results Analysis

2.1 Selection of Web Applications

We focussed our study on the data driven dynamic websites. Our selection of the web sites was based on the Alexa's top websites list in the shopping category [1].

We selected this list because, first, it represents a fairly big sample population and thus provides an accurate and representative sample of current Internet sites in this category. Secondly, this list represents the most popular Web sites, based upon traffic information [2]. This *popularity* is derived from the page views, number of pages viewed on a host, and the reach (number of different users who access a host). The Alexa ranking is a based on the geometric mean of the reach and views quantities.

2.2 Data Collection

To automate the process of data collection we developed a tool to capture the statistics about the distribution of useful information in an HTML page as it

Table 1. Meaning of various HTML statistics

Statistic	Remarks
Tag	Name of the HTML tag
Attribute	Name of attribute of the tag
Attribute size	Size of the attribute value in chars
Attribute size ratio	Ratio of attribute size (in chars) to the total HTML file size (in chars)
Attribute size compression ratio	Used as an indicator of content repetitiveness in the attribute value
Tag count	How many times the tag appeared in the HTML
Text size	Size of the text content of the tag in chars.
Text size ratio	Ratio of tag's text size (in chars) to the total HTML file size (in chars)
Text size compression ratio	Used as an indicator of content repetitiveness in the tag's text value

is served on the browser. From the completeness of the analysis purposes we consider the entire set of HTML elements and their attributes when looking for what data they contain. In practice, however, only the data present in the following places on the HTML is found to be useful:

- Text inside the body of an HTML tag. For instance, text inside the body of `DIV, P, SPAN, A` etc. tags is often found useful.
- Value of the HTML tag attributes (e.g. `src, id, value` and `href` etc.).

We execute the data collection tool on the identified set of web applications and capture the statistics about HTML elements. Table-1 shows what each of the captured statistics mean.

2.3 Results Analysis

We analyse here the results from our study of content distribution inside HTML pages. Based on the insights gained from this analysis, we will look into the opportunities for improving the efficiency of certain web applications in the subsequent sections.

Table-2 shows[1] the overall distribution of the information between the HTML tag's text and attribute values for some of the top shopping web sites. Amongst the entire set of web sites that we studied, the maximum %age of data contained in the tags text was observed to be about 60%, minimum was at about 10% and average was about 24%. Similar numbers for the data contained in tag attribute values was: maximum at about 60%, minimum at about 15% and average was about 36%. All these %ages are w.r.t the total size of the served HTML content.

Another important set of statistics is the attribute-wise distribution of information as shown in the Table-3. We notice that the largest contributor here is the `href` attribute of the `A` tag for majority of the websites. Second largest

[1] For want of space we are showing, in tables 2, 3 and 4, data for a small subset of web applications that we studied.

Table 2. Overall information distribution

Tag Text (chars)	Attr. Text (chars)	% Data in Tags	% Data in Attr.	% Data Total	Host URL
23084	67402	11.48	33.51	44.99	www1.macys.com
41171	85900	16.4	34.22	50.62	www.overstock.com
8109	33171	9.97	40.8	50.77	www.target.com
33603	31935	26.88	25.55	52.43	electronics.shop.ebay.in
11236	25066	17.14	38.24	55.38	autos.yahoo.com
16552	44228	15.19	40.59	55.78	www.tigerdirect.com
11658	43403	12.75	47.48	60.23	www.staples.com
53107	150646	16.03	45.47	61.5	www.alibaba.com
17707	66818	13.7	51.69	65.39	www.barnesandnoble.com
45130	70180	25.91	40.29	66.2	www.buy.com

contributor is the `src` attribute of the `IMG` tag, even though its relative contribution as compared to the top contributor is small (about one third on average). Contribution of all others is less than 5% individually. We also observe that the compression ratio for these top contributors is fairly low (about 0.2) and is an indicator of a fair amount of repeated text there. We investigated these low compression ratio cases further by looking at the actual HTML content of those cases. We observed that the most `href` values had a full URL of which a large part (often upto the path component) was common and only the small query component was changing. Situation with the `src` attribute of the `IMG` tag was very similar. One such example is shown in Listing-1.1 where the repeated URLs are shown in bold underlined font. Further, we analysed the distribution of information amongst the text content appearing directly inside the body of various tags in the served HTML content. These statistics are shown in the Table-4. The largest contributor here is the `SCRIPT` tag whose max contribution in one case is about 55% towards the total size of HTML served, the minimum contribution is about 3% and on average it contributed about 15%. Other top contributors are the `P` (average contribution about 1%) and `A` (average contribution about 3%) tags. Average compression ratios in these cases is relatively high: 0.3 for `SCRIPT`, 0.52 for `P` and 0.4 for `A` tag. This indicates that there's not much repetitiveness in the information contained in these tags. In summary, all these findings indicate the following about the distribution of information in a served HTML page:

- Major chunk of the *useful information* is held in small number of tags and/or their attributes, which often are: `A/href, IMG/src, SCRIPT, P`.
- There is often a fair amount of repetitiveness in the information held by those tags/attributes that are largest contributor towards the HTML page's size.

We'll leverage the findings of our investigation as discussed in this section to propose a technique to improve the web application efficiency.

Table 3. Attribute-wise information distribution

Tag	Attribute	Attr. Size (chars)	% Data in Attr.	Compression Ratio	Host URL
A	href	70088	41.389	0.212	finance.yahoo.com
A	href	31567	34.532	0.215	www.staples.com
A	href	30918	23.916	0.154	www.barnesandnoble.com
A	href	24585	22.561	0.156	www.tigerdirect.com
A	href	32955	18.921	0.195	www.buy.com
A	href	11970	18.262	0.145	autos.yahoo.com
A	href	40645	16.19	0.148	www.overstock.com
A	href	11049	13.591	0.222	www.target.com
A	href	41571	12.547	0.149	www.alibaba.com
IMG	src	15418	9.105	0.135	finance.yahoo.com
A	href	17387	8.645	0.103	www1.macys.com

Table 4. Tag-wise information distribution

Tag	Occurrence	Text Size (chars)	% Data in text	Compression Ratio	Host URL
SCRIPT	7	32474	55.312	0.196	www.istockphoto.com
SCRIPT	43	35008	37.377	0.184	www.walmart.com
LI	33	1508	22.086	0.253	www.netflix.com
SCRIPT	43	36636	21.035	0.218	www.buy.com
STYLE	2	928	13.591	0.48	www.netflix.com
SCRIPT	21	16659	13.328	0.307	electronics.shop.ebay.in
A	611	9381	10.262	0.354	www.staples.com
SCRIPT	41	33529	10.12	0.274	www.alibaba.com
OPTION	1291	11178	8.943	0.375	electronics.shop.ebay.in
SCRIPT	25	5827	8.89	0.334	autos.yahoo.com
SCRIPT	46	13054	7.709	0.266	finance.yahoo.com

Listing 1.1. HTML fragment showing repetitive content

```
<map name='1307012650' id='1307012650'>
  ...
 <area shape='rect' coords='2,89,177,153'
   href='http://www.target.com/gp/browse.html/ref=sc_iw_l_0_2/?node=10218751'
   alt='TVs.' />
 <area shape='rect' coords='2,155,186,209'
   href='http://www.target.com/gp/browse.html/ref=sc_iw_l_0_3/?node=3666481'
   alt='Baby Furniture.' />
  ...
</map>
```

3 Web Application Frameworks - A Literature Review

Following are the major frameworks which are used to build the *core* part of web applications that are developed for various platforms. Recent releases of these frameworks provide support of modern Web 2.0 technologies such as AJAX [3,4] and JSON [5] etc. which can be leveraged to compose efficient solutions. In this paper, these frameworks are grouped into three categories based on how they support building the web UI. Items in each category are not exhaustive; since all frameworks in a given category are conceptually similar therefore only few popular frameworks are listed under each category.

3.1 Frameworks Requiring a Plug-in and/or Scripting Engine in Browser

Frameworks in this category allow creating Rich Internet Applications (RIA) which are aimed at providing the desktop application like user experience. The application is often an executable which is downloaded into the browser and executes via a special scripting engine/plug-in inside the browser. Interactions with the application server are often via RPC style AJAX calls. Popular frameworks in this category are: Google Web Toolkit [6], Microsoft Silverlight [7]

Issues with this Category. Following are the major issues with GWT/Silverlight kind of frameworks,

1. Major part of the UI has to be delivered as a single big script (e.g. .xap for Silverlight and .js files for GWT) which executes within the browser. Though there are different tricks and techniques which can allow a developer to reduce the initial startup time for the application, but the fact remains that for any serious business application the initial download and startup time can be unacceptable, especially over a limited bandwidth connection.
2. Restriction on what can be achieved with a browser-side scripting engine can sometime be a limiting factor for some usecases. For a public facing web application, the assumption about a scripting plugin being available and enabled in the browser may not always be realistic. Heavy reliance on JavaScript (e.g. in GWT like framework) can lead to cross-browser compatibility issues. For instance, in GWT although the code development in Java eases the programmer's effort, however, it is relatively difficult to troubleshoot the generated JavaScript code that finally executes in the browser.
3. Silverlight needs a special browser plug-in in order to execute the application. While this may not be a major issue in newer client machines,for older machines it may be a limitation.
4. Such frameworks use very specialized programming models, hence there is often a significant learning curve and maintenance costs associated.
5. It is difficult to prevent divulging the application code and logic. In case of scripting code based applications the code gets downloaded to the client.

3.2 Frameworks Based on Server-side Tag Libraries and Scripting

Typically, the web application here employs a template engine (e.g. Python Django, Apache Velocity) to combine the data with the presentation markup to create the HTML pages to be served to a browser. In many cases the markup may be mixed with the scriptlets as in Java Server Pages, PHP pages etc. to produce the dynamic HTML pages to be served. Popular frameworks in this category are: Apache Struts [8], Ruby on Rails [9], PHP Zend [10]

Issues with this Category. Most issues in this approach of web application development are related to both server side memory and CPU consumption and more importantly the content sent across the network. Following are the main steps (also shown in Figure-1) that happen on the server for producing a response to a requested dynamic page:

1. Every time a page is requested by the client, the server has to first parse the page (e.g. .jsp or .aspx page etc.) markup to determine what dynamic scripts/tags needs to be instantiated.
2. Instantiate the objects for and execute the scriptlets and tags found on the requested page. This step also performs the data binding, if any, onto the resulting markup.
3. Generated markup which will also contain the data for various UI elements is then sent over the network to the client. Often in the flow of an application, only the data changes between requests to the same page.

Thus the above steps put unnecessary load on the server as well as the network. All that the client needs from server is new data which the client can refresh its display state with.

3.3 Framework Using Component Based User Interface

Here the UI on the server-side is object oriented and created by composing an object graph similar to how it is done for the desktop applications. For instance, a view has a page object and page may have many panel objects and each panel may have various widget objects like text box, label and buttons etc. This component tree is usually rendered as HTML response. Popular frameworks in this category are: Java Server Faces [11], ASP.NET Web Forms [12]

Issues with this Category. In this approach as well the issues are exactly same as in the case of server-side scripting/tags.

4 Exploiting Web 2.0 Technologies — A Hybrid Approach

In each of the frameworks mentioned in previous section it is possible to make use of Web 2.0 technologies such as AJAX, JSON and client-side scripting tools etc.

We exploit the findings of our investigation discussed in section 2.3 to address the issues that have been mentioned for the popular web application frameworks and improve the efficiency. One such technique is discussed below. The key ideas underlying this approach are:

- Separate the data and markup (representing the UI) at the *view* level. Important thing here is the granularity of the *view* (i.e. how many standard UI elements/widgets are packed in the view's markup). Often it is application dependent and can be easily controlled and tuned. The data and the markup of the UI view can travel separately and only *on demand*. Application efficiency increases.
- Use static or one-time dynamically generated markup to create the views in UI. It requires much less server memory and CPU cycles as compared to traditional component/tag-library based UI because it won't be creating the document tree or the object graph on each request for representing the view. Also, manipulation of plain HTML using JavaScript on client side requires cheaper programming skills.
- Use lightweight data interchange mechanism such as JSON to exchange data between client and server.
- The content – both markup and data – can be served by any of the existing server-side framework.

This approach works with plain HTML and JavaScript to create *templatized views* for web UI. A *view* here can be a complete screen (full HTML page) or a section (HTML fragment) of it. These *view templates*, which are plain HTML markup without any data in the start, are incrementally brought to the client as and when they are needed by the user. Any subsequent activation (in a single session) of a view doesn't result in bringing the markup again to the client – only data is fetched from the server as needed. Data binding to UI elements is done on the client-side via DOM manipulation using JavaScript. Following sections provide further details. Request-response interactions occurring in the proposed solution are depicted in Figure-2. For comparison purposes, similar interactions, as they happen in tag-library based approach (which is similar to UI component based approach), are shown in Figure-1. We'd like to mention that this technique does not try to replace the existing frameworks such as those listed in section-3; instead it is aimed at complementing their capabilities to satisfy special efficiency requirements and constraints.

4.1 Use a Compact Data Interchange Format

The data interchange format selection can be based on the following broad criteria:

- For a given amount of information to be exchanged, it should produces a very compact payload.
- Should be easy to deserialize/unmarshal via client scripting tools.
- Availability of very good quality libraries for both client and server side use.

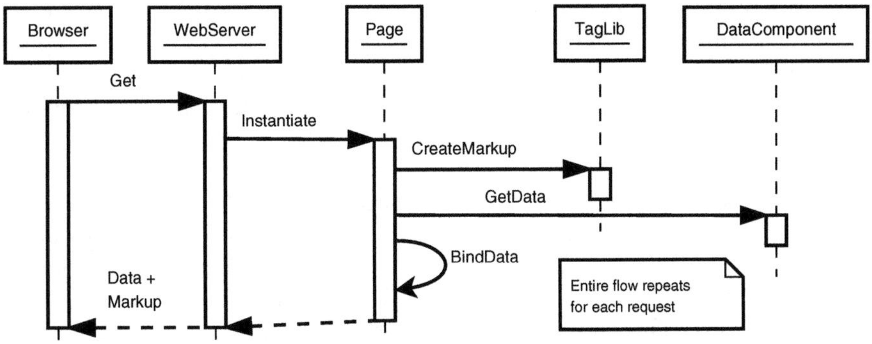

Fig. 1. Request response interactions in tag-lib based approach

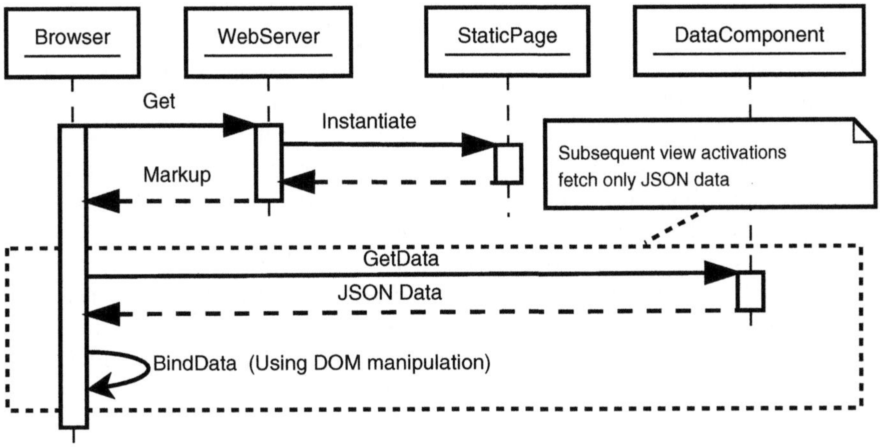

Fig. 2. Request response interactions in proposed solution

One reasonable candidate for web applications is JSON. Use of JSON along with templatized views (as explained in next sub section) helps in reducing the data flowing between client and server. In any session, application views are fetched only once from the server as and when needed. Views are added/updated on the page using DOM manipulation. Data for the view is fetched separately in JSON format. Any subsequent activation of a view requires just the data part to be fetched from server. This results in reducing unnecessary ferrying of "HTML tags" between client and server, thus improving the efficiency of the application.

4.2 Use Static Template Based Views to Construct UI

View template here refers to a piece of HTML markup which defines a screen or its section. Minimal markup is used just enough to indicate the arrangement of UI elements on the view. Assigning proper IDs to different elements is important for later data binding via DOM manipulation using JavaScript. For example, if a view contains a text field and a table containing 4 columns, then the markup will contain just an INPUT tag and a TABLE tag of HTML. Since view templates are static, so no dynamic server-side objects are created when client requests the page/view. This static markup is also cacheable, and even content delivery networks could be leveraged to further improve the performance.

How data is bound to UI elements. Each data-bound HTML element in a view template is assigned a unique ID. The data-bound HTML element also has an attribute to specify which JSON object property holds the data for this element. JSON data fetched from server is bound to UI elements via DOM manipulation using JavaScript. The approach is similar to [13, Ch. 3], except that in our approach we are getting only the data as JSON. There are decent client-side scripting libraries (e.g. JQuery [14], DOJO [15], YUI [16] etc.) available which can ease this task.

Effective use of AJAX. It is common in many web applications to make use of AJAX calls from the client to server for fetching either just the data or the final render-ready HTML hydrated with necessary data. The AJAX interactions between client and server in such a case are at basic UI element level (e.g. a dropdown list of a check-box) and thus are too fine grained. For example, on checking a check-box the application may re-calculate (on server-side) the values shown on some textboxes. Perhaps in some use cases this kind of fine grained interactions is what the application needs. However, it can potentially result in a client being too chatty with the server. If the concurrent user base for the application is large then such a chatty client introduces additional connections load for the server and can be problematic. In the cases where render-ready data-hydrated HTML is fetched over AJAX from the server, the problem is essentially same as described for traditional tag-library based approach. This is because, though the data + markup are brought over AJAX, but still the data *and* markup travel together. In the AJAX technique discussed in this paper we decouple the data and markup at the *coarse grained view* level. Hence it avoids both the above issues as observed with plain use of AJAX.

Trade-offs involved

1. Input validation on server-side will become somewhat manual as compared to other approaches.
2. Use of JavaScript on client side is central to the discussed technique. Hence cross-browser portability can be an issue in situations where browser specific JavaScript features are used in an application.
3. As is common with any AJAX driven web application, page refresh and browser back button require special handling.
4. Also, benefits of the discussed technique are significant only when application use cases involve repeated activations of same views. That is, if a view is activated only once in a session then this approach doesn't provide significant benefit in comparison to the other mentioned approaches.

Table 5. Application implementation styles

Design Method	Description
Method-1	It made use of the proposed technique where markup and data were decoupled.
Method-2: Component based UI	It implemented the dynamic web page using ASP.NET web forms.
Method-3: Tag libs based UI	It implemented the same dynamic web page using ASP.NET MVC framework.

4.3 Experimentation Details and Results

To examine the effectiveness of the proposed technique, a reference implementation was developed for it. We compared the performance against: 1) an application which used a component based UI and 2) an application which used server-side tag library based UI. Functionality wise, the applications showed the users a single dynamic page which displayed a list of products entries similar to a shopping web site product catalogue. A product entry consisted of fields such as: Description summary (a hyperlink), Price, Availability status, User rating (a hyperlink) and a Thumbnail image (a hyperlink).

Each entry was put inside a grid cell on the HTML page. On one page the grid showed about 30-50 rows. This represents a fairly close scenario to most of the web applications that we studied in section-2. Table-5 shows the details about the implementation styles for each of the applications.

Each application was implemented using ASP.NET 2.0 framework on .NET 3.5. Web server was IIS 6.0 on Windows 7 (64bit) running on Intel Core2 Duo T6600 @ 2.2GHz processor with 4GB RAM. Each application was subjected to the load of 100-1500 users making 500 requests each.

Performance Indicator

The Performance Indicator (PI) can be chosen as the CPU usage, Memory usage and Throughput. In the present work, the performance of the proposed technique has been tested with respect to all the above mentioned three criteria. The PI is observed for each method-i and is then normalized with respect to the value of PI for the proposed technique. The normalized index for a PI-r is calculated as:

$$T_r = \frac{T_r^p}{T_r^i} \tag{1}$$

where, T_r^i is value of PI-r as observed with method-i, and T_r^p is the value of same indicator as observed with proposed approach. The results obtained from the experiments are shown in the Figure-3.

We found that with proposed approach the average throughput was about 7 times better than the other two approaches. The server-side memory usage was, on average, about 12% less than that of tag library based UI, and about

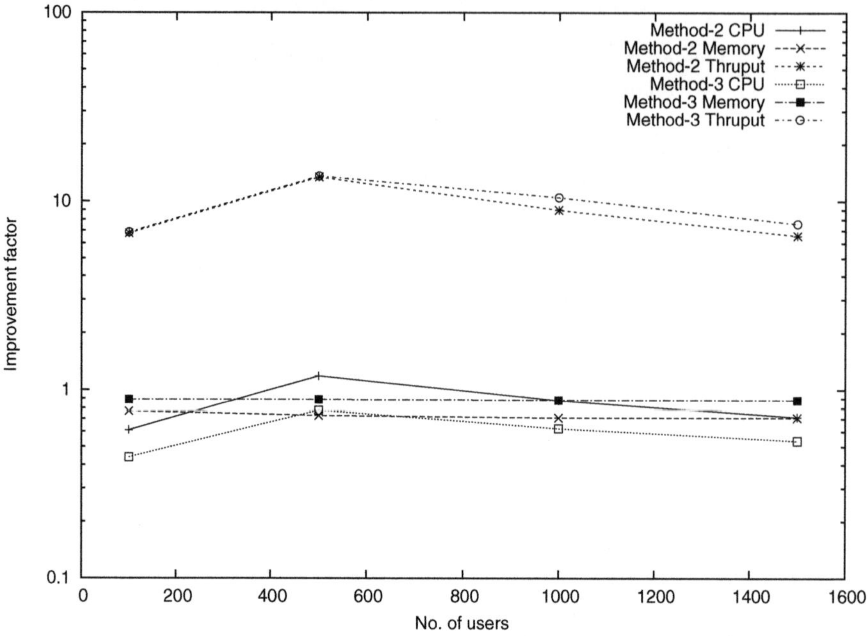

Fig. 3. Efficiency comparison

Table 6. Performance indicator values

Tag Libraries UI			Components Based UI			
CPU	Memory	Thruput	CPU	Memory	Thruput	**Users**
0.439	0.888	6.852	0.610	0.767	6.760	100
0.776	0.888	13.581	1.184	0.728	13.405	500
0.621	0.882	10.454	0.878	0.708	8.969	1000
0.536	0.882	7.591	0.714	0.708	6.562	1500

30-40% less than component based UI approach. CPU consumption was 25-65% less in comparison to tag libraries based UI, and was about 15-24% less than the component based UI approach.

The general trend with the variation of number of concurrent users load is as expected. All performance indicators first slightly improve before they finally plateau out. Initial small improvement with the increase in users load happens due to utilization of cached or one-time created objects. Once the cached objects are built up, then its contribution towards overall performance saturates and doesn't reflect with the further increase in user load.

HTTP requests load for web applications was generated via Apache JMeter [17] and the measurements were done via the following tools: Windows Process Explorer [18], YourKit profiler for .NET [19].

5 Conclusions

We systematically investigated how the *useful information* is spread and delivered via various structural elements of the HTML markup in dynamic web applications. It was observed that a major chunk of a served HTML page contains just the markup; the real useful information content is confined to only a small set of HTML tags and tag attributes. We exploited this finding to propose an efficient technique to deliver dynamic content where we decoupled the markup from the data so that they could travel between client and server independently and only on demand. Our test results show that the proposed technique reduces the use of server-side computing resources such as CPU, memory and network bandwidth.

For instance, we observed that on the www.youtube.com home page just the HTML tags account for about 37% of the HTML size – and we are considering all the tags content as *useful information* here, which in practice is not the case since, for example, the content of *SCRIPT* tag (which often doesn't change) itself is accounting for about 17% of the HTML size here. Average size of the www.youtube.com HTML is about 70000 bytes. So the potential saving per repeated pageview is about $0.37 \times 70000 = 25900$ bytes of bandwidth. According to Alexa statistics [20] www.youtube.com attracts about 25% internet users everyday. By taking into account the reported bounce rate (i.e. the percentage of visits to youtube.com that consist of a single pageview) of about 25%, and assuming that there are only about 1 billion Internet users measured by Alexa per day, simple math shows that youtube.com could potentially save at least about $25900 \times 0.25 \times (1-0.25) \times 1000000000 = 4856250000000$ bytes (i.e. 4522.735 GB) of bandwidth every day. And we are not even looking at the server-side CPU and memory savings at this scale.

The above example clearly shows the usefulness of our technique in heavily used dynamic web applications, particularly the ones deployed in cloud platforms where the resource usage is metered and billed at a very granular level. The other important possible applications of our technique are in low bandwidth clients and handheld devices.

References

1. Alexa Inc. Alexa - top sites by category: Shopping, `http://www.alexa.com/topsites/category/Top/Shopping` (retrieved: March 2011)
2. Alexa Inc. About the alexa traffic rankings, `http://www.alexa.com/help/traffic-learn-more` (retrieved: March 2011)
3. Lin, Q.Z.Z., Wu, J., Zhou, H.: Research on web applications using ajax new technologies. In: MMID 2008, pp. 139–142 (December 2008)
4. Paulson, L.D.: Building rich web applications with ajax. IEEE Computer 38(10), 14–17 (2005)
5. Json, D.C.: The fat-free alternative to xml (January 2011), `http://www.json.org/fatfree.html`

6. Google Inc. Google web toolkit developer guide (January 2011), http://code.google.com/webtoolkit/doc/1.6/DevGuide.html
7. Microsoft Inc. Microsoft silverlight reference documentation (January 2011), http://msdn.microsoft.com/en-us/library/cc838158%28VS.95%29.aspx
8. Apache Software Foundation. Apache struts developer guide (March 2010), http://struts.apache.org/2.1.8/docs/guides.html
9. Ruby on Rails Foundation. Ruby on rails developer guide (March 2010), http://guides.rubyonrails.org
10. Zend. Php zend framework manual (January 2011), http://framework.zend.com/manual/en/
11. Sun Microsystem. Java server faces (jsf) reference documentation (January 2011), http://java.sun.com/javaee/javaserverfaces/reference/docs/index.html
12. Microsoft Inc. Microsoft asp.net reference documentation (2011), http://msdn.microsoft.com/en-us/library/dd394709%28VS.100%29.aspx
13. Gross, C.: Ajax Patterns And Best Practices, ch.3. Dreamtech Press (2007)
14. JQuery. Jquery documentation, http://docs.jquery.com/Main_Page (retrieved: January 2011)
15. The Dojo Foundation. Dojo toolkit guide (March 2011), http://dojotoolkit.org/reference-guide/
16. Yahoo Inc. Yui library manual (March 2010), http://developer.yahoo.com/yui/
17. The Apache Software Foundation. Apache jmeter (March 2010), http://jakarta.apache.org/jmeter/index.html
18. Microsoft TechNet. Windows sysinternals - process explorer v12.03 (February 2011), http://technet.microsoft.com/en-us/sysinternals/bb896653.aspx
19. YourKit LLC. Yourkit profiler 5 for .net (March 2010), http://www.yourkit.com/.net/profiler/index.jsp
20. Alexa Inc. Youtube.com site info., http://www.alexa.com/siteinfo/youtube.com (retrieved: March 2011)

Context-Based Service Recommendation for Assisting Business Process Design

Nguyen Ngoc Chan, Walid Gaaloul, and Samir Tata

Information Department
TELECOM SudParis
UMR 5157 CNRS Samovar, France

Abstract. The WS-BPEL provides a standard for business processes abstraction and execution, in which, the business processes abstraction is the key step for the completeness and success of business processes. The business processes abstraction includes the behavior and interactions between services which are sketched out by business processes designers. The current business process design is labor-intensive and time consuming, especially when it is required to be detailed to ensure the success of the business execution. In this paper, we propose an approach that helps the business process designers facilitate the design step by providing them a list of related services to the current designed model. We propose to capture the requested service's composition context specified through the process fragment surrounding it and recommend the services whose composition context in existing designed service compositions best match the given fragment context. Provided experimental evaluations in this paper show that our approach is efficient in realistic situations.

Keywords: business process modeling; web service composition; workflow pattern; context matching; recommender system.

1 Introduction

The current design of business process models is labor-intensive, especially when such models are required to be detailed to support the development of software systems [20]. It would be inefficient if every time a company engages in modeling and re-designing its process, it did so "from scratch" without consideration of how other companies perform similar processes. Indeed, to avoid the effort of creating process models from scratch, several consortia and vendors have defined so-called reference process models, for example SCOR [18] or SAP [7] models. These models capture proven practices and recurrent business operations in a given domain. They are designed in a generic manner and are intended to be individualized to fit the requirements of specific organizations or IT projects in order to enable systematic reuse of proven practices across process (re-)design projects. However, analysts take the reference models merely as a source of inspiration, but ultimately, they design their own model on the basis of the reference model, with little guidance as to which model elements need to be removed,

C. Huemer and T. Setzer (Eds.): EC-Web 2011, LNBIP 85, pp. 39–51, 2011.

added or modified to address a given requirement. Briefly, the current business process design still has shortcomings: (1) the reference models are human based and provided manually (this work is absolutely error-prone and time-consuming) and (2) they are always studied as a whole while sometimes only some parts of the model need to be considered.

In this paper, we present an original recommendation approach to help the business processes designers facilitate the design step of the business process abstraction. We propose to take into account the composition context specified through the business process fragment surrounding the requested service, and benefit from the modeling and usage of previous service compositions to build our recommendations. Concretely, we propose a process fragment model that computes similarities between services using the relations with their neighbors. The process fragment represents the composition context for a service described in terms of its relations with its neighbors. These relations are described through the control flow patterns. Then, we compute the similarity degrees between services by matching the respective process fragments. Indeed, the composition context informs us about the service behavior and thereafter can unveil its functionality. Therefore, our objective is two-fold: (1) takes into account the composition context, specified through the business process fragment surrounding the composed service, as an input in service discovery, and (2) benefits from the modeling and usage of existing composite services by extracting this implicit knowledge as process fragments to match with the composition context of the requested service. Furthermore, our approach can associate with the functionality-based service recommendation techniques to more precisely retrieve the expected services.

The paper is organized as follows: In section 2 we specify a graph based model to describe a service composition context. Section 3 elaborates the proposed matching algorithm. Section 4 illustrates our implementation and experimental results. Related work is presented in section 5 and we conclude our work in section 6.

2 Graph-Based Modeling of Service Composition Context

In this section, we present a graph-based service composition model whose control flow is modeled using workflow patterns. Firstly, we depict how we use workflow patterns to describe service interactions (see section 2.1). Secondly, we define the relations of each service with its neighbors using new defined layer and zone concepts (see section 2.2). Finally, we specify the composition context graph of each service (see section 2.3).

2.1 Graph-Based Service Composition Model

It is worthwhile to notice that the term composite service is usually used to denote composition of operations offered by different services [2]. Indeed, a composite service, defined using WS-BPEL for instance, is in fact a flow of services' operations and not a flow of services. Thus, in our approach and in order to avoid such confusion, we supposed for simplicity purpose that a service has one operation so that its consumption coincides with its operation invocation.

A composite service implies several services and describes the order of their invocation, and the conditions under which these services are invoked. The control flow (or skeleton in the following) of a composite service specifies the partial ordering of component services (e.g., a service B is executed after the completion of a service A). We use (workflow-like) patterns to define a composite service skeleton. A workflow pattern [21] can be seen as an abstract description of a recurrent class of interactions. Applied to Web services, a pattern defines default dependencies (i.e. interactions) between services. For example, the Synchronize pattern [21] describes an abstract choreography by specifying services dependencies as following: a service is activated after the completion of several other services. We call *atomic pattern* a primitive control flow pattern that can be used in WS-BPEL such as : sequence, parallel split (AND-fork), synchronization (AND-join), multiple choice (OR-fork), an exclusive choice (XOR-fork), or a simple merge (OR-join). In the following we propose a graph-based model of service composition and we use Fig. 1 for all examples in our definitions.

Definition 1 (Direct link pattern). *A direct link pattern is a sequence of atomic patterns which connects two adjacent services. The direct link pattern is directed, and denoted by P. $P_{\mathcal{C}}(s_i, s_j) = p_1 p_2 \dots p_k$ indicates a direct link pattern with a sequence of k atomic patterns from s_i to s_j in the composition $\mathcal{C}$.*

For example, $P_{\mathcal{C}1}(s_1, s_2)$=‘Sequence’, $P_{\mathcal{C}2}(s_3, s_4)$=‘OR-join’‘AND-join’, $P_{\mathcal{C}2}(s_6, s_1)$ =‘’ (there is no direct link pattern from s_6 to s_1 in $\mathcal{C}2$).

Definition 2 (Composition graph). *A composition graph of a service composition $\mathcal{C}$ is a labeled directed graph $G_{\mathcal{C}} = (V_{\mathcal{C}}, L_{\mathcal{C}}, A_{\mathcal{C}})$ in which $V_{\mathcal{C}} \neq \emptyset$ is the set of vertices (services), $L_{\mathcal{C}} \neq \emptyset$ is the set of edge-labels (direct link patterns' names), and $A_{\mathcal{C}} \subseteq V \times V \times L$ is the set of directed edges (direct link patterns) in the composition $\mathcal{C}$. An edge $a =< s_x, s_y, P_{\mathcal{C}}(s_x, s_y) >\in A_{\mathcal{C}}$ is considered to be directed from s_x to s_y and labeled by $P_{\mathcal{C}}(s_x, s_y)$. s_x is called the tailed service, s_y is called the head service and $P_{\mathcal{C}}(s_x, s_y)$ is the direct link pattern from s_x to s_y in $\mathcal{C}$.*

For example, the composition $\mathcal{C}1$ can be presented by a graph $G_{\mathcal{C}1} = (V_{\mathcal{C}1}, L_{\mathcal{C}1}, A_{\mathcal{C}1})$, in which $V_{\mathcal{C}1}$={s_0, s_1, s_2, s_3, s_4}, $L_{\mathcal{C}}$={‘AND-split’, ‘Sequence’, ‘AND-join’}, $A_{\mathcal{C}1}$={< s_0, s_1, ‘AND-split’>, < s_0, s_3, ‘AND-split’>, < s_1, s_2, ‘Sequence’ >, < s_2, s_4, ‘AND-join’>, < s_3, s_4, ‘AND-join’>}.

A path in a composition graph is named as a *pattern path.* A pattern path from s_i to s_j in a composition $\mathcal{C}$ is *indirected* and denoted by $\mathbb{P}_{\mathcal{C}}(s_i, s_j)$. For example, $\mathbb{P}_{\mathcal{C}1}(s_1, s_4) = P(s_1, s_2)P(s_2, s_4)$=‘Sequence’‘AND-join’, $\mathbb{P}_{\mathcal{C}2}(s_3, s_1) = P(s_5, s_3)P(s_5, s_1)$=‘AND-split’‘OR-split’‘AND-split’. The *pattern path's length* is denoted by $Len(\mathbb{P})$ and the *shortest pattern path* is denoted by $SP_{\mathcal{C}}(s_i, s_j)$. For example, $SP_{\mathcal{C}1}(s_0, s_2) = P(s_0, s_1)P(s_1, s_2)$=‘AND-split’‘Sequence’, $SP_{\mathcal{C}2}(s_7, s_6) = P(s_7, s_4)P(s_6, s_4)$=‘OR-join’‘AND-join’‘AND-join’.

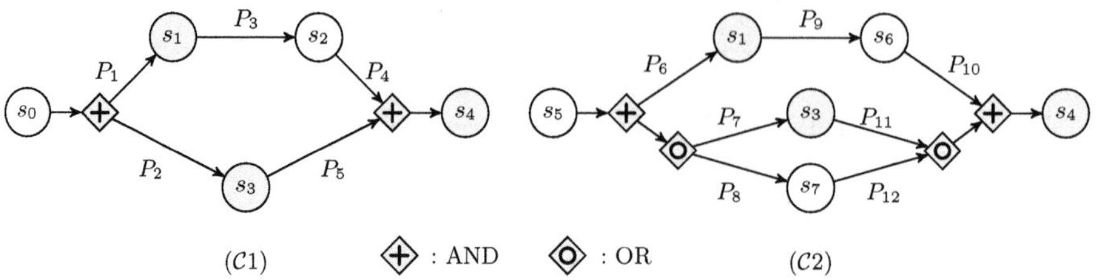

Fig. 1. Example: service compositions

2.2 Service Neighborhood

In this section, we propose some new definitions that are related to services' neighborhood and are used to define the composition context.

Definition 3 (k^{th}-layer neighbor). *A kth-layer neighbor of a service s is a service connected to s via a k-length pattern path ($k \geq 0$). The set of kth-layer neighbors of a service s in a composition $\mathcal{C}$ is denoted by $N^k_{\mathcal{C}}(s)$. $N^0_{\mathcal{C}}(s) = \{s\}$;*

For example, $N^1_{\mathcal{C}1}(s_2) = \{s_1, s_4\}$, $N^2_{\mathcal{C}1}(s_2) = \{s_0, s_3\}$.

Definition 4 (k^{th}-area neighbor). *A kth-area neighbor of a service s is a service connected to s via a l-length pattern path, where $0 \leq l \leq k$. The set of all k^{th}-area neighbors of s in a composition $\mathcal{C}$ creates a process fragment surrounding s and it is denoted by $\mathbb{N}^k_{\mathcal{C}}(s)$. $\mathbb{N}^k_{\mathcal{C}}(s) = \cup^k_{i=0} N^i_{\mathcal{C}}(s)$.*

For example, $\mathbb{N}^1_{\mathcal{C}1}(s_2) = \{s_2, s_1, s_4\}$; $\mathbb{N}^2_{\mathcal{C}1}(s_2) = \{s_2, s_1, s_4, s_0, s_3\}$.

Definition 5 (k^{th}-zone pattern). *A kth-zone pattern of a service $s \in \mathcal{C}$ is a direct link pattern which connects a service in $N^{k-1}_{\mathcal{C}}(s)$ and a service in $N^k_{\mathcal{C}}(s)$. Set of all k^{th}-zone patterns of a service $s \in \mathcal{C}$ is denoted by $Z^k_{\mathcal{C}}(s)$. $Z^0_{\mathcal{C}}(s) = \emptyset$.*

For example, $Z^1_{\mathcal{C}1}(s_1) = \{< s_0, s_1,$ 'AND-split'$>, < s_1, s_2,$ 'Sequence'$>\}$, $Z^2_{\mathcal{C}2}(s_4)$ $= \{< s_1, s_6,$ 'Sequence'$>, < s_5, s_3,$ 'AND-split''OR-split'$>, < s_5, s_7,$ 'AND-split' 'OR-split'$>\}$

2.3 Service Composition Context Graph

We realize that the pattern paths between two services present their relation (closeness). The longer the pattern path is, the weaker their relation is. And if we capture the shortest pattern paths from a service to other, we can measure the best relation between them. On another hand, one edge in the composition graph can belong to more than one zone around a service, depending on the selected pattern paths to the that service. Therefore, we propose to build for each service a specific graph in which each edge belongs to its smallest zone. In other words, we propose to assign the smallest zone number for each direct link patterns computed by the shortest path's length to the associated service and represent the composition graph in another graph, so-call *composition context graph* (definition 6). Concretely, the minimum zone value that is assigned to the pattern connecting s_i and s_j in the composition context graph of s will be $Min(Len(SP_{\mathcal{C}}(s_i,s)), Len(SP_{\mathcal{C}}(s_j,s)))+1$ and the maximum zone value used to assign to all direct link patterns will be $n = Max(Len(SP_{\mathcal{C}}(s_x,s)))+1\ \forall s_x \in \mathcal{C}$.

Definition 6 (Composition context graph). *A composition context graph of a service $s \in \mathcal{C}$ is a labeled directed graph $G_{\mathcal{C}}(s) = (V_{\mathcal{C}}(s), Z_{\mathcal{C}}(s), L_{\mathcal{C}}(s), A_{\mathcal{C}}(s))$ that represents the composition graph $G_{\mathcal{C}} = (V_{\mathcal{C}}, L_{\mathcal{C}}, A_{\mathcal{C}})$ with the minimum k^{th}-zone patterns of s. $V_{\mathcal{C}}$ is the set of vertices (services), $Z_{\mathcal{C}}(s)$ is the minimum set of zones needed to represent the composition graph, $L_{\mathcal{C}}$ is the set of direct link patterns' names and $A_{\mathcal{C}}(s))$ is the set of direct link patterns labeled with their zone numbers. A composition context graph $G_{\mathcal{C}}(s)$ satisfies the followings:*

1. $V_{\mathcal{C}}(s) = V_{\mathcal{C}}$
2. $L_{\mathcal{C}}(s) = L_{\mathcal{C}}$
3. $Z_{\mathcal{C}}(s) = \{1, 2, \ldots, n\}$, *where:* $n = Max(Len(SP_{\mathcal{C}}(s_x, s))) + 1\ \forall s_x \in \mathcal{C}$
4. $A_{\mathcal{C}}(s) = A_{\mathcal{C}} \times Z_{\mathcal{C}}(s)$, *where:* $a_s =< a_c, z_c(s) >=<< s_i, s_j, P(s_i, s_j) >, Min(Len(SP_{\mathcal{C}}(s_i, s)), Len(SP_{\mathcal{C}}(s_j, s))) + 1 >, \forall a_c =< s_i, s_j, P(s_i, s_j) >\in A_{\mathcal{C}}$

For example, a composition context graph $G_{\mathcal{C}1}(s_2) = (V_{\mathcal{C}1}(s_2), Z_{\mathcal{C}1}(s_2), L_{\mathcal{C}1}(s_2), A_{\mathcal{C}1}(s_2))$ of the service s_2 can be inferred from the composition graph $G_{\mathcal{C}1}$ (in Fig. 1), in which: $V_{\mathcal{C}1}(s_2) = \{s_0, s_1, s_2, s_3, s_4\}$, $L_{\mathcal{C}} = \{$'AND-split', 'Sequence', 'AND-join'$\}$, $Z_{\mathcal{C}1}(s_2) = \{1,2,3\}$, $A_{\mathcal{C}}(s) = \{<< s_0, s_1,$ 'AND-split'$>, 2 >, << s_0, s_3,$ 'AND-split'$>, 3 >, << s_1, s_2,$ 'Sequence'$>, 1 >, << s_2, s_4,$ 'AND-join'$>, 1 >, << s_3, s_4,$ 'AND-join'$>, 2 >\}$.

In graphical view, the composition context graphs $G_{\mathcal{C}1}(s_2)$ and $G_{\mathcal{C}2(s_6)}$ of the service s_2 and s_6 can be shown as in Fig. 2. We note that a composition context graph of a service is related to the composition where this service is used, so this composition context graph can differ from one composition to another. For example, the composition context graph of s_3 in $\mathcal{C}1$ is different to the composition context graph of s_3 in $\mathcal{C}2$, ie. $G_{\mathcal{C}1}(s_3) \neq G_{\mathcal{C}2}(s_3)$.

3 Service Recommendation Based on Composition Context Matching

To illustrate each step in the computation, we use an example to compute the pattern matching of two services s_2 and s_6 which respectively belong to the composition $\mathcal{C}1$ and $\mathcal{C}2$ (Fig. 1). The services s_1, s_3, s_4 exist in both compositions. The direct link patterns are: $P_1 = P_2 =$ 'AND-fork', $P_3 =$ 'Sequence', $P_4 = P_5 =$ 'AND-join', $P_6 =$ 'AND-fork', $P_7 = P_8 =$ 'AND-fork''OR-fork', $P_9 =$ 'Sequence', $P_{10} =$ 'AND-join', $P_{11} = P_{12} =$ 'OR-join''AND-join'. The distributions of neighbors of s_2 and s_6 in layers are easily inferred from the compositions and redrawn in Fig. 2. We elaborate step by step how we compute the similarity in the following.

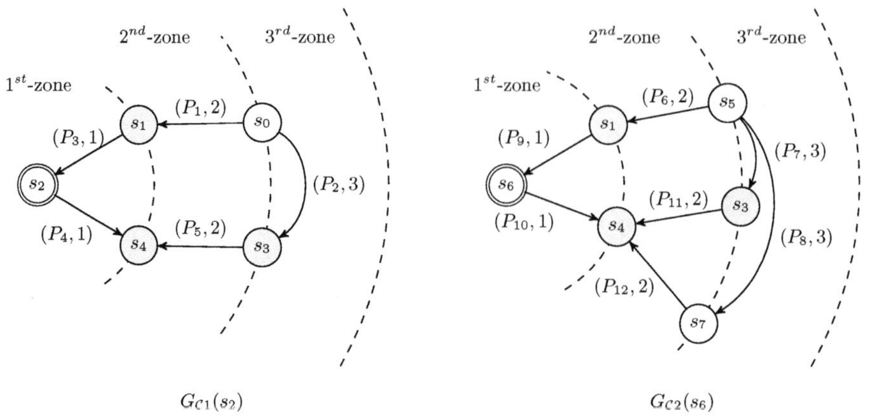

Fig. 2. Composition context graphs inferred from the compositions graph

3.1 Direct Link Pattern Matching

In our approach, the direct link pattern matching is considered as the fundamental weight of the composition context matching. Since each direct link pattern between two adjacent services is a sequence of atomic patterns which can easily mapped to a sequence of characters, we propose to use the Levenshtein distance [13] to compute the matching between two direct link patterns. We consider each atomic pattern as a character, then *a direct link pattern is presented by a sequence of characters* (or string) and the similarity between two direct link patterns can be easily computed.

Concretely, given two direct link patterns $P(s_i, s_j) = p_1 p_2 \dots p_n$ and $P'(s_{i'}, s_{j'}) = p'_1 p'_2 \dots p'_m$, the pattern matching between them is computed by the equation (1).

$$M_p(P, P') = 1 - \frac{LevenshteinDistance(P, P')}{Max(n, m)} \quad (1)$$

The equation (1) also covers two special cases:

① If $P(s_i, s_j) = P(s_{i'}, s_{j'})$,ie.$(m = n) \wedge (p_t = p'_t, \forall t \in [1, n])$,then $M_p(P, P') = 1$
② If $P(s_i, s_j) \subset P(s_{i'}, s_{j'})$, ie. $\exists k < (m - n) : p_t = p'_{(k+t)}, t = \overline{1..n}$, then $M_p(P, P') = \frac{n}{m}$

Since a service in a composition has either the incoming direct link patterns from its precedent services or the outgoing direct link patterns to its following services, *we take into account the direct link pattern's directions* in our computation. Concretely, to compute the direct link pattern matching between s_i and s_j, we match incoming direct link patterns of s_i to incoming direct link patterns of s_j and outgoing patterns of s_i to outgoing direct link patterns of s_j then we sum these matching results to get the final matching value. *The matching between two direct link patterns that have inverse directions is equal to* 0, which means if $P(s_i, s_j)$ and $P(s_{i'}, s_{j'})$ are two direct link patterns from s_i to s_j and $s_{i'}$ to $s_{j'}$ respectively, then $M_p(P(s_i, s_j), P(s_{j'}, s_{i'})) = M_p(P(s_j, s_i), P(s_{i'}, s_{j'})) = 0$.

In our example, when the direct link patterns are mapped to sequences of characters, we have $M_p(P_3, P_9) = M_p$('Sequence','Sequence')=1; $M_p(P_4, P_{10}) = M_p$('AND-join','AND-join')=1; $M_p(P_5, P_{11}) = M_p$('AND-join','OR-join''AND-join')=0.5, and so on.

3.2 Composition Context Matching

The kth-zone neighbors of a service create a fragment composition around it. This fragment contains the composition context of the associated service within k layers. In our approach, we propose to compute the similarity between two services based on the matching of their composition context. Concretely, to compute the similarity between two services s_i and s_j, we *match all direct link patterns that belong to the same zone and are ended by either s_i or s_j or the same services.* By this way, our approach *captures latently the service matching* of two compositions, *focuses only on the related services* and *avoids the time-consuming problem* of redundant matching computations. In our illustrated example, we will match (P_3 and P_9), (P_4 and P_{10}), (P_5 and P_{11}) as they have the same ending services, not (P_1 and P_6) or other pairs.

In formula, suppose that $a =<< s_x, s_y, P_{\mathcal{C}m}(s_x, s_y) >, z >$ is the edge connecting s_x and s_y by the direct link pattern $P_{\mathcal{C}m}(s_x, s_y)$ belongs to zone z in the composition context graph $G_{\mathcal{C}m}(s_i)$, $a \in V_{\mathcal{C}m}(s_i)$. Similarly, $a' =<< s_{x'}, s_{y'}, P_{\mathcal{C}n}(s_{x'}, s_{y'}) >, z' >\in V_{\mathcal{C}n}(s_j)$. The composition context matching of s_i and s_j within k^{th}-area with the direction consideration is given by Equation (2).

$$\mathbb{M}^k_{\mathcal{C}a,\mathcal{C}b}(s_i, s_j) = \frac{\sum\limits_{a \in V_{\mathcal{C}m}(s_i)} \sum\limits_{a' \in V_{\mathcal{C}n}(s_j)} M^*(a, a')}{|Z^k_{\mathcal{C}m}(s_i)|} \tag{2}$$

in which, $M^*(a, a') = M_p(P_{\mathcal{C}m}(s_x, s_y), P_{\mathcal{C}n}(s_{x'}, s_{y'}))$ in cases:

① $(z = z' = 1) \wedge ((s_x = s_i \wedge s_{x'} = s_j \wedge s_y = s_{y'}) \vee (s_x = s_{x'} \wedge s_y = s_i \wedge s_{y'} = s_j))$
② $(1 < z = z' \leq k) \wedge (s_x = s_{x'}) \wedge (s_y = s_{y'}))$

and $M^*(a, a') = 0$ in other cases.

We can easily check that, $\mathbb{M}^k_{\mathcal{C}a,\mathcal{C}b}(s_i, s_j)$ is different from $\mathbb{M}^k_{\mathcal{C}b,\mathcal{C}a}(s_j, s_i)$, and if $Z^k_{\mathcal{C}m}(s_i) \subseteq Z^k_{\mathcal{C}m}(s_j)$, $\mathbb{M}^k_{\mathcal{C}a,\mathcal{C}b}(s_i, s_j)$ will be equal to 1, which means if all patterns from s_i to its kth-layer neighbors are patterns from s_j to its kth-layer neighbors, s_j will be absolutely able to replace s_i.

The kth-area neighbors of a service s create a process fragment surrounding s, which is presented by a sub composition graph. Therefore, the matching problem becomes the graph matching problem which was proved to be a NP-complexity problem [1]. However, in our case, we know the root points of the graph comparison, which are s_i and s_j, and we match only the same pairs of services in both composition graphs, thus *we avoid the NP-complexity problem* of the original graph matching. In another hand, with the composition context graph definition and the direct link patterns presentation in zones, we can compute the composition context matching of any pair of services in compositions. Moreover, direct link patterns locates in the closest zones to the associated service. Therefore, our algorithm run smoothly and returns very high quality results.

The computation given by equation (2) can generate recommendations regardless the zones that a pattern path belongs to. However, in reality, the behavior of a service is strongly reflected by the direct link patterns to its closet neighbors while the interactions among other neighbors in the higher layers do not heavily affect its behavior. Therefore, the impact of kth zones needs to be examined and we propose to assign a weight (w_k) for each kth-zone, so called zone-weight and integrate this parameter into our computation. Since the zone-weight has to have greater values in smaller k zones, we propose to assign the zone-weight a value computed by a polynomial function which is given by equation (3).

$$w_z = \frac{k+1-z}{k} \tag{3}$$

where z is the zone number ($1 \leq z \leq k$), k is the number of considered zones around the service. All direct link patterns connect either to or from the associated service has the greatest weight ($w_1 = 1$) and the direct link patterns connect to/from services in the furthest zone has the smallest weight ($w_k = 1/k$).

With the zone's weight consideration, the pattern matching computation on two services $s_i \in V_{\mathcal{C}a}$ and $s_j \in V_{\mathcal{C}b}$ is the combination of composition context matching (the equation(2)) and the zone-weight impact (the equation(3)), which is given by the equation (4).

$$\mathcal{M}^k_{\mathcal{C}a,\mathcal{C}b}(s_i, s_j) = \frac{2}{k+1} \times \sum_{z=1}^{k} \frac{\sum_{a.z=a'.z'=z} \frac{k+1-z}{k} \times M^*(a, a')}{|Z^z_{\mathcal{C}m}(s_i)| - |Z^{z-1}_{\mathcal{C}m}(s_i)|} \tag{4}$$

where $|Z^z_{\mathcal{C}m}(s_i)| - |Z^{z-1}_{\mathcal{C}m}(s_i)|$ is the number of direct link patterns in the zone z^{th} of $G_{\mathcal{C}m}(s_i)$ (see Definition 5). In case $|Z^z_{\mathcal{C}m}(s_i)| - |Z^{z-1}_{\mathcal{C}m}(s_i)| = 0$, which means there is no direct link pattern in the zone z^{th} of $G_{\mathcal{C}m}(s_i)$, $M^*(a, a')$ is also equal to 0, we consider the fraction $\frac{0}{0}$ as 0.

Return to our example with the zone-weight consideration, in case $k = 1$, $t = 0$, only the nearest neighbors are taken into account, the zone-weight does not affect the results, therefore, the matching values are the same to the case that we do not take into account the zone-weight, which means $\mathcal{M}^1_{\mathcal{C}1,\mathcal{C}2}(s_2, s_6) = \mathbb{M}^1_{\mathcal{C}1,\mathcal{C}2}(s_2, s_6)$ and $\mathcal{M}^1_{\mathcal{C}2,\mathcal{C}1}(s_6, s_2) = \mathbb{M}^1_{\mathcal{C}2,\mathcal{C}1}(s_6, s_2)$. In case $k = 2$, we have: $\mathcal{M}^2_{\mathcal{C}1,\mathcal{C}2}(s_2, s_6) = (1/3) \times (2 \times (M_p(P_{i3}, P_{j3}) + M_p(P_{i4}, P_{j4})/2) + (M_p(P_{i5}, P_{j5})/2)) = 0.75$ and $\mathcal{M}^2_{\mathcal{C}2,\mathcal{C}1}(s_6, s_2) = (1/3) \times (2 \times (M_p(P_{j3}, P_{i3}) + M_p(P_{j4}, P_{i4})/2) + (M_p(P_{j5}, P_{i5})/3)) \approx 0.72$.

The matching values among services present their similarity and they are used to make recommendation. For a selected service, we pick up top-n services which have the highest matching values to recommend it. In our experiments, we recommend the top-5 services for each one.

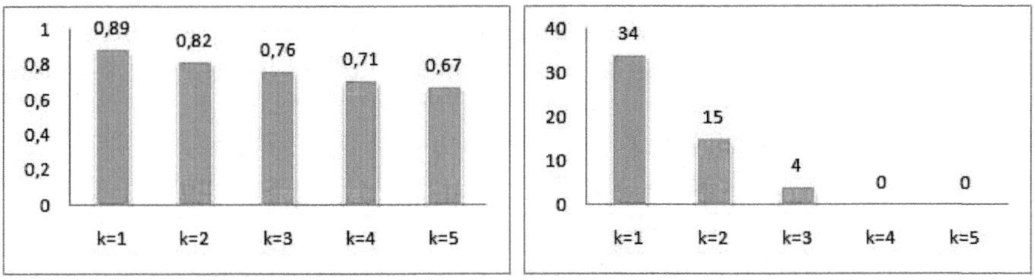

(a) Average matching values **(b)** Services with matching value=1

Fig. 3. Statistics of matching values with different k^{th}-zone

4 Implementation and Experiments

We tried to get experiments from real business process abstracts or web service compositions but finding proper datasets for our approach is really a big challenge. We searched from the Internet in parallel with asking other researchers on our domain but unfortunately we did not found any good dataset or the datasets are under non-disclosure agreements. Finally, we decided to collect manually the scattered business processes and web service compositions (focus on car rental, car selling and travel booking business context) on previous contributions, re-engineer them to be used by our application and added some business processed designed by ourselves. On synthesis of the collected data, we got a database with 46 web services and 27 compositions. The largest composition consists of 14 services and the smallest composition consists of 4 services (in average, 6.8 services per composition). Our application[1] is implemented as a Java applet in order to allow public users adding web services, creating compositions and get recommendations based on our proposed model.

We experiment on asserting *the impact of* k^{th}*-zones on the composition context matching*. For each service, we computed its similarity values with others and selected the most related service which had the highest similarity value. We run the proposed model with different k^{th}-zones. The results showed that the average matching values computed by our algorithm are very high and decrease when k increases (Fig. 3a). When k increases, services and patterns in the further zones are taken into account and in most cases, the matching among these patterns in comparison to the number of patterns in the further zones is lower than the matching in the nearer zones, therefore, it decreases the final matching values.

The kth-zone also affects the number of services which are retrieved with the highest matching values. When k increases, the number of services which are retrieved with high similarity values decreases and the number of services which are retrieved with the lower similarity values increases. Fig. 3b show the distribution of matching values with different k^{th}-zones. With $k = 1$, 34 services were recommended with the similarity equal to 1 (Fig. 3b). When k increases, the unmatched patterns in the further zones around the associated services reduce

[1] `http://www-inf.int-evry.fr/SIMBAD/tools/CMSR/`

the similarity values and the number of services which were retrieved by the highest similarity values also decreased. However, since the nearest neighbors to a service have the greatest weight, most of the results are stable when k increases (Fig. 4).

In practice, the behavior of a service is reflected by its connections to the nearest neighbors (1st-zones). The relations to its higher k^{th}-zone ($k > 1$) neighbors have less impact to its behavior. In our approach, we target to recommend services for business process design, not for an agnostic use. Therefore, widening the kth-zones allows reducing the searching space by taking into account richer composition contexts and get the closer results to the required services. The more zones to a services are considered, the better candidates are retrieved.

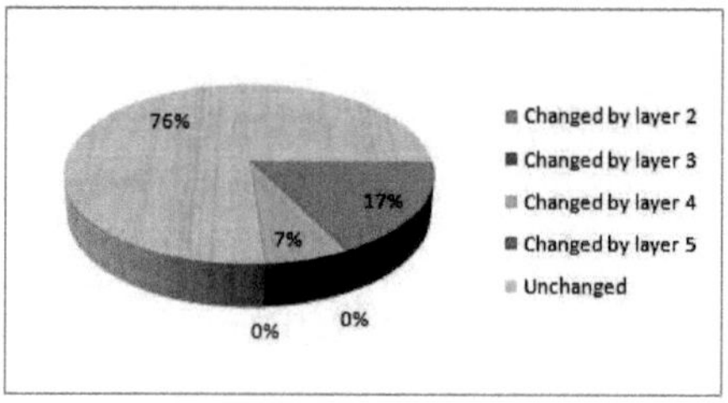

Fig. 4. Statistics of retrieved services

5 Related Work

In recent years, there are many efforts on helping the business process designers to faster and more accurately create new business process models using available reference models. They proposed either to rank the existing business process models in the repository for searching [8,22], or to measure the similarity between them [10,19,14] to create new process models. Some of them [8,22] encountered the NP-complexity graph matching problem and they have to find a compromise between computation complexity and quality of results. Different from them, our approach focused partially on the business process, described as a service composition, to take into account just the composition context to retrieve the most related services. Therefore, we do not face the NP-complexity problem (as we explained in section 3.2). In another hand, we focus on matching a partial context instead of matching the whole business process.

Another contribution that aims at refining business process reference by merging existing process models was recently presented by M.L. Rosa et. al.[16]. However, different from our work, they did not do further to help process designers and users with recommendations. D. Schleicher et. al. [17] also presented an approach based on so-called compliance templates to develop and manage compliant business processes involving different stakeholders. Their work targeted at refining the business process in layers using compliance constraints. These constrains can be composition constraints although the authors did not mention how they can be inferred. In our paper, we propose to implicitly extract them.

Thomas Gschwind et. al. [11] also applied workflow patterns for business process design. They aimed at helping business users understand the context and apply patterns during the editing process. In our work, we help the business users better design a business process by automatically providing them the most related services instead of patterns.

In the web service discovery domain, many solutions for faster reaching to the desired services were also proposed. Most of them based on the traditional service descriptions (WSDL documents) and targeted at finding the similarity between requests from users (query, profile, historic data, etc) and data stored in service repositories. They generated recommendations based on the text processing, including query analysis and web service description similarity. They can be classified in the categories: clustering [9], rating based [15], words analysis [3] and vector space model [12]. Since these approaches are text-based, they can encounter the synonym and polysenym problems (one word can have many meanings and one meaning can be described by different words). In another hand, since they captured only the explicit knowledge described in WSDL files, they lack the implicit knowledge which can be inferred from past usage data.

Our previous contributions [5,4,6] on proposing a web service recommender system based on user's behavior can overcome the shortcomings of the text-based analysis systems. We solved the problem from the user's side and we can provide good recommendations which are close to user's behaviors. However, in our previous work, we did not take into account the relations among web services in compositions. We fulfilled this shortcoming in this work.

Last but not least, it is worth to notice that our approach can associate with the functionality-based service recommendation techniques to generate more precise recommendations since the service connections to its neighbors do not infer fully its functionality. Our approach can be applied as preprocessing step either in the design phase to limit the search space or later in the execution phase to filter the selected recommended services.

6 Conclusion and Future Work

In this paper, we propose an original approach to capture the composition context to generate process design recommendation. Since this composition context presents the requested service's behavior and they can implicitly infer the service's functionality, our approach performed well in recommending related services. Our approach retrieves not only the services for an incomplete abstract process but also possibly the replaceable services to a selected one. It can be very useful in helping the composition designers and managers find suitable services to replace a vulnerable one to enhance the availability of the service compositions. In our future work, we intend to investigate the co-existence of patterns in compositions, as well as the number of time that a web service is used in oder to refine our matching algorithm. We also aim at extending our approach to infer existing service composition from log execution.

Acknowledgement. The work presented in this paper is supported by the ANR French funding under the PAIRSE project.

References

1. Abdulkader, A.M.: Parallel Algorithms for Labelled Graph Matching. PhD thesis, Colorado School of Mines, USA (1998)
2. Alonso, G., Casati, F., Kuno, H., Machiraju, V.: Web Services: Concepts, Architectures and Applications. Springer, Berlin (2003)
3. Blake, M.B., Nowlan, M.F.: A web service recommender system using enhanced syntactical matching. In: ICWS, pp. 575–582 (2007)
4. Ngoc Chan, N., Gaaloul, W., Tata, S.: Collaborative filtering technique for web service recommendation based on user-operation combination. In: Meersman, R., Dillon, T.S., Herrero, P. (eds.) OTM 2010. LNCS, vol. 6426, pp. 222–239. Springer, Heidelberg (2010)
5. Chan, N.N., Gaaloul, W., Tata, S.: Web services recommendation based on user's behavior. In: ICEBE, pp. 214–221 (November 2010)
6. Chan, N.N., Gaaloul, W., Tata, S.: A web service recommender system using vector space model and latent semantic indexing. In: AINA, pp. 602–609 (2011)
7. Curran, T., Keller, G., Ladd, A.: SAP R/3 business blueprint: understanding the business process reference model. Prentice-Hall, Inc., NJ (1998)
8. Dijkman, R., Dumas, M., García-Bañuelos, L.: Graph matching algorithms for business process model similarity search. In: Dayal, U., Eder, J., Koehler, J., Reijers, H.A. (eds.) BPM 2009. LNCS, vol. 5701, pp. 48–63. Springer, Heidelberg (2009)
9. Dong, X., Halevy, A., Madhavan, J., Nemes, E., Zhang, J.: Similarity search for web services. In: VLDB, pp. 372–383 (2004)
10. Ehrig, M., Koschmider, A., Oberweis, A.: Measuring similarity between semantic business process models. In: APCCM 2007, pp. 71–80 (2007)
11. Gschwind, T., Koehler, J., Wong, J.: Applying patterns during business process modeling. In: Dumas, M., Reichert, M., Shan, M.-C. (eds.) BPM 2008. LNCS, vol. 5240, pp. 4–19. Springer, Heidelberg (2008)
12. Kokash, N., Birukou, A., D'Andrea, V.: Web service discovery based on past user experience. In: Abramowicz, W. (ed.) BIS 2007. LNCS, vol. 4439, pp. 95–107. Springer, Heidelberg (2007)
13. Levenshtein, V.: Binary Codes Capable of Correcting Deletions, Insertions and Reversals. Soviet Physics Doklady 10, 707 (1966)
14. Li, C., Reichert, M., Wombacher, A.: On measuring process model similarity based on high-level change operations. In: Li, Q., Spaccapietra, S., Yu, E., Olivé, A. (eds.) ER 2008. LNCS, vol. 5231, pp. 248–264. Springer, Heidelberg (2008)
15. Manikrao, U.S., Prabhakar, T.V.: Dynamic selection of web services with recommendation system. In: NWESP 2005, p. 117. IEEE Computer Society, Washington (2005)
16. La Rosa, M., Dumas, M., Uba, R., Dijkman, R.: Merging business process models. In: Meersman, R., Dillon, T.S., Herrero, P. (eds.) OTM 2010. LNCS, vol. 6426, pp. 96–113. Springer, Heidelberg (2010)
17. Schleicher, D., Anstett, T., Leymann, F., Schumm, D.: Compliant business process design using refinement layers. In: Meersman, R., Dillon, T.S., Herrero, P. (eds.) OTM 2010. LNCS, vol. 6426, pp. 114–131. Springer, Heidelberg (2010)
18. Stephens, S.: Supply chain operations reference model version 5.0: A new tool to improve supply chain efficiency and achieve best practice. Information Systems Frontiers 3, 471–476 (2001)

19. van der Aalst, W.M.P., de Medeiros, A.K.A., Weijters, A.J.M.M.T.: Process equivalence: Comparing two process models based on observed behavior. In: Dustdar, S., Fiadeiro, J.L., Sheth, A.P. (eds.) BPM 2006. LNCS, vol. 4102, pp. 129–144. Springer, Heidelberg (2006)
20. van der Aalst, W.M.P., Dumas, M., Gottschalk, F., ter Hofstede, A.H.M., Rosa, M.L., Mendling, J.: Preserving correctness during business process model configuration. Formal Asp. Comput. 22(3-4), 459–482 (2010)
21. Van Der Aalst, W.M.P., Ter Hofstede, A.H.M., Kiepuszewski, B., Barros, A.P.: Workflow patterns. Distrib. Parallel Databases 14(1), 5–51 (2003)
22. Yan, Z., Dijkman, R., Grefen, P.: Fast business process similarity search with feature-based similarity estimation. In: Meersman, R., Dillon, T.S., Herrero, P. (eds.) OTM 2010. LNCS, vol. 6426, pp. 60–77. Springer, Heidelberg (2010)

Composite Process View Transformation

David Schumm[1], Jiayang Cai[1], Christoph Fehling[1], Dimka Karastoyanova[1], Frank Leymann[1], and Monika Weidmann[2]

[1] Institute of Architecture of Application Systems, University of Stuttgart, Universitätsstraße 38, 70569 Stuttgart, Germany
{Schumm,Fehling,Karastoyanova,Leymann}@iaas.uni-stuttgart.de
[2] Fraunhofer-Institut für Arbeitswirtschaft und Organisation (IAO), Competence Center Electronic Business, 70569 Stuttgart, Germany
Monika.Weidmann@iao.fraunhofer.de

Abstract. The increasing complexity of processes used for design and execution of critical business activities demands novel techniques and technologies. Process viewing techniques have been proposed as means to abstract from details, summarize and filter out information, and customize the visual appearance of a process to the need of particular stakeholders. However, composition of process view transformations and their provisioning to enable their usage in various scenarios is currently not discussed in research. In this paper, we present a lightweight, service-oriented approach to compose modular process view transformation functions to form complex process view transformations which can be offered as a service. We introduce a concept and an architectural framework to generate process view service compositions automatically with focus on usability. Furthermore, we discuss key aspects regarding the realization of the approach as well as different scenarios where process view services and their compositions are needed.

Keywords: Process View, Service Composition, BPM.

1 Introduction

Increasing adoption of Business Process Management (BPM) technologies in industry over the last decade revealed that managing process complexity is a key issue, which needs to be addressed. A large business process may contain hundreds of activities [2], requiring advanced methods and techniques for managing such complexity. Process view transformations have been proposed by various research groups as a means to address this problem. In previous work [4], we have assembled the existing concepts and approaches in the field of process view transformations and distilled them into a unified generic representation in terms of commonly used transformation patterns. As a consequence, we understand a *process view* as the graphical presentation of the result obtained after specific process view transformations have been applied to a process model. The purpose of these transformations is manifold. It ranges from summarizing information in order to reduce complexity, filtering information to abstract from details that are irrelevant for a particular analytical task, translating information to provide a

C. Huemer and T. Setzer (Eds.): EC-Web 2011, LNBIP 85, pp. 52–63, 2011.

perspective for a particular stakeholder, up to linking information to augment a process with related data like runtime information about the execution status.

While algorithms and concepts for process view transformations have been well-established in business process management research [5, 8, 10, 11], there is a lack of investigation of their applicability in practice, their composability, and their integration into given toolsets. We identified approximately 20 different process views so far [4, 6, 7], which provide advanced functions to support process design, process deployment, process monitoring, and process analysis. Based on self-experience as scientific methodology, we observed that these process views have two fundamental aspects in common, which are essential for the work discussed in this paper. The first aspect is that these *process views can be composed* to form complex view transformations. For example, a process can be organized according to the distribution of participants (both human beings and services). This process view can be used as input to another transformation that includes the current status of a particular instance of this process. The output of this transformation can be further transformed to show only the activities which are incomplete. Figure 1 illustrates this composition of process views. The second, fundamental aspect concerns *the way in which process view compositions are defined*: There is little need for complex control constructs like conditions, loops or parallelism. Instead, a sequence of process view transformations typically is being performed, as exemplified in Figure 1. Therefore, we propose defining process view compositions by specifying sequences of service invocations, each representing a particular process view transformation.

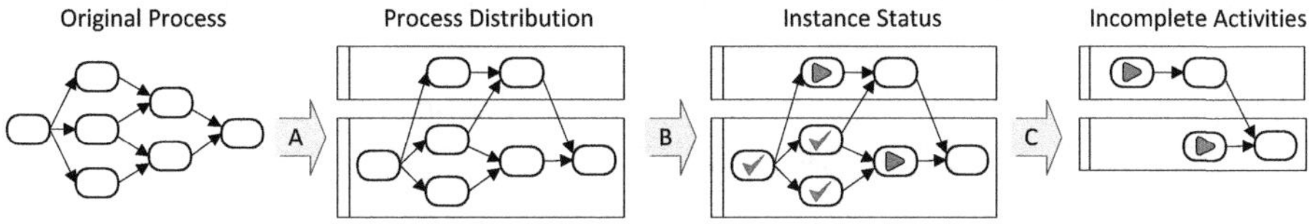

Fig. 1. The result of an exemplary composition of process views: Distribution of participants involved in an input process (A), augmented with the current status of an instance (B), reduced to incomplete activities (C)

The key contribution of this paper is a concept for high-level definition and automatic enactment of service compositions used for composite process view transformation. The concept is intended to empower non-expert users to create pipeline-like service compositions as sequences of service invocations. The approach is to limit the expressiveness of the Business Process Execution Language (BPEL) [1] to a small subset, which allows automatically generating compositions of process view services, out of user-defined composition specifications. Thereby composite process view transformations can be defined that are tailored to the information needs of the different process stakeholders. Moreover, these composites can be provisioned automatically, which is of great advantage. We advance the state of the art regarding the applicability of process view transformation in practice by means of corresponding methods, concepts, and tool support.

The paper's further structure is the following: In Section 2 we introduce a general architecture for service-based composition of process view transformations on a high level. Based on this architecture, Section 3 describes a detailed walk through the different development stages of process view service compositions. These stages embrace building elementary process view services, defining how to compose them, and generating an executable service composition. We discuss advanced aspects and challenges in Section 4. In Section 5 we point out related work in this field. Section 6 concludes the paper.

2 Architecture for a Process View Management Framework

In this section, we present an architecture for a process view management framework, the platform for composition of process view services. We list contained components, describe their interrelation, and give a brief overview of their functionality and purpose. A walk through the key realization aspects of this architecture can be found in Section 3.

We assume three basic roles we target our framework at. The *Process View Service Developer* is responsible for designing and implementing the core functions of the approach, i.e. the process view services. The *Information Designer* is the user and operator of the process view management framework. He/she registers available process view services and creates meaningful view definitions which describe composite process view transformations on a high level of abstraction. Out of these view definitions, executable service compositions are generated automatically by the framework. The *Process View Consumer* finally uses the (composed) services for the creation of views on concrete processes for his/her particular information needs.

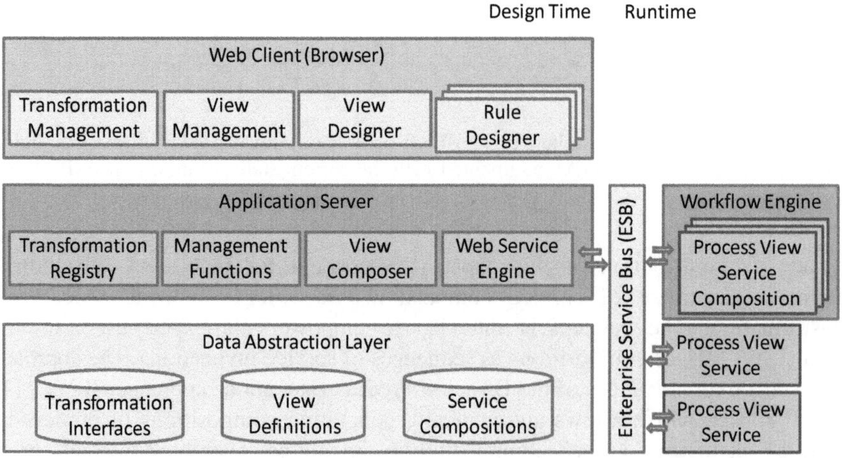

Fig. 2. Architecture for a process view management framework

As shown in Figure 2, we use a three-tier setting for the design time of process view service compositions. Design time is shown on the left part and runtime is shown on the right part of the figure. The upper tier in the design time part of the architecture provides Web-based functions for managing composite process view transformations. In this tier, the *Transformation Management* provides functions for registering and deregistering *Process View Services* (see the runtime part in Figure 2). The *View Management* provides selection menus for creating, deleting, opening and deploying existing view definitions. It may also provide an interface for invocation of process view service compositions which have been deployed to the workflow engine. A view definition represents a composition of process view services on a high level. This definition is abstract and not executable. A view definition is basically a sequential ordering of selected operations of registered process view services. The *View Designer* is the component which is actually used to design and modify view definitions. As process view services need to be parameterized, a set of *Rule Designers* is required. To support the information designer in coping with a diversity of formats, we propose to use the concept of domain-specific languages (DSL) here.

The middle tier represents the backend. The *Transformation Registry* handles requests related to transformation management, extracts interface information and passes them to the *Data Abstraction Layer*; the *Management Functions* provide analogous functionality for requests related to view definitions; the *View Composer* is one of the core components of the framework, responsible for generating an executable *Process View Service Composition* out of a view definition. This composition orchestrates the core of the approach, the *Process View Services.* We propose the use of BPEL [1] as format for executable service compositions.

The generated service compositions can be stored locally, can be registered as process view services for recursive compositions, and can be deployed using the *Web Service Engine* component. This engine integrates with the Web service interfaces provided by the *Workflow Engine*, shown in the right-hand side in Figure 2. The runtime performs the execution of the generated *Process View Service Compositions.*

3 Key Realization Aspects

In this section, we examine the key aspects of our approach from a realization point of view. These aspects concern the development of process view services (Section 3.1), the creation of view definitions (Section 3.2), and the generation of process view service compositions (Section 3.3).

3.1 Development of Process View Services

Process view services are the components which implement process view transformation functionality. They are exposed to the outside using an interface description language like the Web Services Description Language (WSDL). In the following we abstract from the inner implementation of these services and focus on their exposure to the outside and how to control the transformations they perform.

As proposed in our previous work [4] and depicted in Figure 3, the following terms are essential in process view transformations: The *Original Process* is the process model that is subject to a *View Transformation* which results in a *Process View.* We use the term *Target Set* to indicate the process structures in the input process model which should be affected by an elementary transformation *Action.* The action represents the transformation function to be applied. Examples for such functions as described in [4] are structural transformations (aggregation, omission, alteration, abstraction, insertion), data augmentation transformations (runtime, human-assisted, calculated), presentation transformations (appearance, scheme, layout, theme), and transformations with multiple input processes.

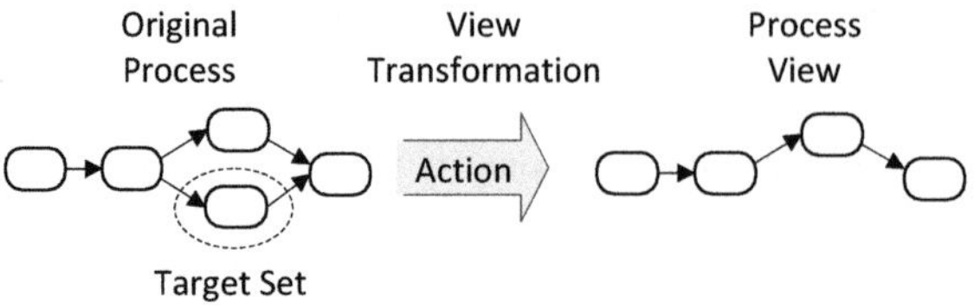

Fig. 3. Process view transformation terminology

Together, a target set and an action make up a *Transformation Rule*. Multiple rules can be applied after one another as in batch processing. For example, a first rule may state to omit all activities for variable assignment. A second rule may state to make service invocation activities "opaque" to state that something is happening at that place, while hiding detailed information. A global *Configuration* is useful to set general parameters valid for all rules. For instance, a parameter in the configuration can switch "executability" on or off. This parameter refers to the preservation of process structures and artifacts that are mandatory for executability, like an instance-creating `<receive>` in BPEL. To support the exposure of process view transformation functionality as a service, as well as to ease their composition, we propose a common structure of transformation instructions as depicted in Figure 4.

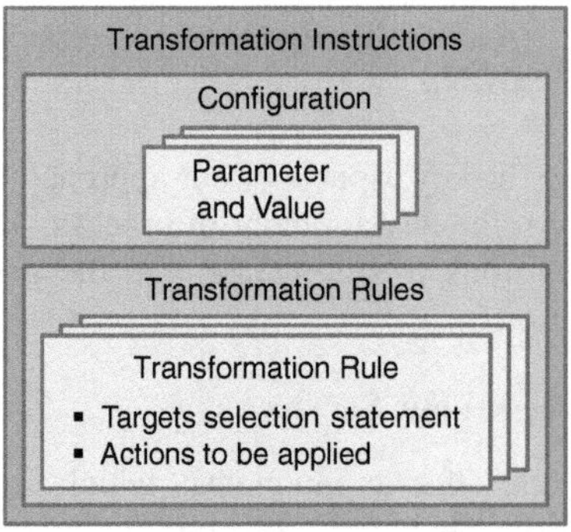

Fig. 4. Common structure of instructions for a process view service

However, our main finding with respect to realization of process view transformations, their exposure as a service, their consumption, and their composition, is that there is no ultimate format or language for describing concrete transformation rules and configuration parameters. Instead, each process view service will likely have a different set of parameters, and will likely use different languages to control the transformation. For example, the target selection statement for a service which removes a process fragment from a given input process will likely be a process fragment itself, while a process view service that provides general filtering functionality will more likely use regular expressions or SQL-like statements. Also, if the same functionality is offered by different vendors, the parameter formats of services may differ. Furthermore, the vocabulary of transformation actions that can be performed will probably differ. As a conclusion, we argue that the concept of DSLs applies here, so each service may use different formats and types of parameters. The architecture presented in Section 2 considers this conclusion with multiple *Rule Designer* components, generated automatically from the service interface description, or directly provided by the process view service vendor.

3.2 Creation of View Definitions

For the presented approach, the main interest lies in the mere use of service offerings as well as in the ability to create own, custom compositions of available services which are possibly provided by different vendors. Besides the functionality that the service needs to offer, the selection of services can be based on process view transformation quality constraints like guarantee of the executability of the process view, or by cost, processing speed, etc. as described in the vision of Web service ecosystems [15] which makes the notion of service procurement explicit. According to [15], a Web service ecosystem is envisioned as a "logical collection of Web services whose exposure and access are subject to constraints characteristic of business service delivery."

Process view services need to be registered in the process view management framework before they can be used in the definition of process view service compositions. As service registration is a common feature in service-oriented application design, we do not discuss this aspect in detail here. The registration of available process view services and hence the information about their input parameter types allows specifying a composition of these services. Parameter and type information is essential for parameterization and configuration of the process view services on a high level. With the term "View Definition" we denote a quite simple form of such composition, with ease-of-use as focal point. We fundamentally constrain the expressiveness of Web service compositions by only allowing the definition of a linear sequence of process view service invocations. The flexibility we provide is focused on the interconnection of output and input parameters of consecutive service invocations. However, process view service compositions which require complex control structures, cycles, and conditional branches cannot be defined in this high-level manner. For such cases the direct usage of process languages like BPEL without an abstraction level on top as we propose here is one possibility (see also Section 4.1). Nevertheless, a lightweight, pipeline-like composition approach may be beneficial for all those cases in which a linear sequence of service invocations is sufficient. Process code can be generated automatically out of the high-level view definition, which is much easier to create than executable process models.

A view definition can be created by iteratively searching and selecting a registered process view service to be used. From this selection one of the operations offered by that service can be chosen. Thereby, a list of process view service invocations comes into being, see Figure 5 (left). The outputs produced by these process view services can be used as input in subsequent service invocations. Thus, the services can be connected by defining data flow between them.

In the creation of view definitions, we can distinguish *dynamic* and *static* parameters. Dynamic parameters are used to make a view definition (and the resulting process view service composition) configurable. This allows adjusting the behavior of the composite view transformation in each invocation without changing and re-deploying its original definition. In contrast, static parameters are used to define constant settings which are valid for all invocations of the resulting process view service composition. For example (see also Figure 5), the first service invocation may augment a process (provided as dynamic parameter "Original Process") with information related to the recognition of a process fragment that is critical for security (customized through the dynamic "Parameter A"). The second service invocation shall extract this fragment, using static transformation instructions specified in the static "Parameter B". The subsequent service invocation takes the original process and the extracted fragment as input, and produces a process view in which this fragment is omitted. The final service invocation in this exemplary view definition produces an SVG rendering of this process, configured statically with "Parameter C". The output "Process View" is finally returned.

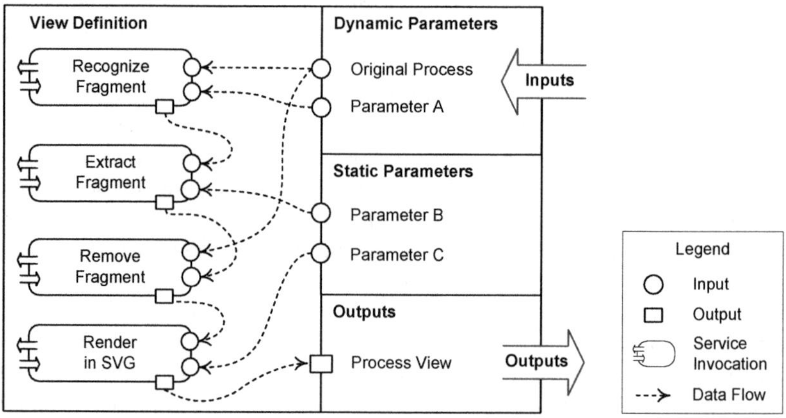

Fig. 5. Definition of a composition of process view services on a high level

Service invocations can be reordered to obtain a view definition that is free of forward dependencies which would make the view definition invalid. When this dependency criterion is met and all service invocation parameters are either connected to dynamic parameters, static parameters, or previous outputs, then this view definition can be used to generate an executable process view service composition.

3.3 Generation of Executable Process View Service Compositions

For the generation of an executable process view service composition several artifacts are necessary. The view definition describes the sequencing of service invocations and the connection of inputs, outputs, and parameters. The WSDL documents of involved process view services contain type definitions and addresses of the services required for execution. Furthermore, as the generated service compositions all have the same basic structure, a template for the service composition is useful. This template consists of a BPEL process skeleton and a WSDL skeleton. The template is instantiated during the generation of executable code from the view definition. The deployment descriptor, which is also required for execution, is rather dependent on the selected services and therefore needs to be generated dynamically.

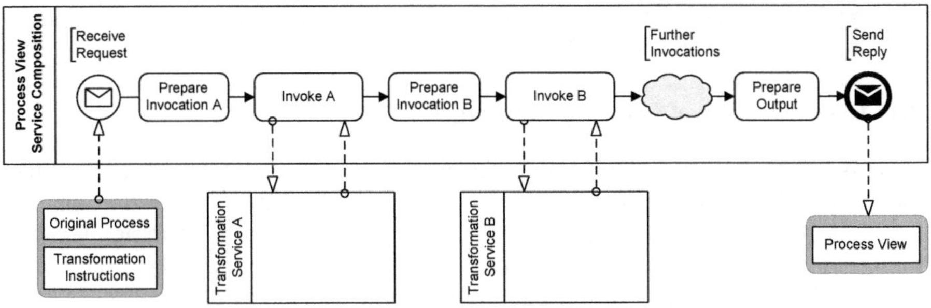

Fig. 6. Generated composition of process view services

The structure of a generated process view service composition is illustrated in Figure 6. In this figure, the Business Process Model and Notation (BPMN) standard [16] is used to visualize the BPEL process, though considering implicit data flow as used in BPEL. The illustration in BPMN is intended to explain the concept, only BPEL code needs to be generated (or: executable BPMN). The process view service composition can be invoked with a request that contains all dynamic parameters, represented by a `<receive createInstance="yes">`. Static parameters are set at process instantiation. For each service invocation specified in the view definition, an `<assign>` activity prepares the input parameters and a subsequent `<invoke>` activity invokes the operation of a service. Finally, the output - the process view - is returned to the service composition consumer by a `<reply>`. Such a generated service composition can be packaged by the *View Composer* component (see Section 2) and be stored in a database, or deployed to a workflow engine to enable execution. A service composition that has been deployed to a workflow engine can also be registered as a new process view service and thus enable recursive compositions.

We developed a prototype of a framework for the management of composite process view transformations on BPEL processes. In comparison to the concept of view definitions presented in Section 3.2, our prototype does not support arbitrary connection of inputs and outputs of services yet. Thus, data mediation is not considered. Currently, one can only configure that a service should use the output produced by the directly prior service invocation as an input for one of its particular parameters. Experiments with our process view services and evaluation of the framework for generating executable service compositions based on BPEL showed that arbitrary connection of output parameters is not necessary in many cases. For instance, the view definition described in Section 3.2 can be implemented that way. Such lightweight compositions can be used to refine a process view step-wise, forming pipeline-like service compositions.

4 Advanced Aspects and Challenges

There are advanced aspects and challenges that need to be addressed before a productive use of (composite) process view services is possible. One aspect is related to the expressiveness of languages involved in the approach (Section 4.1). These languages have significant impact on the flexibility, ease-of-use, and configurability of composite process view transformations. The other aspect we discuss is related to security and privacy (Section 4.2).

4.1 Expressiveness of Involved Languages

Process view services may offer domain-specific languages (DSLs) that allow their parameterization and configuration. To ease usability and to make the approach accessible to a large user group, we also proposed to have a view definition language on top of the execution language which can be used to easily describe sequences of process view service invocations and wire outputs and inputs of these invocations. The question is: How much expressiveness of the involved languages can be provided while still considering ease of use?

Domain-specific languages – The concept of DSLs for parameterizing process view services we presented in Section 3.1 could be extended to provide more flexibility. For example, a rule could conditionally be executed based on the number of activities, control links, or variables contained in an input process. Furthermore, a process view service provider could offer a Web-based rule designer tool to ease the specification of transformation parameters and configuration. Such tools could also be an aid to avoid the definition of inconsistent transformation instructions. A challenge in this lies in the usage of dynamic parameters in a view definition (see Section 3.2). If dynamic parameters have been specified for the view definition, then a new DSL needs to be created to ease invocation of the newly created service composition. This DSL may be composed out of components of the DSLs of the services that are involved in the composition, defining a composition of language profiles.

View definition language – We proposed a view definition to be a sequence of service invocations, where only data flow can be specified in a flexible manner. A major issue in the specification of the data flow is the data mediation that is needed when parts of complex outputs produced by services are used later on as input parameters in invocation of other process view services. To be able to deal with this issue without in-depth technical expertise, a graphical editor is needed to support assigning input and output values. Furthermore, to make the approach more powerful, invocations of process view services could be made conditional, e.g., based on the properties of the process to be transformed. Another feature would be to allow a service invocation to be performed multiple times, for instance invoking an abstraction service until a process contains less than 50 activities. However, if such features are provided there also need to be mechanisms that assure that (i) parameters are properly initialized before any service invocation and (ii) the process is properly routed through the composition, also considering "dead paths" which may arise from conditional service invocations. Standardized process view service parameters which form some kind of basic format for inputs and outputs would make the realization of such features easier.

4.2 Security and Privacy

Well-designed and efficient business processes are an important competitive advantage. Therefore, the corresponding process models are critical intellectual property. If a company uses process view services of third-party providers, business secrets have to be protected. In the following, we discuss three methods to secure the invocation of third-party process view services by (i) hosting them in secure environments, (ii) obfuscation of business process models, and (iii) establishment of a trust relationship between process view service providers and the company using them.

Hosting in secure environments – providing a process view service as an installable package, for example on a CD, allows hosting the service in a private, secure environment. However, service users have to invest in licenses upfront and have to manage updates and patches. Especially, if the service is used seldom, on-demand access and pay-per-use is more desirable.

Obfuscation of business process models – prior to sending process models to insecure process view services, other, internal process view services could be used for process model obfuscation. For example, activity names can be replaced with random identifiers, additional activities and control flow can be added etc. After transformation, an internal deobfuscation service needs to be invoked. This approach can be employed to securely use untrustworthy services. A shortcoming is that it is limited to view transformations that do not require information about process model semantics. Examples for transformations applicable for this approach are aggregation of sequential activities or filtering of particular activity types.

Establishing trust relationships – trust relationships can be established through contracts making providers liable to ensure a certain degree of privacy and security [14]. This method is most likely to be used in practice.

5 Related Work

From academia, significant progress has been made in the field of process views. Process views are applied to various different languages like Event-driven Process Chains (EPC), Petri Nets, BPMN [16], and also to the BPEL [1]. Typically, scientific works on process views concentrate on one particular application scenario. For instance, in [5] process views are used to support service outsourcing by generating "public views". The work presented in [12] focuses on aggregation of activities by making use of part-of relations between activities. A work by Reichert et al. [13] discusses the application of process views to provide access control for process models. In Web service environments, process views can be applied to simplify Web service orchestrations specified in BPEL by omission of activities and aggregation of structures of a BPEL process, as discussed for example in [8]. Our own process view implementations also operate on BPEL processes – in [7] we proposed a process view to remove or extract process structures. However, composition of process views and their provisioning as a service is currently not discussed in research. We argue that all these mentioned process view approaches are well applicable for usage as a software service in the manner we proposed. For instance, a generated public view on a process can subsequently be transformed with advanced aggregation techniques.

Most of the approaches proposed in the field of process views so far have their focus on structural changes of a process model. Recently, graphical aspects and process appearance are taken more and more into account in order to create perspectives which are tailored to the needs of particular stakeholders and scenarios. In this manner, the authors of [17] distinguish between the concrete syntax (appearance) and the abstract syntax (structure) of a process. They argue that changes of the concrete syntax are well-suited to cope with the increasing complexity of process models. Their findings build on literature study, tool and language evaluation, and remarkably, on works related to human perception such as [18]. However, further research is required to cover all aspects of a service-based composition of functions that especially provide transformations of the concrete syntax.

Regarding service composition, the term Composite as a Service (Caas) [9] or Composition as a Service [3] denotes the concept of having a layer on top of Software as a Service (SaaS), which applies process-based application design principles. Defining or executing a composition can be provided as a service which can be offered by a vendor or by a third party. By specifying own compositions, vendor offerings can be combined with services developed in-house. For example, the augmentation of a process with information related to the distribution of activities to the sites of a company may be performed by an in-house service, while an advanced graphical rendering may be provided by a third party.

6 Conclusion

In this paper, we presented an approach for defining and enacting lightweight, service-based applications that form complex process view transformation functionality which can be offered as a service. We introduced an architectural framework and discussed key aspects regarding the realization of such an architecture as well as different scenarios where process view services and their compositions apply. We see our approach as an aid to find a balance between simplicity-of-use on the one hand, and providing flexibility and expressiveness on the other hand, when defining composition of process view services in particular and also when defining service compositions per se. While BPEL provides full flexibility which may be required for specific service compositions, the lightweight approach we presented in this paper is limited, but easy to apply even with little technical skills.

Acknowledgments. The authors D.S. and D.K. would like to thank the German Research Foundation (DFG) for financial support of the project within the Cluster of Excellence in Simulation Technology (EXC 310/1) at the University of Stuttgart. Many thanks go to the EC-Web reviewers for their valuable feedback.

References

1. OASIS: Web Services Business Process Execution Language Version 2.0 (2007)
2. Vanhatalo, J., Völzer, H., Leymann, F.: Faster and more focused control-flow analysis for business process models through SESE decomposition. In: Krämer, B.J., Lin, K.-J., Narasimhan, P. (eds.) ICSOC 2007. LNCS, vol. 4749, pp. 43–55. Springer, Heidelberg (2007)

3. Blake, M., Tan, W., Rosenberg, F.: Composition as a Service. IEEE Internet Computing 14(1), 78–82 (2010)
4. Schumm, D., Leymann, F., Streule, A.: Process Viewing Patterns. In: Proceedings of the 14th IEEE International EDOC Conference, EDOC 2010. IEEE Computer Society Press, Los Alamitos (2010)
5. Eshuis, R., Grefen, P.: Constructing Customized Process Views. Data & Knowledge Engineering 64(2), 419–438 (2008)
6. Schumm, D., Anstett, T., Leymann, F., Schleicher, D.: Applicability of Process Viewing Patterns in Business Process Management. In: Proceedings of the International Workshop on Models and Model-driven Methods for Service Engineering (3M4SE 2010). IEEE Computer Society Press, Los Alamitos (2010)
7. Schumm, D., Leymann, F., Streule, A.: Process Views to Support Compliance Management in Business Processes. In: Buccafurri, F., Semeraro, G. (eds.) EC-Web 2010. Lecture Notes in Business Information Processing, vol. 61, pp. 131–142. Springer, Heidelberg (2010)
8. Zhao, X., Liu, C., Sadiq, W., Kowalkiewicz, M., Yongchareon, S.: Implementing Process Views in the Web Service Environment. WWW Journal 14(1), 27–52 (2011)
9. Leymann, F.: Cloud Computing: The Next Revolution in IT. In: Proceedings of the 52th Photogrammetric Week (2009)
10. Polyvyanyy, A., Smirnov, S., Weske, M.: Business Process Model Abstraction. In: International Handbook on Business Process Management. Springer, Heidelberg (2009)
11. Bobrik, R., Reichert, M., Bauer, T.: View-based process visualization. In: Alonso, G., Dadam, P., Rosemann, M. (eds.) BPM 2007. LNCS, vol. 4714, pp. 88–95. Springer, Heidelberg (2007)
12. Smirnov, S., Dijkman, R., Mendling, J., Weske, M.: Meronymy-Based Aggregation of Activities in Business Process Models. In: Parsons, J., Saeki, M., Shoval, P., Woo, C., Wand, Y. (eds.) ER 2010. LNCS, vol. 6412, pp. 1–14. Springer, Heidelberg (2010)
13. Reichert, M., Bassil, S., Bobrik, R., Bauer, T.: The Proviado Access Control Model for Business Process Monitoring Components. Enterprise Modelling and Information Systems Architectures - An International Journal. German Informatics Society (GI) (2010)
14. Spiller, J.: Privacy-enhanced Service Execution. In: Proceedings of the International Conference for Modern Information and Telecommunication Technologies (2008)
15. Barros, A.P., Dumas, M.: The Rise of Web Service Ecosystems. IT Professional 8(5), 31–37 (2006)
16. Object Management Group (OMG): Business Process Model and Notation (BPMN), Version 2.0, OMG Document Number formal/2011-01-03 (January 2011)
17. La Rosa, M., ter Hofstede, A., Wohed, P., Reijers, H., Mendling, J., van der Aalst, W.: Managing Process Model Complexity via Concrete Syntax Modifications. IEEE Transactions on Industrial Informatics 7(2), 255–265 (2011)
18. Moody, D.L.: The "Physics" of Notations: Toward a Scientific Basis for Constructing Visual Notations in Software Engineering. IEEE Transactions on Software Engineering 35, 756–779 (2009)

A Multi-layer Approach for Customizing Business Services

Yehia Taher[1], Rafiqul Haque[2], Michael Parkin[1], Willem-Jan van den Heuvel[1], Ita Richardson[2], and Eoin Whelan[2]

[1] European Research Institute of Service Science (ERISS), Tilburg University, TIlburg, The Netherlands
{y.taher,m.s.parkin,W.J.A.M.vdnHeuvel}@uvt.nl
[2] Lero – the Irish Software Engineering Research Institute, University of Limerick, Limerick, Ireland
{Rafiqul.Haque,Ita.Richardson}@lero.ie, Eoin.Whelan@ul.ie

Abstract. The reusability of services is a cornerstone of the Service-Oriented Architecture design paradigm as it leads to a reduction in the costs associated with software development, integration and maintenance. However, reusability is difficult to achieve in practice as services are either too generic or over-specified for the tasks they are required to complete. This paper presents our work in defining an approach for achieving service reusability in Service-Based Applications (SBAs) by decomposing the reusability requirements into two layers and then into separate views that allow the customization of business policies, quality of service, tasks and control (i.e., orchestration/choreography) parameters. The objective of defining such an approach is to provide an appropriate solution that will guide the customization of a service's functional and non-functional properties to allow it to be reused in different business contexts.

Keywords: Service, Reusability, Customization, Service Oriented Computing (SOC), Service Based Application (SBA).

1 Introduction

The reusability of services is a cornerstone of Service-Oriented Architectures as it allows the linking together of services to solve an end-to-end business problem or process to create a Service-Based Application (SBA). For instance, services such as *order processing,* and *shipment processing* can be reused to build an *order management* application. Reusability can be deemed as one of the most significant qualities of services within the domain of SBAs for several reasons. In particular, reusability facilitates Just-in-time (JIT) service integration that plays vital role in meeting other important service qualities such as *customer satisfaction*. For example, if a client purchases *goods* from a provider who does not provide an *insurance* service for their delivery and the client asks for shipping insurance the provider should be able to provide this service to promote customer satisfaction, which in turn maximizes the return for provider. In such situations, the provider can integrate a (reusable)

C. Huemer and T. Setzer (Eds.): EC-Web 2011, LNBIP 85, pp. 64–76, 2011.

insurance service with the running business application just in time instead of developing the service from scratch, reducing the up-front costs, for the service provider.

Although reusability has many merits, it has two limitations: generalization and *over-specification*. *Generalization* facilitates designing services from generic point of view; for example, a generic order management application can be designed to meet most requirements by abstracting away its specificity. This means generic services cannot be used in a specific context since they lack the ability to satisfy the specific requirements of any context. Over-specification is the opposite of over-abstraction. An over-specified service has attributes that are highly-specific in a certain context. Unlike generic services, over-specified services may be reused in a specific context, but the target context has to match exactly the source context in terms of requirements. In practice, this is impractical because the requirements between contexts cannot be symmetric. As an example, payment service developed for a business organization operating in the United States cannot be reused directly by any organization in Europe. This example covers wider area; in fact, it is highly unlikely the service could be reused by any other organization in the US. This implies neither generic nor over-specified (reusable) services can be reused to build SBAs directly.

These considerations give the rise to the concept of *customization* that supports fine-tuning generic as well as over-specified services so they may be reused in different target contexts. This method of service customization has been emerging steadily as a concept as the popularity of service oriented computing technologies increases (e.g., WSDL, BPEL, and so on). Earlier research into service customization, including [1], [18] and [10], focused on configurable EPC approach that is limited to service functions, which is obviously important but not adequate for the modern service-driven business environment. The service-driven business environment of today also involves diverse non-functional requirements including quality-of-service, business policy, and security. Customizing services covering such a wide variety of requirements from disparate domains is a non-trivial task and organizations hire experts to perform these tasks, which increases development costs. This implies that it is paramount to enable users to customize both functional and non-functional aspects of services.

In this paper, we propose a multi-layered approach to building SBAs that supports the customization of component services at different layers. The goal of this research is to ease the complexities of service customization and allow non-IT experts without a background in service related technologies (e.g., business analysts) to customize services. The proposed solution provides guidelines for the non-IT expert to allow them to customize services with respect to the specific context.

We organize this article as follows: section 2 describes the motivating example; the proposed solution is explained in section 3; section 4 explains discusses the works related to this research and finally section 5 concludes the research work and briefly outlines the future extension of this research.

2 Motivating Example

In this section we describe an example order management application, composed of reusable services. Figure 1 demonstrates the BPMN model of the application containing services that do not consider any specific context or situation. We have chosen BPMN to represent the application because, in our view, BPMN is an ideal option for service customization in the design phase; it provides graphical notations that are easily understood by non IT-experts, including business analysts.

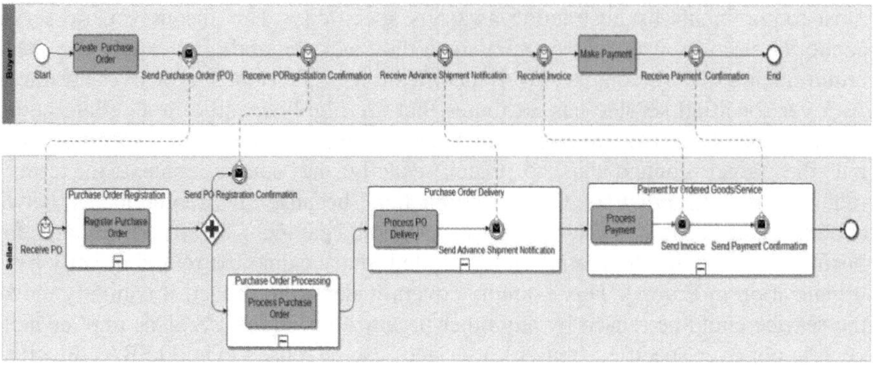

Fig. 1. A purchase order application encapsulates reusable services including order processing, delivery, and payment services

In Figure 1, the two pools represent the partners (*Buyer* and *Seller*) involved in the purchase order process. No specific partner name is given as the process is a generic. The process contains generic activities including *register purchase order, process purchase order*, *process purchase order delivery* and *process payment.* These activities are generic because they are captured from global point of view, i.e., these are activities commonly used by selling organizations. From the perspective of buying organizations, the two generic activities involved in order management are *purchase order creation* and *make payment.* The commonality has also shown in flow of messages between buyer and seller. Besides, the business logic that describes the order of activities has been abstracted (generalized) as well. These generic features of this process facilitate the business organization to reuse it.

As we already mentioned earlier, services designed from global or common perspective cannot be reused directly in a specific context. However, *what exactly are the factors that preclude the direct reusability of generic services*? The simple answer is contextual requirements that vary as the circumstances the service is used in change. For example, the *delivery service* shown in Figure 1 will vary among business types, organizations and the locations it is used in. Another example is the *payment service* which relies on business-specific policies. For example, in business-to-business (B2B) scenarios, buying companies in Europe must issue a *letter of credit* to sellers in South-east Asia before the order is processed, with the letter of credit a legal confirmation from the buyer to credit a certain amount from his account to the seller's account. However, this may not be required for buyers from the United States. The requirements can be more diverse in case of business-to-consumer (B2C) and are enormously important because they are the driving factors that ensure customer satisfaction and provide a competitive advantage for businesses. As discussed above, context-independent reusable services mostly do not adopt these requirements because they are specific to certain context.

Apart from the non-functional perspective, the functional requirements are also important and vary from context to context. Thus, the functional features of a generic service also may not satisfy the requirement of specific context.

The contribution of this research is largely focused on an appropriate solution which will guide the customization of services for a specific context and present our contribution in the following sections.

3 Multi-layer Approach for Customization

The fundamental principles of the proposed approach are *Personalization* and *Localization* that can be viewed primarily from the perspective of service users (e.g., organizations or individuals). These principles have been used extensively within various domains such as web page development. We adopt them in our solution for two very significant reasons. Firstly, they promote reusability by allowing the customization of services recursively for the specific contexts. As an example, a service provider customizes a payment service, taking the organizational policy into account, and stores a description of the customized service in a service repository. The customization function (when considering customization as a function) can be recalled for specific products if the organization has a large number of products in its pipeline as the payment policy may vary based on product type. This is an example of the personalization of services, which allows the tailoring of reusable services according to the requirements of a context and, subsequently, a business object (e.g., product). Furthermore, localization recalls the customization function for diverse requirements of different geographical locations.

Secondly, both personalization and localization provide a comprehensive understanding of what the requirements should be glued with services and when. This helps to ensure the correctness in specifying or choosing the right requirement parameters at the correct time - i.e., services are personalized and localized at different phases of the customization process Thus, it is important for the users to be aware what customization parameters should be used in which phase.

The solution we propose in this paper supports the personalization and localization of services to simplify the service customization process, which is the primary reason to provide a multi-layered approach for service customization. We present the solution as a reference model for service customization. Figure 2 shows the reference model, which has two-layers: the Service-view Segmentation Layer (SSL) and Service Customization Layer (SCL). We describe both layers in the following sections.

3.1 Service-View Segmentation Layer (SSL)

Based on our study ([4], [15]), a service has various views that are categorized into functional and non-functional viewpoints, as in classical requirements engineering. However, we believe this categorization is not adequate to provide a comprehensive understanding on services, especially in a modern, service driven-business environment. Thus, in this research, we refine the classical functional and non-functional views into four, finer grained views: the *task view*, *control view*, *quality view* and *policy view*. This granularity will help magnifying the knowledge on services and their requirements for specific contexts. Additionally, they are vital to simplify the customization process and 'fine-tune' the services to their context. The Service-view Segmentation Layer (SSL) comprises of these four views. The SSL is the top layer of the reference model and initializes the customization process through decomposing a service into the different views which are used to devise its requirements. We now explain these views.

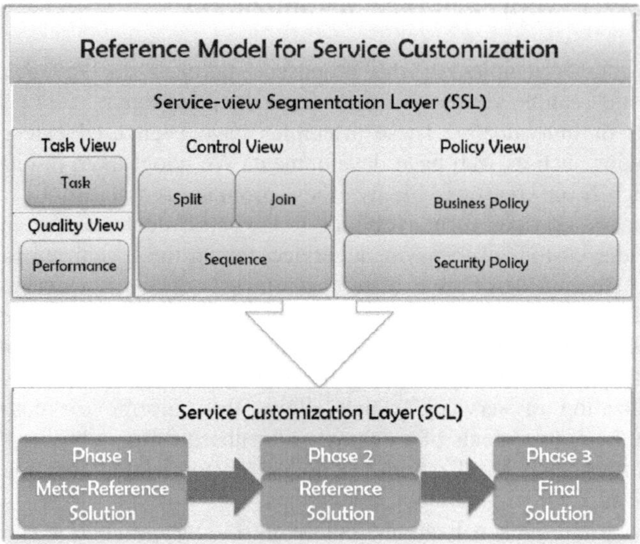

Fig. 2. The Service Customization Reference Model, containing the Service-view Segmentation Layer (SSL) and Service Customization Layer (SCL)

A. Policy View: In a modern-day service-oriented business environment, the business policy is an important requirement of services due to fact that it is the key to gaining a competitive advantage over competitors [17] and differs greatly between organizations. Since business policies are of critical importance for the organization, we separate the policy concern that facilitates explicitness in terms of policy requirements. The policy view helps by analyzing and accumulating the policy requirements of services that can be used during service customization in the Service Customization Layer (SCL). The policy view consists of two types of policies, business policies and security policies. A business policy is a plan, or course of action that is intended to influence and cause decisions and actions, which concern an enterprise in a way that guarantees that the enterprise operates within specified guidelines and regulation [16]. This implies business policies are critical since they influence business decision as well as action.

Furthermore, the advent of the Internet and the Extensible Markup Language (XML) has changed traditional service delivery practices and many services are now delivered electronically. However, the openness of the Internet has made service delivery prone to risks from different types of attacks, such as phishing, through which sensitive business information can be leaked. Thus, security has turned into an important concern for organizations and it is crucial to ensure and ratify the security of payload information during its transfer from sender to receiver. The security policy deals with the security requirements of services and contains technical requirements to ensure secure exchange of business information.

However, policies are also a set of rules or directives intended to influence or guide business behavior [13] and define or constrain some aspect of business [8]. In this research we consider rule as set of constraints that control the service behavior A typical example rule, in this case for the cancellation of an order, is "*a purchase order can be cancelled with money refund if the cancellation request is placed within 15 days from the day order has been placed*". In this example, the number of days is the constraint of the cancellation function. Our solution facilitates specifying such constraints using parameters. Through this research, we target to build a repository of parameters to underpin service customization. We introduce and discuss those parameters in section 3.2.

B. Quality View: non-functional properties described using the general term of Quality of Service (QoS) - "a set of non-functional attributes of those contextual entities that are considered relevant to the interaction between the service and its client, including the service and the client, that bear on the service's ability to satisfy stated or implied needs" [3]. QoS is a concept that accentuates the significance of different issues, such as processing time in services and plays pivotal role in aligning the interests (requirements and offerings) of service users and providers. Thus, QoS is important to both participants, and especially from the service client perspective where QoS could be the primary requirement. The satisfaction of the service client depends on the level of QoS provided by the service provider. Thus, service providers today largely concentrate on the quality requirements of the services. In these circumstances we offer a separate view called the *Quality View* that facilitates the analysis of service quality requirements. These requirements are incorporated with services during customization. Essentially, the key quality aspect of a service is *performance*, which involves time-based measurements such as *Response time*, *Processing Time* and so on.

***C. Task View*:** A service is an action that is performed by an entity (the provider) on behalf of another (the requester) [14] and is often a computational entity located at a specific unique location (e.g., URI) that has an internal state and is able to perform one or more functions [7]. The functions are tasks, such as *registering a purchase order*. A service encapsulates and performs these tasks as a blackbox to the outside world. During customization, a user (customizer) must have knowledge about what tasks are encapsulated in a service because a task may not the target context. In this regard, we separate the *task view* of services. The tasks view is the functional aspect of services. This view helps to analyze the required of target contexts. For instance, in the example shown in Figure 1, the register purchase order task may need to be customized to other tasks including check customer credit and check inventory performed before the registration task. The tasks view is important to ensure the completeness of any functionality in a service. Additionally, it also helps to identify the tasks that are not required to the target context. In summary, this view underpins the capture and specification of the task-related requirements of services.

***D. Control View*:** Services contain tasks that must be performed coherently to produce a desired and effective outcome. Anomalies, such as incorrect task order or deadlock between tasks, jeopardize the service orchestration (the composition of tasks in a composite service) that, in consequence, may produce an incorrect outcome. Simply, tasks need to be controlled in an appropriate manner to obtain a desired outcome. A list of control flow patterns, defined in [2], has been adopted in many successful service technologies, and in particular BPEL. In this research, we create a new view, called the control view, to render the control structure of services. The objective of the control view is to provide users to with an understanding of the process of ordering, splitting and synchronizing of tasks so that the users can define tasks in right order. With this in mind, we include three control connectors: *sequential, split, join* ([2]) that are typically used in service definition. The control view assists in analyzing and defining the connector related requirements for the target service during customization

Form the above description of the reference model for service customization it is clear that the segmentation of views allows a service user to understand the ‘nuts and bolts’ of services and to analyze its requirements. In addition, the visualization of various aspects of service makes the customization process easier for both IT experts as well as non IT experts.

3.2 Service Customization Layer (SCL)

The service customization process consists of three phases. The customizations of service views are performed during these phases taking the requirements of the target contexts into account. The customization of at these phases produces solutions including meta-reference, reference, and final solution but only the final one is deployable. This implies meta-reference and reference solutions are not concrete solutions. The customization starts at the phase of meta-reference solution which is a generic service can be reused to any context. We assume that organizations import such a reusable service for instance, off-the-shelf one at this phase. The customization of this generic service produces a reference solution which is not final solution. Yet another customization is required to generate the final solution that can be deployed on execution engine. It is worth noting that the customizations of meta-reference and reference solution are treated as service personalization and localization respectively.

Now, *what is the most suitable approach for service customization*? Parameterization plays a pivotal role in customization: the parameterization process allows the setting of parameters for a target solution [9]. We believe parameterization is a relatively simple technique for all types of users because it does not require knowledge on technologies and instead only requires a basic understanding of services. In order to support the parameterization of services, we provide a collection of parameters. As we have mentioned above, a process of creating a repository of parameters is ongoing and we will integrate this repository with the customization tool (also ongoing work). However, we present a sample list of parameters in Table 1.

These parameters are extracted from work in diverse fields such as business, legislation, security and so on. We take the services view into special consideration while selecting parameters because views help to analyze and select the suitable parameters for customization. We cluster these parameters into performance, security, policy, and flow controlling. Mapping these clusters to service views, it can be easily understood by service user which parameters should be used for which view. Noticeably, the list of parameters in the table is influenced by [3], [11], and [19]. They explained these parameters extensively.

Table 1. The customization parameters and operators

Parameter				Operator
Performance Parameters	**Security Policy Parameters**	**Business Policy Parameters**	**Flow Controlling Parameters**	
Processing time	Authentication	Availability	MEChoice	Add
Response time	Authorization	Best effort	Before	Prune
Waiting Time	Non-repudiation	Guaranteed	After	Refine
Delay	Intelligibility	Prerequisite	Order	Rename
Throughput	Tamperproof	Co-requisite	Until	Select
		Inclusion	Parallel - Start - Finishes - During - Equal	Aggregate
		Exclusion		
		Segregation of Duty		

In addition, parameterization requires operators which underpin service users to perform customization. In this research, we enlisted a set of operators (see Table 1) that are explained briefly in the followings:

- *Add*: This primitive used to add tasks or functionalities that are required for the target context.
- *Prune*: A task can be removed from a service using this primitive.
- *Refine*: Refine allows a task to be refined into sub-tasks.
- *Aggregate*: Aggregation allows the combination of two or more tasks into a single task.
- *Select*: This operator is used to select tasks or functionalities (that need to be parameterized) and also the parameters. For instance, a user selects task *process payment* of permission process and then selects the performance parameter *processing time*.
- *Rename*: Reaming is used to re-label different parts of services. For instance, a task 'send invoice' of reusable service may be renamed to 'send payment receipt'.
- *Value Tagging*: It is not an operator listed in the table, but we offer value tagging facility for the users. The key idea of value tagging is to facilitate specifying the value of parameters. The framework provides the boolean values of *True* and *False*

as well as a numerical value. Using value tagging, a user can specify the target value for performance parameters for instance, the expected value of the parameter *processing time* equal to *5 days*.

In section 3.3, we briefly explain how to use these operators and parameters with an example.

3.3 Exemplification of Service Customization

In this example we try to show how the proposed solution can be used in practice to customize services. We use the payment service of order management application (see Section 2) for this task. It is a generic service which has been defined without consideration to any specific context (e.g., organization). Now a business analyst in Auto Inc. (a fictitious car-assembling firm) wants to reuse this service and customizes the service using our proposed approach. According to the customization reference model, the analyst places the service at SSL to map the service view and then may perform the following customizations:

A. Task view Customization: The analyst refines the task *process payment* into three different activities including 'create invoice', 'charge credit card', and 'process payment receipt'. Figure 3 shows the refinement. Additionally, the activity 'send invoice' is renamed to 'sent payment receipt'. Two operators *refine* and *rename* are used in this customization.

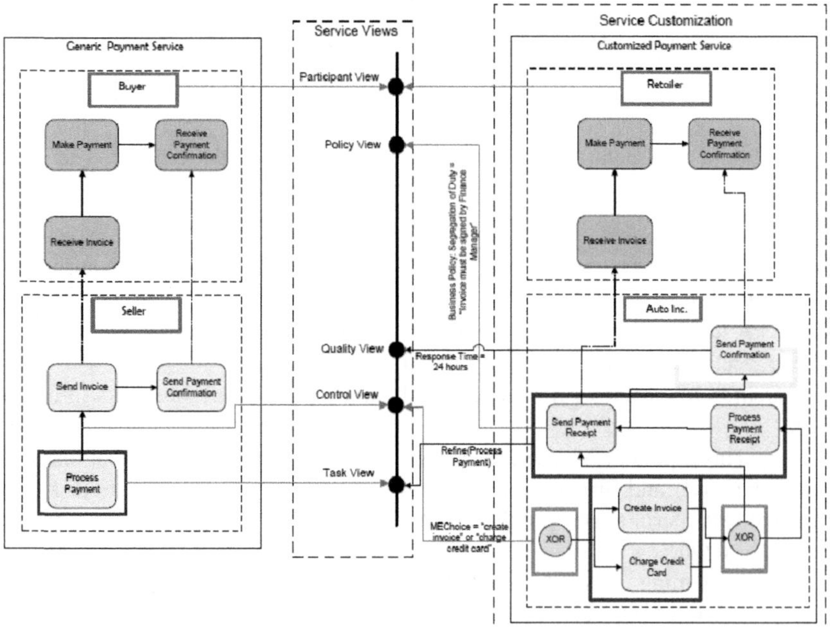

Fig. 3. The figure shows an example of customization of a generic (reusable) service using proposed multi-layer customization solution

B. Control view Customization: The analyst customizes split control the control connectors to connect create invoice and charge credit card activities. Both these activities should not be executed at the same time for the same instances. Thus, the analyst parameterizes the connectors using *MEChoice* parameters (the XOR notation in figure 3) that constrain the execution. *MEChoice* choice means mutually exclusive choice which allows choosing only one of multiple options. This implies, either charge credit card or create invoice should be executed for an instance but not both.

C. Policy view Customization: According to the business policy between the participants' retailer and Auto Inc., the payment receipt must be signed by finance manager. The analyst specifies this policy through parameterizing the 'process payment receipt' task using the business policy parameter *segregation of duty*. This parameter describes how only finance managers are allowed to sign payment receipts (otherwise receipts will not be legally accepted by the retailers).

D. Quality view Customization: In a service-driven business environment there are many quality aspects and we only provide a simple example here. For example, the retailer may require a payment confirmation from Auto Inc. to confirm the company has received the payment and may expect a notification within 24 hours. The analyst parameterizes the task 'send payment confirmation' using *response time* and specifying value 24 hours. In fact, tasks such as 'processing payment receipt' in this example should also be parameterized using quality parameters.

Although the customization in this example looks simple (since we tried to keep it straightforward for the convenience of readers) in practice service customization is enormously complex especially for large scale enterprise applications. This is the very initial phase of our research, and may have several missing points, but from research perspective we believe that this is a highly innovative approach with significant potential because, according to our extensive study, there are tools to customize functional aspects of services but there is no suitable tool for customizing business policies, quality of service and security requirements. Besides, we also believe the combination of view segmentation and parameterization simplifies the customization enormously, which enables any user of the proposed solution to customize services. This is one important contribution that may help to reduce the development costs of services since organizations may not need to hire too many experts from different fields in order to create the service. However, before putting this approach in practice, we plan to provide step-step-step customization guidelines for its users, which will help to reduce costs further.

4 Related Works

In this section we position our solution with related works. This research revolves around two concepts including reusability and customization. Both these concepts are heavily documented throughout various bodies of literature. These concepts are substantial within service engineering domain. To-date, a list of interesting solutions around service customization has been proposed. In particular, [21] proposed a solution that facilitates fragmenting a complex business process into different parts that are intended to be reusable and customizable for target business process model.

The idea of customizing processes through fragmentation is interesting but the solution they proposed is limited to technical aspect and missing technique that facilitates customizing policy related requirements of services.

A collection of reference models (that are used developing business applications) widely known as SAP reference model was produced by [5]. These models are being used in many application services that are developed using technologies from SAP (http://www.sap.com/). This work has been cited heavily, yet criticized by [6]. According to [6], number of SAP reference models is structurally incorrect. Thus, they proposed configurable EPCs within the light of customization concept. Configurable EPCs was investigated by [1], [10], [18], and [12] to identify and model the service variability. They produced interesting results such as *configuration gateways* that support customizing the functional aspects of reusable processes. Noticeably, these works are limited within EPCs and SAP reference model. This means it is not clear whether the proposed solution is applicable to other process model. To solve such a problem, [9] proposed a framework with guidelines to transform a process model to SAP reference model. Now, this framework can map a process model (ignoring the model type) to SAP reference model with customization support. From our perspective, these solutions are too technical for analysts who do not possess solid understanding on different types of technologies (e.g., SAP, ARIS, etc). [22] and [20] proposed relatively simple customization solutions but like many other earlier ones, they ignored the non-functional aspects of services. As we already mentioned the non-functional aspects in particular, security, policy, and quality are critical importance for modern day business environment and thus service engineering.

Now, our multi-layer solution approach is an initiative to simplify service customization through parameterizing both business and technical requirements of services. Some of the earlier solutions also allow parameterizing services but they do not consider business level parameters. Parameterization is relatively simple technique that helps non IT-experts to customize services. Additionally, the segmentation of views helps analyzing the requirements of services especially what customization parameters should be used for the target context.

5 Conclusion

The multi-layer customization solution described in this article aims at supporting non IT experts for customizing services. The proposed solution helps in the customization of services by providing several necessary aspects, including the provision of a service customization reference model (the foundation of the proposed multi-layered solution approach), a comprehensive understanding of services and their customization requirements through service views (the top layer of reference model) and a list of parameters and operators that can be used in the customization of services (the bottom layer of the reference model).

The solution that has been described in this paper is core research in nature that requires extensions and refinement. A simple and user friendly tool implementation is the subject of an ongoing work. We are also developing the tool that will provide step-by-step customization guidelines to the users to ease the customization complexity for non-IT experts. Additionally, we plan to build a repository of parameters which will be integrated with the tool in future. Therefore, we will continue enriching the repository of parameters.

Acknowledgment. The research leading to these results has received funding from the European Community's Seventh Framework Program [FP7/2007-2013] under grant agreement 215482 (S-CUBE).

References

1. van der Aalst, W.M.P., Dreiling, A., Gottschalk, F., Rosemann, M., Jansen-Vullers, M.H.: Configurable process models as a basis for reference modeling. In: Bussler, C.J., Haller, A. (eds.) BPM 2005. LNCS, vol. 3812, pp. 512–518. Springer, Heidelberg (2006)
2. van der Aalst, W.M.P., Hofstede, H.M.A., Kiepuszewski, B., Barros, P.A.: Workflow Patterns. Distributed and Parallel Databases 14(1), 551 (2003)
3. Benbernou, S., Ivona, B., Nitto, D.E., Carro, M., Kritikos, K., Parkins, M.: A Survey on Service Quality Description. ACM Computing Survey V(N), 1–77 (2010)
4. Curbera, Francisco, Khalaf, R., Mukhi, N., Tai, S., Weerawarana, S.: The Next Step in Web Services. Communication of the ACM 46(10), 29–34 (2003)
5. Curran, A.T., Keller, G., Ladd, A.: SAP R/3 Business Blueprint: Understanding the Business Process Reference Model. Enterprise Resource Planning Series. Prentice Hall PTR, Upper Saddle River (1997)
6. van Dongen, B.F., Jansen-Vullers, M.H., Verbeek, H.M.W., van der Aalst, W.M.P.: Verification of the SAP Reference Models using EPC Reduction, State Space Analysis, and Invariants. Technical Report (2006)
7. Guidi, C., Lucchi, R., Gorrieri, R., Busi, N., Tennenholtz, M.: A calculus for service oriented computing. In: Dan, A., Lamersdorf, W. (eds.) ICSOC 2006. LNCS, vol. 4294, pp. 327–338. Springer, Heidelberg (2006)
8. GUIDE Task Force: Defining Business Rules – What Are They (July 2001)
9. van der Heuvel, W.J., Jeusfeld, M.: Model transformation with Reference Models. In: Proc. 3rd International Conference Interoperability for Enterprise Software and Applications, Funchal, Portugal, pp. 63–75 (March 2007)
10. La Rosa, M., Dumas, M.: Configurable Process Models: How To Adopt Standard Practices In Your How Way? BPTrends Newsletter (November 4, 2008)
11. Lu, R., Sadiq, S., Governatori, G.: On Managing Business Processes Variants. Data & Knowledge Engineering Journal 68, 642–664 (2009)
12. Mendling, J., Moser, M., Neumann, G., Verbeek, H.M.W., van Dongen, B.F., van der Aalst, W.M.P.: Faulty ePCs in the SAP reference model. In: Dustdar, S., Fiadeiro, J.L., Sheth, A.P. (eds.) BPM 2006. LNCS, vol. 4102, pp. 451–457. Springer, Heidelberg (2006)
13. OMG's RFP: Organizing Business Plans: The Standard Model for Business Rule Motivation (2002)
14. O'Sullivan, J., Edmund, D., Hofstede, H.M.t.A.: Service Description: A survey of the general nature of services. Technical report (2002)
15. Papazoglou, P.M.: Service Oriented Computing: Concepts, Characteristics, and Directions. In: Proceeding of the Fourth International Conference on Web Information System Engineering, WISE 2003 (2003)
16. Papazoglou, P.M., van der Heuvel, W.J., Leymann, F.: Business Process Management: A Survey. ACM Computing Survey, 1–48 (September 2009)

17. Simchi-Levi, D., Kaminsky, P., Simchi-Levi, E.: Designing and Managing Supply Chain: Concepts Strategies and Case Studies, 3rd edn. McGraw-Hill Irwin, Boston (2008)
18. Stollberg, M., Muth, M.: Efficient Business Service Consumption by Customization with Variability Modeling. Journal of System Integration (2010)
19. UN/CEFACT Modeling Methodology (UMM): UMM Meta Model – Foundation Module Candidate for 2.0 (2009), http://umm-dev.org/ummspecification/
20. Wang, J., Yu, J.: A business-level service model supporting end-user customization. In: Di Nitto, E., Ripeanu, M. (eds.) ICSOC 2007. LNCS, vol. 4907, pp. 295–303. Springer, Heidelberg (2009)
21. Zhilei, M., Leymann, F.: A. Lifecycle Model for Using Process Fragment in Business Process Modelling. In: BPDMS (2008)
22. Zhu, X., Zheng, X.: A Template based Approach for mass Customization of Service Oriented E-business Applications. In: Kishino, F., Kitamura, Y., Kato, H., Nagata, N. (eds.) ICEC 2005. LNCS, vol. 3711, Springer, Heidelberg (2005)

Process Mining for Electronic Data Interchange*

Robert Engel[1], Worarat Krathu[1], Marco Zapletal[1], Christian Pichler[2], Wil M.P. van der Aalst[3], and Hannes Werthner[1]

[1] Vienna University of Technology, Austria
Institute for Software Technology and Interactive Systems
{engel,worarat,marco,werthner}@ec.tuwien.ac.at
[2] Research Studios Austria
Research Studio Inter-Organizational Systems
christian.pichler@researchstudio.at
[3] Eindhoven University of Technology, The Netherlands
Department of Mathematics & Computer Science
w.m.p.v.d.aalst@tue.nl

Abstract. Choreography modeling and service integration received a lot of attention in the last decade. However, most real-world implementations of inter-organizational systems are still realized by traditional *Electronic Data Interchange* (EDI) standards. In traditional EDI standards, the notion of process or choreography is not explicitly specified. Rather, every business document exchange stands for its own. This lack of process awareness in traditional EDI systems hinders organizations from applying Business Process Management (BPM) methods in such settings. To address this shortcoming, we seek to derive choreographies from EDI message exchanges. Thereby, we employ and extend *process mining* techniques, which have so far concentrated on business processes within single organizations. We discover the interaction sequences between the partners as well as the business information conveyed in the exchanged documents, which goes beyond the state-of-the-art in process mining. As a result, we lift the information gained on the IT level to the business level. This enables us to derive new insights that help organizations to improve their performance, e.g., an organization may get insights into the *value* of its business partnerships to support an efficient decision making process. This way we hope to bring the merits of BPM to inter-organizational systems realized by traditional EDI standards.

Keywords: process mining, EDI, EDIFACT, inter-organizational business processes.

1 Introduction

Electronic Data Interchange (EDI) is the exchange of business data between applications based on a format that is understood by all participating parties [9].

* This paper has been produced in the course of the *EDImine* project jointly conducted by the Vienna University of Technology and the Eindhoven University of Technology. *EDImine* is funded by the Vienna Science and Technology Fund (Wiener Wissenschafts-, Forschungs- und Technologiefonds, WWTF - http://www.wwtf.at).

C. Huemer and T. Setzer (Eds.): EC-Web 2011, LNBIP 85, pp. 77–88, 2011.

While recent academic research for Web services and business process modeling places lots of emphasis on modeling choreographies of business processes [2], many inter-organizational business processes are still realized by means of traditional EDI systems. However, traditional EDI systems usually lack the explicit notion of a business process. They are solely responsible for sending and receiving messages. Hence, every exchanged document stands for its own and the process context is lost. This results in a number of shortcomings.

Shortcoming #1. An inter-organizational business process comprises one or more message exchanges between companies for conducting an electronic business transaction. When companies intend to analyze their inter-organizational processes they generally have to rely on a-priori models, if models documenting the business processes exist at all. In case there are models, those may describe the business processes as they were planned, which is not necessarily in sync with the real-world business processes.

Shortcoming #2. EDI documents convey a lot of redundant information, while only a minimal subset of the conveyed information is actually sufficient for a certain step of a transaction. In other words, an inter-organizational business process does not require the exchange of complete business documents as in a paper-based world, but only the appropriate delta of information required to handle the next step in the process. As information is electronic, redundant information does not need to increase the transfer costs. However, it may cause semantic heterogeneity and additional checks.

Shortcoming #3. The specifics of inter-organizational business processes require not only focusing on the executed activities, but also on the actual exchanged business information. However, combined information from process data and business performance data of the exchanged EDI messages, such as EDIFACT messages, is currently not being exploited in a systematic manner. Despite the attainable insights for decision-making there are – to the best of our knowledge – no such approaches for EDI systems.

In this paper we present an approach, though at an early stage, that addresses the three shortcomings presented above. We build upon state-of-the-art process mining techniques [1,16], which we extend for inter-organizational systems realized by means of EDI. Thereby, we focus on EDIFACT [3] since traditional EDI standards like EDIFACT and ANSI X12 still play a dominant role in Business-to-Business (B2B) e-commerce and will presumably continue to be the primary data formats for automated data exchange between companies for years [19]. However, our approach is generic in terms that it is independent of the underlying transfer syntax. Hence, it can also be used for more recent EDI formats such as XML-based business documents.

The remainder of this paper is structured as follows. First, Section 2 introduces process mining as enabling technology. However, thus far process mining is mostly applied within one organization and existing techniques do not exploit the specifics of EDI. Section 3 elaborates on the principal research questions and discusses the resulting challenges. In Section 4, the technical architecture of our approach is described. Section 5 discusses related work. Finally, in Section 6 a summary and conclusion is given.

2 Process Mining

Process mining serves a bridge between data mining and business process modeling [1]. The goal is to extract process-related knowledge from event data stored in information systems. Process mining is an emerging discipline providing comprehensive sets of tools to provide fact-based insights and to support process improvements. This new discipline builds on process model-driven approaches and data mining.

Figure 1 shows that process mining establishes links between the actual processes and their data on the one hand and process models on the other hand. Today's information systems log enormous amounts of events. Classical WFM systems, BPM systems, ERP systems, PDM systems, CRM systems, middleware, and hospital information systems provide detailed information about the activities that have been executed. Figure 1 refers to such data as *event logs*. Information systems that are process-aware provide event logs that can be analyzed directly using existing process mining tools. However, most information systems store such information in unstructured form, e.g., event data is scattered over many tables or needs to be tapped off from subsystems exchanging messages. In such cases, event data exist but some efforts are needed to extract them. Data extraction is an integral part of any process mining effort.

Event logs can be used to conduct three types of process mining: (a) discovery, (b) conformance, and (c) enhancement [1]. The goal of *discovery* is to extract

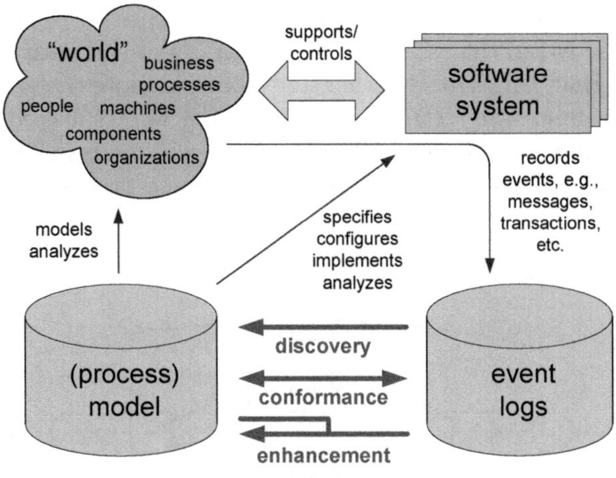

Fig. 1. Three main types of process mining (discovery, conformance, and enhancement) positioned in the classical setting where event logs are collected within a single organization

models from raw event data in information systems (transaction logs, data bases, audit trails, etc.). A discovery technique takes an event log and produces a model without using any a-priori information. An example is the α-algorithm [17] that takes an event log and produces a Petri net explaining the behavior recorded in the log. The second type of process mining is *conformance*. Here, an existing process model is compared with an event log of the same process. Conformance checking can be used to check if reality, as recorded in the log, conforms to the model and vice versa. Techniques as presented in [14] may be used to detect, locate and explain deviations, and to measure the severity of these deviations. The third type of process mining is *enhancement*. Here, the idea is to extend or improve an existing process model using information about the actual process recorded in some event log. Whereas conformance checking measures the alignment between model and reality, this third type of process mining aims at changing or extending the a-priori model, e.g., adding a new perspective to the process model by cross-correlating it with the log. An example is the extension of a process model with performance data. For instance, by combining the timestamps in the event log with the discovered process model it is possible to show bottlenecks, service levels, throughput times, and frequencies.

To illustrate the basic idea of process discovery consider an event log containing information about 50 cases. Each event is characterized by an activity name. (Note that logs also contain timestamps and case data, but we abstract from these in this simple example.) Therefore, we can describe log L as a multiset of traces containing activity names: $L = \{ \langle a,b,d,c,e,g\rangle^{18}, \langle a,b,c,d,e,g\rangle^{12}, \langle a,b,c,d,e,f,b,d,c,e,g\rangle^{7}, \langle a,b,d,c,e,f,b,d,c,e,g\rangle^{5}, \langle a,b,c,d,e,f,b,c,d,e,g\rangle^{3}, \langle a,b,c,d,e,f,b,c,d,e,f,b,d,c,e,g\rangle^{3}, \langle a,b,d,c,e,f,b,c,d,e,f,b,c,d,e,g\rangle^{2}\}$. There are 18 cases that have a trace $\langle a,b,d,c,e,g\rangle$ in the event log, 12 cases followed the path $\langle a,b,c,d,e,g\rangle$, etc. Process discovery algorithms such as the α-algorithm [17] can extract a process model from such a log. Figure 2 shows the resulting process model. All trace in L can be "replayed" by this model. The α-algorithm discovered that all cases start with a and end with g, that c and d are in parallel, that f initiates another iteration, etc. Note that here the process model is represented as a Petri net. However, the notation used is not important. Process mining tools such a ProM can convert the result to the desirable notation. The real challenge is to find the underlying process, not the notation to depict it.

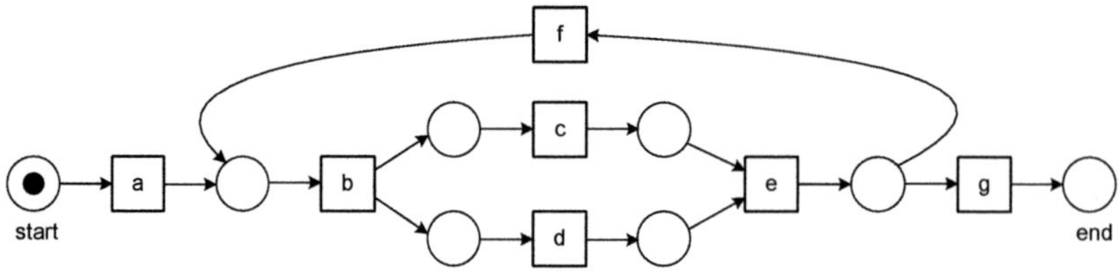

Fig. 2. Process model discovered based on an event log L containing 50 cases characterized by sequences of activity names

Now let us suppose that Figure 2 shows the desired process and log L contains a trace $\sigma = \langle a, b, c, e, g \rangle$. Conformance checking techniques such as the one described in [14] are able to detect that σ deviates. These technique can diagnose an event log, highlight, and quantify deviations.

Figure 2 is a bit misleading given its simplicity and focus on control-flow. Process mining is *not* restricted to the control-flow perspective and may include *other perspectives* such as the resource/organizational dimension, the time/performance dimension, and the object/data dimension. Moreover, process mining techniques can be applied to processes with hundreds of different activities, thousands of cases, etc.

Using ProM, we have applied process mining in over 100 organizations. Most of these applications focus on processes inside one organization. Moreover, despite the omnipresence of EDI, we are not aware of any process mining applications systematically analyzing inter-organizational EDI data. In Figure 2 we assumed the transitions to be activities. *However, in an EDI context these may also correspond to (the sending and/or receiving of) messages.*

3 Challenges and Research Questions

To address the shortcomings presented in Section 1, we identified the following set of research questions.

3.1 Deriving Process Choreographies

A choreography describes the public message exchange between multiple parties [11], with the purpose of supporting interoperability. However, traditional EDI systems lack the explicit notion of a business process, since they are solely responsible for sending and receiving messages. This leads to the first research question, which is to derive choreographies of inter-organizational business processes based on EDI messages that are interchanged between companies.

The hypothesis is that in traditional EDI systems choreographies have been implicitly implemented in the document exchanges, although they have not been explicitly agreed upon beforehand. We intend to develop means for discovering these implicit processes by extending current process mining techniques. However, process mining presupposes the explicit notion of a process (or case) in order to log activities and to correlate them to instances of a process. Hence, we need to group EDI messages to process instances before choreographies can be derived. Thereby, we examine meta-data as well as the actual business data conveyed in the EDI messages, since they carry implicit references to previously sent messages of the same business case. In other words, we use redundantly transferred information in the EDI messages to correlate them to business cases. At the same time, these redundancies are subject to further analyses in EDImine as described in the following section.

3.2 Identifying Redundancies in Business Documents

Redundant information in EDI-based business documents is not problematic for the cost of its transfer, but it may cause undesired semantic heterogeneity. The reason for redundancy is twofold:

First, the strategy for standardizing EDI documents follows a top-down approach [10]. This means, that for designing an EDI business document type the various requirements from different industry domains have been collected and incorporated into the standardization work. The resulting business document type corresponds to a super-set of all the requirements containing a high degree of optional information as well as having the same type of business information positioned in different places.

Second, the absence of an explicit process notion in traditional EDI approaches every business document is rather considered *standalone* and not in the context of a set of document exchanges. This has led to the fact that EDI documents convey a lot of redundant information, while only a minimal subset of the conveyed information is actually sufficient for a certain step of a transaction. In other words, an inter-organizational business process does not require the exchange of complete business documents as in a paper-based world, but only the appropriate *delta* of information required to handle the next step in the process.

This leads us to the second research question which is to develop methods for identifying the minimum as well as the redundant part of information exchanged in the course of a discovered EDI process. Based on this question, the hypothesis is that inter-organizational process mining allows identifying redundantly transferred information and, consequently, allows pointing out the minimal subset of information that is really needed. Our objective is to extend existing mining techniques for identifying redundancies. While such methods for identifying redundancies will be of less utility for already implemented systems, they can highlight current problems in message and process design. The insights gained through process mining will be of value for EDI-related standardization committees. For enabling an appropriate comparison of the similarities as well as the differences between distinct EDI messages it is required to investigate the semantics of the conveyed information. We aim at applying ontological approaches to assign semantically unambiguous meaning to the exchanged information.

3.3 Analyzing Business Performance

Current process mining techniques concentrate on the life cycle of executed activities (e.g., started, finished, canceled, suspended, etc.) and their ordering, to discover the flow of cases in a business process. This is supported by the information contained in log files of a process-aware information system. However, inter-organizational processes need to be monitored in a different manner. The log files of EDI systems are clearly scoped (or limited) to the boundaries of the system – i.e., sending and receiving messages. At the same time, we are able to work with richer information by examining the actual content of the messages that are sent and received by EDI systems. In other words, we do not treat transferred business documents as opaque objects, but combine them with log data.

The resulting research question is whether we can lift the information gained on the IT level (from the log files as well as from the messages) to the business level in order to support companies in decision-making. In addressing this question, semantics is one of the key ingredients. We intend to provide a semantic framework for conceptualizing the process data and business data gained on the IT level. The concepts can then be used to build queries on the business level.

Our goal is to provide a business cockpit comparable to navigation systems supporting car drivers [1]. Such a system will be able to visualize the networks of companies, show the flow of business documents and warn about bottlenecks in document processing. The system may be able to suggest deviations from the regular process flow in case something goes wrong (i.e., detours) – an example may be to order from a different partner, if an order has been sent, but no confirmation was received for a certain time. Consequently, our objective is to answer business-related questions on two levels: (i) business process performance and (ii) general business performance.

Questions on the first level focus on the process performance of an enterprise with the outside world. They cover the discovery, the monitoring/measuring (identification of bottlenecks, average durations, etc.), and the improvement of processes.

Questions on the second level focus on business performance with regard to a company's economic relationships with partners (e.g., number of orders or order volume as indicators of the economic importance of the partnership, etc.). Having information of their value chain at hand, enterprises are able to identify value drivers, cost drivers as well as dependencies on external relationships. By combining process performance and business performance they also gain new insights on the *value* of business partnerships (e.g., does the order volume of a certain partner justify exceptions to the desired workflow leading to higher process costs).

4 Architecture

Our approach conducted in EDImine will be supported and validated by a corresponding tool implementation. Thereby, we do not develop a tool from scratch, but build on an existing open-source solution - the ProM tool[1] [18]. ProM is developed at the Eindhoven University of Technology and is the most prevalent tool in the area of process mining. The architecture of ProM has been designed with extensibility in mind by means of plug-ins. We leverage the extensibility mechanisms of ProM by providing the appropriate plug-ins for the aforementioned research goals.

Figure 3 illustrates the basic architecture of our approach. The starting point for performing the mining tasks is given by two types of data from the EDI systems of an organization: event logs and the contents of EDI messages. In order to allow for further processing in the ProM tool they have to be combined and transformed to a data structure that conforms to the *eXtensible Event Stream*

[1] `http://www.processmining.org` (visited Feb 8, 2011).

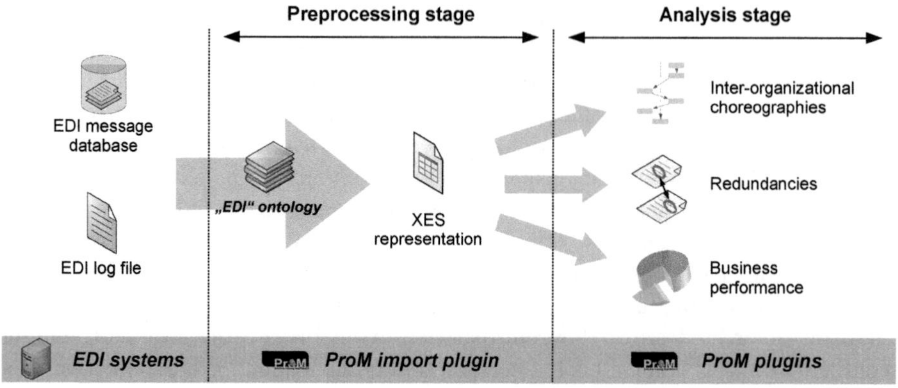

Fig. 3. Preprocessing and analysis stages

(XES) format [18]. XES is an XML-based format for storing event logs and the standard input format for ProM (as of Version 6). The conversion is performed in the preprocessing stage and implemented in a ProM import plug-in. In the subsequent analysis stage, further analyses with regard to the aforementioned research questions can be performed. The tasks of the analysis stage are also implemented by means of corresponding ProM plug-ins. In the following sections, the preprocessing and analysis stages are described in detail.

4.1 Preprocessing Stage

Figure 4 illustrates the architecture of the preprocessing stage in more detail. Business partners participating in an inter-organizational EDI setting record the contents of the exchanged business documents and keep a log of the transactions. Such a log is expected to contain information about sender and receiver of the messages, a timestamp and a reference to the actual message contents. The provided log data and message contents form the primary input for the EDImine preprocessing plug-in which combines them to an XES-conforming representation.

As described in Section 3.1 the log entries have to be grouped according to process instances. However, since EDI systems usually lack awareness of the underlying business processes in whose context they exchange messages, this is not a trivial task. To tackle this challenge, we aim at comparing and matching information of the EDI message exchanges contained in the logs as well as pieces of business information which are repeatedly transferred in the individual messages. This recognition of redundantly transferred information is fostered by a conceptual representation of the transferred business information. The concepts describing business data elements in EDI message types are defined in an external ontology.

Table 1 lists the structural elements of XES documents and their meanings. These elements have to be enriched with attributes in the form of key-value

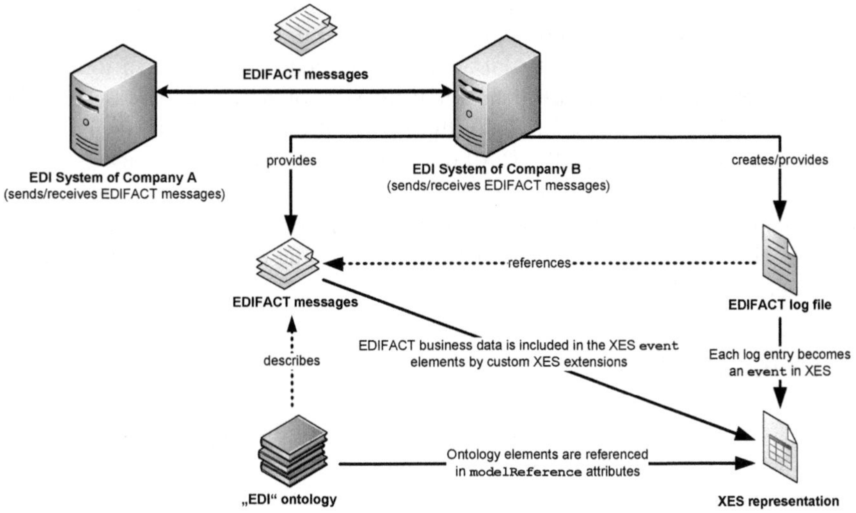

Fig. 4. Preprocessing log data and message contents for mining

Table 1. Structural elements of an XES document

Element	Usage/Meaning
log	Root element of an XES document containing a number of *traces*.
trace	Represents a group of *events* which belong to the same process instance.
event	Contains a single event. In process mining applications this usually corresponds with the execution of a single activity in a process instance.

pairs in order to include actual information about recorded events. The XES standard provides a mechanism through which attributes can be declared in well-defined extensions to the meta-model of XES. In addition, there are a number of predefined *standard extensions* in the XES standard which are generally useful in process mining contexts.

The EDImine preprocessing plug-in converts each log entry from the EDI message exchange log to an *event* element in an XES representation. Furthermore, the business data payload contained in the conveyed EDI messages is included in attributes which we define through extending the XES meta-model. Moreover, the concepts used for conceptualizing the business data are referenced through *modelReference* attributes using XES' standard extension *Semantic*. The *event* elements are grouped to process instances in corresponding *trace* elements.

4.2 Analysis Stage

In the analysis stage the prepared XES data serves as a database for mining the inter-organizational choreographies, for identifying redundancies and for business performance analyses. The conceptualization of the EDI data by means of an ontology as described in Section 4.1 plays a key role for performing the tasks of this stage. First of all, it allows for mapping EDI message types to concrete and human-understandable activity labels in the mined inter-organizational choreographies. Secondly, it permits the identification of redundancies by matching the business data contained in the individual EDI messages with regard to their conceptual belonging. Thirdly, the knowledge in the ontology is used for business performance analyses allowing the user to build sophisticated queries using the concepts from the ontology. These tasks will be realized in ProM plugins; however, the algorithms for these tasks have yet to be developed and are subject to further research.

5 Related Work

Process mining techniques [1,16] extract knowledge about business processes by analyzing event logs. It is seen as part of Business Intelligence (i.e., BP Intelligence [8]) and process mining techniques are also being embedded in commercial BPM suites. So far, the focus has been on the analysis of processes inside a single organization. There exist a few papers on process mining in cross-organizational settings such as [15], which focuses on choreography conformance checking between the mined workflows from event logs of SOAP message exchanges and abstract BPEL models. Similarly, [13] also emphasizes on verifying behavioral properties in Web service choreographies. This reveals that process mining in an inter-organizational context tends to focus on the area of Web services. In practice, however, neither explicit choreography modeling nor Web services are widely employed in electronic business transactions. Rather, *traditional approaches to Electronic Data Interchange (EDI) such as EDIFACT still play an overwhelmingly dominant role* [3,19]. In an unpublished work [12], the topic of mining EDI messages has been approached, but best to our knowledge no further research has been conducted.

In order to achieve the goals of EDImine we intend to conceptualize the data from EDI business documents by means of ontologies. Previous attempts to ontologize various EDI standards include works performed in the course of the Tripcom project[2] [6,7], which aims at creating an ontological infrastructure for business processes and business data. Tripcom defines ontologies for EDI in terms of both syntax and semantics. However, regarding semantics Tripcom focuses on the structure of message types. In contrary, EDImine focuses on building EDI ontologies for business domain specifics (e.g., bank transactions, invoice transactions, etc.) in order to provide a higher conceptual level.

So far, in existing process mining techniques there is little consideration for the semantics of events. For example, activity names are just considered as labels without much consideration for the meaning and their relations to other entities. In the SUPER project[3] [5], a semantic approach has been developed that aims at the deployment of semantic BPM techniques. For instance, the SA-MXML

[2] `http://tripcom.org/ontologies` (visited March 14, 2011).
[3] `http://www.ip-super.org` (visited March 14, 2011).

(Semantically Annotated Mining XML) format, an annotated version of the MXML format, was developed to collect and store event logs such that events are linked to ontologies. The use of ontologies and reasoners causes an immediate benefit to process mining techniques by raising the level of abstraction from the syntactic level to the semantic level [4]. However, the MXML format has shown several limitations which is the reason for choosing the XES format [18].

6 Conclusion

In this paper we introduced our approach for mining inter-organizational business processes. We discussed the lack of process awareness in common Electronic Data Interchange (EDI) systems and three shortcomings resulting thereof: (i) the unavailability of information about real-world business process execution, (ii) redundancies in the transferred business documents and (iii) the lack of support for systematic analyses of business performance and decision-making. We further described how we intend to address these shortcomings by extending existing process mining techniques and applying them on inter-organizational systems. Lastly, we proposed a two-staged technical architecture for our approach that integrates with the existing process mining tool ProM by means of plug-ins.

We expect that the unveiling of the inter-organizational choreographies will help companies to rediscover and document the relationships in their business network. Furthermore, we believe that insights gained from the combination of process and business performance data will aid companies in decision-making with regard to their interactions with business partners. Finally, methods to identify redundancies in message exchanges will be less relevant for already implemented EDI solutions, but can help standardization bodies to streamline future business document standards. The overall goal is to bring the merits of Business Process Management (BPM) to inter-organizational systems realized by means of EDI.

References

1. van der Aalst, W.M.P.: Process Mining: Discovery, Conformance and Enhancement of Business Processes. Springer, Heidelberg (2011)
2. Barros, A., Dumas, M., Oaks, P.: Standards for Web Service Choreography and Orchestration: Status and Perspectives. In: Bussler, C.J., Haller, A. (eds.) BPM 2005. LNCS, vol. 3812, pp. 61–74. Springer, Heidelberg (2006)
3. Berge, J.: The EDIFACT Standards. Blackwell Publishers, Inc., Malden (1994)
4. de Medeiros, A.K.A., Pedrinaci, C., van der Aalst, W.M.P., Domingue, J., Song, M., Rozinat, A., Norton, B., Cabral, L.: An Outlook on Semantic Business Process Mining and Monitoring. In: Chung, S., Herrero, P. (eds.) OTM-WS 2007, Part II. LNCS, vol. 4806, pp. 1244–1255. Springer, Heidelberg (2007)
5. de Medeiros, A.K.A., van der Aalst, W.M.P., Pedrinaci, C.: Semantic Process Mining Tools: Core Building Blocks. In: 16th European Conference on Information Systems (2008)

6. Foxvog, D., Bussler, C.: Ontologizing EDI: First Steps and Initial Experience. In: Proceedings of International Workshop on Data Engineering Issues in E-Commerce, pp. 49–58 (2005)
7. Foxvog, D., Bussler, C.J.: Ontologizing EDI semantics. In: Roddick, J., Benjamins, V.R., Si-said Cherfi, S., Chiang, R., Claramunt, C., Elmasri, R.A., Grandi, F., Han, H., Hepp, M., Lytras, M.D., Mišić, V.B., Poels, G., Song, I.-Y., Trujillo, J., Vangenot, C. (eds.) ER Workshops 2006. LNCS, vol. 4231, pp. 301–311. Springer, Heidelberg (2006)
8. Grigori, D., Casati, F., Castellanos, M., Shan, M., Dayal, U., Sayal, M.: Business Process Intelligence. Computers in Industry 53(3), 321–343 (2004)
9. Hill, N., Ferguson, D.: Electronic Data Interchange: A Definition and Perspective. EDI Forum: The Journal of Electronic Data Interchange 1, 5–12 (1989)
10. Liegl, P., Huemer, C., Pichler, C.: A Bottom-up Approach to Build XML Business Document Standards. In: Proceedings of the 7th IEEE International Conference on e-Business Engineering, pp. 56–63. IEEE, Los Alamitos (2010)
11. Peltz, C.: Web Services Orchestration and Choreography. Computer 36, 46–52 (2003)
12. Pham, T.T.: Mining of EDI Data for Performance Measurement of a Supply Chain. DICentral Corporation (2003) (unpublished)
13. Rouached, M., Gaaloul, W., van der Aalst, W.M.P., Bhiri, S., Godart, C.: Web Service Mining and Verification of Properties: An Approach Based on Event Calculus. In: Meersman, R., Tari, Z. (eds.) OTM 2006. LNCS, vol. 4275, pp. 408–425. Springer, Heidelberg (2006)
14. Rozinat, A., van der Aalst, W.M.P.: Conformance Checking of Processes Based on Monitoring Real Behavior. Information Systems 33(1), 64–95 (2008)
15. van der Aalst, W.M.P., Dumas, M., Rozinat, A., Ouyang, C., Verbeek, H.: Choreography Conformance Checking: An Approach based on BPEL and Petri nets. ACM Transactions on Internet Technology 8(3), 29–59 (2008)
16. van der Aalst, W.M.P., Reijers, H.A., Weijters, A.J.M.M., van Dongen, B.F., de Medeiros, A.K.A., Song, M., Verbeek, H.M.W.: Business Process Mining: An Industrial Application. Information Systems 32, 713–732 (2007)
17. van der Aalst, W.M.P., Weijters, A., Maruster, L.: Workflow Mining: Discovering Process Models from Event Logs. IEEE Transactions on Knowledge and Data Engineering 16(9), 1128–1142 (2004)
18. Verbeek, H.M.W., Buijs, J.C.A.M., van Dongen, B.F., van der Aalst, W.M.P.: XES, XESame, and ProM 6. In: van der Aalst, W.M.P., Mylopoulos, J., Sadeh, N.M., Shaw, M.J., Szyperski, C., Soffer, P., Proper, E. (eds.) Information Systems Evolution. LNBIP, vol. 72, pp. 60–75. Springer, Heidelberg (2011)
19. Vollmer, K., Gilpin, M., Stone, J.: B2B Integration Trends: Message Formats. Forrester Research (2007)

InCarMusic: Context-Aware Music Recommendations in a Car

Linas Baltrunas[1], Marius Kaminskas[1], Bernd Ludwig[1], Omar Moling[1], Francesco Ricci[1], Aykan Aydin[2], Karl-Heinz Lüke[2], and Roland Schwaiger[2]

[1] Faculty of Computer Science
Free University of Bozen-Bolzano
Piazza Domenicani 3, 39100 Bolzano, Italy
fricci@unibz.it
[2] Deutsche Telekom AG, Laboratories
Innovation Development
Ernst-Reuter-Platz 7, D-10587 Berlin, Germany
Karl-Heinz.Lueke@telekom.de

Abstract. Context aware recommender systems (CARS) adapt to the specific situation in which the recommended item will be consumed. So, for instance, music recommendations while the user is traveling by car should take into account the current traffic condition or the driver's mood. This requires the acquisition of ratings for items in several alternative contextual situations, to extract from this data the true dependency of the ratings on the contextual situation. In this paper, in order to simplify the in-context rating acquisition process, we consider the individual perceptions of the users about the influence of context on their decisions. We have elaborated a system design methodology where we assume that users can be requested to judge: a) if a contextual factor (e.g., the traffic state) is relevant for their decision making task, and b) how they would rate an item assuming that a certain contextual condition (e.g., traffic is chaotic) holds. Using these evaluations we show that it is possible to build an effective context-aware mobile recommender system.

1 Introduction

Recommender Systems (RSs) are software tools and techniques providing suggestions for items to be of use to a user [11]. In this paper we focus on a particular approach for RSs, Collaborative Filtering (CF). In CF, explicit ratings for items, given by a population of users, are exploited to predict the ratings for items not yet evaluated by the users [6]. Often, system generated recommendations can be more compelling and useful if the contextual situation of the user is known. For instance, in a music recommender, the traffic condition or the mood of the driver may be important contextual conditions to consider before suggesting a music track to be played in her car. Context-aware recommender systems (CARSs) are gaining ever more attention and various techniques have been introduced to improve their performance [1].

C. Huemer and T. Setzer (Eds.): EC-Web 2011, LNBIP 85, pp. 89–100, 2011.

To adapt recommendations to the user's context, the dependency of the user preferences (i.e., the ratings in CF) on the contextual situations must be modeled. Hence, a major initial issue for the correct design of CARSs is the assessment of the contextual factors that are worth considering when generating recommendations. This is not an easy problem: it requires informed conjectures to be formulated regarding the influence of some data, before collecting the data. Moreover, after a meaningful set of contextual factors is identified, a model, which predicts how the ratings will change depending on the contextual factors, must be built. For a set of items, this step requires the collection of explicit ratings from a population of users under several distinct contextual situations.

The main contribution of this paper is the description of a methodology for supporting the development cycle of a Context-Aware Collaborative Filtering system, as sketched above. This methodology has been previously applied to a completely different application scenario, for recommending places of interest [2], and it is adapted here to the problem of recommending music tracks to a group of users in a car. The methodology comprises four steps: context factors relevance assessment; in-context acquisition of ratings; context-aware rating prediction; and context-aware recommendation generation and visualization for a user. Each of these steps is supported by a specific system and technique. First, in order to quantitatively estimate the dependency of the user preferences on a candidate set of contextual factors, we developed a tool for acquiring context relevance subjective judgments. Second, we developed a user interface that actively asks the users to rate items under certain contextual conditions. Next, a predictive model was built, which has the goal of predicting the user's ratings for items under target contextual situations where these ratings are not known. We show that this model, which extends classical matrix factorization, can generate accurate recommendations, i.e., can better predict the true ratings, compared with a system that does not take into account the contextual information. Finally, a mobile recommender system (InCarMusic) was built to present the recommendations to the user. The recommendations have the highest predicted rating for the user's contextual situation with the joint preferences of all the passengers in the car considered, i.e., providing group recommendations [5,3].

The rest of this paper is organized as follows: in Section 2 we discuss some of the related work. In Section 3, we introduce our context-aware recommender system prototype (InCarMusic) to give immediately the motivations of our technological development. In Section 4, we explain our approach for acquiring the data describing the relationships between user preferences and contextual situations. In Section 5, we present our algorithm for context-aware recommendations and we illustrate the results of the evaluation of the proposed model. We finally draw our conclusions and list some open issues that call for future work.

2 Related Work

Context-awareness in recommender systems as a research topic has been receiving considerable attention in the last years [1]. To the best of our knowledge, the specific problem of in-car context-aware music recommendation has not been addressed until now. There is a body of work, however, on the related problem of context-aware music recommendation, which typically addresses different recommendation scenarios. For instance, [8] has improved a music recommender service with context awareness using case-based reasoning. The used context factors include the season, month, weekday, weather and temperature information. Listening cases have been obtained by aligning users' listening history data with weather bureau information. In [10] a context-aware music recommender for urban environments is presented. The context factors include the location of the user (in terms of a ZIP code), time of day, weekday, noise/traffic level, temperature and weather data. The system was bootstrapped by manually annotating the tracks in the user's library with the values of the selected contextual factors.

A common feature of these systems is the usage of a generic context model, mostly consisting of time- and weather-related information. We note that these research works do not formally address the issues of context factor selection and system bootstrapping as we do in the presented work. The choice of the most informative context factors has not been informed by any data mining experiment, and the impact of individual context factors on music perception has not been investigated.

Another area of context-aware music recommendation is dedicated to adapting music content to other types of multimedia, e.g., web pages [4] or images [9]. These systems typically use machine learning methods for learning relations between music and the context information (i.e., text or images).

3 InCarMusic Mobile Application

InCarMusic is a mobile application (Android) offering music recommendations to the passengers of a car after they have entered ratings for some items using a web application that will be illustrated in the next section. If the user did not previously enter any ratings, then the recommendations are adapted solely to the contextual situation and not to the user long term preferences described by her ratings.

First, the *Channels* tab allows the user to specify and edit channels (see Fig. 1(a)). A channel is meant to provide a certain kind of music to the user. In the channel specification the user can detail, for instance, that the channel "Happy-Classic" is appropriate when she is "happy" and would like to listen mostly to classical music and a bit of jazz. Creating such a channel enables the user to quickly switch to this type of music whenever she likes. A default channel is also provided for recommending music without asking the user to create one. Second, the *Passengers* tab allows the user to identify the passengers that are present in the car (see Fig. 1(b)). We note that the user, is always included in the passengers list. Passengers can be imported from the local contacts and should have previously provided some ratings, as it is requested to the user (see Fig. 1(c)). This means that they should have registered to the Web portal that provides the music content to our system.

(a) Editing a Channel (b) Setting the Group (c) Editing the Passengers

Fig. 1. InCarMusic user interface

The *Play* tab allows the user to retrieve music recommendations (tracks) adapted to the selected channel and the passengers (see Fig. 2(a)). Due to lack of space, in this paper we will not explain how the recommendations are adapted to the group of passengers. For that purpose, we exploit recommendation aggregation techniques illustrated in [3]. Hence, for the rest of this paper we will consider only the scenario where a single user is present in the car. While the user is listening to a music track, she can rate it (see Fig. 2(b)). These ratings are "in-context", i.e., as we explained in the introduction, the system collects the ratings together with the description of the current contextual situation of the user. We note that these ratings are immediately uploaded to the recommender server component and can be exploited for the computation of the next recommendations.

Finally, the *Profile* tab allows the user to modify her profile and define some application settings (see Fig. 2(c)). In particular, the user can set her current contextual situation and current music genre preferences (see Fig. 2(d)). These settings are used in the default channel, if the user has not selected a particular channel. We note that this last interface is pretty similar to that used for channel configuration (see Fig. 1(a)), as the operation is the same: here the user is just configuring a particular channel, the default one.

4 Rating Acquisition

In order to offer the service described in the previous section we collected the users' assessment of the effect of context on their music preferences using two web applications that are described here . In fact, there was no ready-to-use application for collecting ratings from car drivers and other passengers while in the car. As any effort to record these conditions during a trip in a car was considered not easily solvable, we developed two web-based tools, which were

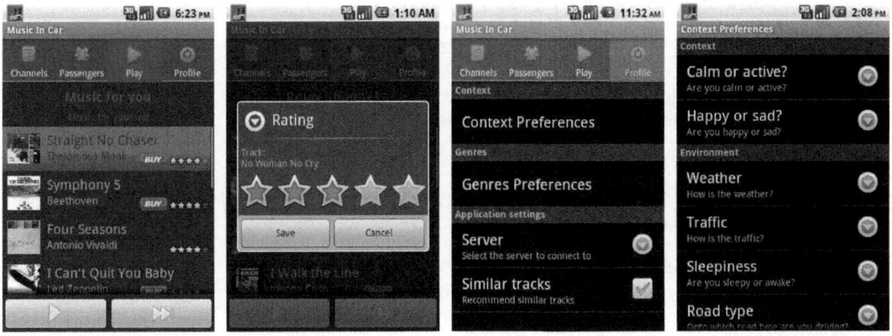

(a) Tracks Proposed to Play (b) Rating a Track (c) Editing the User Profile (d) Configuring the Recommender

Fig. 2. InCarMusic user interface (cont)

used in two consecutive phases, for simulating situations occurring in a car. In the first phase, the users were asked to evaluate the effect of certain contextual conditions on the propensity to listen to music of a particular genre, while in the second phase the users entered ratings for tracks assuming that certain contextual conditions hold (see below for more details).

4.1 Context Model and Music Track Corpus

In order to understand the influence of context on the music preferences of car passengers, context was modeled as a set of independent contextual factors. The factors are assumed to be independent in order to get a tractable mathematical model. This assumption, even if it is clearly false, as in other probabilistic models such as the naive Bayes classifier, still does not prevent the generation of reliable rating predictions. We identified the following factors and their possible values, *contextual conditions*, as potentially relevant for in car music recommendations:

Contextual Factor	**Contextual Conditions**
driving style (DS)	relaxed driving, sport driving
road type(RT)	city, highway, serpentine
landscape (L)	coast line, country side, mountains/hills, urban
sleepiness (S)	awake, sleepy
traffic conditions (TC)	free road, many cars, traffic jam
mood (M)	active, happy, lazy, sad
weather (W)	cloudy, snowing, sunny, rainy
natural phenomena (NP)	day time, morning, night, afternoon

Music tracks were of ten different genres. We observe that there is no unified music genre taxonomy, and we have chosen to use the genres defined in [12]: classical, country, disco, hip hop, jazz, rock, blues, reggae, pop and metal. For phase one, i.e., the relevance assessment of different contextual factors, five representative tracks per genre were manually selected. This resulted in

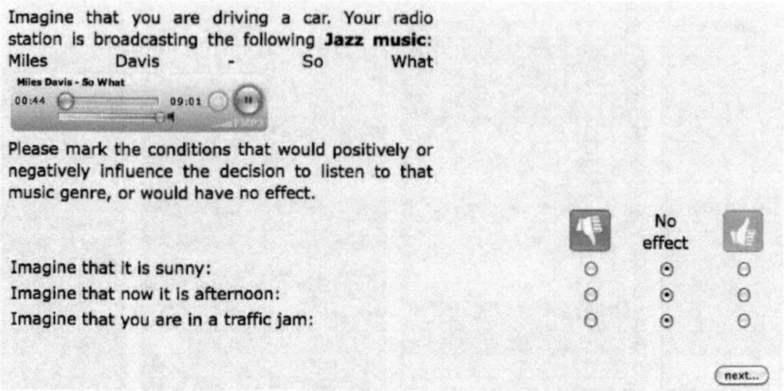

(a) Interface for Acquiring Context Relevance Judgments

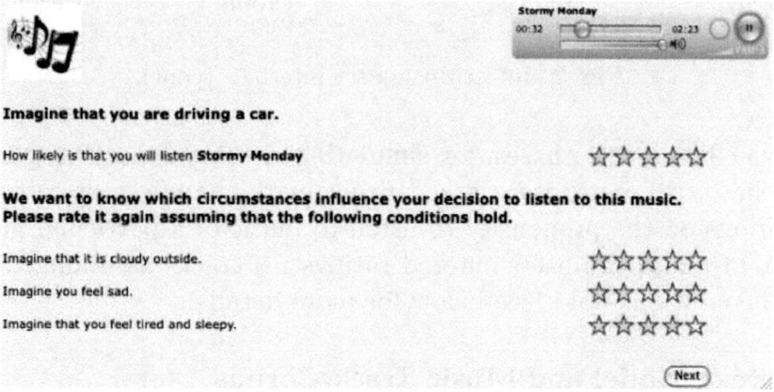

(b) Interface for Collecting Ratings with And without Context

Fig. 3. Tools for collecting user data in phase one and two

a dataset of 50 music tracks. For phase two, i.e., the assessment of the impact of contextual conditions for particular tracks, 89 additional tracks (belonging to pop, disco and hip hop genres) were added to the dataset from the MusicLoad (`http://www.musicload.de/`) download site.

4.2 Relevance of the Contextual Factors

In order to estimate the relevance of the selected contextual factors, we developed a tool for acquiring subjective judgments about the impact of these factors on the users' listening preferences. For this purpose, the users were requested to evaluate if a particular contextual condition, e.g., "today is sunny", has a positive or negative influence in her propensity to listen to music of a particular genre (see Figure 3(a)). In phase one, we acquired 2436 evaluations from 59 users with the help of our web based interview tool.

Then, for estimating the relevance of the considered contextual factors, we computed the probability distribution $P(I|F,G)$, where I is the random (response) variable of the user's answer (one out of $+1$ "increase", -1 "decrease", or 0 "no effect"), F is a contextual factor (the value of this random variable may

Table 1. Relevance of contextual factors rel(I, F, G) for different music genres

Blues music	Classical music	Country music	Disco music	Hip Hop music
DS 0.324193188	DS 0.77439747	S 0.469360938	M 0.177643232	TC 0.192705142
RT 0.216609802	S 0.209061123	DS 0.363527911	W 0.17086365	M 0.151120854
S 0.144555483	W 0.090901095	W 0.185619311	S 0.147782999	S 0.105843345
TC 0.118108963	NP 0.090509983	M 0.126974621	TC 0.129319405	NP 0.105765981
NP 0.112002402	M 0.088905397	L 0.112531867	DS 0.098158779	W 0.066024976
L 0.107824176	L 0.055675749	RT 0.109261318	RT 0.057335072	L 0.049526929
W 0.085346042	RT 0.020526969	TC 0.098999258	NP 0.049819373	DS 0.047180469
M 0.063156392	TC 0.015991764	NP 0.037183774	L 0.048588262	RT 0.01483038
Jazz music	**Metal music**	**Pop music**	**Reggae music**	**Rock music**
S 0.168519565	DS 0.462220717	S 0.418648658	S 0.549730059	TC 0.238140493
RT 0.127974728	W 0.264904662	DS 0.344360938	DS 0.382254696	S 0.224814184
W 0.106333439	S 0.196577939	RT 0.268688459	TC 0.321430505	DS 0.132856064
DS 0.100983424	L 0.122791055	TC 0.233933032	M 0.167722198	L 0.111553065
NP 0.08421736	TC 0.096436983	M 0.137086672	L 0.145512313	RT 0.096436983
L 0.053389487	M 0.06953522	NP 0.098963857	W 0.131936343	M 0.087731308
TC 0.04519683	RT 0.05580976	W 0.072377398	NP 0.105242236	W 0.083079089
M 0.035043738	NP 0.046507175	L 0.051131981	RT 0.07481265	NP 0.078288105

be any of the contextual conditions assigned to this dimension – see previous section), and G is the genre of the item. The effect of F can be measured by comparing $P(I|F, G)$ with $P(I|G)$ that does not take any context into account. For this purpose, we computed the normalized mutual information $\mathrm{rel}(I, F, G)$ of the random variables I and F for each music genre G:

$$\mathrm{rel}(I, F, G) = \frac{H(I|G) - H(I|F, G))}{H(I|G)}$$

where $H(X)$ is the entropy of the discrete random variable X taking values from $\{1, \ldots, n\}$: $H(X) = -\sum_{i=1}^{n} P(X = i) \log(P(X = i))$. $\mathrm{rel}(I, F, G)$ gives a measure of the relevance of the contextual factor F: the bigger this value, the greater the relevance. In Table 1, we rank the contextual factors, for each genre, according to their influence on I, as measured by $\mathrm{rel}(I, F, G)$. These figures indicate the contextual factors that are likely to influence a recommendation either positively of negatively. In particular, the factors F with higher $\mathrm{rel}(I, F, G)$ (for each genre G) are those providing more information to the knowledge of the influence variable I (representing the change of the propensity to listen to that music). But these values do not say what conditions, i.e., values of the factors, are likely to produce positive or negative influences I. To find out these conditions we searched for the values that maximize the probability to have a positive (negative) influence, i.e., the contextual conditions c_p and c_n such that: $c_p = \mathrm{argmax}_c P(I = +1|F = c)$ and $c_n = \mathrm{argmax}_c P(I = -1|F = c)$. Due to space constraints, we present, for each genre, only the two most influential contextual conditions (see Table 2). In fact, these results could be immediately used in a context-aware recommender system: given a particular contextual condition one can look in Table 2 and find the music genres, which are preferred or not (high or low probability) by the user in that condition.

Table 2. Influence of context on the driver's decision to select a certain Genre

genre	F	c_n	$P(-1\|c_n)$	c_p	$P(+1\|c_p)$
Blues	DS	sport driving	0.89	relaxed driving	0.6
	RT	serpentine	0.44	highway	0.6
Classics	DS	sport driving	0.9	relaxed driving	0.4
	S	sleepy	0.6	awake	0.33
Country music	S	sleepy	0.67	sleepy	0.11
	DS	sport driving	0.6	relaxed driving	0.67
Disco music	M	sad	0.5	happy	0.9
	W	cloudy, rainy	0.33	sunny	0.8
Hip Hop music	TC	many cars, traffic jam	0.22	free road	0.6
	M	sad	0.56	happy	0.78
Jazz music	S	sleepy	0.7	awake, sleepy	0.2
	RT	city, highway	0.4	highway	0.4
Metal music	DS	relaxed driving	0.56	sport driving	0.7
	W	snowing	0.56	cloudy	0.78
Pop music	S	sleepy	0.8	awake	0.44
	DS	relaxed driving	0.5	sport driving	0.67
Reggae music	S	sleepy	0.5	awake	0.44
	DS	sport driving	0.5	relaxed driving	0.89
Rock music	TC	traffic jam	0.8	free road, many cars	0.44
	S	sleepy	0.44	awake	0.44

4.3 The Impact of Contextual Conditions on Ratings

The aim of phase one was to find out the contextual factors that are more influential in changing the propensity of the user to listen to music of different genres. Conversely, in the second phase of our study, we were interested in individual tracks and their ratings, and we wanted to measure if there were any differences in these ratings in the two following cases: without considering any contextual condition, and under the assumption that a certain contextual condition holds. Therefore, we implemented a second web tool, where we asked the users to rate a track without assuming any particular context and also imagining three different contextual conditions (see Fig. 3(b)). The users rated the played tracks on a scale from 1 (*I do not like the track at all*) to 5 (*I like the track very much*). The contextual factors occurred in the questionnaires randomly but proportionally to their relevance as assessed in phase one.

In this phase, 66 different users rated music tracks; overall, 955 interviews (see the screenshot in Fig. 3(b)) were conducted. As in each interview three ratings in context were collected, the data consists of 955 ratings without context and 2865 ratings with context. In Table 3, we present the analysis of the collected data. We compare the average rating for all the items: rated under the assumption that the given context factor holds (*Mean with context* – MCY) and rated without assuming any contextual condition (*Mean without context* – MCN). We conducted t-tests in order to find out the contextual conditions that produce significant differences between MCN and MCY. The table illustrates that for many contextual conditions there are statistically significant differences. This illustrates that in this application context-awareness is relevant, as the user rating behavior is dependent on context. This hypothesis will be further validated in the next section.

Table 3. Influence of contextual conditions on the average rating of music tracks

Condition	ratings	p-value	MCN	MCY	Influence	Significance
- *Driving style*						
relaxed driving	167	0.3891	2.382876	2.275449	↓	
sport driving	165	0.3287	2.466782	2.345455	↓	
- *Landscape*						
coast line	119	0.6573	2.420207	2.487395	↑	
country side	118	0.02989	2.318707	2.033898	↓	*
mountains/hills	132	0.1954	2.530208	2.348485	↓	
urban	113	0.02177	2.456345	2.141593	↓	*
- *Mood*						
active	97	0.01333	2.552778	2.154639	↓	*
happy	96	0.5874	2.478322	2.385417	↓	
lazy	97	0.07	2.472376	2.185567	↓	.
sad	97	0.01193	2.552632	2.134021	↓	*
- *Natural phenomena*						
afternoon	92	0.9699	2.407186	2.413043	↑	
day time	98	0.09005	2.381215	2.132653	↓	.
morning	98	0.6298	2.559441	2.479592	↓	
night	90	0.1405	2.516224	2.777778	↑	
- *Road type*						
city	123	0.551	2.479029	2.398374	↓	
highway	131	0.2674	2.457348	2.618321	↓	
serpentine	127	0.07402	2.542066	2.291339	↓	.
- *Sleepiness*						
awake	69	0.3748	2.561437	2.739130	↑	
sleepy	80	0.0009526	2.60371	2.01250	↓	* * *
- *Traffic conditions*						
free road	117	0.7628	2.491131	2.538462	↑	
many cars	132	0.3846	2.530444	2.409091	↓	
traffic jam	127	1.070e-06	2.478214	1.850394	↓	* * *
- *Weather*						
cloudy	103	0.07966	2.647727	2.378641	↓	.
rainy	77	0.6488	2.433453	2.519481	↑	
snowing	103	0.02056	2.601759	2.252427	↓	*
sunny	97	0.6425	2.570236	2.649485	↑	

Significance: * * *: $p < 0.001$; * *: $0.001 \leq p < 0.01$; *: $0.01 \leq p < 0.05$; .: $0.05 \leq p < 0.1$

It is also notable that in the majority of the cases, context has a negative influence on the users' ratings. This may be a consequence of the low overall rating for the music tracks that we observed in the study: for the average user who did not like the tracks, there was no context that could change this attitude. We observe however, that for single users who provided many ratings and had a more positive attitude towards the tracks we could find several contextual factors that had a positive influence on the ratings.

5 Prediction Model

The rating prediction component computes a rating prediction for all the items, while assuming that the current user context holds. The current context is partially specified by the user, using the system GUI (as we illustrated in Section 3). Then the items with the highest predicted ratings are recommended. In this section, we present this algorithm, which extends Matrix Factorization (MF), and incorporates contextual information to adapt the recommendation to the user's contextual situation.

In [6] the authors present a Matrix Factorization approach to CF that uses "baseline" parameters, i.e., additional model parameters for each user and item. They indicate the general deviation of the rating of a user for an item from the global average. So for instance, a user baseline will be positive if it refers to a user that tends to rate higher than the average users' population. Baseline parameters can also be used to take into account the impact of context. This has been already shown by [7], where the authors introduced baseline parameters to model the time dependency of the ratings.

We have extended and adapted this approach to the music domain by incorporating the selected contextual factors into the MF model. We have introduced one model parameter for each contextual condition (value for a factor) and music track genre pair. This provides an opportunity to learn how a contextual condition affects the ratings and how they deviate from the standard personalized prediction. This deviation is the *baseline* for that contextual condition and genre combination. In principle, we could introduce parameters for each contextual condition and music track, however, this would require much more data to train the model.

More formally, in the collected context-aware rating data base a rating $r_{uic_1\dots c_k}$ indicates the evaluation of the user u for the item i made in the context $c_1, \dots, c_k$, where $c_j \in \{0, 1, \dots, z_j\}$ is the set of possible (index) values of the contextual factor j, and 0 means that the contextual factor j is unknown. The tuples $(u, i, c_1, \dots, c_k)$ for which $r_{uic_1\dots c_k}$ is known are stored in the set $R = \{(u, i, c_1, \dots, c_k) | r_{uic_1\dots c_k} \text{ is known}\}$. Note that in our collected data set, there are ratings where only one contextual condition is known and all others are unknown. We recall that MF aims at factorizing the ratings matrix into two $m \times d$ and $n \times d$ dimensional matrices V and Q respectively. A user is then represented with a vector $\boldsymbol{v}_u$ and an item i with a vector $\boldsymbol{q}_i$. We propose the following model for the computation of a personalized context-dependent rating estimation.

$$\hat{r}_{uic_1\dots c_k} = \boldsymbol{v}_u \cdot \boldsymbol{q}_i + \bar{\imath} + b_u + \sum_{j=1}^{k} b_{g_i j c_j} \tag{1}$$

where $\boldsymbol{v}_u$ and $\boldsymbol{q}_i$ are d dimensional real valued vectors representing the user u and the item i. $\bar{\imath}$ is the average of the item i ratings in the data set R, $b_{g_i j c_j}$ is the baseline of the contextual condition c_j and genre g_i of item i. If a contextual factor is unknown, i.e., $c_j = 0$, then the corresponding baseline $b_{g_i j c_j}$ is set to 0. In this way, one can learn the influence only of the known contextual conditions.

Model Training. In order to generate rating predictions, the model parameters should be learned using the training data. We defined the learning procedure as an optimization problem:

$$\min_{v_*, q_*, b_*} \sum_{r \in R} [(r_{uic_1\dots c_k} - \boldsymbol{v}_u \cdot \boldsymbol{q}_i - \bar{\imath} - \sum_{j=1}^{k} b_{g_i j c_j})^2 + \lambda(\|\boldsymbol{v}_u\|^2 + \|\boldsymbol{q}_i\|^2 + \sum_{j=1}^{k} b_{g_i j c_j}^2)]$$

where $r = (u, i, c_1, \dots, c_k)$. For better generalization performance, a regularization term, λ, is added, as it is usual in this type of models. As λ grows the model

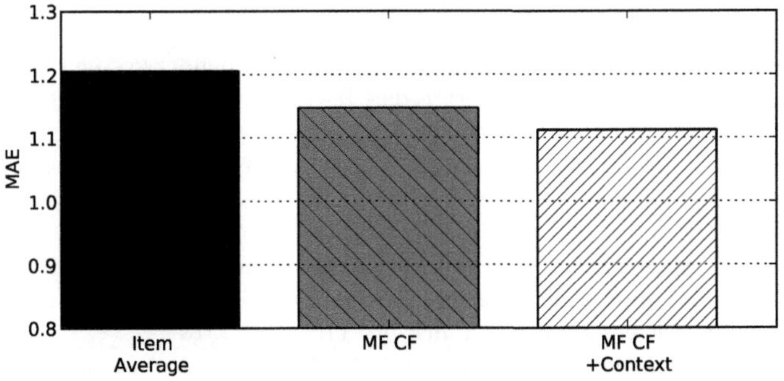

Fig. 4. Mean Absolute Error of different prediction models

becomes more "rigid", and fits less the variability in the training data. Model parameters were learned using stochastic gradient descent, which has been already proven to be efficient [6].

The Mean Absolute Error (MAE) of the considered models is shown in Figure 4. The largest improvement with respect to the non-personalized model based on the item average is achieved, as expected, by personalizing the recommendations ("MF CF" in the figure). This gives an improvement of 5%. However, the personalized model can be further improved by contextualization ("MF CF + Context") producing an improvement of 7% with respect to the item average prediction, and a 3% improvement over the personalized model. We conclude that the modeling approach and the rating acquisition process described in the previous sections can substantially improve the rating prediction accuracy when taking into account the contextual information.

6 Conclusions

In this paper we have illustrated a methodology for acquiring subjective evaluations about the relevance and the impact of certain contextual conditions on the ratings for music tracks. We have shown that using this approach a useful and effective set of ratings can be collected and a context-aware recommender system can be bootstrapped. The off-line evaluation of the predictive model, which extends Matrix Factorization (MF), has shown that it can substantially improve a non-personalized prediction, but also a classical personalized prediction based on MF, hence showing the practical advantage of the proposed approach. The mobile application that we have developed can offer context-aware and personalized music recommendations to users in a car scenario.

In the future we plan to perform a field study to validate the usability of the prototype and to incorporate a technique for extrapolating the item ratings from user actions on the items; e.g., listening to a track for a certain time in a contextual situation may be interpreted as a graded sign that this context is suited for the track. The challenge here is to filter noisy signs and build a reliable predictive model of the rating by using the user actions as predictive features.

References

1. Adomavicius, G., Tuzhilin, A.: Context-aware recommender systems. In: Ricci, F., Rokach, L., Shapira, B., Kantor, P. (eds.) Recommender Systems Handbook, pp. 217–256. Springer, Heidelberg (2011)
2. Baltrunas, L., Ludwig, B., Peer, S., Ricci, F.: Context relevance assessment and exploitation in mobile recommender systems. Personal and Ubiquitous Computing (to appear, 2011)
3. Baltrunas, L., Makcinskas, T., Ricci, F.: Group recommendations with rank aggregation and collaborative filtering. In: RecSys 2010: Proceedings of the 2010 ACM Conference on Recommender Systems, pp. 119–126 (2010)
4. Cai, R., Zhang, C., Wang, C., Zhang, L., Ma, W.Y.: Musicsense: contextual music recommendation using emotional allocation modeling. In: MULTIMEDIA 2007: Proceedings of the 15th International Conference on Multimedia, pp. 553–556. ACM, New York (2007)
5. Jameson, A., Smyth, B.: Recommendation to groups. In: Brusilovsky, P., Kobsa, A., Nejdl, W. (eds.) Adaptive Web 2007. LNCS, vol. 4321, pp. 596–627. Springer, Heidelberg (2007)
6. Koren, Y.: Factorization meets the neighborhood: a multifaceted collaborative filtering model. In: KDD 2008: Proceeding of the 14th ACM SIGKDD International Conference on Knowledge Discovery and Data Mining, pp. 426–434. ACM, New York (2008)
7. Koren, Y.: Collaborative filtering with temporal dynamics. In: KDD 2009: Proceedings of the 15th ACM SIGKDD International Conference on Knowledge Discovery and Data Mining, pp. 447–456. ACM, New York (2009)
8. Lee, J.S., Lee, J.C.: Context awareness by case-based reasoning in a music recommendation system. In: Ichikawa, H., Cho, W.-D., Chen, Y., Youn, H.Y. (eds.) UCS 2007. LNCS, vol. 4836, pp. 45–58. Springer, Heidelberg (2007)
9. Li, C.T., Shan, M.K.: Emotion-based impressionism slideshow with automatic music accompaniment. In: MULTIMEDIA 2007: Proceedings of the 15th International Conference on Multimedia, pp. 839–842. ACM Press, New York (2007)
10. Reddy, S., Mascia, J.: Lifetrak: music in tune with your life. In: HCM 2006: Proceedings of the 1st ACM International Workshop on Human-Centered Multimedia, New York, NY, USA, pp. 25–34 (2006)
11. Ricci, F., Rokach, L., Shapira, B.: Introduction to recommender systems handbook. In: Ricci, F., Rokach, L., Shapira, B., Kantor, P. (eds.) Recommender Systems Handbook, pp. 1–35. Springer, Heidelberg (2011)
12. Tzanetakis, G., Cook, P.: Musical genre classification of audio signals. IEEE Transactions on Speech and Audio Processing 10(5), 293–302 (2002)

Semantic Contextualisation of Social Tag-Based Profiles and Item Recommendations

Iván Cantador, Alejandro Bellogín,
Ignacio Fernández-Tobías, and Sergio López-Hernández

Departamento de Ingeniería Informática, Universidad Autónoma de Madrid
28049 Madrid, Spain
{ivan.cantador,alejandro.bellogin}@uam.es,
ign.fernandez01@estudiante.uam.es, sergio.lopez@uam.es

Abstract. We present an approach that efficiently identifies the semantic meanings and contexts of social tags within a particular folksonomy, and exploits them to build contextualised tag-based user and item profiles. We apply our approach to a dataset obtained from Delicious social bookmarking system, and evaluate it through two experiments: a user study consisting of manual judgements of tag disambiguation and contextualisation cases, and an offline study measuring the performance of several tag-powered item recommendation algorithms by using contextualised profiles. The results obtained show that our approach is able to accurately determine the actual semantic meanings and contexts of tag annotations, and allow item recommenders to achieve better precision and recall on their predictions.

Keywords: social tagging, folksonomy, ambiguity, semantic contextualisation, clustering, user modelling, recommender systems.

1 Introduction

Among the formats of user generated content available in the so called Web 2.0, *social tagging* has become a popular practice as a lightweight mean to classify and exchange information. Users create or upload content (resources), annotate it with freely chosen words (tags), and share these annotations with others. In this context, the nature of tagged resources is manifold: photos (Flickr[1]), music tracks (Last.fm[2]), video clips (YouTube[3]), and Web pages (Delicious[4]), to name a few.

In a social tagging system, the whole set of tags constitutes an unstructured collaborative knowledge classification scheme that is commonly known as *folksonomy*. This implicit classification serves various purposes, such as for resource organisation, promotions, and sharing with friends or with the public. Studies have shown, however, that tags are generally chosen by users to reflect their interests. Golder and Huberman [9] analysed tags on Delicious, and found that (1) the

---

[1] Flickr, Photo sharing, `http://www.flickr.com`
[2] Last.fm, Internet radio and music catalogue, `http://www.last.fm`
[3] YouTube, Online video-sharing, `http://www.youtube.com`
[4] Delicious, Social bookmarking, `http://delicious.com`

C. Huemer and T. Setzer (Eds.): EC-Web 2011, LNBIP 85, pp. 101–113, 2011.

overwhelming majority of tags identify the topics of the tagged resources, and (2) almost all tags are added for personal use, rather than for the benefit of the community. These findings lend support to the idea of using tags to derive precise user preferences and item descriptions, and bring with new research opportunities on personalised search and recommendation.

Despite the above advantages, social tags are free text, and thus suffer from various vocabulary problems [12]. Ambiguity (polysemy) of the tags arises as users apply the same tag in different domains (e.g., `bridge`, the architectonical structure vs. the card game). At the opposite end, the lack of synonym control can lead to different tags being used for the same concept, precluding collocation (e.g., `biscuit` and `cookie`). Synonym relations can also be found in the form of acronyms (e.g., `nyc` for `new york city`), and morphological deviations (e.g., `blog`, `blogs`, `blogging`). Multilinguality also obstructs the achievement of a consensus vocabulary, since several tags written in different languages can express the same concept (e.g., `spain`, `españa`, `spagna`). Moreover, there are tags that have single meanings, but are used in different semantic contexts that should be distinguished (e.g., `web` may be used to annotate items about distinct topics such as Web design, Web browsers, and Web 2.0).

To address such problems, in this paper, we present an approach that efficiently identifies semantic meanings and contexts of social tags within a particular folksonomy (Section 3), and exploits them to build contextualised tag-based user and item profiles (Section 4). These enhanced profiles are then used to improve a number of tag-powered item recommendation algorithms (Section 5). To evaluate our approach, we conduct two experiments on a dataset obtained from Delicious social bookmarking system (Section 6): a user study consisting of manual judgements of tag disambiguation and contextualisation cases, and an offline study that measures the performance of the above recommenders. The obtained results show that our approach is able to accurately determine the actual semantic contexts of tag annotations, and allows item recommenders to achieve better precision and recall on their predictions.

2 Related Work

Current social tagging systems facilitate the users with the organisation and sharing of content. The way users can access the resources, however, is limited to searching and browsing through the collections. User-centred approaches, such as personalised search and recommendation, are not yet supported by most of such systems, although these functionalities are proven to provide a better user experience, by facilitating access to huge amounts of content, which, in the case of social tagging systems, is created and annotated by the community of users.

Recent works in the research literature have investigated the adaptation of personalised search [10, 15, 21] and recommendation [5, 6, 14, 16, 22] techniques to social tagging systems, but they have a common limitation: they do not deal with **semantic ambiguities** of tags. For instance, given a tag such as `sf`, existing content retrieval strategies do not discern between the two main meanings of that tag: *San Francisco* (the Californian city) and *Science Fiction* (the literary genre). This phenomenon occurs too frequently to be ignored by a social tagging system. As an example, as for March 2011, Wikipedia contains[5] over 192K disambiguation entries.

Semantic ambiguity of tags is being investigated in the literature. There are approaches that attempt to identify the actual meaning of a tag by linking it with **structured knowledge bases** [2, 7, 18]. These approaches, however, rely on the availability of external knowledge resources, and so far are preliminary and have not been applied to personalisation and recommendation.

Other works are based on the concept of tag co-occurrence, that is, on extracting the actual meaning of a tag by analysing the occurrence of the tag with others in describing different resources. These approaches usually involve the application of **clustering techniques** over the co-occurrence information gathered from the folksonomy [3, 4, 20], and have been exploited by recent personalisation and recommendation approaches [8, 17]. Their main advantage is that an external knowledge source is not required. Nonetheless, they present several problems:

- *Lack of scalability.* Current approaches are not incremental; small changes in the folksonomy imply re-computing clusters within the whole folksonomy. This lack of scalability is undesired for a social tagging system, as its community of users is constantly adding new resources and annotations, resulting in a highly dynamic folksonomy.
- *Need for a stop criterion.* Current approaches have to define a stop criterion for the clustering processes. For instance, a hierarchical clustering [17] needs to establish the proper level at which clusters are selected, whereas an approach using a partitional clustering technique such as K-means needs to define beforehand how many clusters to build [8]. These values are difficult to define without proper evaluation, and have a definite impact on the outcome of the clustering process, and ultimately, on the semantic disambiguation or contextualisation approach. Moreover, these approaches define and evaluate the above parameter values over static test collections, and thus may not be easily adjustable over real social tagging systems.
- *Lack of explicit contextualisation.* Current approaches do not use clustering information to explicitly build contextualised user and item models. This information is rather incorporated into the retrieval and filtering algorithms, and cannot be exploited by other systems. Thus, these approaches do not offer a real contextualisation of tags, since they do not extract the context in which tags are used. For instance, a desired outcome of a disambiguation approach would be to provide a new contextualised tag description of the user's interests rather than her original raw tag values. Following the previous example, `sf` tag would be properly contextualised if it is defined within one of its possible meanings, such as `sf|San_Francisco` and `sf|Science_Fiction`. Recent works have investigated the contextualisation of folksonomies [3], but lack proper user and item models, and usually require humans to manually label each context.

As explained in subsequent sections, the approach presented herein addresses the above limitations by exploiting a fast graph clustering technique proposed by

[5] Wikipedia disambiguation pages, `http://en.wikipedia.org/wiki/Category:All_disambiguation_pages`

Newman and Girvan [13], which automatically establishes an optimal number of clusters. Moreover, for a particular tag, the approach does not have to be executed in the whole folksonomy tag set but in a subset of it, and explicitly assigns semantic contexts to annotations with such tag.

3 Semantic Contexts of Social Tags

In the literature, there are approaches that attempt to determine the different semantic meanings and contexts of social tags within a particular folksonomy by clustering the tags according to their co-occurrences in item annotation profiles [3, 8, 17]. For example, for the tag `sf`, often co-occurring tags such as `sanfrancisco`, `california` and `bayarea` may be used to define the context "San Francisco, the Californian city", while co-occurring tags like `sciencefiction`, `scifi` and `fiction` may be used to define the context "Science Fiction, the literary genre".

In this paper, we follow a clustering strategy as well, but in contrast to previous approaches, ours provides the following benefits:

- Instead of using simple tag co-occurrences, we propose to use more sophisticated tag similarities, which were presented by Markines et al. in [11], and are derived from established information theoretic and statistical measures.
- Instead of using standard hierarchical or partitional clustering strategies, which require defining a stop criterion for the clustering processes, we propose to apply the graph clustering technique presented by Newman and Girvan [13], which automatically establishes an optimal number of clusters. Moreover, to obtain the contexts of a particular tag, we propose not to cluster the whole folksonomy tag set, but a subset of it.

In the following, we briefly describe the above tag similarities and clustering technique.

3.1 Tag Similarities

A folksonomy $\mathcal{F}$ can be defined as a tuple $\mathcal{F} = \{\mathcal{T}, \mathcal{U}, \mathcal{I}, \mathcal{A}\}$, where $\mathcal{T}$ is the set of tags that comprise the vocabulary expressed by the folksonomy, $\mathcal{U}$ and $\mathcal{I}$ are respectively the sets of users and items that annotate and are annotated with the tags of $\mathcal{T}$, and $\mathcal{A} = \{(u, t, i)\} \in \mathcal{U} \times \mathcal{T} \times \mathcal{I}$ is the set of assignments (annotations) of each tag t to an item i by a user u.

To compute semantic similarities between tags, we follow a two step process. First, we transform the tripartite space of a folksonomy, represented by the triples $\{(u, t, i)\} \in \mathcal{A}$, into a set of tag-item relations $\{(t, i, w_{t,i})\} \in \mathcal{T} \times \mathcal{I} \times \mathbb{R}$ (or tag-user relations $\{(t, u, w_{t,u})\} \in \mathcal{T} \times \mathcal{U} \times \mathbb{R}$), where $w_{t,i}$ (or $w_{t,u}$) is a real number that expresses the relevance (importance, strength) of tag t when describing item profile i (or user profile u). In [11], Markines et al. call this transformation as tag assignment "aggregation", and present and evaluate a number of different aggregation methods. In this paper, we focus on two of these methods, *projection* and *distributional* aggregation, which are described with a simple example in Figure 1. Projection aggregation is based on the Boolean use of a tag for annotating a particular item, while distributional aggregation is based on the popularity (within the community of users) of the tag for annotating such item.

Second, in the obtained bipartite tag-item (or tag-user) space, we compute similarities between tags based on co-occurrences of the tags in item (or user) profiles. In [11], the authors compile a number of similarity metrics derived from established information theoretic and statistical measures. In this paper, we study some of these metrics, whose definitions are given in Table 1.

Tag assignments [user, tag, item]

Alice	conference	recommender	research
dexa.org/ecweb2011	1	1	
delicious.com		1	
ir.ii.uam.es		1	1

Bob	conference	recommender	research
dexa.org/ecweb2011	1	1	1
delicious.com		1	
ir.ii.uam.es			

⇩

Tag assignment aggregation [tag, item]

Projection	conference	recommender	research
dexa.org/ecweb2011	1	1	1
delicious.com		1	
ir.ii.uam.es		1	1

Distributional	conference	recommender	research
dexa.org/ecweb2011	2	2	1
delicious.com		2	
ir.ii.uam.es		1	1

Fig. 1. An example of projection and distributional tag assignment aggregations. Two users, Alice and Bob, annotate three Web pages with three tags: *conference*, *recommender* and *research*.

Table 1. Tested tag similarity metrics. $I_1, I_2 \subseteq I$ are the sets of items annotated with $t_1, t_2 \in \mathcal{T}$.

Similarity	***Projection aggregation***	***Distributional aggregation***
Matching	$sim(t_1,t_2) = \lvert I_1 \cap I_2 \rvert$	$sim(t_1,t_2) = -\sum_{t \in I_1 \cap I_2} \log p(t)$
Overlap	$sim(t_1,t_2) = \frac{\lvert I_1 \cap I_2 \rvert}{\min(I_1, I_2)}$	$sim(t_1,t_2) = \frac{\sum_{t \in I_1 \cap I_2} \log p(t)}{\max(\sum_{t \in I_1} \log p(t), \sum_{t \in I_2} \log p(t))}$
Jaccard	$sim(t_1,t_2) = \frac{\lvert I_1 \cap I_2 \rvert}{\lvert I_1 \cup I_2 \rvert}$	$sim(t_1,t_2) = \frac{\sum_{t \in I_1 \cap I_2} \log p(t)}{\sum_{t \in I_1 \cup I_2} \log p(t)}$
Dice	$sim(t_1,t_2) = \frac{2\lvert I_1 \cap I_2 \rvert}{\lvert I_1 \rvert + \lvert I_2 \rvert}$	$sim(t_1,t_2) = \frac{2\sum_{t \in I_1 \cap I_2} \log p(t)}{\sum_{t \in I_1} \log p(t) + \sum_{t \in I_2} \log p(t)}$
Cosine	$sim(t_1,t_2) = \frac{I_1}{\sqrt{\lvert I_1 \rvert}} \cdot \frac{I_2}{\sqrt{\lvert I_2 \rvert}} = \frac{\lvert I_1 \cap I_2 \rvert}{\sqrt{\lvert I_1 \rvert \cdot \lvert I_2 \rvert}}$	$sim(t_1,t_2) = \frac{I_1}{\lVert I_1 \rVert} \cdot \frac{I_2}{\lVert I_2 \rVert}$

3.2 Tag Clustering

We create a graph G, in which nodes represent the social tags of a folksonomy, and edges have weights that correspond to semantic similarities between tags. By using the similarity metrics presented in Section 3.1, G captures global co-occurrences of tags within item annotations, which in general, are related to *synonym* and *polysemy* relations between tags. Note that G is undirected. Using asymmetric metrics (e.g. those of [11] based on collaborative filtering), we may obtain directed graphs that would provide different semantic relations between tags, e.g. *hypernym* and *hyponym*.

Once G is built, we apply the graph clustering technique presented by Newman and Girvan [13], which automatically establishes an optimal number of clusters. However, we do not cluster G, but subgraphs of it. Specifically, for each tag $t \in \mathcal{T}$, we select its T_1 most similar tags and then, for each of these new tags, we select its T_2 most similar tags[6] to allow better disinguising semantic meanings and contexts ot t within the set of T_1 tags. With all the obtained tags (at most $1 + T_1 T_2$), we create a new graph G_t, whose edges are extracted from G. We have implemented an online demo[7] that obtains the contexts of tags in stored folksonomies. Table 2 shows examples of contexts retrieved by our system for Delicious tags. Centroids are representative tags of the contexts, and are automatically identified by our approach, as explained in Section 4.

Table 2. Examples of semantic contexts identified for different Delicious tags

tag	context centroid	context popularity	context tags
sf	fiction	0.498	fiction, scifi, sciencefiction, schi-fi, stores, fantasy, literature
	sanfrancisco	0.325	sanfrancisco, california, bayarea, losangeles, la
	restaurants	0.082	restaurants, restaurant, dining, food, eating
	events	0.016	events, event, conferences, conference, calendar
web	webdesign	0.434	webdesign, webdev, web_design, web-design, css, html
	web2.0	0.116	web2.0, socialnetworks, social, socialmedia
	javascript	0.077	javascript, js, ajax, jquery
	browser	0.038	browser, browsers, webbrowser, ie, firefox
london	england	0.263	england, uk, britain, british, english
	transport	0.183	transport, tube, underground, transportation, train, bus, map
	theatre	0.030	theatre, theater, tickets, entertainment, arts
	travel	0.030	travel, vacation, flights, airlines
holiday	christmas	0.336	christmas, xmas
	travel	0.274	travel, trip, vacation, tourism, turismo, planner
	airlines	0.104	airlines, arline, flights, flight, cheap
	rental	0.019	rental, apartment, housing, realestate

4 Tag-Based Profiles

We define the profile of user u as a vector $\mathbf{u} = (u_1, \dots, u_T)$, where u_t is a weight (real number) that measures the "informativeness" of tag t to characterise contents annotated by u. Similarly, we define the profile of item i as a vector $\mathbf{i} = (i_1, \dots, i_T)$, where i_t is a weight that measures the relevance of tag t to describe i. There exist different schemes to weight the components of tag-based user and item profiles. Some of them are based on the information available in individual profiles, while others draw information from the whole folksonomy.

TF Profiles

The simplest approach for assigning a weight to a particular tag in a user or item profile is by counting the number of times such tag has been used by the user or the number of times the tag has been used by the community to annotate the item. Thus, our first profile model for user u consists of a vector $\mathbf{u} = (u_1, \dots, u_T)$, where

[6] In the conducted experiments, $T_1 = 25$ and $T_2 = 3$ gave the best results.

[7] CTag Context Viewer, `http://ir.ii.uam.es/reshet/results.html`

$$u_t = tf_u(t),$$

$tf_u(t)$ being the tag frequency, i.e., the number of times user u has annotated items with tag t. Similarly, the profile of item i is defined as a vector $\mathbf{i} = (i_1, \ldots, i_T)$, where

$$i_t = tf_i(t),$$

$tf_i(t)$ being the number of times item i has been annotated with tag t.

TF-IDF Profiles

In an information retrieval environment, common keywords that appear in many documents of a collection are not informative, and are generally not helpful to distinguish relevant documents for a given query. To take this into account, the TF-IDF weighting scheme is usually applied to the document profiles. We adopt that principle, and adapt it to social tagging systems, proposing a second profile model, defined as follows:

$$u_t = tfiuf_u(t) = tf_u(t) \cdot iuf(t),$$
$$i_t = tfiif_i(t) = tf_i(t) \cdot iif(t)$$

where $iuf(t)$ and $iif(t)$ are inverse frequency factors that penalise tags that frequently appear (and thus are not informative) in tag-based user and item profiles respectively. Specifically, $iuf(t) = \log(M/m_t), m_t = |\{u \in \mathcal{U} | u_t > 0\}|$, and $iif(t) = \log(N/n_t), n_t = |\{i \in \mathcal{I} | i_t > 0\}|$. Note that we incorporate both user and item tag distribution global importance factors, iuf and iif, following the vector space model principle that as more rare a tag is, the more important it is for describing either a user's interests or an item's content.

BM25 Profiles

As an alternative to TF-IDF, the Okapi BM25 weighting scheme follows a probabilistic approach to assign a document with a ranking score given a query. We propose an adaptation of such model by assigning each tag with a score (weight) given a certain user or item. Our third profile model has the following expressions:

$$u_t = bm25_u(t) = \frac{tf_u(t) \cdot (k_1 + 1)}{tf_u(t) + k_1\left(1 - b + b \cdot {|u|}/{avg(|u|)}\right)} \cdot iuf(t),$$

$$i_t = bm25_i(t_l) = \frac{tf_i(t) \cdot (k_1 + 1)}{tf_i(t) + k_1\left(1 - b + b \cdot {|i|}/{avg(|i|)}\right)} \cdot iif(t)$$

where b and k_1 are set to the standard values 0.75 and 2, respectively.

Profiles with Semantically Contextualised Tags

We propose to apply our semantic contextualisation approach to each of the profile models defined before – TF, TF-IDF and BM25. A tag t is transformed into a semantically contextualised tag t^u (or t^i), which is formed by the union of t and the semantic context $c_{t,u}$ (or $c_{t,i}$) of t within the corresponding user profile u (or item profile i). For instance, tag `sf` in a user profile with tags like `city`, `california` and `bayarea` may be transformed into a new tag `sf|sanfrancisco`, since in that profile, "sf" clearly refers to San Francisco, the Californian city. With this new tag, matchings with item profiles containing contextualised tags such as `sf|fiction`, `sf|restaurants` or `sf|events` would be discarded by a personalised search or recommendation algorithm because they may annotate items related to Science Fiction, or more specific topics of San Francisco like restaurants and events in the city.

More formally, the context (centroid) $c_{t,u}$ (or $c_{t,i}$) of tag t within the user profile u (or item profile i), and the corresponding contextualised tag t^u (or t^i) are defined as follows:

$$\forall(u,t,i)\in\mathcal{A},\quad \begin{aligned} c_{t,u} &= c(t,u) = \arg\max_{c_t} cos(\mathbf{c}_t, \mathbf{u}) \Rightarrow t^u = t \cup c_{t,u} \\ c_{t,i} &= c(t,i) = \arg\max_{c_t} cos(\mathbf{c}_t, \mathbf{i}) \Rightarrow t^i = t \cup c_{t,i} \end{aligned}$$

where $\mathbf{c}_t = (c_1, \ldots, c_T)$ is the weighted list of tags that define each of the contexts c_t of tag t within the folksonomy (see Table 2).

Table 3 shows some examples of contextualised tag-based profiles generated by our approach. We have implemented another online demo[8] that allows contextualising profiles manually defined by the user or automatically extracted from Delicious.

Table 3. Examples of 4 semantically contextualised tag-based item profiles. Each original *tag* is transformed into a *tag|context* pair.

culture|philosophy	essay|interesting	fiction|sf	future|scifi	futurism|philosophy
god|science	interesting|science	literature|scifi	mind|philosophy	read|philosophy
religion|philosophy	research|science	sci-fi|sf	sciencefiction|sf	scifi|writing
sf|fiction	storytelling|fiction	toread|philosophy	universe|philosophy	writing|fiction
bayarea|sf	california|sf	city|sustainability	conservation|green	eco|green
environment|recycle	government|activism	green|environment	home|green	local|sanfrancisco
recycle|environment	recycling|environment	sanfrancisco|sf	**sf|sanfrancisco**	solar|environment
sustainability|recycling	sustainable|green	trash|green	urban|sustainability	volunteer|environmental
ajax|javascript	css|javascript	design|web	embed|webdesign	framework|javascript
gallery|jquery	html|javascript	icons|web	javascript|ajax	jquery|webdev
js|javascript	library|javascript	plugin|webdev	programming|javascript	site|webdev
toolkit|webdev	tutorials|webdev	**web|javascript**	web2.0|web	webdev|javascript
articles|web	blogs|web2.0	idea|community	internet|tools	library|opensource
network|tools	podcasts|education	rdf|web	reading|education	school|educational
semantic|semanticweb	semanticweb|web	semweb|semanticweb	software|utilities	technology|web2.0
tim|web	trends|technology	**web|web2.0**	web2.0|social	wiki|web2.0

5 Tag-Powered Item Recommenders

Adomavicius and Tuzhilin [1] formulate the recommendation problem as follows. Let $\mathcal{U}$ be a set of users, and let $\mathcal{I}$ be a set of items. Let $g{:}\,\mathcal{U}\times\mathcal{I}\rightarrow\mathcal{R}$, where $\mathcal{R}$ is a totally ordered set, be a utility function such that $g(u,i)$ measures the gain of usefulness of item i to user u. Then, for each user $u \in \mathcal{U}$, we want to choose items $i^{\max,u} \in \mathcal{I}$, unknown to the user, which maximise the utility function g:

$$\forall u \in \mathcal{U},\quad i^{\max,u} = \arg\max_{i\in\mathcal{I}} g(u,i)$$

In content-based recommendation approaches, g is formulated as:

$$g(u,i) = sim(ContentBasedUserProfile(u), Content(i)) \in \mathcal{R}$$

where $ContentBasedUserProfile(u) = \mathbf{u} = (u_1,\ldots,u_K) \in \mathbb{R}^K$ is the content-based preferences of user u, i.e., the item content features that describe the interests, tastes and needs of the user, and $Content(i) = \mathbf{i} = (i_1,\ldots,i_K) \in \mathbb{R}^K$ is the set of content features characterising item i. These descriptions are usually represented as vectors of

[8] CTag Profile Builder, `http://ir.ii.uam.es/reshet/results.html`

real numbers (weights) in which each component measures the "importance" of the corresponding feature in the user and item representations. The function *sim* computes the similarity between a user profile and an item profile in the content feature space. From the previous formulations, in this paper, we consider social tags as the content features that describe both user and item profiles (as explained in Section 4), and present a number of recommenders that we presented and evaluated in [6].

TF-based Recommender

To compute the preference of a user for an item, Noll and Meinel [15] propose a personalised similarity measure based on the user's tag frequencies. In their model, we introduce a normalisation factor that scales the utility function to values in the range [0,1], without altering the user's item ranking:

$$g(u,i) = tf(u,i) = \frac{\sum_{t:i_t>0} tf_u(t)}{\max_{v\in\mathcal{U},t\in\mathcal{T}}\left(tf_v(t)\right)}$$

TF-IDF Cosine-based Recommender

Xu et al. [21] use the cosine measure to compute the similarity between user and item profiles. As profile component weighting scheme, they use TF-IDF. We adapt their approach with the proposed tag-based profile models as follows:

$$g(u,i) = cos_{tf\text{-}idf}(u,i) = \frac{\sum_t tf_u(t)\cdot iuf(t)\cdot tf_i(t)\cdot iif(t)}{\sqrt{\sum_t\left(tf_u(t)\cdot iuf(t)\right)^2}\cdot\sqrt{\sum_t\left(tf_i(t)\cdot iif(t)\right)^2}}$$

BM25 Cosine-based Recommender

Xu et al. [21] also investigate the cosine measure with a BM25 weighting scheme. They use this model on personalised Web Search. We adapt and define it for social tagging as follows:

$$g(u,i) = cos_{bm25}(u,i) = \frac{\sum_t\left(bm25_u(t)\cdot bm25_i(t)\right)}{\sqrt{\sum_t\left(bm25_u(t)\right)^2}\cdot\sqrt{\sum_t\left(bm25_i(t)\right)^2}}$$

Recommenders with Semantically Contextualised Tag-based Profiles

We propose to evaluate the previous recommenders (1) by using tag-based user and item profiles existing in a real dataset, and (2) by contextualising these profiles with the approach presented in Section 4.

6 Experiments

To evaluate our tag-based profile contextualisation approach and its impact on the presented tag-powered recommendation models, we used a dataset obtained from Delicious system. Delicious is a social bookmarking site for Web pages. By the end of 2008, the service claimed more than 5.3 million users and 180 million unique bookmarked URLs. As a collaborative social tagging platform, Delicious contains tagged items (Web pages) belonging to practically any domain.

Our dataset was formed by 2,203 Delicious users, randomly selected from the set of users who tagged top Delicious bookmarks of 14th May 2009, and had at least 20 bookmarks in their profiles. By extracting the latest 100 bookmarks of each user, and filtering out those bookmarks with less than 20 tags, the final dataset contained 146,382 different bookmarks and 54,618 distinct tags. On average, each user profile had 77 bookmarks and 195 tags, and each item profile had 19 tags.

Once the dataset was built, we ran our clustering technique to obtain the semantic contexts of 2,893 tags: those belonging to at least 200 bookmarks. Although these tags are only 5.3% of the total set of tags in our dataset, they appear in 80.6% of the gathered tag assignments, and as we shall show in Section 6.2, they were enough to improve significantly the performance of the recommenders. Before that, in Section 6.1, we present an experiment to evaluate the accuracy of the contextualisation approach.

6.1 Evaluating Tag Contextualisation

We performed a preliminary user study to manually evaluate context assignments to tag annotations of user and item profiles. 30 PhD students and academic staff of our department participated in the experiment. They were requested to select the proper semantic context of 360 annotations (50% of them in user profiles and the remaining 50% in item profiles) of 78 distinct tags. Each annotation was evaluated by 3 different subjects, providing a total of 1,080 evaluation tests. An evaluation test consisted of presenting a subject with a particular tag, the profile the tag belonged to, and the set of possible semantic contexts of the tag. These semantic contexts were shown as coloured clusters in a tag co-occurrence based graph to ease the evaluation task. In each test, a subject could select one, two or three options for the proper semantic context of the tag. These options had to be selected sorted by decreasing preference. Moreover, in case a subject did not feel confident with the evaluation of a certain test, she could state that test was "unknown" for her. There was a substantial agreement among subjects. Fleiss' Kappa statistic measuring subjects' agreement was $\kappa = 0.636$ (a value $\kappa = 1$ means complete agreement) for the first context choice in known tests.

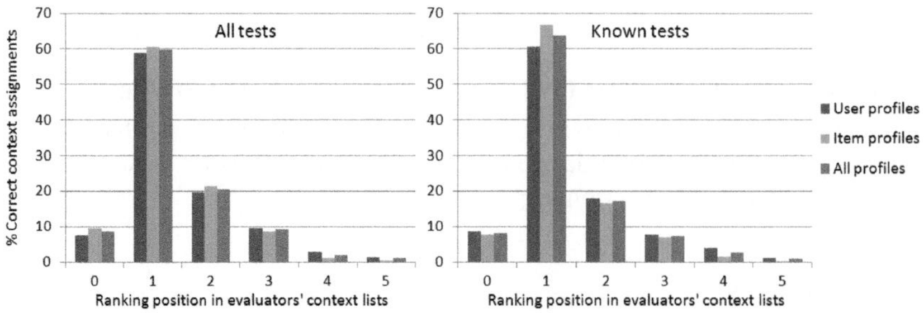

Fig. 2. Accuracy of the proposed semantic contextualisation approach

The contexts provided by the subjects were then used as ground truth to measure the accuracy of our contextualisation approach. For each test, we made a ranked list with the contexts selected by the subjects, ordered according to their positions in the subjects' choices lists (the more preferred choice, the higher the ranking score), and the number of such lists in which they appeared (the higher the number of lists, the higher the ranking score). Figure 2 shows the percentages of correct context assignments corresponding to the 1st to 5th positions in the rankings. Position 0 means the contexts assigned by our approach was not selected by any subject in the tests. For known tests, our approach assigned the correct context in 63.8% of the cases in the 1st positions of the ranked lists. The accuracy was 60.6% for annotations in user profiles, and 66.7% for annotations in item profiles, which was expected since user profiles contain more diverse tags (user preferences) than item profiles (content descriptions). Summing the correct context assignments for the 2 and 3 top choices of each subject, we respectively obtained accuracy values of 81.1% and 88.4% (being 86.3% for user profiles, and 90.5% for item profiles). Only 8.2% of the context assignments were wrong.

6.2 Evaluating Contextualised Tag-Powered Item Recommendations

To evaluate the performance of each recommender, we assume a content retrieval scenario where a system provides the user a list of *N* recommended items based on her tag-based profile. We take into account the percentage and ranking of relevant items appearing in the provided lists, computing four metrics often used to evaluate information retrieval systems: Precision and Recall at the top *N* ranked results (P@*N*, R@*N*), Mean Average Precision (MAP), and Discounted Cumulative Gain (DCG). *Precision* is defined as the number of retrieved relevant items divided by the total number of retrieved items. *MAP* is a precision metric that emphasises ranking relevant items higher. *Recall* is the fraction of relevant items that are successfully retrieved by the system. Finally, *DCG* measures the usefulness of an item based on its position in a result list. In our evaluation framework, retrieved items were all the items belonging to each test set (see below). Thus, a test set may contain (1) items belonging to the active user's profile, considered thus as "relevant", and (2) items from other users' profiles, assumed as "non relevant" for the active user.

We randomly split the set of items in the database into two subsets. The first subset contained 80% of the items for each user, and was used to build the recommendation models (training). The second subset contained the remaining 20% of the items, and was used to evaluate the recommenders (test). We built the recommendation models with the whole tag-based profiles of the training items, and with those parts of the users' tag-based profiles formed by tags annotating the training items. We evaluated the recommenders with the tag-based profiles of the test items. In the evaluation, we performed a 5-fold cross validation procedure.

Table 4. Improvements on the performance of the recommenders, by using contextualised profiles (those marked with *). The results were achieved with the *cosine similarity* and *distributional aggregation*. No significant differences were obtained with the other similarities.

	P@5	P@10	P@20	MAP	R@5	R@10	R@20	NDCG
tf	0.073	0.056	0.041	0.023	0.024	0.036	0.054	0.061
tfidf	0.135	0.103	0.074	0.044	0.044	0.067	0.096	0.113
bm25	0.149	0.109	0.077	0.048	0.048	0.071	0.100	0.121
tf*	0.093	0.069	0.049	0.029	0.030	0.045	0.064	0.077
tfidf*	0.162	0.117	0.083	0.052	0.053	0.076	0.107	0.131
bm25*	**0.171**	**0.123**	**0.085**	**0.069**	**0.055**	**0.080**	**0.109**	**0.136**
tf*	27.20%	23.18%	18.54%	23.77%	28.40%	23.98%	19.25%	24.81%
tfidf*	19.68%	14.49%	12.15%	18.07%	19.37%	14.18%	11.62%	18.07%
bm25*	15.25%	13.09%	9.85%	16.97%	15.09%	12.57%	9.13%	12.64%

The results are shown in Table 4. As found in previous studies [6], BM25 recommender achieved the best precision and recall values. But more importantly, all the recommenders were improved by using contextualised tag-based profiles. The table also shows the performance improvement percentages, which range from 24% for the TF recommender to 13% for the BM25 recommender, in all the computed metrics. It is important to note that these improvements were obtained by using a simple contextualisation approach (Section 4) that achieved 63.8% of accuracy according to our user study (Section 6.1), and which was applied to only 5.3% of the tags.

7 Conclusions

In this paper, we have presented an approach to semantically contextualise social tag-based profiles within a particular folksonomy. Our approach utilises a clustering technique that exploits sophisticated co-occurrence based similarities between tags, and is very efficient since it is not executed on the whole tag set of the folksonomy, and provides an automatic stop criterion to establish the optimal number of clusters.

We have applied the approach on tag-based user and item profiles extracted from Delicious bookmarking system, and evaluated it with a number of state of the art tag-powered item recommenders. The obtained results are encouraging. By contextualising 5.3% of the tags available in the dataset, we achieved an accuracy on context assignments of 63.8% (according to manual judgements of a conducted user study), and 13% to 24% precision/recall improvements on the tested recommenders.

For future work, we plan to extend our study by investigating alternative contextualisation strategies, evaluating them on additional (collaborative filtering and hybrid) recommenders, and using larger datasets from different social tagging systems. An empirical comparison with other clustering approaches, and a deep analysis to determine which folksonomy characteristics have more impact on the effectiveness of contextualised tag-based profiles in recommendation will be done as well.

Acknowledgements. This work was supported by the Spanish Ministry of Science and Innovation (TIN2008-06566-C04-02), and the Community of Madrid (CCG10-UAM/TIC-5877).

References

1. Adomavicius, G., Tuzhilin, A.: Toward the Next Generation of Recommender Systems: A Survey and Possible Extensions. IEEE Transactions on Knowledge & Data Engineering 17(6), 734–749 (2005)
2. Angeletou, S., Sabou, M., Motta, E.: Improving Folksonomies Using Formal Knowledge: A Case Study on Search. In: Gómez-Pérez, A., Yu, Y., Ding, Y. (eds.) ASWC 2009. LNCS, vol. 5926, pp. 276–290. Springer, Heidelberg (2009)
3. Au Yeung, C.M., Gibbins, N., Shadbolt, N.: Contextualising Tags in Collaborative Tagging Systems. In: 20th Conference on Hypertext and Hypermedia, pp. 251–260. ACM Press, New York (2009)
4. Benz, D., Hotho, A., Stützer, S., Stumme, G.: Semantics Made by You and Me: Self-emerging Ontologies Can Capture the Diversity of Shared Knowledge. In: 2nd Web Science Conference (2010)
5. Bogers, T., Van Den Bosch, A.: Recommending Scientific Articles Using Citeulike. In: 2nd ACM Conference on Recommender Systems, pp. 287–290. ACM Press, New York (2008)

6. Cantador, I., Bellogín, A., Vallet, D.: Content-based Recommendation in Social Tagging Systems. In: 4th ACM Conference on Recommender Systems, pp. 237–240. ACM Press, New York (2010)
7. García-Silva, A., Szomszor, M., Alani, H., Corcho, O.: Preliminary Results in Tag Disambiguation using DBpedia. In: 1st International Workshop on Collective Knowledge Capturing and Representation (2009)
8. Gemmell, J., Ramezani, M., Schimoler, T., Christiansen, L., Mobasher, B.: The Impact of Ambiguity and Redundancy on Tag Recommendation in Folksonomies. In: 3rd ACM Conference on Recommender Systems, pp. 45–52. ACM Press, New York (2009)
9. Golder, S.A., Huberman, B.A.: Usage Patterns of Collaborative Tagging Systems. Journal of Information Science 32(2), 198–208 (2006)
10. Hotho, A., Jäschke, R., Schmitz, C., Stumme, G.: Information Retrieval in Folksonomies: Search and Ranking. In: Cruz, I., Decker, S., Allemang, D., Preist, C., Schwabe, D., Mika, P., Uschold, M., Aroyo, L.M. (eds.) ISWC 2006. LNCS, vol. 4273, pp. 411–426. Springer, Heidelberg (2006)
11. Markines, B., Cattuto, C., Menczer, F., Benz, D., Hotho, A., Stumme, G.: Evaluating Similarity Measures for Emergent Semantics of Social Tagging. In: 18th Intl. Conference on WWW, pp. 641–650. ACM Press, New York (2009)
12. Mathes, A.: Folksonomies - Cooperative Classification and Communication through Shared Metadata. Computer Mediated Communication. University of Illinois Urbana-Champaign, IL, USA (2004)
13. Newman, M.E.J., Girvan, M.: Finding and Evaluating Community Structure in Networks. Physical Review E 69, 26–113 (2004)
14. Niwa, S., Doi, T., Honiden, S.: Web Page Recommender System based on Folksonomy Mining for ITNG 2006 Submissions. In: 3rd International Conference on Information Technology: New Generations, pp. 388–393. IEEE Press, Los Alamitos (2006)
15. Noll, M.G., Meinel, C.: Web Search Personalization Via Social Bookmarking and Tagging. In: Aberer, K., Choi, K.-S., Noy, N., Allemang, D., Lee, K.-I., Nixon, L.J.B., Golbeck, J., Mika, P., Maynard, D., Mizoguchi, R., Schreiber, G., Cudré-Mauroux, P. (eds.) ASWC 2007 and ISWC 2007. LNCS, vol. 4825, pp. 367–380. Springer, Heidelberg (2007)
16. Sen, S., Vig, J., Riedl, J.: Tagommenders: Connecting Users to Items through Tags. In: 18th International Conference on WWW, pp. 671–680. ACM Press, New York (2009)
17. Shepitsen, A., Gemmell, J., Mobasher, B., Burke, R.: Personalized Recommendation in Social Tagging Systems using Hierarchical Clustering. In: 2nd ACM Conference on Recommender Systems, pp. 259–266. ACM Press, New York (2008)
18. Specia, L., Motta, E.: Integrating Folksonomies with the Semantic Web. In: Franconi, E., Kifer, M., May, W. (eds.) ESWC 2007. LNCS, vol. 4519, pp. 624–639. Springer, Heidelberg (2007)
19. Vallet, D., Cantador, I., Jose, J.M.: Personalizing Web Search with Folksonomy-Based User and Item Profiles. In: Gurrin, C., He, Y., Kazai, G., Kruschwitz, U., Little, S., Roelleke, T., Rüger, S., van Rijsbergen, K. (eds.) ECIR 2010. LNCS, vol. 5993, pp. 420–431. Springer, Heidelberg (2010)
20. Weinberger, K.Q., Slaney, M., Van Zwol, R.: Resolving Tag Ambiguity. In: 16th International ACM Conference on Multimedia, pp. 111–120. ACM Press, New York (2008)
21. Xu, S., Bao, S., Fei, B., Su, Z., Yu, Y.: Exploring Folksonomy for Personalized Search. In: 31st Annual Intl. Conf. on Research and Development in Information Retrieval, pp. 155–162. ACM Press, New York (2008)
22. Zanardi, V., Capra, L.: Social Ranking: Uncovering Relevant Content using Tag-based Recommender Systems. In: 2nd Conference on Recommender Systems, pp. 51–58. ACM Press, New York (2008)

Multi-agent Negotiation in Electricity Markets

Fernando Lopes[1] and Helder Coelho[2]

[1] LNEG – National Research Institute
Estrada do Paço do Lumiar 22, 1649-038 Lisbon, Portugal
fernando.lopes@lneg.pt
[2] University of Lisbon, Department of Computer Science
Bloco C6, Piso 3, Campo Grande, 1749-016 Lisbon, Portugal
hcoelho@di.fc.ul.pt

Abstract. The electricity industry throughout the world, which has long been dominated by vertically integrated utilities, has experienced major changes. Basically, liberalization has separated the contestable functions of electricity generation and retail from the natural monopoly functions of transmission and distribution. This, in turn, has led to the establishment of electricity markets (EMs)—systems for effecting the purchase and sale of electricity using supply and demand to set energy prices. Ideally, competition and innovation would lead to lower prices and better uses of energy resources. However, the analysis of important EMs yields the main observation that they are still far from liberalized. Stated simply, tariffs do not reflect the pressure of competition. This article addresses the challenge of using software agents with negotiation competence to help manage the complexity of EMs towards ensuring the full benefits of deregulation. Specifically, it presents a multi-agent electricity market composed of a collection of autonomous agents and describes a generic framework for bilateral negotiation. Market participants equipped with the framework are able to enter into fixed price forward contracts and to reach (near) Pareto-optimal agreements.

Keywords: Electricity markets, multi-agent systems, intelligent software agents, automated negotiation, bilateral contracts.

1 Introduction

The electrical power industry provides the production and delivery of electricity to businesses and households through a grid. Electricity is most often produced at power stations, transmitted at high-voltages to multiple substations near populated areas, and distributed at medium and low-voltages to consumers. Traditionally, electric power companies owned the whole infrastructure from generating stations to transmission and distribution infrastructures. Deregulation began in the earlier nineties and has basically separated the contestable functions of electricity generation and retail from the natural monopoly functions of transmission and distribution. This, in turn, has led to the establishment of a wholesale market for electricity generation and a retail market for electricity retailing.

C. Huemer and T. Setzer (Eds.): EC-Web 2011, LNBIP 85, pp. 114–123, 2011.

Practically speaking, electricity markets (EMs) are systems for effecting the purchase and sale of electricity using supply and demand to set energy prices. Two primary motives for restructuring are ensuring a secure and efficient operation and decreasing the cost of electricity utilization. To achieve these goals, three major market models have been considered [16]: pools, bilateral contracts, and hybrid models. A pool, or power exchange, is a market place where electricity-generating companies submit production bids and corresponding market-prices, and consumer companies submit consumption bids. A market operator uses a market-clearing tool, typically a standard uniform auction, to set market prices. Bilateral contracts are negotiable agreements on delivery and receipt of power between two traders. These contracts are very flexible since the negotiating parties can specify their own terms. The hybrid model combines several features of pools and bilateral contracts.

Ideally, opening up the electrical power industry to competition would be an important tool to improve efficiency and benefit energy customers. Competitive forces would drive companies to innovate and operate in more efficient and economic ways. Innovation would lead to lower prices and better uses of energy resources. However, the analysis of important EMs yields the main observation that they are still far from liberalized. Today there is still a lack of both theoretical and practical understanding and important challenges are still waiting to be addressed more thoroughly. Chief among these are the additional complexities to coordinate technical and economic issues, and the technical difficulties to understand EMs internal dynamics. Stated simply, tariffs do not reflect the pressure of competition.

Multi-agent systems (MAS) have generated lots of excitement in recent years because of their promise as a new paradigm for designing and implementing complex software systems (see, e.g., [18]). MAS can deal with complex dynamic interactions and support both artificial intelligence techniques and numerical algorithms. Agent technology has been used to solve real-world problems in a range of industrial and commercial applications. Accordingly, this work looks at using software agents with negotiation competence to help manage the complexity of EMs, particularly retail markets, towards ensuring long-term capacity sustainability. Specifically, the purpose of this paper is twofold:

1. to design a multi-agent electricity market composed of a collection of autonomous agents, each responsible for one or more market functions, and each interacting with other agents in the execution of their responsibilities;
2. to equip agents with a negotiation framework enabling them to enter into forward bilateral contracts and to reach (near) Pareto-optimal agreements.

This paper builds on our previous work in the areas of automated negotiation [6,7,8,10,11] and electricity markets [9]. In particular, it tries to present an integrated and coherent view of bilateral negotiation in electricity markets. It also describes a case study involving interaction between a retailer agent and an industrial customer agent—results show that market participants can enter into efficient bilateral contracts, helping to protect them from price risks (related to high prices volatilities, mainly at times of peak demands and supply shortages).

The remainder of the paper is structured as follows. Section 2 describes a multi-agent electricity market, placing emphasis on the individual behavior of autonomous agents. Section 3 presents a negotiation framework for market participants, focusing on the social behavior of agents. Section 4 illustrates how autonomous agents equipped with the framework operate in a negotiation setting—a simplified retail market. Finally, related work and concluding remarks are presented in sections 5 and 6 respectively.

2 Multi-agent Electricity Market

Multi-agent systems are essentially loosely coupled networks of software agents that interact to solve problems beyond the capabilities of each individual agent. Conceptually, a multi-agent approach in which autonomous agents are capable of flexible action in order to meet their design objectives is an ideal fit to the naturally distributed domain of a deregulated electricity market. Accordingly, we consider the following types of agents:

1. *system operator*: maintains the system security, administers transmission tariffs, and coordinates maintenance scheduling [12];
2. *market operator*: regulates pool negotiations, and thus, is present only in a pool or hybrid market [12];
3. *sellers and buyers*: sellers represent entities able to sell electricity and buyers represent distribution companies or electricity consumers.
4. *virtual power players*: responsible for managing coalitions of producers [17];
5. *traders*: promote liberalization and competition, and simplify dealings either between sellers/buyers and the market operator or between sellers and buyers.

The agents are autonomous computer systems capable of flexible problem solving and able to communicate, when appropriate, with other agents. They are equipped with a generic model of individual behavior [6]. Specifically, each agent has the following key features:

A1 a set of *beliefs* representing information about the agent itself and the market; beliefs are formulae of some logical language (the precise nature of the language is not relevant to our model);

A2 a set of *goals* representing world states to be achieved; goals are also formulae of some logical language;

A3 a library of *plan templates* representing simple procedures for achieving goals; a plan template *pt* has an header and a body; the header defines a name for *pt*; the body specifies either the decomposition of a goal into more detailed subgoals or some numerical computation;

A4 a set of *plans* for execution, either immediately or in the near future; a plan is a collection of plan templates structured into a hierarchical and temporally constrained And-tree.

The generation of a plan *p* from the plan templates stored in the library is performed through an iterative procedure involving four main tasks:

1. *plan retrieval*: searching the library for any plan template whose header unifies with the description of a goal;
2. *plan selection*: selecting the preferred plan template *pt* (from the set of retrieved plan templates);
3. *plan addition*: adding the preferred plan template to *p*;
4. *plan interpretation*: selecting a composite plan template from *p*, say *pt*, establishing a temporal ordering for the elements of its body, and picking the first ordered element (which is interpreted as a new goal).

Now, in order to move towards the benefits of deregulation, we put forward the following requirements for market design:

- market participants should be able to enter into hedge contracts to protect themselves from volatility, notably price volatility;
- participants should be able to effectively negotiate various issues at the table (e.g., three-rate tariffs or even hour-wise tariffs);
- participants should be capable of exhibiting strategic behaviour and considering Demand Response (DR), with the objective of distributing demand over time.

The structure of hedge contracts varies due to different conventions and market structures. However, the two simplest and most common forms are fixed price forward contracts and contracts for differences. A forward contract is an agreement to buy or sell electricity at a specified point of time in the (near) future. A contract for differences is similar to a forward contract, but considers a strike price and allows refunds. For instance, if the actual electricity price in a given period of time is higher than the strike price, a generator will refund the difference to a retailer. Similarly, a retailer will refund the difference when the actual price is less than the strike price.

Energy consumption is typically distributed unevenly along a day—consumers have similar and time synchronous behaviors leading to different energy peaks. Utility companies need to guarantee that they can supply electrical power to all customers, regardless of the amount of energy demanded. Furthermore, they need to be prepared for not only the usual, predictable demand-peaks, but also for any possible peak loads. To this end, there have been a number of initiatives, grouped under the general term of demand-side-management (DSM), to distribute demand over time to avoid peak loads. In particular, many companies have already presented a two-rate tariff to smooth the daily demand profile (cheaper night tariff). This dual peak/off-peak tariff can easily be extended and refined if companies can offer a three-rate tariff (a peak/medium/off-peak tariff) or even an hour-wise DSM-tariff (an hourly-rate tariff). Furthermore, there is still another mechanism that refines the preference elicitation of agents: dynamic pricing tariffs. Specifically, Demand Response has been implemented in several markets and has proved to bring relevant benefits to market players [1].

3 Multi-agent Negotiation

Negotiation, like other forms of social interaction, often proceeds through several distinct phases, notably a beginning or initiation phase, a middle or problem-solving phase, and an ending or resolution phase. This paper concentrates on the operational and strategic process of preparing and planning for negotiation (usually referred to as pre-negotiation), and the central process of moving toward agreement (usually referred to as actual negotiation).

3.1 Pre-negotiation

Pre-negotiation involves mainly the creation of a well-laid plan specifying the activities that negotiators should attend to before actually starting to negotiate. More specifically, negotiators who carefully prepare and plan will make efforts to perform a number of activities, including [4,15]:

- defining the agenda and prioritizing the issues;
- defining the limits and targets;
- selecting an appropriate protocol.

Effective preparation requires that negotiators establish a negotiating agenda—a final set of issues to be deliberated. This task often involves interaction with the opponent. Specifically, every negotiator discloses its list of issues in order to reach agreement about what will be discussed during actual negotiation. The next step is to prioritize the issues at stake. Prioritization usually involves two steps: (i) determining which issues are most important and which are least important, and (ii) determining whether the issues are connected or separate. Priorities can be set in a number of ways (e.g., to rank-order the issues, or to use standard techniques, such as the nominal group technique). For the sake of simplicity, we consider that negotiators set priorities by ranking-order the issues.

Effective preparation also requires that negotiators define two key points for each issue at stake: the *resistance point* or *limit*—the point where every negotiator decides to stop the negotiation rather than to continue, because any settlement beyond this point is not minimally acceptable, and the *target point* or *level of aspiration*—the point where every negotiator realistically expects to achieve a settlement.

Additionally, effective preparation requires that negotiators agree on an appropriate protocol that defines the rules governing the interaction. The protocol can be simple, allowing agents to exchange only proposals. Alternatively, the protocol can be complex, allowing agents to provide arguments to support their negotiation stance. However, most sophisticated protocols make considerable demands on any implementation (see, e.g., [8]). Therefore, we consider an alternating offers protocol. Two agents bargain over the division of the surplus of $n \geq 2$ issues by alternately proposing offers at times in $T = \{1, 2, \ldots\}$. A proposal (or offer) is a vector specifying a division of the surplus of all the issues. The agents have the ability to unilaterally opt out of the negotiation when responding to a proposal.

The agents' preferences are modelled by the well-known additive model—the parties assign numerical values to the different levels on each issue and add them to get an entire offer evaluation [15]. This model is simple, and probably the most widely used in multi-issue negotiation. However, it is only appropriate when mutual preference independence exists between issues.

3.2 Actual Negotiation

The negotiation protocol defines the possible states, the valid actions of the agents in particular states, and the events that cause states to change. It often marks branching points at which negotiators have to make decisions according to their strategies. Accordingly, this subsection describes two groups of strategies that have attracted much attention in negotiation research, namely [14]:

1. *concession making or yielding*: negotiators reduce their demands or aspirations to accommodate the opponent;
2. *problem solving or integrating*: negotiators maintain their aspirations and try to find ways of reconciling them with the aspirations of their opponent.

Concession strategies are functions that model significant opening positions and typical patterns of concessions. Practically speaking, three different opening positions (extreme or high, reasonable or moderate, and modest or low) and three levels of concession magnitude (large, substantial, and small) have attracted much attention in negotiation research. They may be associated with a number of strategies, including [13]:

1. *starting high and conceding slowly*: negotiators adopt an optimistic opening position and make small concessions throughout negotiation;
2. *starting reasonable and conceding moderately*: negotiators adopt a realistic opening position and make substantial concessions during the course of negotiation.

Lopes et al. [6,10] present a formal definition of these and other relevant concession strategies.

Problem solving behaviour aims at finding agreements that appeal to all sides, both individually and collectively. The host of existing problem solving strategies includes [3]:

1. *logrolling*: two parties agree to exchange concessions on different issues, with each party yielding on issues that are of low priority to itself and high priority to the other party;
2. *nonspecific compensation*: one party achieves its goals and pays off the other for accommodating its interests.

The formal definition of relevant logrolling strategies and other important problem solving strategies appears elsewhere [7,11].

4 Case Study: Multi-agent Retail Market

A multi-agent electricity market system, involving a wholesale market and a retail market, is currently being developed using the JAVA programming language and the JADE framework. At present, market participants can exhibit simple goal-directed behavior and interact, when appropriate, with other agents to meet their design objectives. Also, they can enter into simple fixed-price forward bilateral contracts for physical delivery.

In general, retailers operate in a fine zone between profit and loss. Specifically, if the price to end-users is too high then no customer signs on. Also, if the price from producers is higher than prices in contracts with end-users, then retailers will lose money. Therefore, it is essential that retailers select the right strategies to negotiate with end-users, while entering into favorable contracts with producers.

For illustrative purposes, we present below a specific scenario involving negotiation between a retailer and a customer:

> "David Colburn, CEO of N2K Power, and Tom Britton, executive at SCO Corporation, are still at it. Colburn and Britton have already gone through the numbers—N2K has offered a three-rate DSM-tariff in accordance with global demand: peak-load period (45€/MWh), medium-load period (42€/MWh), and off-peak period (40€/MWh). This rating scheme was proposed to incentive SCO to move consumption into cheaper hours. However, Britton saw the offer in a slightly different light and has insisted on 40€/MWh for the medium-load period. Colburn and Britton are discussing and, so far, have accomplished little more than making each other angry. Can they resolve their differences?"

The following key characteristics can be noted from this scenario:

1. negotiation involves two parties (bilateral negotiation) and three issues (multi-issue negotiation); specifically, Colburn (electricity retailer) and Britton (industrial customer) are negotiating a three-rate DSM-tariff: `price#1` (for peak-load period), `price#2` (for medium-load period), and `price#3` (for off-peak period);
2. negotiation involves elements of both competition and cooperation; specifically, negotiation is inter-organizational and thus competitive in nature (the parties want to maximize their individual payoff); however, N2K Power seeks to make SCO Corporation as satisfied as possible to establish a long-term relationship (Colburn is thus concerned with Britton's outcome).

Table 1 shows the negotiation issues, the (normalized) weights, and the limits of the Retailer agent. The weights are numbers that express the preferences of Colburn for the issues at stake. As noted, Colburn has set the hourly rates in accordance with the global demand, and thus the first issue (`price#1`) is the most important to N2K Power.

Figure 1 shows the joint utility space for Colburn and Britton. The abscissa represents the utility to Colburn, and the ordinate the utility to Britton. The

Table 1. Issues, preferences and limits (Retailer agent)

Negotiation Issue	Time Period	Weight	Limit
`price#1`	07 – 12 14 – 20	0.40	35
`price#2`	12 – 14	0.35	35
`price#3`	00 – 07 20 – 24	0.25	35

solid line OCO' represents the Pareto optimal or efficient frontier *i.e.*, the locus of achievable joint evaluations from which no joint gains are possible [15]. The small squares depict a few options for settling the issues at stake.

Now, we take up a few strategies and examine their impact on the negotiation outcome. Practically speaking, negotiators who demand too much will often fail to reach agreement. Those who demand too little will usually reach agreement but achieve low benefits. The most successful negotiators are often those who are moderately firm. However, if negotiators do not try to devise new alternatives by means of problem solving, the result will probably be a compromise agreement with low benefits to both sides. For instance, Colburn and Britton can agree on the outcome represented by point A in Figure 1.

Suppose now that it is of higher priority for Britton to settle the medium-load rate, rather than the off-peak rate. Colburn and Britton have the makings of a logrolling deal. Accordingly, the two agents can reach the agreement represented by point B in Figure 1. This agreement is better for both agents than the compromise agreement represented by point A. Noticeably, logrolling strategies can permit negotiators to fully exploit the differences in the valuation of the issues and to capitalize on Pareto optimal agreements. In this way, Colburn and Britton can pursue specific logrolling strategies and agree on the optimal agreement represented by point C in Figure 1. This agreement lies along the efficient frontier.

5 Related Work

Multi-agent energy markets have received some attention lately and a number of prominent tools have been proposed in the literature, notably EMCAS—software agents with negotiation competence use strategies based on machine-learning and adaptation to simulate electricity markets [2], and AMES—open-source computational laboratory for studying wholesale power markets, restructured in accordance with U.S. Federal Energy Regulatory Commission [5].

Also, worthy to mention is the work of Vale et al. [12,17]. They developed the MASCEM system, a multi-agent simulator of EMs supporting a diversity of market models and capturing relevant features of market players. Specifically, it includes a market operator, a system operator, virtual power producers,

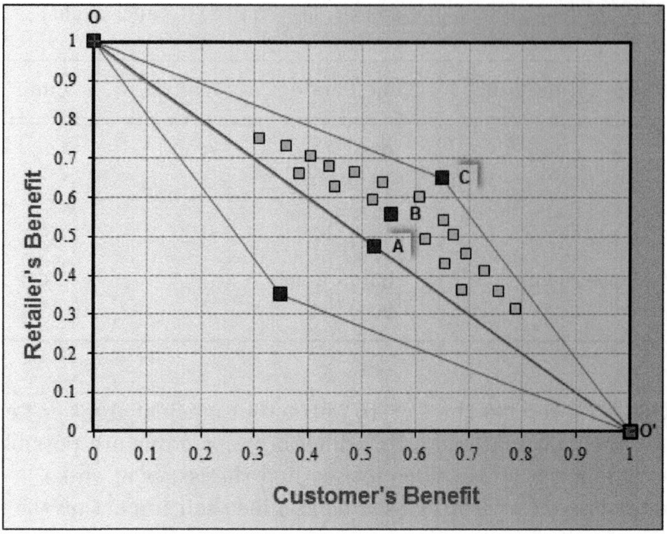

Fig. 1. Joint utility space for the Retailer-Customer negotiation situation

buyers, sellers, and traders. Additionally, it can simulate pool markets, forward markets, balancing markets, complex markets, and bilateral contracts. Furthermore, it integrates (real) data from the Iberian Market, allowing users to define realistic scenarios.

Nevertheless, despite the power and elegance of MASCEM and other existing EM simulators, they often lack generality and flexibility, mainly because they are limited to particular market models, specific types of market participants, and particular features of market players. Currently, there is a pressing need to go a step forward in the development of EM simulators, since they are crucial for tackling the complex challenges posed by electricity markets.

6 Conclusion

This article has addressed, at least partially, the challenges created by competitive energy markets towards ensuring the benefits of deregulation. Specifically, it has presented a multi-agent electricity market composed of multiple software agents and described a generic framework for automated negotiation. Results from a simplified multi-agent retail market, involving interaction between a retailer and an industrial customer, shown that a computational negotiation approach can help protect market participants from price volatility, without making use of significant computational resources.

As this research progresses, we aim to tackle increasingly more complex and realistic scenarios. We also aim to develop agents capable of both entering into various concurrent bilateral negotiations and negotiating more complex bilateral contracts, helping them to transfer financial risks between different market participants.

References

1. Cappers, P., Goldman, C., Kathan, D.: Demand Response in U.S. Electricity Markets: Empirical Evidence. Energy 35, 1526–1535 (2010)
2. Koritarov, V.: Real-World Market Representation with Agents: Modeling the Electricity Market as a Complex Adaptive System with an Agent-Based Approach. IEEE Power & Energy Magazine, 39–46 (2004)
3. Lax, D., Sebenius, J.: The Manager as Negotiator. Free Press, New York (1986)
4. Lewicki, R., Barry, B., Saunders, D., Minton, J.: Negotiation. McGraw Hill, New York (2003)
5. Li, H., Tesfatsion, L.: Development of Open Source Software for Power Market Research: The AMES Test Bed. Journal of Energy Markets 2, 111–128 (2009)
6. Lopes, F., Mamede, N., Novais, A.Q., Coelho, H.: A Negotiation Model for Autonomous Computational Agents: Formal Description and Empirical Evaluation. Journal of Intelligent & Fuzzy Systems 12, 195–212 (2002)
7. Lopes, F., Mamede, N., Novais, A.Q., Coelho, H.: Negotiation Strategies for Autonomous Computational Agents. In: 16th European Conference on Artificial Intelligence (ECAI-2004), pp. 38–42. IOS Press, Amsterdam (2004)
8. Lopes, F., Wooldridge, M., Novais, A.Q.: Negotiation Among Autonomous Computational Agents: Principles, Analysis and Challenges. Artificial Intelligence Review 29, 1–44 (2008)
9. Lopes, F., Novais, A.Q., Coelho, H.: Bilateral Negotiation in a Multi-Agent Energy Market. In: Huang, D.-S., Jo, K.-H., Lee, H.-H., Kang, H.-J., Bevilacqua, V. (eds.) ICIC 2009. LNCS, vol. 5754, pp. 655–664. Springer, Heidelberg (2009)
10. Lopes, F., Coelho, H.: Concession Behaviour in Automated Negotiation. In: E-Commerce and Web Technologies, pp. 184–194. Springer, Heidelberg (2010a)
11. Lopes, F., Coelho, H.: Bilateral Negotiation in a Multi-Agent Supply Chain System. In: E-Commerce and Web Technologies, pp. 195–206. Springer, Heidelberg (2010b)
12. Praça, I., Ramos, C., Vale, Z., Cordeiro, M.: MASCEM: A Multi-Agent System that Simulates Competitive Electricity Markets. IEEE Intelligent Syst. 18, 54–60 (2003)
13. Pruitt, D.: Negotiation Behavior. Academic Press, New York (1981)
14. Pruitt, D., Kim, S.: Social Conflict: Escalation, Stalemate, and Settlement. McGraw Hill, New York (2004)
15. Raiffa, H.: The Art and Science of Negotiation. Harvard University Press, Cambridge (1982)
16. Shahidehpour, M., Yamin, H., Li, Z.: Market Operations in Electric Power Systems. John Wiley & Sons, Chicester (2002)
17. Vale, Z., Pinto, T., Praça, I., Morais, H.: MASCEM - Electricity markets simulation with strategically acting players. IEEE Intelligent Systems 26(2) (2011)
18. Wooldridge, M.: An Introduction to MultiAgent Systems. John Wiley & Sons, Chichester (2009)

How to Make Specialists NOT Specialised in TAC Market Design Competition? Behaviour-Based Mechanism Design*

Dengji Zhao[1,2], Dongmo Zhang[1], and Laurent Perrussel[2]

[1] Intelligent Systems Laboratory, University of Western Sydney, Australia
{dzhao,dongmo}@scm.uws.edu.au
[2] IRIT, University of Toulouse, France
laurent.perrussel@univ-tlse1.fr

Abstract. This paper proposes an approach to design behaviour-based double auction mechanisms that are adaptive to market changes under the Trading Agent Competition Market Design platform. Because of the dynamics of the market environment, it is not feasible to test a mechanism in all kinds of environments. Since the strategies adopted by traders are well classified and studied, we will analyse and utilise the behaviour of traders with each kind of strategy, design specific (trader-dependent) mechanisms for attracting them, and finally integrate these trader-dependent mechanisms to achieve adaptive mechanisms.

Keywords: Adaptive Mechanism Design, Double Auction, Behaviour-based Mechanism, E-Commerce, Trading Agent Competition.

1 Introduction

A double auction market allows multiple buyers and sellers to trade commodities simultaneously. Most modern exchange markets, e.g. the New York Stock Exchange, use double auction mechanisms. In a typical double auction market, buyers submit *bids* (buy orders) to the auctioneer (the market maker) offering the highest prices they are willing to pay for a certain commodity, and sellers submit *asks* (sell orders) to set the lowest prices they can accept for selling the commodity. The auctioneer collects the orders and tries to match them using certain market clearing policies in order to make transactions.

An annual Trading Agent Competition (TAC) Market Design Tournament (CAT Tournament) was established in 2007 to foster research in the design of double auction market mechanisms in a dynamic and competitive environment, particularly mechanisms able to adapt to changes in the environment [1,2]. A CAT tournament consists of a series of games, and each game is a simulation of double auction markets including traders (buyers and sellers) and specialists

* This research was supported by the Australian Research Council through Discovery Project DP0988750.

C. Huemer and T. Setzer (Eds.): EC-Web 2011, LNBIP 85, pp. 124–135, 2011.

(market makers). Traders are simulated and provided by the tournament organiser, while each specialist is a double auction market set up and operated by a competitor. Traders dynamically swap between specialists to trade, while specialists compete with each other by attracting traders, executing more transactions and gaining more profit. Therefore, the CAT tournament environment simulates not only the dynamics of traders but also competition among specialists, which renders the market design particularly challenging.

Although certain winning market mechanisms under the TAC competition platform have been published [3,4,5,6], they cannot guarantee that a winning mechanism is also competitive when the environment changes. This also explains why a winning specialist could not win all games in the final in past tournaments. This is further demonstrated by Robinson *et al.* through one post-tournament evaluation [7]. They showed that most specialists are susceptible to environmental changes. *This phenomenon raises the question of how to design a competitive double auction market that is adaptive to environmental changes.*

Central to becoming a winning specialist in the CAT tournament is attracting as many good traders as possible in order to receive more good shouts, generate more transactions and therefore create more profit for both traders and the market maker. This is also true for a real exchange market, as people normally choose a market based on market liquidity and the number of traders in the market. Moreover, there often does not exist a uniform mechanism that is attractive to all kinds of traders, which also explains why different exchange markets use different policies to target different traders in the real world. *Therefore, it is very important for a market maker to fully understand the market environment and target the right customers.* A key way to understanding the market environment is analysing historical market information.

Therefore, in this paper we propose an approach based on traders' behaviour to design competitive mechanisms that are also adaptive to environmental changes. By classifying and utilising traders' behaviour, we first design mechanisms that are competitive in environments with one kind of trader, and then integrate these trader-dependent mechanisms to obtain competitive mechanisms for any complex environment that is not known in advance.

This paper is organised as follows. After a brief introduction to the CAT tournament platform in Sect. 2, we show how to classify traders based on their behaviour in Sect. 3. Section 4 presents a way to utilise traders' behaviour in the design process and shows an experimental example. In Section 5 we introduce a more general extension of this approach, and conclude in Sect. 6 with some suggested directions for future work.

2 Preliminary

This section will introduce the CAT tournament platform, called JCAT [8]. JCAT provides the ability to run CAT games. A CAT game consists of a CAT server and CAT clients including traders (buyers and sellers) and specialists (market makers). The CAT server works as a communication hub between CAT clients and records all game events and validates requests from traders and specialists. A CAT game lasts a certain number of days, say 500, and each day consists of rounds. Each trading agent is equipped with a specific bidding strategy and can only choose one specialist to trade in each day, while each specialist is a combination of policies. Traders are configured by the competition organiser, and each specialist is set by a competitor.

Each trader is configured with a private value (i.e. its valuation of the goods it will trade), a *market selection strategy* and a *bidding strategy*. The market selection strategy determines a specialist to trade in each day, and the bidding strategy specifies how to make offers. The main market selection strategies used in previous competitions are based on an n-armed bandit problem where daily profits are used as rewards to update the value function. Bidding strategies integrated in JCAT are those that have been extensively studied in the literature, namely ZIC (Zero Intelligence-Constrained [9]), ZIP (Zero Intelligence Plus [10]), GD (Gjerstad Dickhaut [11]), and RE (Roth and Erev [12]).

Each specialist operates one exchange market and designs its own market rules in terms of five components/policies, namely accepting policy, clearing policy, matching policy, pricing policy and charging policy. Accepting policy determines what shouts/orders are acceptable. Clearing policy schedules clearing time during a trading day. Matching policy specifies which ask is matched with which bid for clearing. Pricing policy calculates a transaction price for each match given by matching policy. Charging policy is relatively independent from other policies and determines the charges a specialist imposes on a trading day, e.g. fees for each transaction.

3 Behaviour-Based Trader Classification

Given an unknown environment, the key to understanding it is analysing traders' behaviour. Especially when the strategies adopted by traders can be clearly classified, we want to find out traders' behaviour patterns for different strategies, i.e. the relationship between traders' strategies and their behaviour. Therefore, we can distinguish traders in terms of their behaviour and apply different policies for different traders. In this section, based on JCAT, we introduce how to collect traders' behaviour-related information, define the categories of traders and finally show how to classify traders based on their behaviour.

3.1 Data Acquisition

In JCAT, for each trader i and each specialist s, all specialists can obtain the following trader-related historical information.

- Accepted shouts of i by s.
- Cleared/Matched shouts of i by s.

The above information is also the only information about each trader available for all specialists. The trader of a rejected shout is never revealed to any specialist, even the specialist whom the shout was submitted to. Therefore, the acceptance of a shout cannot depend on the sender's historical information. Given the above information about each trader, we need to pre-process it depending on what we need for the design process, e.g. the average clearing price for a trader in a specialist during a period of time and a trader's trading time distribution.

3.2 Defining Categories of Trader

Given the perfect equilibrium price p_e^* of a market[1], we classify traders into two different categories, intra-marginal and extra-marginal:

- *Intra-marginal*: A seller (buyer) i with private valuation v_i is intra-marginal if $v_i \leq p_e^*$ ($v_i \geq p_e^*$).
- *Extra-marginal*: Otherwise.

The reason for classifying traders into these two categories is that intra-marginal traders can bring profitable shouts to a market, while extra-marginal traders do not. Therefore, a competitive specialist needs to attract more intra-marginal traders. We can further classify intra-marginal traders in terms of their bidding strategies.

3.3 Category Recognition from Behaviour

We say a trader is attracted by a specialist if the trading time the trader spent in that specialist is much greater than the time it spent in any other specialist. We know that a profit-seeking trader chooses a specialist that has given it the highest profit in some past period. In order to give a trader profit, a specialist has to match its shouts as many as possible with profitable clearing prices. Therefore, intra-marginal traders are more likely to be attracted. Thus, a trader's trading time distribution (i.e. stability) will be the main information to be considered in its category recognition.

Trading Time Distribution. As the main market selection strategy adopted in CAT competitions, *ϵ-greedy selection* determines what is the most profitable specialist for a trader and then selects this specialist with probability of $1-\epsilon$ and the others randomly with probability ϵ. This selection strategy uses reinforcement learning method based on the profit a trader received from each specialist. ϵ is mostly set to be 0.1 in CAT competitions.

Based on the above market selection strategy, we recognised the following trading time distribution patterns. We say a trader i is more stable if the time (w.r.t. the number of days) that i spent in each market varies significantly, i.e. the standard deviation of the trading time is higher. Generally speaking, intra-marginal traders are much more stable than extra-marginal traders under the same bidding strategy, but the degree of stability varies with bidding strategies.

- *Under the same bidding strategy.* All intra-marginal traders have similar trading time distribution, in other words, intra-marginal traders with valuations

[1] The equilibrium of a market where traders truthfully report their demand and valuations.

far from the perfect market equilibrium are not more stable than those with valuations close to the perfect market equilibrium. Extra-marginal traders with valuations close to the perfect equilibrium are less stable than intra-marginal traders, but they still have preferences between markets. When valuations of extra-marginal traders are far from the perfect market equilibrium, they have no strict preference for any market, i.e. the times spent in each specialist are very close to each other.
- *Degree of stability with different strategies.* Given similar valuations, GD, ZIP and ZIC traders are more stable than RE traders. One reason is that an RE trader uses the profit that it was able to obtain in the most recent trading in a market to adjust (increase) its bidding price, so it will keep increasing its bidding price in a market until finally its shouts cannot be successfully matched, which will cause the trader to move to another market.

Stability vs Intra-marginality. As we have mentioned in the above, most intra-marginal traders are very stable. However, some extra-marginal traders with valuations close to the perfect equilibrium can also be very stable if there are some specialists that have very high probability to match their shouts while others cannot do so. Therefore, a stable trader doesn't need to be intra-marginal. To find out whether or not a stable trader is intra-marginal, we need further information about their behaviour, e.g. bidding prices. If a stable seller's (buyer's) average bidding price is above (under) the equilibrium price, then it maybe not intra-marginal. In general, the selected information should be able to efficiently classify traders into the categories you defined.

4 Behaviour-Based Policy Design

A mechanism in a specialist is a combination of different policies and the relationship between these policies are not completely clear, so searching a competitive combination without restriction under this setting will be computationally intractable. In general, we limited the search space for each policy to certain well-known alternatives that are normally trader-independent. Moreover, there often exist many policy combinations that are competitive under the same market environment, which can be seen from the results in [6]. However, in our approach, since we have gained an understanding of traders' behaviour, we are able to further limit the search space by utilising traders' behaviour. More importantly, we want to further utilise traders' behaviour information to design trader-dependent mechanisms that attract one kind of trader, and integrate those trader-dependent mechanisms to achieve adaptive mechanisms that are attractive to all kinds of traders. In the rest of this section we will define the policies of a specialist by using traders' behaviours and propose a two-step method to search adaptive mechanisms.

4.1 A Search Space of Behaviour-Based Policies

Combined with traders' behaviours, the following policies are adapted from the literature.

Accepting Policy. Once a specialist gets a new shout, it has to first decide whether or not to accept it. If too many extra-marginal shouts are accepted, they will not be matched and therefore the transaction rate will be very low. So why does not a specialist only accept shouts from traders that it wants to attract? Unfortunately, a specialist does not know who is the sender of a shout before the shout is accepted in CAT competitions. Instead some other general market information can be used here, e.g. the equilibrium price of historical shouts received in a market. We will use the equilibrium price of historical shouts to set up a maximum (minimum) acceptable ask (bid) price for each day, as historical equilibrium can approximately distinguish between intra-marginal and extra-marginal shouts.

Given current day t, most recent M historical shouts H_t^M, the maximum acceptable ask price A_t^a and minimum acceptable bid price A_t^b are defined as:

$$A_t^a = E(H_t^M) + \theta^a * F_t^a$$
$$A_t^b = E(H_t^M) - \theta^b * F_t^b$$

where $E(H_t^M)$ is the equilibrium price of H_t, $F_t^a, F_t^b \geq 0$ are relaxations, and $\theta^a, \theta^b \in [0, 1]$ are the relaxation rates. F_t^a and F_t^b are calculated for each day, and θ^a, θ^b are dynamically updated during a day, say, updated after each round.

Matching Policy. The two most used matching policies are *equilibrium matching* and *maximal matching*. Equilibrium matching is used to find the equilibrium price p_e which balances the bids and the asks going to be matched so that all the bids with price $p \geq p_e$ and all the asks with price $p \leq p_e$ are matched [13]. The aim of maximal matching is to maximise the number of transactions/matches by matching high intra-marginal shouts with lower extra-marginal shouts if necessary. The main difference between these two matchings is that maximal matching moves some profit from high intra-marginal traders to lower extra-marginal traders so that lower extra-marginal traders are attracted. Actually maximal matching can also be used for other proposes, e.g. stabilising some high intra-marginal traders, which can be seen in a mechanism for attracting GD traders in Section 4.3. But one disadvantage of maximal matching is that if it moves too much profit from high intra-marginal traders, they will leave the market so that other intra-marginal traders will be affected recursively. At the same time, since equilibrium matching always gives more profit to high intra-marginal traders, some profit seeking traders, like ZIC and RE traders, will keep increasing their profit margin so that their shouts are difficult to match.

Because of the availability of each traders' behaviour information, we will adopt this information for the matching policy. The following are the two additional policies we used in this framework.

1. *Double Equilibrium Matching.* We run two matchings one after another. The first matching is an equilibrium matching based on the bidding price of shouts. The second matching rematches the matched shouts given by the first matching in terms of the average clearing price of each sender's current

Algorithm 4.1. Modified Discriminatory k-pricing Policy

```
Input: a: ask, b: bid
Output: p̂: clearing price
begin
    if best(s(a)) = m_i and best(s(b)) = m_i then k = 0.5;
    else if best(s(a)) = m_i (or best(s(b)) = m_i) then
        if s(b) (or s(a)) is attractable then k = minK (or k = 1 − minK);
        else k = 0.5;
    else
        if s(a) is more attractive than s(b) then k = 1 − minK;
        else k = minK;
    end
    if p*(a) ≤ p*(b) then p_a = max(p*(a), p(a)); p_b = min(p*(b), p(b));
    else p_a = p(a); p_b = p(b);
    p̂ = p_a + k * (p_b − p_a);
end
```

best market[2], called best clearing price. The second matching matches two shouts if the gap between their best clearing prices is very small. This is because their best clearing prices are good enough to attract them and also don't give them too much space to increase their profit margin.

2. *Behaviour-based Maximal Matching.* Maximal matching is guided by traders' behaviour so that extra-marginal shouts are matched only if the senders are those whom we want to attract, i.e. stable traders.

Pricing Policy. Pricing policy will also play a very important role not only in attracting traders but also in stabilising traders. We use a modified *discriminatory k-pricing policy*, where k is dynamically determined for each match according to the two corresponding traders' behaviour. Let $p(x)$ indicate the bidding price of shouts x, $s(x)$ indicate the sender of shout x, $best(t)$ indicate the current best market of trader t, and $p^*(t)$ is the average clearing price for trader t in $best(t)$. Assume the current specialist is m_i, Algorithm 4.1 gives the pseudo-code of the modified pricing policy, where $minK \in [0, 1]$ is what we have to set up for each different goal. The key idea of this policy is stabilising/keeping traders a specialist has already attracted and attracting those that are not attracted yet. The attractability of a trader is dependent on the overall design goal.

Clearing Policy. There are two main clearing policies used in TAC competitions, round-based and continuous. Round-based clearing clears at the end of each round, while continuous clearing clears whenever there is a new match available. Matching policy is sensitive to clearing policy. For instance, maximal matching will be useless with continuous clearing. Moreover, traders will have chances to revise their shouts if the market does not clear for some rounds during a day. We use a modified version of round-based clearing policy in this framework. Instead of clearing in each round, we choose a fixed number of clearing time

[2] The current best market of a trader is the market where it trades most.

points according to the number of goods each trader has, for example, we clear 5 times a day if each trader requires to exchange 3 items. Then we distribute clearing time points into the 10 rounds of a day by giving greater preference to the first 5 rounds. Thus, we clear more in the beginning of a day while waiting longer near the end of a day, because intra-marginal traders become less and less when it is approaching the end of a day and we want to give unsatisfied traders more chances to improve their shouts.

Charging Policy. Charging is a trade-off between traders' profits and a specialist's profit. It is not closely related to the above policies, but it affects traders' market selection. Therefore, most specialists in previous competitions do not charge in the beginning of a TAC game in order to attract traders. However, for most high intra-marginal traders, charging does not affect their profit too much, because they already reserved a large profit margin by bidding a very low (high) price to buy (sell). This framework will only focus on profit fee, as other fees, i.e. registration fee, transaction fee and information fee, could lead to 0 profit even for a trader who has successfully traded in the market.

4.2 Searching Adaptive Mechanisms

We know the main challenge for stabilising/attracting traders is stabilising their bidding prices, which depends on their bidding strategies. In other words, we might not be able to find a uniform mechanism that is attractive to traders with any kind of bidding strategy. Therefore, instead of searching for competitive mechanisms in a mixed environment from the very beginning, we propose a two-step approach. We first identify trader-dependent mechanisms that are competitive in an environment with only one kind of trader. Then we combine trader-dependent mechanisms together to achieve mechanisms that are competitive in any environment.

Trader-dependent Mechanism Design. Given the goal of a trader-dependent mechanism that we want to achieve (or a function of trader-dependent mechanism to maximise), we first set up the testing environment according to the goal and an initial mechanism as the current best mechanism, and then monotonically modify only one of the parameters in the search space to compete with the current best to find the next best one that increases the goal function the most, until we cannot find any modification that has any significant improvement of the function. Note that we require the modification of each parameter to be monotonic, i.e. update/change in one direction. Algorithm 4.2 describes the searching process for trader-dependent mechanisms. This algorithm will return mechanisms that locally maximise the goal function. In order to get an overall optimal mechanism, we can repeat this process with different initialisations.

Adaptive Mechanisms with Trader-dependent Mechanisms. Once we get trader-dependent mechanisms for each kind of trader offline, we will adapt

Algorithm 4.2. Searching Trader-dependent Mechanism

Input: m_0: initial mechanism, f_m: a function of mechanism to maximise, δ: the minimum improvement
Output: m^*: the local best mechanism

begin
  $CurrBest \leftarrow m_0$;
  repeat
    $m^* \leftarrow CurrBest$;
    foreach *policy parameter* r **do**
      $m' \leftarrow$ monotonically update r in m^*;
      if $f_m(m') > f_m(CurrBest)$ **then** $CurrBest \leftarrow m'$;
    end
  until $f_m(CurrBest) < f_m(m^*) + \delta$;
end

them online for any market environment. The main idea is to use the classification learned in Section 3 to determine each trader's category and apply the corresponding trader-dependent mechanism. However, we might end up with many inconsistent trader-dependent mechanisms that are required to run together for some environments. In such a case, we have to either apply only one of them or mix them by giving different priority to apply each of them. In order to make such a discrimination, we need to ascertain which trader-dependent mechanism will attract more good traders, which can be done, for example, by statistical analysing traders' behaviour.

4.3 Experiments

In this section, we show a trader-dependent mechanism that is attractive to intra-marginal traders with GD bidding strategy, which is also the most attractive bidding strategy adopted by traders [14].

GD traders use the market history of submissions and transactions to form their beliefs over the likelihood of a bid or ask being accepted, and use this belief to guide their bidding [11]. Then the bidding strategy is to submit the shout that maximises a trader's expected profit, i.e. the product of its belief function and its linear utility function.

Based on the search space given in Section 4.1 and our specialist agent *jackaroo*[3], we identified a trader-dependent mechanism that is very good at attracting intra-marginal GD traders. The value of each parameter of the mechanism is given in Table 1, where A_r and B_r are respectively the accepted asks and bids until round r in one day. We have tested this trader-dependent mechanism (JaGD) with other competitive agents available from the TAC agents repository[4], *CUNY.CS.V1* (Cu09.1), *CUNY.CS.V2* (Cu09.2), *Mertacor* (Me09), *cestlavie* (Ce09), *jacakroo* (Ja09) from CAT 2009 final, and *PoleCat* (Po10), *Mertacor* (Me10) from CAT 2010 final. Tables 2 and 3 show the average trading time

[3] Achieved 3rd, 1st, and 2nd in CAT Tournament 2008, 2009, and 2010, respectively.
[4] `http://www.sics.se/tac/`

Table 1. GD Attractive Mechanism

Policy	Parameter	Value
Accepting	F_t^a,F_t^b	6
	θ^a	$1 - \max(0, \frac{A_r - B_r}{A_r})$
	θ^b	$1 - \max(0, \frac{B_r - A_r}{B_r})$
Matching	Behaviour-based Maximal Matching	
Pricing	*minK*	0.15
Clearing	Modified Round-based	
Charging	12% profit fee	

Table 2. Average Trading Time Distribution of Each Type of Trader

	Specialists								Standard Deviation
	Cu09.1	Cu09.2	Me09	Me10	Po10	Ce09	Ja09	JaGD	
ZIC Sellers	39.60	40.40	54.20	**136.27**	56.83	55.07	42.87	74.77	31.95
ZIC Buyers	41.77	36.13	46.23	**125.53**	67.13	53.93	46.17	83.10	29.64
ZIP Sellers	15.43	16.77	50.00	**179.20**	62.50	50.83	59.40	65.87	51.04
ZIP Buyers	18.30	21.07	49.00	**197.83**	64.50	40.90	45.37	63.03	57.24
GD Sellers	20.73	22.46	49.29	77.80	87.43	62.37	37.84	**142.09**	40.21
GD Buyers	22.91	19.57	51.23	69.50	79.84	69.66	41.34	**145.94**	40.26
RE Sellers	53.10	47.31	53.59	**89.76**	69.46	67.90	55.91	62.97	13.43
RE Buyers	55.19	51.56	55.61	**86.56**	73.07	64.94	55.07	58.00	11.91

distribution of one CAT game (500 days), where the bold value in each row shows which market the traders in this row selected most and the underlined value in each column indicates which kind of traders were attracted most by the specialist in that column. The environment is mixed with 70 GD, 70 RE, 30 ZIC, and 30 ZIP buyers and sellers respectively, with valuations uniformly distributed in [60,160], i.e. the perfect market equilibrium is 110. From Table 2 we can see that *JaGD* attracted about 30% of GD traders' trading time (the average for each market is 12.5%). Table 3 further shows that most traders attracted by *JaGD* are intra-marginal GD traders, and some lower extra-marginal traders are also attracted because of the use of maximal matching. It is worth mentioning that, except GD traders, this trader-dependent mechanism is not appealing to other traders, and it is also the case vice versa which can be seen from *Me10*.

5 A Framework for Behaviour-Based Mechanism Design

In this section, we want to summarise our behaviour-based design approach to a more general adaptive mechanism design framework based on traders' behaviour. This framework consists of *data acquisition*, *behaviour-based classification of traders*, *defining behaviour-based policies*, *trader-dependent mechanism design* and *integrating trader-dependent mechanisms*.

1. *Data acquisition* collects and aggregates market information, especially trader related information, which will be the foundation of the other components. Some statistical and data mining methods can be adapted here.

Table 3. Average Trading Time Distribution of Buyers

	Specialists								Standard Deviation
	Cu09.1	Cu09.2	Me09	Me10	Po10	Ce09	Ja09	JaGD	
intra-marginal buyers (with valuations between 160 and 110)									
ZIC	27.60	17.27	34.13	**181.27**	65.27	46.20	36.73	91.53	53.39
ZIP	18.70	20.85	42.10	**256.15**	58.85	27.40	40.90	35.05	79.31
GD	23.97	18.64	36.72	70.92	75.42	64.81	18.53	**191.00**	57.02
RE	42.53	39.88	48.84	**113.66**	82.91	68.22	47.84	56.13	25.12
lower extra-marginal buyers (with valuations between 110 and 90)									
ZIC	48.25	49.38	56.13	79.38	71.88	58.75	50.38	**85.88**	14.62
ZIP	16.60	23.40	46.00	89.80	71.80	60.20	34.20	**158.00**	45.77
GD	28.44	21.44	38.89	47.67	108.89	65.22	33.56	**155.89**	46.81
RE	68.86	57.86	55.14	66.00	**70.29**	62.71	59.14	60.00	5.43
other extra-marginal buyers (with valuations between 90 and 60)									
ZIC	64.71	61.43	60.86	58.86	**65.71**	65.00	61.57	61.86	2.39
ZIP	18.40	19.60	79.60	72.60	**79.80**	75.60	74.40	80.00	26.99
GD	19.40	20.24	76.56	75.32	75.76	**78.24**	77.00	77.48	26.36
RE	**65.16**	62.19	62.71	63.23	63.55	62.06	61.61	59.48	1.64

2. *Behaviour-based classification of traders* distinguishes traders in terms of their behaviour. This step heavily depends on the information obtained in the first step. Some machine learning methods, e.g. decision tree leaning, might be useful here.
3. *Defining behaviour-based policies* determines how to utilise behaviour in specialist policies. The main contribution of traders' behaviour in this stage is connecting the loosely coupled policies to reduce the search space.
4. *Trader-dependent mechanism design* identifies mechanisms that are competitive in environments with only one of kind of trader.
5. *Integrating trader-dependent mechanisms* combines all trader-dependent mechanisms to achieve mechanisms that are competitive under an environment containing a mixture of any kinds of traders.

6 Conclusion

We have introduced a behaviour-based adaptive mechanism design approach under the Trading Agent Competition Market Design platform. This approach consists of behaviour-based trader classification, mechanism design for specific environments (called trader-dependent mechanism design) and integrating trader-dependent mechanisms for any complex environments that are not known in advance. To the best of our knowledge, this is the first market design framework heavily depending on traders' behaviour (i.e. market history). By integrating traders' behaviour into market policies, we are able to constrain the search space of double auction mechanisms. More importantly, because of gaining an understanding of the market environment from traders' behaviour, the resulting mechanisms will apply differential policies for attracting different traders and therefore be more focused, more competitive and adaptive.

However, how to use traders' behaviour information more efficiently in trader classification and specialist policy design is worth further investigation. For instance, we might be able to use certain well studied methods from data mining, e.g. decision tree learning, in behaviour-based trader classification, and even build a clearer relationship between the loosely coupled policies of specialist by using traders' behaviour information to further improve the design quality.

References

1. Cai, K., Gerding, E., Mcburney, P., Niu, J., Parsons, S., Phelps, S.: Overview of cat: A market design competition version 2.0. Technical report, University of Liverpool (2009)
2. Parkes, D.C.: Online mechanisms. In: Algorithmic Game Theory. Cambridge University Press, Cambridge (2007)
3. Vytelingum, P., Vetsikas, I.A., Shi, B., Jennings, N.R.: Iamwildcat: The winning strategy for the tac market design competition. In: Proceeding of the 18th European Conference on Artificial Intelligence, pp. 428–432 (2008)
4. Stavrogiannis, L.C., Mitkas, P.A.: Cat 2008 post-tournament evaluation: The mertacors perspective. In: IJCAI Workshop on Trading Agent Design and Analysis (2009)
5. Honari, S., Ebadi, M., Foshati, A., Gomrokchi, M., Benatahr, J., Khosravifar, B.: Price estimation of persiancat market equilibrium. In: IJCAI Workshop on Trading Agent Design and Analysis, TADA (2009)
6. Niu, J., Cai, K., Parsons, S.: A grey-box approach to automated mechanism design. In: Proceedings of the 9th International Conference on Autonomous Agents and Multiagent Systems: volume 1 - Volume 1. AAMAS 2010, pp. 1473–1474 (2010)
7. Robinson, E., McBurney, P., Yao, X.: How specialised are specialists? Generalisation properties of entries from the 2008 and 2009 TAC market design competitions. In: David, E., Gerding, E., Sarne, D., Shehory, O. (eds.) AMEC 2009. LNBIP, vol. 59, pp. 178–194. Springer, Heidelberg (2010)
8. Niu, J., Cai, K., Parsons, S., Gerding, E., McBurney, P., Moyaux, T., Phelps, S., Shield, D.: Jcat: a platform for the tac market design competition. In: AAMAS 2008 (2008)
9. Gode, D.K., Sunder, S.: Allocative efficiency of markets with zero-intelligence traders: Market as a partial substitute for individual rationality. Journal of Political Economy 101(1), 119–137 (1993)
10. Cliff, D.: Minimal-intelligence agents for bargaining behaviors in market-based environments. Technical report (1997)
11. Gjerstad, S., Dickhaut, J.: Price formation in double auctions. In: E-Commerce Agents, Marketplace Solutions, Security Issues, and Supply and Demand, pp. 106–134. Springer, London (2001)
12. Erev, I., Roth, A.E.: Predicting how people play games: Reinforcement learning in experimental games with unique, mixed strategy equilibria. American Economic Review 88(4), 848–881 (1998)
13. Friedman, D., Rust, J.: The Double Auction Market: Institutions, Theories, And Evidence. Westview Press, Boulder (1993)
14. Phelps, S., Mcburney, P., Parsons, S.: Evolutionary mechanism design: a review. Autonomous Agents and Multi-Agent Systems 21, 237–264 (2010)

Argumentation with Advice

John Debenham[1] and Carles Sierra[2]

[1] QCIS, UTS, Broadway, NSW 2007, Australia
[2] IIIA, CSIC, Campus UAB, 08193 Bellaterra, Catalonia, Spain

Abstract. This paper is concerned with *rhetorical argumentation* that aims to alter the beliefs of the listener, and so to influence his future actions, as opposed to *classical argumentation* that is concerned with the generation of arguments, usually as logical proofs, for and against a given course of action. Rhetorical argumentation includes rhetoric moves such as *Threat*, *Reward* and *Appeal*. Rhetorical argumentative utterances generated by an agent contribute to the strength of its relationship with the listener. This paper examines advice and the rhetoric particle *"I advise you ..."* that may be used to strengthen such relationships.

1 Introduction

The study of argumentation is in two camps: first, *classical argumentation* that is concerned with the generation of arguments, usually as logical proofs, for and against a given course of action that support decision making processes; and second, *rhetorical argumentation* that aims to alter the beliefs of the listener, and is the focus of this paper. The seminal work [1] builds on the notion of one argument "attacking" another; we are more interested in how to *counter* the effect of the partner agent's arguments rhetorically, and how to lead a dialogue towards some desired outcome. Rhetorical argumentation includes moves such as *Threat*, *Reward* and *Appeal*; although no formal model of the meaning of these speech acts has been proposed yet. *Argumentation* in this sense is concerned with building (business) *relationships* through shaping another agent's reasoning, beliefs and expectations [2].

Agents may attempt to counter their partner's arguments with *Inform* statements. The subject of an inform may be factual, e.g. "today is Tuesday", or non-factual, e.g. "this movie is exciting". *Opinions* are non-factual informative speech acts, they are the speaker's evaluation of a particular aspect of a thing in context, and may be used in an attempt to build relationships with the listener. *Advice* is opinion that is uttered with the aim of either changing the listeners beliefs or influencing the listener's future actions, e.g. "if I were you I would buy the Nikon". We give the semantics of advice utterances and describe their strategic use advice in argumentative dialogue [3].

In this paper an agent's rationality is based on two basic suppositions: *everything* in the world is constantly changing and not *all* facts can be known by an agent. An agent will have its model of: the world, of the other agents and of itself evolving at all time, and does not have, for instance, a *fixed* set of preferences. As it continually receives information from the environment, i.e. it is situated in it, its beliefs change. In particular, an agent changes its models both to *manage* its future dialogue and *because* of what has already been said.

C. Huemer and T. Setzer (Eds.): EC-Web 2011, LNBIP 85, pp. 136–147, 2011.

When agents engage in argumentative dialogue they may attempt to discover the objectives, needs or preferences of the other agent. This has the direct consequence of updating the model of the other agent and so enabling the conversation to progress. Section 2 discusses the communication language and advice illocutions. Section 3 proposes a rational agent architecture that contains the necessary components to give (higher-order) semantics to these illocutions in Section 4. Section 5 concludes.

2 Communication Framework

The communication language we consider, U, contains three fundamental primitives:[1] $\mathrm{Commit}(\alpha, \beta, \varphi)$ to represent, in φ, what is the world α aims at bringing about and that β has the right to verify, complain about or claim compensation for any deviations from, $\mathrm{Observe}(\alpha, \varphi)$ to represent that a certain state of the world, φ, is observed, and $\mathrm{Done}(u)$ to represent the event that a certain action u[2] has taken place. In our language, norms, contracts, and information chunks will be represented as instances of $\mathrm{Commit}(\cdot)$ where α and β can be individual agents or institutions, U is the set of expressions u defined as:

$$
\begin{aligned}
u &::= \mathit{illoc}(\alpha, \beta, \varphi, t) \mid u; u \mid \textbf{Let } \mathit{context} \textbf{ In } u \textbf{ End} \\
\varphi &::= \mathit{term} \mid \mathrm{Done}(u) \mid \mathrm{Commit}(\alpha, \beta, \varphi) \mid \mathrm{Observe}(\alpha, \varphi) \mid \varphi \wedge \varphi \mid \\
&\qquad \varphi \vee \varphi \mid \neg\varphi \mid \forall v.\varphi_v \mid \exists v.\varphi_v \\
\mathit{context} &::= \varphi \mid \mathit{id} = \varphi \mid \mathit{prolog\_clause} \mid \mathit{context}; \mathit{context}
\end{aligned}
$$

where φ_v is a formula with free variable v, illoc is any appropriate set of illocutionary particles, ';' means sequencing, and *context* represents either previous agreements, previous illocutions, or code that aligns the ontological differences between the speakers needed to interpret an action u, and term represents logical predicates. t represents a point in time.[3] We will note by Φ the set of expressions φ used as the propositional content of illocutions.

For example, we can represent the following offer: "If you spend a total of more than €100 in my shop during October then I will give you a 10% discount on all goods in November", as:

$$
\begin{aligned}
&\mathrm{Offer}(\alpha, \beta, \mathtt{spent}(\beta, \alpha, \mathtt{October}, \mathrm{X}) \wedge \mathrm{X} \geq €100 \rightarrow \\
&\quad \forall\, \mathrm{y}.\ \mathrm{Done}(\mathrm{Inform}(\xi, \alpha, \mathrm{pay}(\beta, \alpha, \mathrm{y}), \mathrm{November})) \rightarrow \mathrm{Commit}(\alpha, \beta, \mathrm{discount}(\mathrm{y}, 10\%)))
\end{aligned}
$$

or, "If I tell you who I buy my tomatoes from then would you keep that information confidential?" as:

$$
\begin{aligned}
&\mathrm{Offer}(\alpha, \beta, \exists\delta.\ (\mathrm{Commit}(\alpha,\beta,\mathrm{Done}(\mathrm{Inform}(\alpha,\beta,\mathrm{provider}(\delta,\alpha,\mathrm{tomato})))) \wedge \\
&\qquad \forall\gamma.\ \forall\, \mathrm{t}.\ \mathrm{Commit}(\beta,\alpha,\neg\mathrm{Done}(\mathrm{Inform}(\beta,\gamma,\mathrm{provider}(\delta,\alpha,\mathrm{tomato}), \mathrm{t}))))
\end{aligned}
$$

[1] We will not detail this language as our focus is on new illocutionary moves requiring higher-order semantics.

[2] Without loss of generality we will assume that all actions are dialogical.

[3] Usually dropped in the examples to simplify notation.

In order to define the *terms* of the language introduced above (e.g. $pay(\beta, \alpha, y)$ or $discount(y, 10\%)$) we need an ontology that includes a (minimum) repertoire of elements: a set of *concepts* (e.g. quantity, quality, material) organised in a is-a hierarchy (e.g. platypus is a mammal, australian-dollar is a currency), and a set of relations over these concepts (e.g. price(beer,AUD)).[4]

We model ontologies following an algebraic approach [4] as: An ontology is a tuple $\mathcal{O} = (C, R, \leq, \sigma)$ where:

1. C is a finite set of concept symbols (including basic data types);
2. R is a finite set of relation symbols;
3. $\leq$ is a reflexive, transitive and anti-symmetric relation on C (a partial order)
4. $\sigma : R \to C^+$ is the function assigning to each relation symbol its arity

where $\leq$ is a traditional *is-a* hierarchy, and R contains relations between the concepts in the hierarchy.

The concepts within an ontology are closer, semantically speaking, depending on how far away they are in the structure defined by the $\leq$ relation. Semantic distance plays a fundamental role in strategies for information-based agency. How signed contracts, $Commit(\cdot)$ about objects in a particular semantic region, and their execution $Observe(\cdot)$, *affect* our decision making process about signing future contracts on nearby semantic regions is crucial to modelling the common sense that human beings apply in managing trading relationships. A measure [5] bases the *semantic similarity* between two concepts on the path length induced by $\leq$ (more distance in the $\leq$ graph means less semantic similarity), and the *depth* of the subsumer concept (common ancestor) in the shortest path between the two concepts (the deeper in the hierarchy, the closer the meaning of the concepts). Semantic similarity could then be defined as:

$$\theta(c, c') = e^{-\kappa_1 l} \cdot \frac{e^{\kappa_2 h} - e^{-\kappa_2 h}}{e^{\kappa_2 h} + e^{-\kappa_2 h}}$$

where l is the length (i.e. number of hops) of the shortest path between the concepts, h is the depth of the deepest concept subsuming both concepts, and κ_1 and κ_2 are parameters scaling the contribution of shortest path length and depth respectively.

Agents give advice when they perceive that the listener has less experience in an area. Advice is thus a rhetorical move that uses the asymmetry of information between two agents. It is a genuine ecological move as it makes full sense in the context of a dialogue where both sides are revealing their positions and thus its meaning can only be determined in the context of the agents' mutual evolving models of each other.

In the context of negotiation advice makes sense before the signing of the contract — warning the other agent about potential consequences, "I advise you not buy a reflex camera for your grand mother, they are too bulky", or afterwards to justify a contract violation, "if I were you I would be happy with receiving bottles from the 2008 vintage instead of 2007, they are much better". They are naturally composed of a comparison between contracts or options and a justification.

[4] Axioms defined over the concepts and relations are omitted here.

3 Argumentation Agent Architecture

This Section describes how argumentative interactions are managed by our agent using the LOGIC illocutionary framework [6] that was originally proposed for agents whose sense of distributive justice spanned equity, equality and need. [6] focussed heavily on the *prelude stage* of a negotiation where agents prepare using the five LOGIC dimensions [7]. The five LOGIC dimensions are quite general:

- Legitimacy concerns *information* that may be part of or relevant to contracts signed.
- Options concerns *contracts* where a contract is a set of commitments one for each agent in the contract.
- Goals are the *objectives* of the agents.
- Independence concerns the agent's *outside options* — i.e. the set of agents are capable of satisfying the agent's needs.
- Commitments are the *commitments* that an agent may have.

and are used in this paper to manage all incoming communications including the exchange of "I advise you..." argumentative illocutions. A more formal representation model for LOGIC is:

- $L = \{B(\alpha, \varphi)\}$, that is a set of *beliefs*.
- $O = \{\text{Plan}(\langle \alpha_1, \text{Do}(p_1)\rangle, \ldots, \langle \alpha_n, \text{Do}(p_n)\rangle\}$, that is a set of *joint plans*
- $G = \{D(\alpha, \varphi)\}$, that is a set of *desires*.
- $I = \{\text{Can}(\alpha, Do(p))\}$, that is a set of *capabilities*.
- $C = \{I(\alpha, \text{Do}(p))\} \cup \{\text{Commit}(\alpha, \text{Do}(p))\}$, that is a set of *commitments* and *intentions*.

Our description is from the point of view of agent α in a *multiagent system* with a finite number of other agents $\mathcal{B} = \{\beta_1, \beta_2, \ldots\}$, and a finite number of *information providing agents* $\Theta = \{\theta_1, \theta_2, \ldots\}$ that provide the *context* for all events in the system — Θ^t denotes the state of these agents at time t. The only thing that α 'knows for certain' is its *history* of past communication that it retains in the repository $\mathcal{H}_\alpha^t$. Each *utterance* in the history contains: an illocutionary statement, the sending agent, the receiving agent, the time that the utterance was sent or received. Utterances are organised into dialogues, where a *dialogue* is a finite sequence of related utterances.

α acts to satisfy a *need*, ν, that are considered in context (ν, Θ^t), and does so by communicating an utterance, (μ, β), containing an illocutionary statement, $\mu \in U$, to another agent, $\beta \in \mathcal{B}$. If an utterance is part of a complete dialogue, *d*, that aimed to satisfy a need then the dialogue is tagged with: the triggering need, ν, the prevailing context, Θ^t, and an *ex post* rating $r \in R$ of how satisfactorily the dialogue satisfied the need. Such a *rated dialogue* has the form: $\boldsymbol{d} = (d, \nu, \Theta^t, r) \in \mathcal{H}_\alpha^t$.

Agent α observes the actions of another agent β in the context Θ^t. Observations are of little value unless they can be verified. α may not posses a sufficient variety of sensory input devices. Sensory inadequacy is dealt with by invoking a truthful *institution agent*, ξ, that promptly reports what it sees. So if β commits to delivering twelve sardines at 6:00pm, or states that "it will rain tomorrow" and is committed to the truth of that prediction, then α will eventually verify those commitments when ξ advises what occurs. If β passes an "I advise you..." message to α, or even a simple Inform(...) message, we assume that β is committed to the validity of the contents.

All communication is recorded in $\mathcal{H}_\alpha^t$ that in time may contain a large amount of data. To make this data useful to α's strategies it is summarised and categorised using the LOGIC framework. To achieve this α requires a categorising function $v : U \rightarrow \mathcal{P}(\{\mathsf{L,O,G,I,C}\})$ where U is the set of utterances. The power set, $\mathcal{P}(\{\mathsf{L,O,G,I,C}\}$, is required as some utterances belong to multiple categories. For example, "I will not pay more for Protos[5] than the price that John charges" is categorised as both Option *and* Independence.

World Model. α's world model, $\mathcal{M}^t$, is the first way in which $\mathcal{H}_\alpha^t$ is summarised. α's proactive reasoning machinery identifies the aspects of the world that α is interested in. They are represented in $\mathcal{M}^t$ as probability distributions, (X_i), in first-order probabilistic logic $\mathcal{L}$. Each of α's plans, s, contains constructors for a set of distributions $\{X_i\} \in \mathcal{M}^t$ together with associated *update functions*, $K_s(\cdot)$, such that $K_s^{X_i}(\mu)$ is a set of linear constraints on the posterior distribution for X_i. $\mathcal{M}^t$ is then maintained from utterances received using *update functions* that transform utterances into constraints on $\mathcal{M}^t$.

Proactive reasoning is described in [8]. For example, in a simple multi-issue contract negotiation α may estimate $\mathbb{P}^t(\text{acc}(\beta, \alpha, \delta))$, the probability that β would accept contract δ, by observing β's responses. The distribution $\mathbb{P}^t(\text{acc}(\beta, \alpha, \delta))$ is classified as an Option in LOGIC. Using shorthand notation, if β sends the message $\text{Offer}(\delta_1)$ then α may derive the constraint: $K^{\text{acc}(\beta,\alpha,\delta)}(\text{Offer}(\delta_1)) = \{\mathbb{P}^t(\text{acc}(\beta, \alpha, \delta_1)) = 1\}$, and if this is a counter offer to a former offer of α's, δ_0, then: $K^{\text{acc}(\beta,\alpha,\delta)}(\text{Offer}(\delta_1)) = \{\mathbb{P}^t(\text{acc}(\beta, \alpha, \delta_0)) = 0\}$. In the not-atypical special case of multi-issue bargaining where the agents' preferences over the individual issues *only* are known and are complementary to each other's, maximum entropy reasoning can be applied to estimate the probability that any multi-issue δ will be acceptable to β by enumerating the possible worlds that represent β's "limit of acceptability" [9]. As another example, the predicate $\text{canDo}(\alpha, \beta, \nu)$ meaning β is able to satisfy α's need ν — this predicate is classified as Independence in LOGIC.

Updating $\mathcal{M}^t$ is complicated when the integrity of utterances received are questionable — it would certainly be foolish for α to believe completely every utterance received. For completeness the procedure for doing this, and for attaching an *a priori* belief to utterances (see Equation 7), is summarised in Section 3.1. If at time t, α receives such an utterance u that may alter this world model then the (Shannon) *information* in u with respect to the distributions in $\mathcal{M}^t$ is: $\mathbb{I}^t(u) = \mathbb{H}(\mathcal{M}^t) - \mathbb{H}(\mathcal{M}^{t+1})$. Let $\mathcal{N}^t \subseteq \mathcal{M}^t$ be α's model of agent β. If β sends the utterance u to α then the *information* about β within u is: $\mathbb{H}(\mathcal{N}^t) - \mathbb{H}(\mathcal{N}^{t+1})$. $\mathcal{M}^t$ may contain distributions in any of the five LOGIC categories, where $\mathbb{H}$ is Shannon entropy.

Intimacy and Balance Model. The *intimacy* and *balance* model is the second way in which $\mathcal{H}_\alpha^t$ is summarised. *Intimacy* is degree of closeness, and *balance* is degree of fairness. Informally, *intimacy* measures how much one agent knows about another agent's private information, and *balance* measures the extent to which information revelation

[5] A fine wine from the 'Ribera del Duero' region, Spain.

between the agents is 'fair'. The *intimacy* and *balance* model is structured using the LOGIC illocutionary framework and the ontology $\mathcal{O}$[6]. For example, the communication $\text{Accept}(\beta, \alpha, \delta)$ meaning that agent β accepts agent α's previously offered deal δ is classified as an Option, and $\text{Inform}(\beta, \alpha, \textit{info})$ meaning that agent β informs α about *info* and commits to the truth of it is classified as Legitimacy. The *intimacy* and *balance* model contains two components per agent: first α's model of β's private information, and second, α's model of the private information that β has about α.

The *intimacy* of α's relationship with β_i, I_i^t, is the amount that α knows about β_i's private information and is represented as real numeric values over $\{\mathsf{L,O,G,I,C}\} \times \mathcal{O}$. Suppose α receives utterance u from β_i and that category $f \in v(u)$. For any concept $c \in \mathcal{O}$, define $\Theta(u, c) = \max_{c' \in u} \theta(c', c)$. Denote the value of I_i^t in position (f, c) by $I_{i(f,c)}^t$ then: $I_{i(f,c)}^t = \rho \times I_{i(f,c)}^{t-1} + (1 - \rho) \times \mathbb{I}^t(u) \times \Theta(u, c)$ for any c, where ρ is the discount rate and $\mathbb{I}^t(u)$ is as defined above. α's estimate of β_i's intimacy on α, J_i^t, is constructed similarly. The *balance* of α's relationship with β_i, B_i^t, is the element by element numeric difference of I_i^t and J_i^t.

Trust, Reliability and Honour. The third way in which α summarises $\mathcal{H}_\alpha^t$ is with trust, reliability and honour measures. These concepts are all concerned with the relationship between commitment and enactment. Trust is concerned with the relationship between a signed contract (the commitment) and the execution of the contract (the enactment). Reliability is is concerned with the relationship between information (where the truth of the information is the commitment) and its subsequent verification (the enactment). Honour is similarly concerned with arguments.

We represent the relationship between commitment and enactment using conditional probabilities, $\mathbb{P}(u'|u)$. If u is a commitment and u' the corresponding subsequent observation then $\mathbb{P}(u'|\, u)$ is the probability that u' will be observed given that u had been promised. For example, if u is an "I advise you..." message from agent β then the conditional probability, $\mathbb{P}(u'|u)$, is an estimate of α's expectation of what will eventually be observed, and the uncertainty in the validity of β's communication is the entropy $\mathbb{H}(u'|u)$.

[10] describes three aspects of the relationship between commitment and enactment:

1. as the difference between our expectation $\mathbb{P}(u'|\, u)$ and a distribution that describes what we would ideally like to observe $\mathbb{P}_I(u'|\, u)$:

$$1 - \sum_{u'} \mathbb{P}_I^t(u'|u) \log \frac{\mathbb{P}_I^t(u'|u)}{\mathbb{P}_\beta^t(u'|u)}$$

2. as expected preferability of the enactment compared to the commitment:

$$\sum_{u'} \mathbb{P}^t(\text{Prefer}(u', u)) \mathbb{P}_\beta^t(u'|u)$$

[6] Only a subset of the ontology is required. The idea is simply to capture "How much has Carles told me about wine", or "how much do I know about his commitments (possibly with other agents) concerning cheese".

3. as predictability of those enactments that are preferable to the commitment:

$$1 + \frac{1}{B^*} \cdot \sum_{u' \in \Phi_+(u,v,\kappa)} \mathbb{P}^t_+(u'|u) \log \mathbb{P}^t_+(u'|u)$$

where if $u \leq v$ in the ontology let: $\Phi_+(u, v, \kappa) = \{u' \mid \mathbb{P}^t(\text{Prefer}(u', u, v)) > \kappa\}$ for some constant κ, and $\mathbb{P}^t_+(u'|u)$ is the normalisation of $\mathbb{P}^t_\beta(u'|u)$ for $u' \in \Phi_+(u, v, \kappa)$,

$$B^* = \begin{cases} 1 & \text{if } |\Phi_+(u, v, \kappa)| = 1 \\ \log |\Phi_+(u, v, \kappa)| & \text{otherwise} \end{cases}$$

There is no neat function mapping the concepts of trust, reliability and honour into the five LOGIC categories. For example, the relationship between contractual commitment and contractual enactment is concerned with both Options *and* Commitment. Alternatively, the relationship between the commitment and enactment of an argument is concerned with Legitimacy *and* what ever else the argument is about. However the five LOGIC categories together provide a complete framework for representing these concepts.

Self Model. Finally, α's *self model* is not directly related to communication. It represents the LOGIC relationships between the agent's components and the various summaries of the communications received.

3.1 Updating $\mathcal{M}^t$

α's world model, $\mathcal{M}^t$, at time t is a set of random variables, $\mathcal{M}^t = \{X_i, \ldots, X_n\}$ each representing an aspect of the world that α is interested in. In the absence of in-coming messages the integrity of $\mathcal{M}^t$ decays. α may have background knowledge concerning the expected integrity as $t \to \infty$. Such background knowledge is represented as a *decay limit distribution*. One possibility is to assume that the decay limit distribution has maximum entropy whilst being consistent with observations. Given a distribution, $\mathbb{P}(X_i)$, and a decay limit distribution $\mathbb{D}(X_i)$, $\mathbb{P}(X_i)$ decays by:

$$\mathbb{P}^{t+1}(X_i) = \Delta_i(\mathbb{D}(X_i), \mathbb{P}^t(X_i)) \tag{1}$$

where Δ_i is the *decay function* for the X_i satisfying the property that $\lim_{t\to\infty} \mathbb{P}^t(X_i) = \mathbb{D}(X_i)$. For example, Δ_i could be linear: $\mathbb{P}^{t+1}(X_i) = (1 - \nu_i) \times \mathbb{D}(X_i) + \nu_i \times \mathbb{P}^t(X_i)$, where $\nu_i < 1$ is the decay rate for the i'th distribution. Either the decay function or the decay limit distribution could also be a function of time: Δ^t_i and $\mathbb{D}^t(X_i)$.

The following procedure updates $\mathcal{M}^t$ for all utterances $u \in U$. Suppose that α receives a message u from agent β at time t. Suppose that this message states "I advise you that something is so" with probability z, and suppose that α attaches an epistemic belief $\mathbb{R}^t(\alpha, \beta, u)$ to u — a method for estimating $\mathbb{R}^t(\alpha, \beta, u)$ is given below. Each of α's active plans, s, contains constructors for a set of distributions $\{X_i\} \in \mathcal{M}^t$ together with associated *update functions*[7], $K_s(\cdot)$, such that $K^{X_i}_s(u)$ is a set of linear

[7] A sample update function for the distribution $\mathbb{P}^t(acc(\beta, \alpha, \delta))$ is given above.

constraints on the posterior distribution for X_i. Denote the prior distribution $\mathbb{P}^t(X_i)$ by $\boldsymbol{p}$, and let $\boldsymbol{p}_{(u)}$ be the distribution with minimum relative entropy[8] with respect to $\boldsymbol{p}$: $\boldsymbol{p}_{(u)} = \arg\min_{\boldsymbol{r}} \sum_j r_j \log \frac{r_j}{p_j}$ that satisfies the constraints $K_s^{X_i}(u)$. Then let $\boldsymbol{q}_{(u)}$ be the distribution:

$$\boldsymbol{q}_{(u)} = \mathbb{R}^t(\alpha, \beta, u) \times \boldsymbol{p}_{(u)} + (1 - \mathbb{R}^t(\alpha, \beta, u)) \times \boldsymbol{p} \tag{2}$$

and then let:

$$\mathbb{P}^t(X_{i(u)}) = \begin{cases} \boldsymbol{q}_{(u)} & \text{if } \boldsymbol{q}_{(u)} \text{ is "more interesting" than } \boldsymbol{p} \\ \boldsymbol{p} & \text{otherwise} \end{cases} \tag{3}$$

A general measure of whether $\boldsymbol{q}_{(u)}$ is *more interesting* than $\boldsymbol{p}$ is: $\mathbb{K}(\boldsymbol{q}_{(u)} \| \mathbb{D}(X_i)) > \mathbb{K}(\boldsymbol{p} \| \mathbb{D}(X_i))$, where $\mathbb{K}(\boldsymbol{x} \| \boldsymbol{y}) = \sum_j x_j \ln \frac{x_j}{y_j}$ is the Kullback-Leibler distance between two probability distributions $\boldsymbol{x}$ and $\boldsymbol{y}$.

Finally merging Equation 3 and Equation 1 we obtain the method for updating a distribution X_i on receipt of a message u:

$$\mathbb{P}^{t+1}(X_i) = \Delta_i(\mathbb{D}(X_i), \mathbb{P}^t(X_{i(u)})) \tag{4}$$

This procedure deals with integrity decay, and with two probabilities: first, the probability z in the utterance u, and second the belief $\mathbb{R}^t(\alpha, \beta, u)$ that α attached to u.

$\mathbb{R}^t(\alpha, \beta, u)$ is an epistemic probability that takes account of α's personal caution. An empirical estimate of $\mathbb{R}^t(\alpha, \beta, u)$ may be obtained by measuring the 'difference' between commitment and observation. Suppose that u is received from agent β at time t and is verified by the institution agent, ξ, as u' at some later time t'. Denote the prior $\mathbb{P}^u(X_i)$ by $\boldsymbol{p}$. Let $\boldsymbol{p}_{(u)}$ be the posterior minimum relative entropy distribution subject to the constraints $K_s^{X_i}(u)$, and let $\boldsymbol{p}_{(u')}$ be that distribution subject to $K_s^{X_i}(u')$. We now estimate what $\mathbb{R}^u(\alpha, \beta, u)$ should have been in the light of knowing *now*, at time t', that u should have been u'.

The idea of Equation 2, is that $\mathbb{R}^t(\alpha, \beta, u)$ should be such that, *on average* across $\mathcal{M}^t$, $\boldsymbol{q}_{(u)}$ will predict $\boldsymbol{p}_{(u')}$ — no matter whether or not u was used to update the distribution for X_i, as determined by the condition in Equation 3 at time u. The *observed reliability* for u and distribution X_i, $\mathbb{R}^t_{X_i}(\alpha, \beta, u)|u'$, on the basis of the verification of u with u', is the value of k that minimises the Kullback-Leibler distance:

$$\mathbb{R}^t_{X_i}(\alpha, \beta, u)|u' = \arg\min_k \mathbb{K}(k \cdot \boldsymbol{p}_{(u)} + (1-k) \cdot \boldsymbol{p} \;\|\; \boldsymbol{p}_{(u')})$$

The predicted *information* in u with respect to X_i is:

$$\mathbb{I}^t_{X_i}(\alpha, \beta, u) = \mathbb{H}^t(X_i) - \mathbb{H}^t(X_{i(u)}) \tag{5}$$

---

[8] Given a probability distribution $\boldsymbol{p}$, the *minimum relative entropy distribution* $\boldsymbol{q} = (q_1, \ldots, q_I)$ subject to a set of n linear constraints $\boldsymbol{g} = \{g_j(\boldsymbol{p}) = \boldsymbol{a_j} \cdot \boldsymbol{q} - c_j = 0\}, j = 1, \ldots, n$ (that must include the constraint $\sum_i q_i - 1 = 0$) is: $\boldsymbol{q} = \arg\min_{\boldsymbol{r}} \sum_j r_j \log \frac{r_j}{p_j}$. This may be calculated by introducing Lagrange multipliers $\boldsymbol{\lambda}$: $L(\boldsymbol{q}, \boldsymbol{\lambda}) = \sum_j q_j \log \frac{q_j}{p_j} + \boldsymbol{\lambda} \cdot \boldsymbol{g}$. Minimising L, $\{\frac{\partial L}{\partial \lambda_j} = g_j(\boldsymbol{p}) = 0\}, j = 1, \ldots, n$ is the set of given constraints $\boldsymbol{g}$, and a solution to $\frac{\partial L}{\partial q_i} = 0, i = 1, \ldots, I$ leads eventually to $\boldsymbol{q}$. Entropy-based inference is a form of Bayesian inference that is convenient when the data is sparse [11] and encapsulates common-sense reasoning [12].

that is the reduction in uncertainty in X_i where $\mathbb{H}(\cdot)$ is Shannon entropy. Equation 5 takes account of the value of $\mathbb{R}^t(\alpha,\beta,u)$.

If $\mathbf{X}(u)$ is the set of distributions in $\mathcal{M}^t$ that u affects, then the *observed reliability* of β on the basis of the verification of u with u' is:

$$\mathbb{R}^t(\alpha,\beta,u)|u' = \frac{1}{|\mathbf{X}(u)|}\sum_i \mathbb{R}^t_{X_i}(\alpha,\beta,u)|u' \tag{6}$$

For any concept $c \in \mathcal{O}$, $\mathbb{R}^t(\alpha,\beta,c)$ is α's estimate of the reliability of information from β concerning c. In the absence of incoming communications the integrity of this estimate will decay in time by: $\mathbb{R}^t(\alpha,\beta,c) = \chi \times \mathbb{R}^{t-1}(\alpha,\beta,c)$ for decay constant $\chi < 1$ and close to 1. On receipt of communication u is subsequently verified as u':

$$\mathbb{R}^t(\alpha,\beta,c) = \mu \times \mathbb{R}^{t-1}(\alpha,\beta,c) + (1-\mu) \times \mathbb{R}^t(\alpha,\beta,u)|u' \tag{7}$$

where μ is the learning rate, that estimates the reliability of β's advice on any concept c. If $\mathbf{X}(u)$ are independent the predicted *information* in u is:

$$\mathbb{I}^t(u) = \sum_{X_i \in \mathbf{X}(u)} \mathbb{I}^t_{X_i}(\alpha,\beta,u) \tag{8}$$

Suppose α sends message u to β where u is α's private information, then assuming that β's reasoning apparatus mirrors α's, α can estimate $\mathbb{I}^t(\beta,\alpha,u)$. This completes the the update process for $\mathcal{M}^t$.

4 Advice Interaction

An *opinion* is a speaker's evaluation of a particular aspect of a thing in context. *Advice* is a speaker's evaluation of a particular aspect of a thing in the context of the speaker's beliefs of the listener's context. An "I advise you..." illocution is a form of advice [13]. It is a directive in Searle's classification of speech acts. This illocution gives advice to the listener to take some action, for example, "I advise you I would buy that Ferrari." It is not an assertive. Such advice will only be considered seriously by the listener if he believes that the speaker's beliefs about him are accurate. In terms of this work, this is indicated by a degree of intimacy in the appropriate section of the LOGIC framework.

An agent may be motivated to issue an "I advise you..." illocution *either* to develop a reputation for giving good advice — in the LOGIC framework this develops intimacy particularly in the L dimension — *or* to directly influence the listener's actions possibly to the benefit of the speaker "If I were you I would accept the offer I made you yesterday". The rational effect of these two examples are different. In the first example, whether the listener follows the advice is not important, what matters is whether he believes at some time that the advice was good, in the second example, the intention is that the listener will follow the advice.

"I advise you..." illocutions may be issued with varying degrees of knowledge of the state of the listener. For example, "I advise you to buy the Ferrari." assumes that the speaker has beliefs about the listener's intentions — such as he intends to buy a car. Another example, "If I were you I would offer them €100 now" assumes that the speaker has beliefs about both the listener's intentions *and* the state of his active plans. For simplicity we restrict these beliefs to the listener's intentions.

In common usage, an "I advise you..." illocution may contain advice *either* to act (i.e. advice that the listener should utter) as described above, *or* that the listener should modify his mental attitudes "I advise you to count on tomorrow being fine". The first of these is an *"I advise you" action*, and the second, that advises the agent to modify his beliefs, is an *"I advise you" belief change*[9]. In addition, such advice may advise the listener to modify his goals, his intentions or his plans — these three cases are omitted for brevity. A definition of an *"I advise you" action* is given in Table 1. The definition of an *"I advise you" belief change* is not presented here.

5 Discussion

In this paper we have argued that a a rich model of rationality is required to properly model agents in a changing world. Particularly important is the need to model dialogical moves that refer to the agent's internal models (beliefs, or goals) that are updated as a dialogue develops. Traditional constructivist approaches share a more static view of the world. Dialogues may influence internal models along a number of dimensions. In this paper we have followed a simplified version of the approach of [6] classifying them as beliefs, plans, desires, capabilities and intentions. This model is very flexible and clear in representing and classifying the evolving pieces of information that an agent's memory requires in order to correctly interpret and generate illocutionary moves. We have given a precise model of how this evolution of the memory can be implemented using concepts drawn from information-theory. Finally, a formal description of a prototypical dialogical move, "I advise you ...", is given. We have argued, that if agents are to be situated in a changing world, they need to incorporate an ecological mind that among other things requires a higher order interpretation of communication languages. This is so, because self-reference and the reference to whole dialogues is unavoidable in argumentative information exchanges.

As future lines of work, we plan to extend this approach to further advice-giving illocutions, and to revisit other classical dialogical moves such as those found in negotiation dialogues (e.g. propose, accept, reject). The *evolution* of our information-theoretic agents is being further examined in the development of negotiation agents in the Diplomacy game: we plan to use a Diplomacy testbed (www.dipgame.org) to obtain experimental results from agents interacting with human beings using rich languages that have illocutionary moves similar to the one modelled here.

---

[9] In line with the remarks at the beginning of this section the assertive "Tomorrow will be fine" may be treated as an Inform; when that statement is verified by the listener he will feed that into his estimate of the speaker's reliability as in Section 3.1. The directive "I advise you to count on tomorrow being fine." is a richer statement. It relies on the speaker's weather forecasting ability *and* on the accuracy of his beliefs of the listener. In particular, it relies on the accuracy of the speaker's beliefs concerning the significance of tomorrow's weather to what ever the listener is doing. That is it relies on a level of intimacy. The subsequent evaluation of this piece of advice will then effect the speaker's intimacy represented in the LOGIC model.

Table 1. Advice actions in FIPA-style format. The two feasibility preconditions are alternative representations of i's beliefs of the superiority of his knowledge, and the two rational effects represent two possible motives for uttering the illocution.

Summary	The sender (for example, i) informs the receiver (for example, j) that the sender believes the receiver should perform some action (for example, a) if the receiver's intentions includes some goal (for example, c)
Message Content	A tuple consisting of an action expression denoting the action that is advised, and an intention that the receiver may hold.
Description	I_Advise_You indicates that the sending agent: • believes he knows the receiving agent holds a particular intention • believes his knowledge of facts concerning the receiving agent's intention is better than the receiving agent's knowledge of it • intends the receiving agent to believe that the action is in his interests • believes that the receiving agent may act otherwise
Formal Model	$<i,\ \mathtt{i\_advise\_you}(j,a,c)>$ FP1: $B_i\ I_j\ c \wedge B_i\ W_i(c) \rightarrow W_{j\backslash i}(c) \wedge B_i\ \mathrm{Agent}(j,\ a) \wedge \neg B_i\ I_j\ \mathrm{Done}(a)$ FP2: $B_i\ I_j\ c \wedge B_i\ (\mathbb{H}(W_i(c)) < \mathbb{H}(W_{j\backslash i}(c))) \wedge B_i\ \mathrm{Agent}(j,\ a)\ \neg B_i\ I_j\ \mathrm{Done}(a)$ RE1: $B_j\ I_i\ \mathrm{Done}(<j,\ \mathrm{rates}(a,\ x)>,\phi)$ where $\mathrm{rates}(a,x)$ is the action of rating action a as x, and ϕ is true when the rating is performed RE2: $\mathrm{Done}\ (a)$ $W_i(c)$ denotes all of i's beliefs concerning c — i.e. that part of i's world model $W_{j\backslash i}(c)$ denotes i's beliefs concerning all of j's beliefs concerning c $W_i(c) \rightarrow W_{j\backslash i}(c)$ denotes that everything in $W_{j\backslash i}(c)$ can be derived from a subset of $W_i(c)$ $\mathbb{H}(S)$ denotes the overall uncertainty of the set of beliefs S — possibly as entropy

Examples	Agent i advises agent j that from his understanding of agent j's intentions agent j should accept an offer from agent k to sell a Nikon camera to agent j.
	`(i_advise_you`
	`:sender (agent-identifier :name i)`
	`:receiver (set (agent-identifier :name j))`
	`:content`
	`"((advise-action (agent-identifier :name j)`
	`(accept-proposal`
	`:sender (agent-identifier :name j)`
	`:receiver (set (agent-identifier :name k))`
	`:content`
	`"accept the Nikon"`
	`("want camera"))"`
	`:language fipa+if_I_were_you+advise-action)`
	where `advise-action` is an action that the receiver is advised to perform

Acknowledgements. Research supported by the Agreement Technologies CONSOLIDER project under contract CSD2007-0022 and INGENIO 2010 and by the Agreement Technologies COST Action, IC0801.

References

1. Dung, P.M.: On the Acceptability of Arguments and its Fundamental Role in Nonmonotonic Reasoning, Logic Programming and n-Person Games. Artificial Intelligence 77, 321–358 (1995)
2. Greene, K., Derlega, V.J., Mathews, A.: Self-disclosure in personal relationships. In: Vangelisti, A., Perlman, D. (eds.) Cambridge Handbook of Personal Relationships, pp. 409–427. Cambridge University Press, Cambridge (2006)
3. Krause, A., Horvitz, E.: A utility-theoretic approach to privacy and personalization. In: Fox, D., Gomes, C.P. (eds.) Proceedings of the Twenty-Third AAAI Conference on Artificial Intelligence, AAAI 2008, Chicago, Illinois, USA, pp. 1181–1188. AAAI Press, Menlo Park (2008)
4. Kalfoglou, Y., Schorlemmer, W.M.: IF-map: An ontology-mapping method based on information-flow theory. In: Spaccapietra, S., March, S., Aberer, K. (eds.) Journal on Data Semantics I. LNCS, vol. 2800, pp. 98–127. Springer, Heidelberg (2003)
5. Li, Y., Bandar, Z.A., McLean, D.: An approach for measuring semantic similarity between words using multiple information sources. IEEE Transactions on Knowledge and Data Engineering 15, 871–882 (2003)
6. Sierra, C., Debenham, J.: The LOGIC Negotiation Model. In: Proceedings Sixth International Conference on Autonomous Agents and Multi Agent Systems AAMAS 2007, Honolulu, Hawai'i, pp. 1026–1033 (2007)
7. Fischer, R., Ury, W., Patton, B.: Getting to Yes: Negotiating agreements without giving in. Penguin Books (1995)
8. Sierra, C., Debenham, J.: Information-based deliberation. In: Padgham, L., Parkes, D., Müller, J., Parsons, S. (eds.) Proceedings Seventh International Conference on Autonomous Agents and Multi Agent Systems AAMAS 2008, Estoril, Portugal, ACM Press, New York (2008)
9. Sierra, C., Debenham, J.: Information-based agency. In: Proceedings of Twentieth International Joint Conference on Artificial Intelligence, IJCAI 2007, Hyderabad, India, pp. 1513–1518 (2007)
10. Sierra, C., Debenham, J.: Trust and honour in information-based agency. In: Stone, P., Weiss, G. (eds.) Proceedings Fifth International Conference on Autonomous Agents and Multi Agent Systems AAMAS 2006, Hakodate, Japan, pp. 1225–1232. ACM Press, New York (2006)
11. Cheeseman, P., Stutz, J.: On the relationship between bayesian and maximum entropy inference. In: Fischer, R., Preuss, R., von Toussaint, U. (eds.) Bayesian Inference and Maximum Entropy Methods in Science and Engineering, pp. 445–461. American Institute of Physics, Melville (2004)
12. Paris, J.: Common sense and maximum entropy. Synthese 117, 75–93 (1999)
13. Decapua, A., Huber, L.: 'If I were you ...': Advice in American English. Multilingua 14, 117–132 (1995)

On Collaborative Filtering Techniques for Live TV and Radio Discovery and Recommendation

Alessandro Basso[2], Marco Milanesio[3,*], André Panisson[1], and Giancarlo Ruffo[1]

[1] Dipartimento di Informatica, Università degli Studi di Torino, Turin, Italy
{panisson,ruffo}@di.unito.it
[2] Emporos Systems Corporation, Charlotte, NC, USA
alessandro.basso@gmail.com
[3] Eurecom, Sophia Antipolis, France
marco.milanesio@eurecom.fr

Abstract. In order to integrate properly recording services with other streaming functionalities in a DMR (e.g., AppleTV, PS3) we need a way to put live TV and radio events into friendly catalogs. But recordings are based on parameters to be set by the users, such as timings and channels, and event discovery can be not trivial. Moreover, personalized recommendations strongly depend on the information quality of discovered events.

In this paper, we propose a general collaborative strategy for discovering and recommending live events from recordings with different timings and settings. Then, we present an analysis of collaborative filtering algorithms using data generated by a real digital video and radio recorder.

Keywords: TV and Radio Broadcasts, Recommender Systems, Collaborative Filtering.

1 DMR Context, Motivations and Related Work

Digital Media Receivers (DMRs), such as the AppleTV, or other devices that integrate also DMR functionalities, such as the PS3 and the XBox 360, are rapidly spreading worldwide revolutionizing the way we use our TVs and how we access to streaming content. The major attractiveness of a DMR is in the integration of several functionalities that usually come with different devices: a user can (1) watch (or listen), pause and record live television (or radio); (2) play and store music albums and view related art; (3) view, store, and edit digital pictures; (4) rent or buy new music and movies from catalogs; and so on.

DMR functionalities can be accessed through in-house as well as external services (or *channels*); for instance, the AppleTV allows the user to rent a movie from Apple store and also from Netflix. Moreover, the user can stream a media file stored in another computer connected to the home network, or from other

* Please note that co-authors A. Basso and M. Milanesio contributed to an earlier stage of the work presented in this paper when they were affiliated at the University of Turin as research assistants.

C. Huemer and T. Setzer (Eds.): EC-Web 2011, LNBIP 85, pp. 148–159, 2011.

on-line services like YouTube. However, no matter where the content streams from, the DMR provides an integrated user interface that allows users to browse, search and playback media resources as they were contained in a larger digital library.

This kind of interaction shifts the user's attention from *timing* (e.g., "my favorite TV shows starts at 8:00 p.m.") to *availability* (e.g., "the last movie of my favorite actor is already in my library"). This has implications over recording, because broadcasters schedule timings for their transmissions, and it is up to the user to set parameters accordingly such as the channel, starting and ending times, and so on. It is not surprising that popular applications that offer personalized podcasts, news, TV and radio shows (e.g., Stitcher), usually present lists of available shows to the user, before aggregating media resources together into custom channels. Hence, we need a way to automatically *discover* live TV and radio events and to present them to the user. Probably, this capability is still missing because of the aforementioned timing problem, but also due to the lack of a standard format for structuring the description of events and the unreliability of many Electronic Program Guides (EPGs) (when they are available) [1]. Even if recommendation in the IPTV domain has been studied previously (e.g., [2,3]), there is still room for the discovery of live events to be recorded through custom settings.

After discovery, *recommendation* is a second factor for successful recording services into the DMR context. A recommender system must suggest the user to program the recording of a live event before it occurs. This suggestion must be based on user preferences, and ratings can be used to improve the accuracy of the system.

We are conscious that it is risky to look for general conclusions from a specific case study; for this reason, we decided to remove as many biases as possible. We did not use EPGs and descriptions on timings and content distributed by broadcasters. Moreover, we did not use explicit user ratings. This comes with the observation that feedbacks are not always available, due to user data management strategies (e.g., privacy can be a concern) and unreliability of ratings; in fact, users do not always use explicity feedbacks correctly, due to lazyness or carelessness [12].

Furthermore, given such lack of descriptive information, we cannot use *Content-Based* (*CB*) systems at this stage of the analysis, whereas *Collaborative Filtering* (*CF*) techniques can be easily executed here. We know that CF performances can be improved in practice with the benefits that come with a CB engine, and so we propose a comparative analysis to identify which CF system (and under which assumptions) over performs the others in a real world scenario.

Section 2 gives a brief introduction of the experimental environment. The event discovery procedure is presented in (Section 3). Then, we describe the analyzed recommendation algorithms (Section 4). Finally, the evaluation of the chosen algorithms is presented in Section 5, before drawing conclusions.

2 Discussion on Data Collection

Our analysis is based on real data generated by the *Faucet PVR* system, integrated in a web-based podcasting service named *VCast* (`http://www.vcast.it/`). Faucet allows users to record their favorite (Italian) TV and Radio programs, and to further download them into their devices (e.g., iPod, PC, notebook). User can set up her own programming and see or download their recordings through a simple web interface.

Faucet's users can record their preferred live events in a very traditional way: they can set a list of parameters like the channel, the periodicity, as well as starting and ending times. They are also asked to assign a name to each of their recordings. After the customized event has been recorded, the user can download and reproduce it.

As we said in the introduction, data coming from a general purpose recording system are not immediately usable to identify events such as the transmissions, but assume the form of unstructured information, which have to be properly processed. Intuitively, let T be the set of transmissions during a day and t_i be a specific transmission broadcasted on channel c_{t_i}, starting at time b_{t_i} and ending at time f_{t_i}. Then, in principle, t_i can be directly used in the recommendation engine, as well as $\forall t \in T$. However this is not the case in the real world: if we look at data collected by monitoring the activity of many users, such transmissions are not trivially identifiable, mainly because users set different timings for the same event. This is due to two reasons: (1) users set timings according to clocks that are not in synch each other: this can produce differences in timings in the order of minutes; (2) Users are interested on different parts of the same TV or radio show: in this case, we can have critical differences in timings.

As a final observation, broadcasting is characterized by the *expiration* of some events: we can suggest the user to record only future broadcasts, and even if some shows are serialized, the recording of the single episode should be programmed in advance. This phenomenon is (partially) due to copyright management, since the content provider are not willing to authorize service providers to store previously recorded event for further distribution. Nevertheless, recording of a broadcast is still allowed, because it is seen as a single user activity. As a consequence, we have to deal (also) with volatile content, and this differs very much with the VoD domain, that has been exhaustively explored in the context of recommendation.

The anonymized dataset that we used for our experiments is publicly available at: `http://secnet.di.unito.it/vcast`.

3 Data Processing and Discovery of Events

Even if the DMR environment is perfect for dealing with catalogs of *discrete* events, we cannot prevent the users from setting timing parameters when they want to record live shows. However, we can provide a discovery method that identifies recordings programmed by other users, and that inserts found events in a dynamic catalog: some events can be added when new recordings are observed;

other events are removed when their timings expire. Once we have detected our set of discrete events, we can run our recommender algorithms to create personalized catalogs.

The first step is the identification of the broadcasted transmissions from the amount of unstructured data resulting from the recording process. This is a multi-step procedure that extracts a set of *discrete elements* as the representatives of the broadcasted *events*. Basically, a discrete element is obtained as the result of the aggregation of several different recordings. A preliminary investigation on the extraction of events from recordings is given in [1].

Let $U = \{u_1, u_2, ..., u_k\}$ be the set of distinct users in the Faucet platform. Each user recorded some programs in the past and scheduled some for the future. To schedule a program, a user must choose a channel c among a list of predefined channels C, a periodicity p among the possible periodicities allowed in the digital recorder (for example, daily, weekly, no-repeat), the start and the end of the recording. Besides, the user is required to annotate his/her recording with a (possibly) meaningful title.

Let $R = \{r_1, r_2, ..., r_m\}$ be the set of the recorded programs. Each recording in R is a tuple $r =< u, c, p, tl, b, f >$ set by a user $u \in U$ who recorded on the channel c with periodicity p a program titled tl starting at time b and finishing at time f. Thus, we can assume that there exists a function mapping every user to her recordings.

The set R is first processed by means of **clustering**; then, **aggregation** and **merging** are carried out in sequence on the output of the clustering. The three phases are described in the following.

Clustering: Due to the lack of information about the content of each recording, they are clustered wrt the channel, the periodicity and the difference between timings. Specifically, $\forall r_i, r_j \in R | c_{r_i} = c_{r_j} \wedge p_{r_i} = p_{r_j}$ we have that

$$r_i \uplus r_j \text{ iff } |b_{r_i} - b_{r_j}| < \delta_b \wedge |f_{r_i} - f_{r_j}| < \delta_f,$$

where $\uplus$ is the clustering operator and δ_b, δ_f determine the maximum clustering distance for the start and end times, respectively. The identified clusters contain recordings equal in the channel and periodicity, and similar in the timing. The recording that minimizes the intra-cluster timing distances is chosen as the centroid of the cluster. Each cluster identifies a new event.

Aggregation: As the system produces new recordings continuously, we perform the clustering once an hour obtaining the set of newly generated events. A further step is then required to aggregate the new events with those previously created. Such an operation is performed by comparing each new event with the existing events wrt channel, periodicity and timings; if the timings are similar, we correct the properties of existing events with the values of the newly created ones. The list of users associated to the event is updated accordingly.

Merging: Similar events, i.e. with the same channel and periodicity but timings within a fixed range, are merged into a single event. All features of the new events are computed by means of the values of the merged ones. This operation is required because events can be created in subsequent moments, by aggregating recordings referring to the same broadcasted transmissions. Due to the high variability of the timings, especially when a new transmission appears, such events slowly and independently converge to more stable timeframes, determining the need of merging them into single events.

As a result of the whole process, we obtain a number of events, each being a tuple defined as $e =< U_e, c, tl, b, f, p >$ where U_e is the list of users who set a recording referring to event e, c is the channel, tl is a title chosen among those given by users using a majority rule, b and f are the the starting and ending times and p is the periodicity. More detail on event detection and title selection can be found in [1].

We observed the behavior of the system in a one year timeframe, i.e., from June 2008 to June 2009, wrt the number of users, events and recordings. As the number of active recordings and events tends to increase over time, the number of users follows a different, less constant, trend. Specifically, we can notice a considerable increase in the number of registered users in the system between November 2008 ($<$ 35.000 users) and March 2009 ($>$ 45.000). In July 2009 we observed an interesting average number of 20.000 users with at least one scheduled recording. The relative success of the service reflected in the number of recordings: we had about until 200K recordings in June 2008 (the service was launched few months ago), and approximately 900K recordings one year after. Analogously, the number of events generated by the aggregations of the recordings grows up: we could detect almost 32K different events in June 2008. The overall number of detected events was about 130k after one year.

4 Recommendation

Two well-known recommendation techniques are considered in this work: (1) the memory based *collaborative filtering* approach named k-Nearest Neighbors (kNN) [9]; (2) the model based approach based on the *SVD transform* [10].

Exploiting the basic idea of the *nearest neighbors* approach, we apply both variants of the kNN algorithm: the user-based one [5], by identifying users interested in similar contents; and the item-based approach [4], by focusing on items shared by two or more users. The *MostPopular* items can be considered as a special case of the user-based kNN approach, where all users are considered as neighbors. In addition, we also analyze the performance of a variant of the SVD technique based on implicit ratings, presented in [6].

User-based kNN. In the *user-based* kNN algorithm, the weight of an element e for a user u can be defined as:

$$\mathrm{w}(u,e) = \sum_{v \in N(u)} \mathrm{r}(v,e) \cdot \mathrm{c}(u,v), \tag{1}$$

$$\text{where} \quad \mathrm{r}(v,e) = \begin{cases} 1 \text{ if } & e \in E_v \\ 0 \text{ if } & e \notin E_v \end{cases}$$

E_v is the set of elements recorded by user v, whilst $N(u)$ is the neighborhood of user u, limited by considering only the top-N neighbors ordered by user similarity. $c(u, v)$ is calculated using a similarity metric, $S(u, v)$, and we considered several well known measures, such as: the *Jaccard*'s coefficient, the *Dice*'s coefficient, the *Cosine* similarity and the *Matching* similarity [8]. All similarity metrics are calculated using the implicit binary ratings $r(v, e)$. Then, $\forall u$, we can compute the subset $N_u \subseteq U$ of *neighbors* of user u by sorting all users v by similarity with u. Only the k users most similar to u and with $S(u, v) > 0$ will be present on N_u.

If the number of neighbors is limited by the chosen similarity to a number lower than k, we can also consider the 2nd-level neighbors, i.e., for each user v belonging to $N(u)$ we compute $N(v)$. The overall set of 1st-level and 2nd-level users is then used to define the users similar to u, as previously described. It is worth noting that, in case of considering 2nd-level neighbors, the coefficient $c(u, v)$ in eq. (1) has to be computed taking into account the similarity between the considered neighbor and further ones. For example, considering user u, her neighbor v and her 2nd-level neighbor x, we have:

$$c(u, x) = S(u, v) * S(v, x),$$

that is a combination of the similarities computed between the neighbors pairs for the considered user.

MostPopular. The *MostPopular* algorithm can be also defined by means of eq. (1), assuming the number of neighbors unbounded, which implies $N(u) = U, \ \forall u \in U$; and $c(u, v) = 1, \ \forall u, v \in U$.
The weight of an element e to a user u is therefore defined as:

$$w(u, e) = \sum_{v \in U} r(v, e) \tag{2}$$

All elements are sorted in descendant order by weight. The set of neighbors is independent of the user in the *MostPopular* algorithm. As consequence, all users receive the same recommended elements, i.e., the most popular elements.

Item-based kNN. In the *item-based* kNN algorithm, the weight of an element e for a user u is defined as:

$$w(u, e) = \sum_{f \in N(e)} r(u, f) \cdot c(e, f), \tag{3}$$

$N(e)$ is the set of n items most similar to e and recorder by u, and $c(e, f)$ is the neighbor's weight wrt item e.

Differently from the user-based case, using $k = \infty$ in the item-based approach does not lead to the *Most Popular* set of elements. In fact, the algorithm simply takes all items $f \in E_u$ as neighbors of e, making $N(e)$ user-dependent.

The similarity among items, $S(e, f)$, is based on the same measures already mentioned before, yet redefined considering two items e, f and their sets of users U_e, U_f who recorded them. $\forall e \in E$ we can compute the subset $N_e \subseteq E$ of *neighbors* of item e. An item f such that $U_e \cap U_f \neq \emptyset$ is thus defined as a neighbor of e. Starting from the neighborhood of e, similarity with e is computed for each pair $< e, f >$ such that $f \in N_e$ using the implicit binary ratings $\mathrm{r}(u, e)$ as defined in (1), and the weights are calculated according to (3).

SVD. The Singular Value Decomposition technique analyzed in this work makes use of implicit feedbacks and implements the method proposed in [6]. Specifically, given the observations of the behavior of user u wrt item i, r_{ui}, we can define the user's preference p_{ui} as equal to the implicit binary rating r_{ui}. Note that r_{ui} is set to 1 when u records item i, 0 otherwise.

After associating each user u with a user-factors vector $x_u \in \mathbb{R}^f$ and each item i with an item-factors vector $y_i \in \mathbb{R}^f$, we can predict the unobserved value by user u for item i through the inner product: $x_u^T y_i$. Factors are computed by minimizing the following function [6]:

$$\min_{x*y*} \sum_{u,i} (p_{ui} - x_u^T y_i)^2 + \lambda \left(\sum_u \|x_u\|^2 + \sum_i \|y_i\|^2 \right)$$

5 Experimental Results

Our evaluation is based on measuring the accuracy of each recommendation algorithm in predicting the elements that users would program. This is achieved by computing precision and recall on the predicted items. The more accurate is this prediction, the more valuable elements are recommended. It is important to underline that we do not consider any feedback related to the user's interest in the recommended items, but we only focus on the prediction ability of the algorithms analyzed.

To evaluate a recommendation algorithm, we fix an arbitrary time t in the data collection interval, and use the information about the user recordings before time t to predict the elements recorded by each user after time t. The collected data start at January 2008 and end November 2009, thus we choose uniformly distributed values of t varying from June 2008 to June 2009 in order to not have biased results by scarcity of training data or by lack of test data.

Given the set E of events in our framework, we define the following subsets:

- $A(t) \subset E$, define the active events at time t ($b_e > t$);
- $R(u, t) \subset E$, define the events recorded by user u before time t;
- $V(u, t) \subset A(t)$, define the events recorded by user u after time t;
- $Rec(u, t) \subset A(t)$, define the events recommended to user u at time t.

It is important to notice that $A(t)$ is also the set of all elements suitable for recommendation at time t. The aim of our recommendation algorithms is to predict which events are in $V(u, t)$. For that, for each user, the algorithms associate a weight for each element in $A(t)$ that are not present in $R(u, t)$. To recommend items to users, we use the top n recommended elements $Rec(n, u, t) \subset Rec(u, t)$, ordered by weight. The *precision* values for the top n recommended elements at time t are computed as the average of $(Rec(n,u,t) \cap V(u,t))/Rec(n,u,t)$ for all users. The same for *recall* values, computed as the average of $(Rec(n,u,t) \cap V(u,t))/V(u,t)$ for all users [10]. Finally, we compute the precision and recall for the top n recommended elements as the average of the precision and recall at different ts.

Our evaluation does not use user's feedbacks regarding his interest in unconsidered items (i.e., not programmed, nor downloaded). Thus in this context, as in [6], recall measures are more suitable than precision measures. In fact, we can assume that e_i is of any interest for user u only if $e_i \in V(u,t)$, otherwise no assumption on user's interests can be made. Anyway, for sake of completeness, we also report the analysis of precision values.

5.1 Evaluation

We start our evaluation showing how different similarity functions affect the results of user-based kNN recommendation algorithms. We can observe from Figure 1(a) that, in case of the user-based algorithm, all chosen similarities show nearly the same performances. In all cases, we used a neighborhood of $k = 300$, however the results are similar for other values of k. When it comes to the item-based algorithm, the Matching similarity considerably outperforms the other measures, as displayed in Figure 1(b). Again, both Dice and Jaccard show a very similar behavior, being clearly superior to the Cosine metric when more than 5 elements are recommended. In both Figures 1(a) and 1(b), the Jaccard similarity is not shown being almost identical to the Dice.

In Figure 2(a) we evaluate the consequences of adding second-level neighbors in the neighborhood of user-based kNN recommendation algorithms. We can observe that increasing the number of first level neighbors (when it is lower than k) by adding the second level ones implies a better performance of the algorithms. In this example, we used Dice similarity and $k = 300$, however the results are similar when applying second-level neighbors to other similarities.

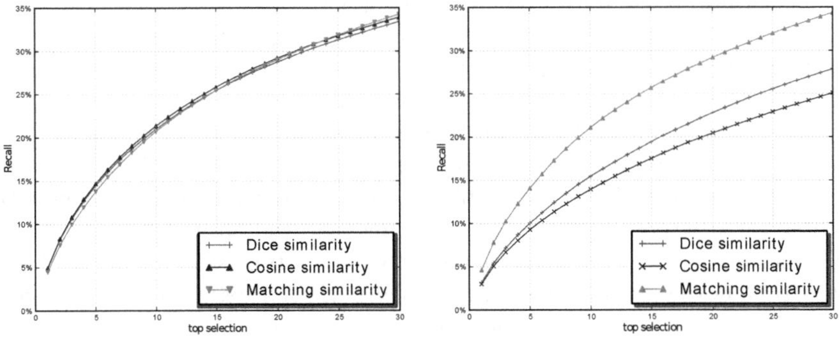

(a) User-based kNN (b) Item-based kNN

Fig. 1. Comparison between similarity functions in user-based and item-based kNN

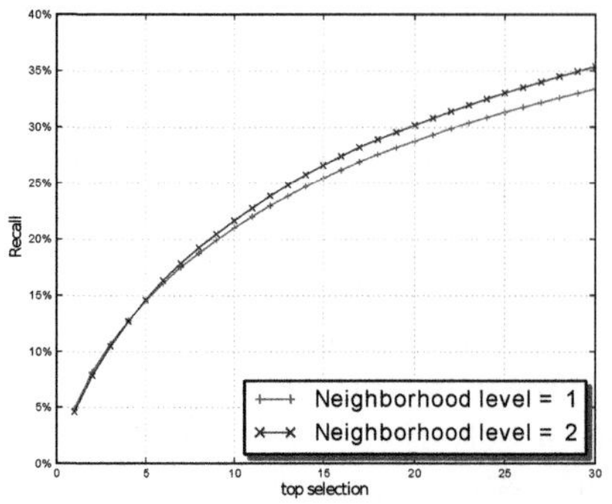

(a) Recall values for one-level and two-level neighborhoods for user-based kNN

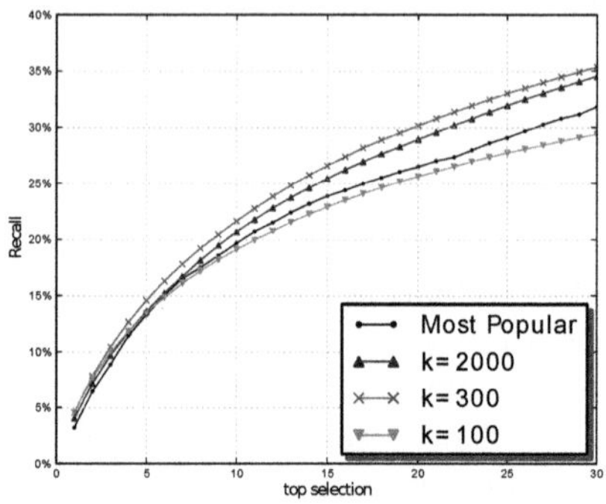

(b) Recall values for different neighborhood sizes in user-based kNN

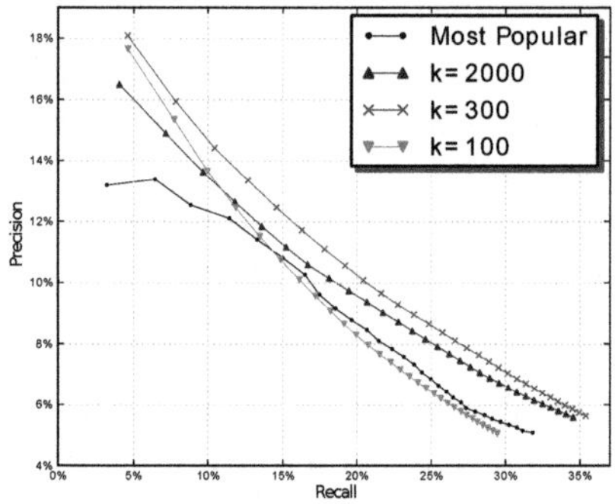

(c) Precision vs Recall for different neighborhood sizes in user-based kNN

Fig. 2. Neighborhoods comparison, precision and recall for user-based kNN

In the next tests, we try to find an optimal value for k in the user-based kNN algorithm. Fig. 2(b) shows the results of kNN user-based for different values of k and the *MostPopular* recommender. We used Dice similarity, but the results are similar with other similarity functions, as previously explained. We can observe that a value $k = 100$ is not sufficient to outperform the *MostPopular* algorithm, due to the lower value of the recall. On the other side, a very high number of neighbors allows to perform better than the *MostPopular*. However, we could notice that for high values of k the algorithm starts to converge to the *MostPopular*, characterized by an unbounded number of neighbors. We found that $k = 300$ is a good compromise between the ability of providing valuable recommendations and the resource consumption in calculating the neighborhood.

To better observe the trend of both recall and precision, Figure 2(c) shows the two values combined. Again, $k = 300$ performs better if we take the top 10 recommended elements, as it also yields to good results in terms of precision. Considering more than 10 recommendations, it would seem appropriate to increase the number of neighbors, as the results for precision and recall are slightly better. Nevertheless, considering the algorithm performance also in terms of computational requirements, $k = 300$ is still a good choice when we take into account the precision metric.

An interesting comparison among the three kNN algorithms analyzed, i.e., user-based, item-based and *MostPopular*, is depicted in Figure 3(a). We can observe that the latter is clearly outperformed by the other two algorithms in terms of recall, especially when more recommended items are considered. The user-based kNN performs slightly better than the item-based version, although the gap is mostly noticeable when more items are recommended. In general, item-based algorithms tend to perform better because usually the number of items is considerably lower than the users [9]. Such a property does not hold in our domain, hence making the user-based version superior in terms of recall, as we initially expected.

A final experiment was made in order to compare the performance of the SVD approach to the kNN. The implementation of the SVD algorithms described in Section 4 is tested with different parameters, with the purpose of identifying the more suitable ones in our context. In particular, we try different sizes for

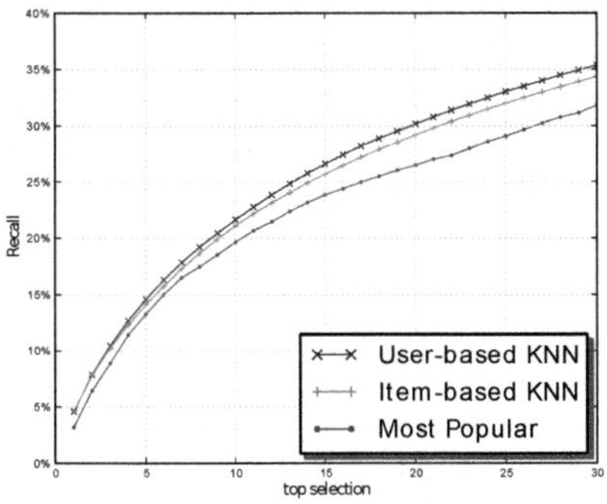

(a) Recall for user-based kNN ($k = 300$), item-based kNN and MostPopular

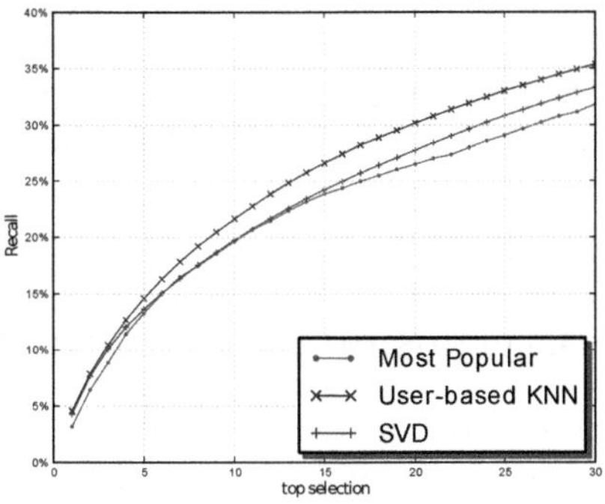

(b) Recall values for SVD wrt user-based kNN ($k = 300$) and MostPopular

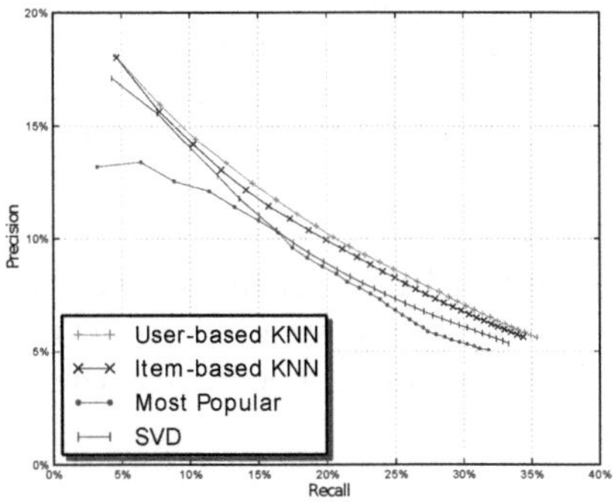

(c) Precision vs Recall for user-based kNN ($k = 300$), SVD and MostPopular

Fig. 3. Precision and recall for the analyzed algorithms

user-factors and item-factors vectors, values for the λ parameter and number of training steps. Results are depicted in Figure 3(b). The best prediction is obtained with 100 features, $\lambda = 500$ and 15 training steps. However, the performance of the SVD approach in the analyzed context is worse if compared to a neighborhood model such as kNN. Similarly, results related to the precision (Figure 3(c)) show an analogous performance of the kNN algorithms wrt SVD, with the *Most Popular* being considerably less precise than others.

It could appear surprising that the prediction performance of the SVD recommender is worse than other techniques, as this algorithm normally performs better in several other contexts [10,7,6]. We believe that the motivations for such an unusual behavior reside in the dataset characteristics. In particular, a reason might be identified in the so called *cold start problem*, whose effects involve users, items and communities [11]. In our context, the cold start problem is particularly noticeable with items and is due to the lack of relevant feedbacks when a new event first appears in the system. Such an issue is made worse by the fact that items to recommend are generally new ones, i.e. those events having a starting time in the future. This property holds for no-repeat events as well as for repetitive ones (the starting time is updated according to their periodicity). So, events whose starting time has passed are no longer eligible for recommendation.

The fact that recommendations are affected by the cold start problem is one key factor that may influence SVD performance, as this algorithm needs support of user's preferences to perform well. On the contrary, a neighborhood-based approach such as kNN appears to better deal with newly introduced items, as also reported in [2].

6 Conclusion and Future Work

We proposed a methodology to detect live TV and radio events from a set of independently programmed recordings. Assuming that such events can be browsed, searched and played back as other digital resources as they are included in a large digital library, it emerges the importance of suggesting recordings to user. Thus, we experimented with data of a real digital recording service to compare collaborative filtering techniques. Our findings showed that neighborhood based strategies, such as kNN, can return in good prediction accuracy and, if correctly tuned, they can outperform SVD-based techniques as well as *most popular* strategies, which dangerously leverage the phenomenon of many users concentrated on very few relevant events.

The evaluation of a content-based recommender system in this domain is planned. This was not possibile at this stage of the work because of the difficulty of getting descriptions about recorded events with earlier versions of the analysed DMR system.

Acknowledgements. This work has been partially produced within the "SALC" (Service à la carte) project, supported by Finpiemonte, ("Progetto Polo ICT"). Of course, we are grateful to InRete and Giorgio Bernardi that provided us the access to the *VCast* digital recording system data.

References

1. Basso, A., Milanesio, M., Ruffo, G.: Events discovery for personal video recorders. In: EuroITV 2009: Proceedings of the 7th European Interactive TV Conference, pp. 171–174. ACM, New York (2009)
2. Cremonesi, P., Turrin, R.: Analysis of cold-start recommendations in IPTV systems. In: RecSys 2009: Proc. of the 3rd ACM conf. on Recommender Systems, pp. 233–236. ACM, New York (2009)
3. Cremonesi, P., Turrin, R., Bambini, R.: A Recommender System for an IPTV Service Provider: a Real Large-Scale Production Environment. In: Kantor, P., Ricci, F., Rokach, L., Shapira, B. (eds.) Recommender Systems Handbook, vol. ch.30, pp. 200–220. Springer, Heidelberg (2009)
4. Deshpande, M., Karypis, G.: Item-based top-n recommendation algorithms. ACM Trans. Inf. Syst. 22(1), 143–177 (2004)
5. Herlocker, J.L., Konstan, J.A., Borchers, A., Riedl, J.: An algorithmic framework for performing collaborative filtering. In: SIGIR 1999: Proc. of the 22nd Annual Intern. ACM SIGIR Conf. on Research and Development in Information Retrieval, pp. 230–237. ACM, New York (1999)
6. Hu, Y., Koren, Y., Volinsky, C.: Collaborative filtering for implicit feedback datasets. In: ICDM 2008: : Proc. of the 2008 Eighth IEEE Intl. Conf. on Data Mining, pp. 263–272. IEEE Computer Society, Washington, DC (2008)
7. Koren, Y.: Collaborative filtering with temporal dynamics. Commun. CACM 53(4), 89–97 (2010)
8. Markines, B., Cattuto, C., Menczer, F., Benz, D., Hotho, A., Stumme, G.: Evaluating similarity measures for emergent semantics of social tagging. In: WWW 2009: Proc. of the 18th Int. Conf. on World Wide Web, pp. 641–650. ACM, New York (2009)
9. Sarwar, B., Karypis, G., Konstan, J., Reidl, J.: Item-based collaborative filtering recommendation algorithms. In: WWW 2001: Proc. of the 10th Int. Conf. on World Wide Web, pp. 285–295. ACM, New York (2001)
10. Sarwar, B.M., Karypis, G., Konstan, J.A., Riedl, J.T.: Application of dimensionality reduction in recommender system - a case study. In: ACM WebKDD Workshop (2000)
11. Schafer, J.B., Konstan, J., Riedi, J.: Recommender systems in e-commerce. In: EC 1999: Proceedings of the 1st ACM Conference on Electronic Commerce, pp. 158–166. ACM Press, New York (1999)
12. Smyth, B., Wilson, D.: Explicit vs. implicit profiling a case-study in electronic programme guides. In: Proc. of the 18 th In. Joint Conf. on Artificial Intelligence (IJCAI 2003), pp. 9–15 (2003)

Rating Elicitation Strategies for Collaborative Filtering

Mehdi Elahi, Valdemaras Repsys, and Francesco Ricci

Free University of Bozen-Bolzano,
Piazza Domenicani 3, Bozen-Bolzano, Italy
mehdi.elahi@stud-inf.unibz.it
valdemaras@gmail.com
fricci@unibz.it
http://www.unibz.it

Abstract. The accuracy of collaborative filtering recommender systems largely depends on two factors: the quality of the recommendation algorithm and the nature of the available item ratings. In general, the more ratings are elicited from the users, the more effective the recommendations are. However, not all the ratings are equally useful and therefore, in order to minimize the users' rating effort, only some of them should be requested or acquired. In this paper we consider several rating elicitation strategies and we evaluate their system utility, i.e., how the overall behavior of the system changes when these new ratings are added. We simulate the limited knowledge of users, i.e., not all the rating requests of the system are satisfied by the users, and we compare the capability of the considered strategies in requesting ratings for items that the user experienced. We show that different strategies can improve different aspects of the recommendation quality with respect to several metrics (MAE, precision, ranking quality and coverage) and we introduce a voting-based strategy that can achieve an excellent overall performance.

Keywords: Recommender Systems, Active Learning, Rating Elicitation.

1 Introduction

Recommender Systems (RSs) support users in choosing the right products or services to consume by providing personalized suggestions that match the user's needs and constraints [11]. In this paper we are concerned with collaborative filtering (CF) RSs [5]; these systems use item ratings provided by a population of users to predict unknown ratings of the current user, and recommend the items with the largest predicted ratings. CF rating prediction accuracy does depend on the characteristics of the prediction algorithm, but also on the ratings known by the system. The more (informative) ratings are available the higher the recommendation accuracy is. In fact, in [10] it is shown that the recommendation accuracy can be improved to a larger extent if the ratings are acquired with a well designed selection strategy compared with the "classic" strategy where the users self-select the items to rate.

C. Huemer and T. Setzer (Eds.): EC-Web 2011, LNBIP 85, pp. 160–171, 2011.

Rating elicitation has been also tackled in some previous research works [8,9,1,4,3] but these papers focused on a different problem, namely the benefit of rating elicitation for a single user, e.g., in the sign up stage. Conversely, we consider the impact of several (some original) elicitation strategies on the system overall effectiveness (more details are provided in Section 5). We measured their effect using several evaluation metrics, including: the rating prediction accuracy (Mean Absolute Error), the number of acquired ratings, the recommendation precision, the system coverage, and the effectiveness of the recommendations' ranking, measured with normalized discounted cumulative gain (NDCG).

Moreover, we explore another new aspect, i.e., the performance of an elicitation strategy taking into account the size of the rating database, and we show that different strategies can improve different aspects of the recommendation quality at different stages of the rating database development. In this context, we have verified an hypothesis made originally by [9], i.e., that certain strategies, for instance, requesting users to rate the items with the largest predicted ratings, may generate, a system-wide bias, i.e., they can increase, rather than decrease, the system error.

In order to perform such an evaluation, we have created a system which simulates a real process of rating elicitation in a community of users, the consequent rating database growth starting from a relatively small set of data (cold-start), and the system adaptation (retraining) to the new data. In these simulations we used a state of the art Matrix Factorization recommender algorithm [5]; so that the results here presented can provide useful guidelines for managing real operational RSs.

In conclusion in this paper we provide a realistic, comprehensive evaluation of several, applicable and novel, rating elicitation strategies, providing guidelines and conclusions that would help their exploitations in real RSs. This is an important and necessary preliminary step for the application of any rating elicitation strategy in a real operational and possibly conversational system; having the goal to reduce the effort spent by users in rating (unnecessary) items and to improve the quality of the recommendations for all. We note that in this paper we extend a previous work [2] by describing and evaluating more strategies, including the voting one, and evaluating their behaviors on larger and a more realistic data set.

The rest of the paper is structured as follow. In section 2 we introduce the rating elicitation strategies that we have analyzed, and in section 3 we present the simulation procedure that we designed to evaluate their effects. The results of our experiments are shown in section 4. In section 5 we review some related research, and finally in section 6 we summarize the results of this research and we outline some future work.

2 Elicitation Strategies

A rating dataset R is an $n \times m$ matrix of real values (ratings) with possible null entries. The variable r_{ui}, denotes the entry of the matrix in position (u, i), and contains the rating assigned by the user u to the item i. r_{ui} can store a null value representing the fact that the system does not know yet the opinion of the user on that item. In the Movielens dataset, which was used in our experiments, ratings are integers between 1 and 5 included. A rating elicitation strategy S is a function $S(u, N, K, C_u) = L$ which returns a list of $M \leq N$ items $L = \{i_1, \ldots, i_M\}$ whose ratings should be asked to the user u, where N is the maximum number of ratings to be elicited. K is the $n \times m$ matrix containing the known ratings, in other words, the ratings (of all the users) that have been already acquired by the RS. Finally, C_u is the set of candidate items whose ratings have not yet been asked to u, hence potentially interesting to be acquired. In fact, a strategy must not ask a user to rate the same item twice, i.e., the items in L must be removed from C_u.

Every strategy we propose analyzes the dataset of known ratings K and assigns a score to each item in C_u measuring how valuable it is to acquire the user opinion for that item. Then the N items with the highest score are identified, if the strategy can compute N scores, otherwise a smaller number of requests (M) is returned. Then, these items are actually presented to the user u to provide his ratings. It is important to note that the user may not have experienced some of these items; in this case the system will obtain less ratings.

We have considered many strategies; the first three below have been reported previously, while the rest are either original or have not been tested previously.

Popularity: the score for the item i is equal for all the users, and it is the number of not null ratings for i in K, i.e., those already acquired by the system. More popular items are more likely to be known by the users, and hence it is more likely that a request for such a rating will really expand the rating database [1] [9].

log(popularity)∗entropy: the score for the item i is computed by multiplying the logarithm of the popularity of i with the entropy of the ratings for i in K. This strategy tries to combine the effect of the popularity score, which is discussed above, with the heuristics that items with more diverse ratings (larger entropy) bring more useful information about the user preferences [1] [9].

Binary Prediction: the matrix K is transformed into a matrix B with the same number of rows and columns, by mapping null entries in K to 0, and not null entries to 1. A factor model is built using B as training data and then the prediction $\hat{b}_{ui}$ for each item i in C_u is computed and assigned as the score for the item. This strategy tries to predict what items the user has experienced, to maximize the probability that the requested ratings could be added to K (similarly to the popularity strategy).

Highest Predicted: a rating prediction $\hat{r}_{ui}$ is computed for all the items i in C_u (using the ratings in K) and the score for i is set to this predicted rating $\hat{r}_{ui}$. The idea is that the best recommendations could also be more likely to have been experienced by the user and their ratings could also reveal useful information on what the user likes. This is the default strategy for RSs, i.e., enabling the user to rate the recommendations.

Lowest Predicted: for each item in the C_u a rating prediction $\hat{r}_{ui}$ is computed (using the ratings in K). Then the score for item i is $M_r - \hat{r}_{ui}$, where M_r is the maximum rating value (e.g., 5). Lowest predicted items are likely to reveal what the user does not like, but should actually collect a few ratings, since the user is unlikely to have experienced all the items that he does not like.

Highest and Lowest Predicted: for each item i in C_u a prediction $\hat{r}_{ui}$ is computed (using the set of ratings in K). Then the score for i is $|\frac{M_r - m_r}{2} + m_r - \hat{r}_{ui}|$, where M_r (m_r) is the maximum (minimum) rating value. This strategy tries to ask for information on items that the user may or may not like.

Random: the score for an item is a random number. This is just a baseline strategy, used for comparison.

Voting: the score for the item i is the number of votes given by a committee of strategies including *popularity, variance* [12] , *entropy* [9], *highest-lowest predicted, binary prediction,* and *random.* Each of these strategies produces its top 100 candidates for rating elicitation, and then the items appearing more often in these lists are selected. This strategy depends on the selected voting strategies, and we included random to impose an exploratory behavior that should improve the system coverage.

Finally, we would like to note that we have also evaluated other strategies: *variance, entropy,* and $log(pop) * variance$. But, since their observed behaviors are very similar to some of the previously mentioned strategies, due to lack of space they are not described here.

3 Evaluation Approach

In order to study the effect of the considered elicitation strategies we set up a simulation procedure. The goal was to simulate the evolution of the RS's performance exploiting these strategies. In order to run such simulations we partition (more details on the partition method are given later) all the available (not null) rating data in R into three different matrices with the same number of rows and columns as R:

- K: contains the ratings that are considered to be known by the system at a certain point in time.
- X: contains the ratings that are considered to be known by the users but not by the system. These ratings are incrementally elicited, i.e., they are transferred into K if the system asks for them from the (simulated) users.
- T: contains the ratings that are never elicited and are used only to test the strategy, i.e., to estimate the evaluation measures (defined later).

We also note that if $i \in C_u$ then its rating is worth acquiring because "unclear" to the system and candidate for elicitation, i.e., k_{ui} is null and the system has not yet asked for this rating from u. That request may end up with a new (not null) rating $k_{ui} = x_{ui}$ inserted into K, if the user has experienced it, which is simulated by the fact that x_{ui} is not null in X, or in a no action, if this rating is not found in X. The system, in any case will remove that item from C_u, i.e., will not try to collect the same rating twice. It is important to note that in real scenarios the system may ask later on for a rating that the user is unable to provide at a certain point in time: because he may have experienced that item after the first request. This case is not considered in our simulation. Moreover, we observe that these three matrices partition the full dataset R: if r_{ui} has a not null value then either k_{ui} or x_{ui} or t_{ui} has that value, and only one of them is not null. The testing of a strategy S proceeds in the following way:

1. The not null ratings in R are partitioned into the three matrices K, X, T.
2. MAE, Precision, Coverage and NDCG are measured on T, training the prediction model on K.
3. For each user u:
   (a) Only the first time that this step is executed, C_u, the candidate set of user u is initialized to all the items i such that k_{ui} is null in K.
   (b) Using the strategy S a set of items $L = S(u, N, K, C_u)$ is computed.
   (c) L_e, which contains only items from L that have not null rating in X is created.
   (d) Assign to the corresponding entries in K the ratings for items in L_e as found in X and remove them from X.
   (e) Remove the items in L from C_u: $C_u = C_u \setminus L$.
4. Train the prediction model on K and compute MAE, Precision, Coverage and NDCG on T.
5. Repeat steps 3-4 (Iteration) for I times.

The MovieLens rating database were used for our experiments. Movielens consists of 1,000,000 ratings from 6,040 users on 3,900 movies. The experiments were conducted partitioning (randomly) the 1,000,000 not null ratings in the data set R in the following way: 2000 in K (i.e., very limited knowledge at the beginning), 698,000 in X, and 300,000 in T. Moreover, $|L| = N = 10$, i.e., the system at each iteration asks a simulated user for his ratings on 10 items. The number of iterations was $I = 200$, and the number of factors in the SVD prediction model was set to 16. It should be noted that we have also experimented with a denser initial matrix K containing 20,000 ratings. But, in spite of this difference similar results, as discussed below, were obtained.

When deciding how to split the available data into the three matrices K, X and T an obvious alternative choice was to respect the time evolution of the dataset, i.e., to insert into K the first 2000 ratings acquired by the system, then to use the second temporal segment of 698,000 ratings to populate X and finally to use the remaining ratings for T. Actually, it is not significant to test the performance of the proposed strategies for a *particular* evolution of the rating dataset.

Since we want to study the evolution of a rating data set under the application of a new strategy we cannot test it only against the temporal distribution of the data that was generated by a particular (unknown) previously used elicitation strategy. Hence we followed the approach also used in [3], i.e., to random split the rating data but we generated some (5) random splits of the ratings into K, X and T, and averaged the results. Besides, in this way we were able to generate users and items that had no ratings initially in the known dataset K. We believe this approach provided us with a realistic and hard experimental setup, allowing us to address the new user and new item problems [11]. In any case, additionally we performed the same experiments with the data partitioned by the natural order of acquisition time. The results were very similar to those observed in the random partitioning, confirming that the partitioning method does not impose any significant bias on the experiments.

We have considered four evaluation measures: mean absolute error (MAE), precision, coverage and normalized discounted cumulative gain (NDCG). Precision is computed considering, for each user, the top 10 recommended items (whose rating value appear in T) and judging relevant the items with ratings (in T) equal to 4 or 5. The coverage is measured as the proportion of the full set of items over which the system can form predictions or make recommendations [11]. Normalized Discounted Cumulative Gain (DCG) is a measure originally used to evaluate the effectiveness of information retrieval systems [7], but it is now becoming popular in RSs as well [13] [6]. NDCG measures the quality of a ranking comparing it to the best attainable one, i.e., the ranking where the recommendations are ordered in decreasing value of their actual ratings.

4 Experimental Results

4.1 Mean Absolute Error

MAE computed on the test ratings in T at successive iterations of the application of the considered elicitation strategies is depicted in Figure 1. Excluding the voting strategy, which needs particular discussion, there are two clearly distinct groups of strategies:

1. Strategies monotonically decreasing the error: lowest predicted, lowest-highest predicted, and random.
2. Strategies non monotonically decreasing the error: binary predicted, highest predicted, popularity, log(pop)∗entropy.

The monotonically error decreasing strategies have overall a better performance (MAE) during the learning process, except at the end. During the iterations 1-40 the best strategy is random, and the second best is lowest predicted. During iterations 40-90 the non monotonic strategies log(pop)∗entropy and popularity are the best performing. Starting from iteration 120 the MAE of popularity, log(pop)*entropy, and of all the prediction-based strategies does not change anymore. This is because these strategies are not able to add any new

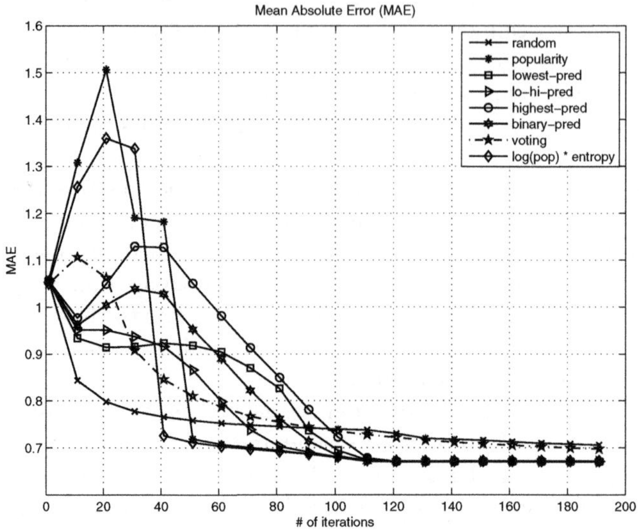

Fig. 1. MAE of the considered strategies (MovieLens data set)

ratings to K. The system MAE during the application of the random and voting strategies keeps decreasing until all the ratings in X are acquired, i.e., moved to K. In fact, it is important to note that prediction based strategies (e.g., highest predicted) cannot elicit ratings for which the prediction can not be made, i.e., for movies and users that don't have ratings in K.

The strategies that are not monotonically decreasing the error can be further divided into two groups. Binary prediction and highest predicted first slightly decrease MAE (iterations 1-10), then they increase MAE (10-30), and finally they keep decreasing the error. While popularity and log(pop)∗entropy, first increase the error (iterations 1-20) and then they keep decreasing it. The explanation for such a behavior is that these strategies have a strong selection bias. For instance, the highest predicted strategy attempts to elicit ratings that have high predicted values. As a result it ends up with adding more high (than low) ratings to the known matrix (K), which biases the rating prediction. This negatively affects MAE at the beginning of the process, because the ratings that they are requesting are more likely to be present in X since it is larger. In a second stage of the process, i.e., after they have collected all the ratings in X with their selection bias, they slowly add the remaining ratings, hence producing in K a distribution of ratings that is closer to the overall distribution in the full data set. In fact, for instance, looking into the data we discovered that at iteration 30 the highest-predicted strategy has already elicited most of the high ratings. Then the next ratings that are elicited are actually ratings with average or low values (but erroneously predicted with high values) and this reduces the bias in K and also the prediction error.

Voting, as explained before, is very much dependent on the strategies that vote for the items. So it can be seen that voting produces an error that is close to the average MAE of the six voting strategies and shows only a minor non monotonic behavior.

4.2 Number of Acquired Ratings

It is important to measure how many ratings are added by the considered strategies. In fact, certain strategies can acquire more ratings, by better guessing what items the user actually experienced. This occurs in our simulation if a strategy asks the simulated user for more ratings present in the matrix X. Conversely, a strategy may not be able to acquire many ratings but those actually acquired are more useful to generate better recommendations.

Table 1 shows the percentage of the requested ratings that have been actually acquired in a particular iteration because present in X. This is a key issue for an elicitation strategy since those strategies that are not able to find movies that users are able to rate will not increase the size of the ratings data set. For instance, random at the iteration 20 can only acquire 3.1% of the requested ratings. Other strategies are more effective, e.g., not surprisingly, binary predicted and highest predicted, at the same iteration can collect more than 20% of the requested ratings.

It is important to note that these ratios underestimates what could be observed in a real scenario. In fact, here X contains all the ratings that can be acquired by a strategy. But, this is only a subset of the ratings that a generic MovieLens user could provide, since it includes only those actually collected by MovieLens. To illustrate better this situation, we conducted a small experiment by extracting a random subset of 50 movies from MovieLens and asking our colleagues (20) to indicate how many movies they could rate. On average they indicated 6 movies, i.e., a ratio of 12%, i.e., more than 4 times larger than the reply ratio of the random strategy in this simulation. This indicates that in reality, users could rate many more movies requested by the various strategies. This is also illustrated by the findings described in [9]. In their live user experiments, popularity strategy (for instance) could acquire on average 50% of the requested

Table 1. The ratio of the ratings acquired over those requested at different iterations

	acquired/requested ratings ratio			
Strategy	iteration=20	iteration=40	iteration=60	iteration=100
Random	3.1%	3.1%	3.1%	2.8%
Popularity	13.8%	11.3	9.9%	7.3%
Lowest predicted	7.7%	8.3%	8.8%	9.5%
Low-high predicted	13.4%	12.6%	12.0%	11.5%
Highest predicted	20.8%	18.7%	16.1%	12.3%
Binary prediction	20.5%	16.9%	15.7%	12.6%
Voting	12.1%	8.3%	6.7%	4.7%
Log(pop)*entropy	13.0%	10.1	10.0%	7.3%

ratings and pop∗entropy, which is similar to our log(pop)∗entropy strategy, could also acquire a similar percentage of ratings. These results clearly illustrate that many of the strategies presented here could already be applicable in a realistic scenario. But obviously there is still space for defining new strategies that can identify a larger percentage of items that users can actually rate.

4.3 Normalized Discounted Cumulative Gain

We measured NDCG on the first top 10 recommendations with not null values in T (of each user) (Figure 2). Random is the best strategy at the beginning of the active learning process, but at iteration 40 voting passes random and then remains the best strategy. Excluding the random strategy, voting and highest predicted are the best overall. Lowest predicted is by far the worst, and this is very different from its performance with respect to MAE. Moreover, another striking difference from the MAE results, is that all the considered strategies improve NDCG monotonically. Analyzing the experiment data we discovered that lowest predicted is not effective for NDCG because it is eliciting more user ratings on the lowest ranked items and this is useless to predict the ranking of the top items. It is also important to note that here voting is by far the best. We should also note that voting and random also have the best behavior in term of coverage (not shown here for lack of space) since they can actually elicit ratings for new items and new users. We have also evaluated the strategies with respect to precision. These results are very similar to those shown previously for NDCG hence due to the lack of space they are not shown here.

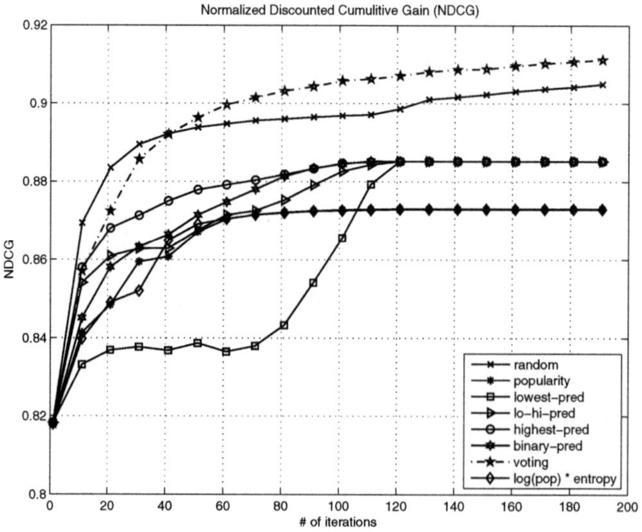

Fig. 2. NDCG of the all strategies

In conclusion from these experiments we can see that *there is not a clear best strategy* that dominates the others for all the evaluation measures (among those that we evaluated). The *voting* strategy is the best for NDCG, whereas for MAE one should suggest *random* at the beginning and successively Popularity and log(pop)*entropy. We observe that voting represents a good compromise which can improve the quality of the ranking of the top items and reduce substantially the prediction error. Similar results have been obtained by running the same experiments on another data set, that is NetFlix: which reinforces the support for the conclusions that we have derived.

5 Related Work

Active learning in RS aims at actively acquiring user preference data to improve the output of the RS [12]. [9] Proposes six techniques that collaborative filtering recommender systems can use to learn about new users in the sign up process. They considered: pure *entropy* where items with the largest entropy are preferred; *random*; *popularity*; $log(popularity) * entropy$ where items that are both popular and have diverse rating values; and finally *item-item personalized*, where the items are proposed randomly until one rating is acquired, then a recommender is used to predict the items that the user is likely to have seen. They studied the behavior of an item-to-item RS only with respect to MAE, and designed an offline experimental study that simulates the sign up process. The process was repeated and averaged for all the test users. In this scenario the $log(popularity) * entropy$ strategy was found to be the best. It is worth noting that these results are not comparable with ours as they measured how a varying set of ratings elicited from one user are useful in predicting the ratings of the same user. In our experiments we simulate the simultaneous acquisition of ratings from all the users, by asking each user in turn for 10 ratings, and repeating this process several times. This simulates the long term usage of a recommender system where users come again and again to get new recommendations and the rating provided by a user is exploited to generate better recommendations to others (system performance).

In [3] is noted that the Bayesian active learning approach introduced in [4] makes an implicit and unrealistic assumption that a user can provide rating for any queried item. Hence, the authors proposed a revised Bayesian selection approach, which does not make such an assumption, and introduces an estimation of the probability that a user has consumed an item in the past and is able to provide a rating. Their results show that personalized Bayesian selection outperforms Bayesian selection and the random strategy with respect to MAE. Their simulation setting is similar to that used in [9], hence for the same reason their results are not directly comparable with ours. There are other important differences between their experiments and ours: their strategies elicit only one rating per request; they compare the proposed approach only with the random strategy; they do not consider the new user problem, since in their simulations all the users have 3 ratings at the beginning of the experiment, whereas in our experiments, there might be users that have no ratings at all in the initial stage of the experiment; they use a completely different rating prediction algorithm (Bayesian vs. Matrix Factorization).

In [1] again a user-focussed approach is considered. The authors propose a set of techniques to intelligently select ratings when the user is particularly motivated to provide such information. They present a conversational and collaborative interaction model which elicits ratings so that the benefit of doing that is clear to the user, thus increasing the motivation to provide a rating. Item-focused techniques that elicit ratings to improve prediction on a specific item are proposed. Popularity, entropy and their combination are tested, as well as their item focused modifications. Results have shown that item focused strategies are constantly better than unfocused ones. Also in this case, their results are complementary to our findings, since the elicitation process and the evaluation metrics are different.

6 Conclusions and Future Work

In this work we have addressed the problem of selecting ratings to ask users also defined as the ratings elicitation problem. We have proposed and evaluated a set of ratings elicitation strategies. Some of them have been proposed in a previous work [9] (popularity, random, log(pop)∗entropy), and some, which we define as prediction-based strategies, are new: binary-prediction, highest-predicted, lowest-predicted, highest-lowest-predicted. We have also proposed a voting strategy combining six different strategies which shows very good performances for several evaluation metrics (MAE, NDCG, precision, coverage). We have evaluated these strategies for their system-wide effectiveness implementing a simulation loop that models the day-by-day process of rating elicitation and rating database growth. We have taken into account the limited knowledge of the users, i.e., the fact that the users will not know all the possible ratings, and this is a small percentage of all of them. During the simulation we have measured several metrics at different phases of the rating database growth.

The performed evaluation has shown that different strategies can improve different aspects of the recommendation quality and in different stages of the rating database development. Moreover, we have discovered that some strategies may incur the risk of increasing MAE if they keep adding only ratings with a certain value, e.g., the highest-predicted strategy that is an approach often adopted in real RSs. In addition, prediction-based strategies neither address the problem of new users, nor of new items. Whereas, voting, popularity and log(pop)*entropy strategies are able to select items for new users, but can not select items that have no ratings.

In the future we want to study the effect of different prediction algorithms, e.g., K-Nearest Neighbor [11], on the performance of the selected strategies. Moreover, we want to better explore the possibility of combining strategies using different heuristics depending on the state of the target user, and the data set, hence building a more adaptive approach.

References

1. Carenini, G., Smith, J., Poole, D.: Towards more conversational and collaborative recommender systems. In: Proceedings of the 2003 International Conference on Intelligent User Interfaces, Miami, FL, USA, January 12-15, pp. 12–18 (2003)
2. Elahi, M., Ricci, F., Repsys, V.: System-wide effectiveness of active learning in collaborative filtering. In: Bonchi, F., Buntine, W., Gavalda, R., Guo, S. (eds.) Proceedings of the International Workshop on Social Web Mining, Co-located with IJCAI, Barcelona, Spain (July 2011)
3. Harpale, A.S., Yang, Y.: Personalized active learning for collaborative filtering. In: SIGIR 2008: Proceedings of the 31st Annual International ACM SIGIR Conference on Research and Development in Information Retrieval, pp. 91–98. ACM, New York (2008)
4. Jin, R., Si, L.: A bayesian approach toward active learning for collaborative filtering. In: UAI 2004: Proceedings of the 20th Conference in Uncertainty in Artificial Intelligence, Banff, Canada, July 7-11, pp. 278–285 (2004)
5. Koren, Y., Bell, R.: Advances in collaborative filtering. In: Ricci, F., Rokach, L., Shapira, B., Kantor, P. (eds.) Recommender Systems Handbook, pp. 145–186. Springer, Heidelberg (2011)
6. Liu, N.N., Yang, Q.: Eigenrank: a ranking-oriented approach to collaborative filtering. In: SIGIR 2008: Proceedings of the 31st Annual International ACM SIGIR Conference on Research and Development in Information Retrieval, pp. 83–90. ACM, New York (2008)
7. Manning, C.: Introduction to Information Retrieval. Cambridge University Press, Cambridge (2008)
8. McNee, S.M., Lam, S.K., Konstan, J.A., Riedl, J.: Interfaces for eliciting new user preferences in recommender systems. In: Brusilovsky, P., Corbett, A.T., de Rosis, F. (eds.) UM 2003. LNCS, vol. 2702, pp. 178–187. Springer, Heidelberg (2003)
9. Rashid, A.M., Albert, I., Cosley, D., Lam, S.K., Mcnee, S.M., Konstan, J.A., Riedl, J.: Getting to know you: Learning new user preferences in recommender systems. In: IUI 2002: Proceedings of the 2002 International Conference on Intelligent User Interfaces, pp. 127–134. ACM Press, New York (2002)
10. Rashid, A.M., Karypis, G., Riedl, J.: Learning preferences of new users in recommender systems: an information theoretic approach. SIGKDD Explorations 10(2), 90–100 (2008)
11. Ricci, F., Rokach, L., Shapira, B., Kantor, P.B. (eds.): Recommender Systems Handbook. Springer, Heidelberg (2011)
12. Rubens, N., Kaplan, D., Sugiyama, M.: Active learning in recommender systems. In: Ricci, F., Rokach, L., Shapira, B., Kantor, P. (eds.) Recommender Systems Handbook, pp. 735–767. Springer, Heidelberg (2011)
13. Weimer, M., Karatzoglou, A., Smola, A.: Adaptive collaborative filtering. In: RecSys 2008: Proceedings of the 2008 ACM Conference on Recommender Systems, pp. 275–282. ACM, New York (2008)

Information Retrieval and Folksonomies together for Recommender Systems

Max Chevalier[1], Antonina Dattolo[2], Gilles Hubert[1], and Emanuela Pitassi[2]

[1] IRIT, Université P. Sabatier, 118 rte de Narbonne, F-31062 Toulouse, France
{Max.Chevalier,Gilles.Hubert}@irit.fr
[2] University of Udine, Via delle Scienze 206, I-33100 Udine, Italy
{antonina.dattolo,emanuela.pitassi}@uniud.it

Abstract. The powerful and democratic activity of social tagging allows the wide set of Web users to add free annotations on resources. Tags express user interests, preferences and needs, but also automatically generate folksonomies. They can be considered as gold mine, especially for e-commerce applications, in order to provide effective recommendations. Thus, several recommender systems exploit folksonomies in this context. Folksonomies have also been involved in many information retrieval approaches. In considering that information retrieval and recommender systems are siblings, we notice that few works deal with the integration of their approaches, concepts and techniques to improve recommendation. This paper is a first attempt in this direction. We propose a trail through recommender systems, social Web, e-commerce and social commerce, tags and information retrieval: an overview on the methodologies, and a survey on folksonomy-based information retrieval from recommender systems point of view, delineating a set of open and new perspectives.

Keywords: Information Retrieval, Folksonomy, Recommendation, e-commerce.

1 Introduction

The advent of social Web has significantly contributed to the explosion of Web content and, as side effect, to the consequent explosive growth of the information overload. So, users need a computer-supported help in order to choose what to buy, how to spend their leisure time, how to select among several options: this help is historically offered by Recommender Systems (RS). RS automate specific strategies with the goal of providing affordable, personal, and high-quality recommendations, and so supporting online users, specially in electronic commerce, in decision-making, planning and purchasing processes. The attention of the international scientific community on RS is active and is largely demonstrated by the significant number of conferences, workshops, books, surveys and special issues on this research area (see in particular two recent books [1,2] and two surveys [3,4]).

In the past, in the mid 1990s, the first RS in e-commerce provided recommendations based mainly on specific attributes of the products or on aggregated

C. Huemer and T. Setzer (Eds.): EC-Web 2011, LNBIP 85, pp. 172–183, 2011.

data of purchases, such as the top overall sellers on a site, the demographics of the customer, or the analysis of the past buying behavior of the customer as a prediction for future buying behavior [5]. These systems used only a small subset of the available information about customers, and they substantially provided not-personalized recommendations. Examples of these generation of RS for e-commerce were provided in Amazon, eBay, Moviefinder.com, Reel.com, Levis or cdnow.

Currently the extensive use of social applications is emphasizing the central role of users and their (cor)relations, in spite of the previous methodologies in the major part applied only on products and purchases: the focus is on the customer profile, her preferences, needs, and feedbacks, the reputation of buyers and sellers, the relationships established between user communities and sub-communities, and last but not least the personal way of each user to classify the huge amount of information at her disposal, applying on it a set of freely chosen keywords, called tags. The social tagging activity generates *folksonomies*, which play a strategic role in the generation of recommendations. As a consequence, specific attention is given to that part of e-commerce dedicated to the use of social aspects, the so-called *social commerce* [6].

Historically, RS and Social Web have been closely interconnected, and the use of folksonomies in RS is widely recognized as a core subject [3]. Nevertheless, another relevant research area has been often associated to RS: *Information Retrieval* (IR). IR and RS appear siblings, share similar objectives, and similar measures (even for evaluation). Both IR and RS are faced with similar filtering and ranking problems. In [7], the author argues, for example, that RS is not clearly separated from IR. The individualized criteria that RS try to achieve probably are the core differences between RS and IR [1].

This work proposes an overview on the methodologies, and a survey of folksonomy-based IR from RS point of view. Through the study of RS and IR and their evolution due to social web (with particular attention to folksonomies), this work underlines the complementarity between these two research areas, delineating the currently applied contributions of IR for RS, but also identifying which IR techniques and approaches could be exploited to improve RS in e-commerce context.

The paper is organized as follows. Section 2 presents the basic concepts and techniques related to RS. Section 3 compares IR basics and RS ones. Folksonomy and social Web are then described in Section 4 in order to show their positive impact. Finally, Section 5 proposes a survey of integration approaches between folksonomy, IR and RS in order to improve recommendations, and a set of perspectives, in order to show the real potential of such integration.

2 Basics of RS

The increasing volume of information on the Web is the main motivation for RS: they support users during their interaction with large information spaces, and direct them toward the information they need. RS model user interests, goals, knowledge, and tastes, by monitoring and modeling the (implicit or explicit) feedbacks provided by the user. A traditional classification [8] of RS is based on how item suggestions are generated and distinguishes three categories: (a) *CF (Collaborative Filtering)* uses social knowledge to generate recommendations. It may be further differentiated into: Model-based approaches, which build a probabilistic model for predicting the future rating assignments of a user, on the basis of her personal history; Memory-based approaches, which use statistical techniques for identifying the users, called neighbors, with common behaviour (user-based approaches) or items evaluated in a similar way by the community (item-based approaches); (b) *CB (Content-based)* analyzes past user activities looking for resources she liked; it models the resources by extracting some features (for example, topics or relevant concepts) from documents. The user profile is then defined describing what features are of interest for the user. The user relevance of a new resource is computed by matching a representation of the resource to the user profile; (c) *HF (Hybrid Filtering)* combines CB and CF approaches.

A more general taxonomy has been proposed in [9], where current recommendation technologies are discussed considering three dimensions:

1. the **Recommendation Algorithms** dimension includes discussed *CF, CB, HF recommenders*, and also adds *KB (Knowledge-based)* recommenders, that use domain knowledge to generate recommendations.
2. the **User Interaction** dimension includes: (a) *Conversational RS*, which directly interact with the user by asking her to give feedback (Candidate/Critique systems) or to answer questions (Question/Answer systems); (b) *Single-shot RS* where each interaction is used for suggesting recommendation independently;
3. the **User Models** dimension includes the *Persistent User Model*, which deduces the user interests and preferences from user inputs accumulated over the time, and the *Ephemeral User Model*, which infers the intentions/interests of the user solely on input from the current session. In [4], the authors have recently highlighted the centrality of the user model and its specific importance in the e-commerce field, both for Web browsing and purchase recommendation.

3 IR and RS

RS and IR can be considered as siblings, since they share the same objectives. This section compares IR and RS techniques focusing on their similarities.

Basics of IR. Salton in 1968 [10] defined IR as a field concerned with the structure, analysis, organization, storage searching, and retrieval of information. The objective of IR is to provide information corresponding to (matching) a need expressed by the user (query). Research was devoted, for the most part, to propose techniques to represent both documents and users' information needs and to match these representations. The different steps of the IR process are described

in [11]. The most important steps of this process are related to the indexing step and the evaluation: the *indexing step* is related to the way information is described. It is based on various theoretical models, such as the well-known Vector Space Model (VSM) [12], probabilistic model [13], and language model [14]. In addition to these models, in order to distinguish the importance of various features that describe the document, weighting schemes have been proposed like tf.idf [15] and bm25 [16].
The *evaluation of matching* between a document and a query. To evaluate such a matching, many measures have been proposed associated to a given model. For instance the cosine measure is commonly associated to the well-known vector space model.

Relevant documents (those that match the most the query) are then displayed to the user through a common ranked list visualization.

Comparison between IR and RS. IR systems and RS are very close fields. Kumar and Thambidurai [4] argue that "The different [Recommender] systems use various methods, concepts and techniques from diverse research areas like: IR, Artificial Intelligence, or Behavorial Science" . Burke in 2007 [7] underlines that "a recommender system can be distinguished from an IR system by the semantics of its user interaction. A result from a recommender system is understood as a recommendation, an option worthy of consideration; a result from an IR system is interpreted as a match to the user's query. RS are also distinguished in terms of personalization and agency. A recommender system customizes its responses to a particular user. Rather than simply responding to queries, a recommender system is intended to serve as an information agent." As underlined in [7], this latter distinction is more and more blurred because nowadays IR systems integrate personalized features and new criteria in addition to strict "matching" (using tags, social networks...). Furthermore, RS are based on information filtering techniques that have been considered since 1992 as close to IR techniques [17]. This latter paper also presents two figures illustrating the similarities between these two techniques. So, as a consequence IR and RS are two fields that share techniques: indexation models and similarity measures like the famous PageRank algorithm used by Google have been adapted to RS [18]. At the same time, CF techniques have also been integrated in IR process [19]. As a conclusion, IR and RS, having the same objective, are similar at a general point of view.

4 Social Web and Its Impact on IR and RS

During the last years the advent of Social Web has greatly changed the role of the Web users, providing them with the opportunity to become key actors, to share knowledge, opinions and tastes thanks to the interaction through on line media.

End users are playing an increasing active role within the recommendation process in several fields, and in particular in the e-commerce; in fact, both their choices and feedbacks on purchased items, and the folksonomies generated on them improve and enrich the recommendation process. Recently a new trend of e-commerce, the *Social Commerce*, has grown, leveraging Web 2.0 technologies and on line social media like blogs, web forums, virtual communities, and social networks. In the social shopping tools the customer ratings, their reviews, recommendations and referrals are fundamental to create a trusted environment. In particular, Social Commerce highlights two relevant aspects: the *friendship relations*, typical of social networks like Facebook, and the *word-of-mouth*, that generates the viral marketing. This is generated when customers promote a product or service by telling others about their positive experience with it [20].

In this context users contribute each other to the sale of goods and services due to their positive and negative feedbacks, reviews, ratings and testimonials regarding their past and present experiences [21].

Examples of relevant Social Commerce are the on-line purchase clubs, as Buy Vip and Vente-privee, the Facebook shops, like Wishpot, and the the on-line social coupon services, where promotional coupons are sold to customers for having discounts on several different items and services. See for example Glamoo and Kgb Deals.

Social Web and its impact on e-commerce become now available as new user knowledge, and offer great opportunities both for recommender technologies and IR techniques; these last in turn can positively stimulate the grow of social phenomenon, allowing more effective and personalized user interface.

4.1 RS and Social Web

Social tagging systems are recently receiving increasing attention from the scientific community: the growing number of scientific publications concerning this issue on one hand, and the development of real social tagging systems on the other, such as for example, BibSonomy, delicious, and Last.fm, confirm this tendence.

As deeply investigated in [3] through social Web applications users upload and share resources within a community, and mainly introduce personal and cheap classifications, applying on them specific tags. A tag is a term freely chosen by a user and it represents a meta data describing the item in order to be useful as a keyword to identify or to find later again a resource. The collection of all the tag assigned by a user constitutes her *personomy*, while the collection of all personomies in a system, is called *folksonomy*.

Due to the freedom of social annotation, it suffers from some limitations like (1) the *ambiguity* of tags which could be written using different lexical forms, (2) the *synonymy* or *polysemy* problem, (3) the different *levels of expertise* and *specificity* used for annotating resources. Nevertheless tags contain rich and potentially useful, social/semantic information, and their nature can be understood by analyzing the user motivations and goals in performing tagging activity. Using tags corresponds to a specific intent of a user, such as describe the aim of a resource, its content, the document type, some quality or property specification, the association of tasks to it as a self-reminder, and so on [22].

Tags are particularly used in social networks, social bookmarking applications, sharing systems, and recently also in the e-commerce field. In this extent the same *Amazon.com*, one of the bigger e-commerce applications, added to classical recommendations, a new recommendation mechanism based on the *amazon folksonomy*, generated by customer tagging activity.

Introducing folksonomies as basis for recommendations means that the usual binary relation between users and resources, which is largely employed by traditional RS, changes into a ternary relation between users, resources, and tags, more complex to manage.

Different surveys [4,3] analyze the use of social tagging activities for recommendations, focusing their attention in particular on the following aspects:

- **RS improvement thanks to tags:** an interesting overview on social tagging systems and their impact on RS is presented in [23]; while a methodology to improve RS thanks to Web 2.0 systems and particularly to social bookmarking platforms is offered by [24]; moreover, the same work [25] provides a recommender system model based on tags.
- **Role of tag recommendation:** the system presented in [26] exploits a factorization model to propose personalized tag recommendations, while the work [27] illustrates a strategy used in a Web page recommender system exploiting affinities between users and tags. In addition to these affinities, [28] proposes a recommender system exploiting tag popularity and representativeness to recommend web pages.
- **Tags & User modeling:** since RS rely on a user model to generally personalize recommendations, [29] proposes an original way to enhance modeling to improve tag recommendation. In a general context, [30] and [31] also illustrates how tag activity can improve user modeling.

Nevertheless very few works highlight how to employ folksonomies in the field of e-commerce recommendation: for example, in the e-commerce area, [32] proposes a product recommender system based on tagging features. This leads us to think that further researches, evaluation studies and insights are needed.

4.2 IR and Social Web

In this section we introduce a state of art related to Social IR, i.e. IR that uses folksonomies. From IR point of view, tags and particularly the relations between tags have been studied as a novel knowledge base related to information exploited in IR process:

- As a pull approach, users retrieving information need to understand what information is available to identify which one is relevant to their need. Tag cloud has been used in this context to offer an original and improved visual IR interface [33,34]. Such an interface allows user browsing information. A more powerful visualization based on tag clusters [35] is considered as better than tag cloud.

- FolkRank [36] is a new search algorithm for folksonomies. It can also be used to identify communities within the folksonomy that are used to adapt information ranking. This algorithm is inspired from the famous PageRank model from Google. Information ranking (scoring) has also been studied according to query [37]. Another document ranking based on relations extracted from (user, tag, resource) is illustrated in [38].
- IR have also been improved thanks to folksonomies and two original measures [39] SocialPageRank that computes the popularity of web pages, and SocialSimRank that calculates the similarity between tags and queries.
- Query expansion based on tag co-occurrence has been studied in [40], [41], [42]. Results show that such an approach consistently improves retrieval performance.

5 Current and New Perspectives

In previous sections we underlined that folksonomies have a real and positive impact on RS and IR even if only few works deal with the use of folksonomies to improve e-commerce. This section presents the potential contribution of IR to RS and then describes a set of trails we identified to improve recommendation using IR and folksonomies.

5.1 Contribution of IR for RS

As underlined in [4], "RS are characterized by *cross-fertilization* of various research fields such as: Information Retrieval, Artificial Intelligence, Knowledge Representation, Discovery and Data/Text Mining, Computational Learning and Intelligent and Adaptive Agents". As a result IR and RS research areas are complementary and can participate together to improve recommendation quality. Many examples have already shown on the role of IR for improving RS. Here, we describe the most representative works in this field in order to propose new trails to make converging IR & RS.

Similarity measures. In order to achieve efficient filtering, a similarity value has to be computed between user and item features. In this domain IR has a big experience. So, for instance [43] proposes the reformulation of the performance prediction problem in the field of IR to that of the RS. Moreover [44] defines information channels used in CF as close to the IR vector-space model.

RS process replacement. Following an original direction, in [45] the authors investigate the possibility to reformulate a collaborative RS problem in an IR one. They use common IR process as a part of the RS process and show they obtain a decrease of the MSRE (Mean Square Root Error) rather than a real collaborative RS. This paper presents "an experimental investigation of possible relations between IR and RS".

Prediction. [43] analyzes how to adapt the query clarity technique to CF to predict neighbor performance, and then use the proposed predictor within a CF algorithm, enhancing the selection and weighting of neighbors.

5.2 Possible Contribution of IR for RS

Previous section present recent works related to RS improvements using IR techniques. As we can see, these works are quite recent and many other trails could be investigated. Indeed, to achieve its aim an IR system relies on an effective information process: indexing. Recently, IR indexing schemes integrate external evidence sources (i.e. folksonomies and social networks) to characterize in a more precise way information content. Indeed, we can ascertain that the information raw content itself is not sufficient and today work consider more usage-based characteristics. Such work is emergent and huge trails in this scope have been identified. RS may benefit from this evolution of IR indexing techniques and related similarity measures. Moreover another IR trend concerns the way IR systems model communities and users in a more contextual way. Such improvement allows IR systems to better meet users' needs and requirements and can be applied to RS to enhance matching between users for instance. Next sections illustrates the most representative improvements that IR techniques can provide to RS.

Data source selection issue. In [46], the authors point out that important issues for RS are the selection of the most appropriate information source to get the most relevant information to be recommended and the integration of the information. A response to the selection issue can be inspired by IR works such as GlOSS [47] that aims to better describe any source content to improve its selection. More recently, works related to integrated IR (sometimes called desktop search [48]) emerged bringing hints to address source integration issue. Such IR techniques may be applied to RS to identify adapted information sources that could be suitable to compute more accurate recommendations. Furthermore RS may compute more diversified recommendation list thanks to these various information sources and adapted IR similarity measures.

User & Item modeling. Personalized features are more and more developed in IR. For example, in the context of personalized search, folksonomy-based user and document profiles [49], [50] have been proposed to improve IR techniques. Such modeling could be adapted to RS in order to improve recommendation accuracy and more particularly the way the matching between users is computed thanks to adapted IR similarity measures. To limit the required resources and to decrease the number of processed tags, Peters et al. [51] for instance propose to only consider relevant tags called "power tags". In addition, some IR techniques have been proposed aiming at identifying user behavior and interests through implicit modeling [52] and determining the kind of information searched [48]. Such techniques could be integrated to RS in order to improve contextual user modeling.

Cold-start issue. An important issue in RS concerns new users [53]. Indeed, RS might have enough information related to a new user to recommend relevant information. In addition to IR user modeling techniques, community identification techniques applied to IR (i.e. [36]) can be used for instance as stereotypes in order to tackle cold-start issue.

5.3 Possible Evolution of RS for E-Commerce

The improvement of RS allowed by IR (cf. section 5.2) can be directly applied to e-commerce context i.e. cold-start, scalability, similarity measures, user & item modeling. Other evolutions could be adapted to e-commerce to improve recommendations.

Filtering information issue. In order to improve content-based recommendations for e-commerce as explained in section 5.2, one might exploit semantic retrieval techniques to identify (filter) items to be recommended to a specific user. For instance, [54] describes a product IR system based on opinion mining or unlike [55] exploits an ontology to identify/filter products.

Data source selection issue. To improve data source selection for e-commerce, one might propose to associate metadata to common data sources for every product or product category. Such metadata could be based on tags, ratings or comments on these data sources.

6 Conclusion

Folksonomies in IR and RS are mostly considered as an additional knowledge base related to the relations between users, resources and tags. Through these relations, systems can improve for instance resource or user modeling. Such techniques are quite developed in IR field and would be quickly adapted to RS. Indeed, this is a high value-added knowledge base because coming from real users' activity.

In this paper, we proposed a perspective view of the convergence of folksonomy, IR and RS to improve recommendations related to information. Some trails are encouraging; as highlighted by [45], a full association between IR and RS could be envisaged. We identified a set of perspectives that compose our future research road-map towards the implementation of these trails in e-commerce context (i.e. considering product as a specific information).

References

1. Ricci, F., Rokach, L., Shapira, B., Kantor, P.B. (eds.): Recommender Systems Handbook, 1st edn. Hardcover (2011)
2. Jannach, D., Zanker, M., Felfernig, A., Friedrich, G. (eds.): Recommender Systems An Introduction. Hardback (November 2010)
3. Dattolo, A., Ferrara, F., Tasso, C.: On social semantic relations for recommending tags and resources using folksonomies. In: Hippe, Z.S., Kulikowski, J.L., Mroczek, T. (eds.) Human-Computer Systems Interaction. Backgrounds and Applications, vol. 2. Springer, Heidelberg (in press)
4. Kumar, A., Thambidurai, P.: Collaborative web recommendation systems a survey approach. Global Journal of Computer Science and Technology 9(5), 30–36 (2010)
5. Schafer, B.J., Konstan, J., Riedl, J.: Recommender systems in e-commerce. In: ACM Conference on Electronic Commerce, pp. 158–166 (1999)

6. Zimmermann, H.D.: From eCommerce to eCommerce 2.0: The Changing Role of the Customer. In: Antlová, K. (ed.) Proceedings of the Liberec Informatics Forum, November 4-5, pp. 171–179 (2010)
7. Burke, R.: The adaptive web, pp. 377–408. Springer, Heidelberg (2007)
8. Malone, T.W., Grant, K.R., Turbak, F.A., Brobst, S.A., Cohen, M.D.: Intelligent information-sharing systems. Commun. ACM 30, 390–402 (1987)
9. Ramezani, M., Bergman, L., Thompson, R., Burke, R., Mobasher, B.: Selecting and applying recommendation technology. In: International Workshop on Recommendation and Collaboration in Conjunction with 2008 International ACM Conference on Intelligent User Interfaces, IUI 2008 (2008)
10. Salton, G.: Automatic Information Organization and Retrieval. McGraw Hill Text, New York (1968)
11. Manning, C.D., Raghavan, P., Schtze, H.: Introduction to Information Retrieval. Cambridge University Press, New York (2008)
12. Salton, G., Wong, A., Yang, C.S.: A vector space model for automatic indexing. Commun. ACM 18, 613–620 (1975)
13. Robertson, S.E.: The probabilistic character of relevance. Inf. Process. Manage. 13(4), 247–251 (1977)
14. Ponte, J.M., Croft, W.B.: A language modeling approach to information retrieval. In: Proceedings of the 21st Annual International ACM SIGIR Conference on Research and Development in Information Retrieval, SIGIR 1998, pp. 275–281. ACM, New York (1998)
15. Salton, G., Buckley, C.: Term-weighting approaches in automatic text retrieval. Inf. Process. Manage. 24(5), 513–523 (1988)
16. Robertson, S.E., Walker, S., Hancock-Beaulieu, M., Willet, P.: Okapi at TREC-7: Automatic ad hoc, filtering, VLC and interactive track. In: TREC-7: The 7th Text REtrieval Conference, National Institute of Standards and Technology (NIST), pp. 253–264 (1998)
17. Belkin, N.J., Croft, W.B.: Information filtering and information retrieval: two sides of the same coin? Commun. ACM 35, 29–38 (1992)
18. Jiang, F., Wang, Z.: Pagerank-based collaborative filtering recommendation. In: Zhu, R., Zhang, Y., Liu, B., Liu, C. (eds.) ICICA 2010. LNCS, vol. 6377, pp. 597–604. Springer, Heidelberg (2010)
19. Jeon, H., Kim, T., Choi, J.: Personalized information retrieval by using adaptive user profiling and collaborative filtering. AISS 2(4), 134–142 (2010)
20. Linda, ling Lai, S.: Social commerce: e-commerce in social media context. World Academy of Science, Engineering and Technology, 39–44 (2010)
21. Weisberg, J., Te'eni, D., Russo, M.L.A.: Past purchase and intention to purchase in e-commerce: the mediation of social presence and trust. Internet Research 21(1) (2011)
22. Golder, S.A., Huberman, B.A.: Usage patterns of collaborative tagging systems. J. Inf. Sci. 32, 198–208 (2006)
23. Milicevic, A., Nanopoulos, A., Ivanovic, M.: Social tagging in recommender systems: a survey of the state-of-the-art and possible extensions. Artificial Intelligence Review 33, 187–209 (2010), 10.1007/s10462-009-9153-2
24. Siersdorfer, S., Sizov, S.: Social recommender systems for web 2.0 folksonomies. In: Proceedings of the 20th ACM Conference on Hypertext and Hypermedia, HT 2009, pp. 261–270. ACM, New York (2009)
25. Xia, X., Zhang, S., Li, X.: A personalized recommendation model based on social tags. In: DBTA 2010, pp. 1–5 (2010)

26. Rendle, S., Lars, S.T.: Pairwise interaction tensor factorization for personalized tag recommendation. In: Proceedings of the Third ACM International Conference on Web Search and Data Mining, WSDM 2010, pp. 81–90. ACM, New York (2010)
27. Niwa, S., Doi, T., Honiden, S.: Web page recommender system based on folksonomy mining for itng 2006 submissions. In: Proceedings of the Third International Conference on Information Technology: New Generations, pp. 388–393. IEEE Computer Society, Washington, DC (2006)
28. Durao, F., Dolog, P.: A personalized tag-based recommendation in social web systems. Adaptation and Personalization for Web 2.0, 40 (2009)
29. Wetzker, R., Zimmermann, C., Bauckhage, C., Albayrak, S.: I tag, you tag: translating tags for advanced user models. In: WSDM 2010, pp. 71–80 (2010)
30. Carmagnola, F., Cena, F., Cortassa, O., Gena, C., Torre, I.: Towards a tag-based user model: How can user model benefit from tags? In: Conati, C., McCoy, K., Paliouras, G. (eds.) UM 2007. LNCS (LNAI), vol. 4511, pp. 445–449. Springer, Heidelberg (2007)
31. Simpson, E., Butler, M.H.: Collaborative and Social Information Retrieval and Access: Techniques for Improved User Modeling, IGI Global, pp. 43–64 (2009)
32. Jiao, Y., Cao, G.: A collaborative tagging system for personalized recommendation in b2c electronic commerce. In: International Conference on Wireless Communications, Networking and Mobile Computing, WiCom 2007, pp. 3609–3612 (September 2007)
33. Hassan-Montero, Y., Herrero-Solana, V.: Improving tag-clouds as visual information retrieval interfaces. In: InScit 2006: International Conference on Multidisciplinary Information Sciences and Technologies (2006)
34. Bar-Ilan, J., Zhitomirsky-Geffet, M., Miller, Y., Shoham, S.: Tag, cloud and ontology based retrieval of images. In: Proceeding of the Third Symposium on Information Interaction in Context, IIiX 2010, pp. 85–94. ACM, New York (2010)
35. Knautz, K., Soubusta, S., Stock, W.G.: Tag clusters as information retrieval interfaces. In: Proceedings of the 2010 43rd Hawaii International Conference on System Sciences, HICSS 2010, pp. 1–10. IEEE Computer Society, Washington, DC (2010)
36. Hotho, A., Jäschke, R., Schmitz, C., Stumme, G.: Information retrieval in folksonomies: Search and ranking. In: Sure, Y., Domingue, J. (eds.) ESWC 2006. LNCS, vol. 4011, pp. 411–426. Springer, Heidelberg (2006)
37. Liu, D., Hua, X.S., Wang, M., Zhang, H.: Boost search relevance for tag-based social image retrieval. In: Proceedings of the 2009 IEEE International Conference on Multimedia and Expo, ICME 2009, pp. 1636–1639. IEEE Press, Piscataway (2009)
38. Bender, M., Crecelius, T., Kacimi, M., Michel, S., Neumann, T., Parreira, J.X., Schenkel, R., Weikum, G.: Exploiting social relations for query expansion and result ranking. In: Data Engineering for Blogs, Social Media, and Web 2.0, ICDE 2008 Workshops, pp. 501–506 (2008)
39. Bao, S., Xue, G., Wu, X., Yu, Y., Fei, B., Su, Z.: Optimizing web search using social annotations. In: Proceedings of the 16th International Conference on World Wide Web, WWW 2007, pp. 501–510. ACM, New York (2007)
40. Wang, J., Davison, B.D.: Explorations in tag suggestion and query expansion. In: Proceeding of the 2008 ACM Workshop on Search in Social Media, SSM 2008, pp. 43–50. ACM, New York (2008)

41. Biancalana, C., Micarelli, A.: Social tagging in query expansion: A new way for personalized web search. In: Proceedings IEEE CSE 2009, 12th IEEE International Conference on Computational Science and Engineering, August 29-31, pp. 1060–1065. IEEE Computer Society, Vancouver (2009)
42. Jin, S., Lin, H., Su, S.: Query expansion based on folksonomy tag co-occurrence analysis. In: 2009 IEEE International Conference on Granular Computing, pp. 300–305. IEEE, Los Alamitos (2009)
43. Bellogín, A., Castells, P.: A performance prediction approach to enhance collaborative filtering performance. In: Gurrin, C., He, Y., Kazai, G., Kruschwitz, U., Little, S., Roelleke, T., Rüger, S., van Rijsbergen, K. (eds.) ECIR 2010. LNCS, vol. 5993, pp. 382–393. Springer, Heidelberg (2010)
44. Gemmell, J., Schimoler, T., Mobasher, B., Burke, R.D.: Resource recommendation in collaborative tagging applications. In: Buccafurri, F., Semeraro, G. (eds.) EC-Web 2010. LNBIP, vol. 61, pp. 1–12. Springer, Heidelberg (2010)
45. Costa, A., Roda, F.: Recommender systems by means of information retrieval. CoRR (a more recent version of this paper will be published in WIMS 2011) abs/1008.4815 (2010)
46. Aciar, S., Herrera, J.L., de la Rosa, J.L.: Integrating information sources for recommender systems. In: CCIA 2005, pp. 421–428 (2005)
47. Gravano, L., García-Molina, H., Tomasic, A.: Gloss: text-source discovery over the internet. ACM Trans. Database Syst. 24, 229–264 (1999)
48. Kim, J., Croft, W.B.: Ranking using multiple document types in desktop search. In: Proceeding of the 33rd International ACM SIGIR Conference on Research and Development in Information Retrieval, SIGIR 2010, pp. 50–57. ACM, New York (2010)
49. Vallet, D., Cantador, I., Jose, J.: Personalizing Web Search with Folksonomy-Based User and Document Profiles. In: Gurrin, C., He, Y., Kazai, G., Kruschwitz, U., Little, S., Roelleke, T., Rüger, S., van Rijsbergen, K. (eds.) ECIR 2010. LNCS, vol. 5993, pp. 420–431. Springer, Heidelberg (2010)
50. Lu, C., Hu, X., Chen, X., Park, J.R., He, T., Li, Z.: The topic-perspective model for social tagging systems. In: Proceedings of the 16th ACM SIGKDD International Conference on Knowledge Discovery and Data Mining, KDD 2010, pp. 683–692. ACM, New York (2010)
51. Peters, I., Stock, W.G.: Power tags in information retrieval. Library Hi Tech. 28(1), 81–93 (2010)
52. Shen, X., Tan, B., Zhai, C.: Implicit user modeling for personalized search. In: Proceedings of the 14th ACM International Conference on Information and Knowledge Management, CIKM 2005, pp. 824–831. ACM, New York (2005)
53. Lam, X.N., Vu, T., Le, T.D., Duong, A.D.: Addressing cold-start problem in recommendation systems. In: Proceedings of the 2nd International Conference on Ubiquitous Information Management and Communication, ICUIMC 2008, pp. 208–211. ACM, New York (2008)
54. Wei, H., Xin, C., Haibo, W.: Product information retrieval based on opinion mining. In: 2010 Seventh International Conference on Fuzzy Systems and Knowledge Discovery (FSKD), vol. 5, pp. 2489–2492 (August 2010)
55. Zhang, L., Zhu, M., Huang, W.: A Framework for an Ontology-based E-commerce Product Information Retrieval System. Journal of Computers 4(6), 436–443 (2009)

An Exploratory Work in Using Comparisons Instead of Ratings

Nicolas Jones[1], Armelle Brun[1], Anne Boyer[1], Ahmad Hamad[2]

[1]LORIA - Nancy Université, KIWI Group
[2] Sailendra SAS
BP 239, 54506 Vandœuvre-lès-Nancy, France
{nicolas.jones,armelle.brun,anne.boyer,ahmad.hamad}@loria.fr

Abstract. With the evolution of the Web, users are now encouraged to express their preferences on items. These are often conveyed through a rating value on a multi-point rating scale (for example from one to five). Ratings have however several known drawbacks, such as imprecision and inconsistency. We propose a new modality to express preferences: comparing items ("I prefer x to y"). In this initial work, we conduct two user-studies to understand the possible relevance of comparisons. This work shows that users are favorably predisposed to adopt this new modality. Moreover, it shows that preferences expressed as ratings are coherent with preferences expressed trough comparisons, and to some extent equivalent. As a proof of concept, a recommender is implemented using comparison data, where we show encouraging results when confronted to a classical rating-based recommender. As a consequence, asking users to express their preferences through comparisons, in place of ratings, is a promising new modality for preference-expression.

1 Introduction

With the emergence of the Web 2.0, users are encouraged to express their preferences about events, websites, products, etc. These preferences are exploited by personalized services to adapt the content to each user. For example, the collaborative filtering (CF) approach in recommender systems uses these preferences to suggest some items that comply with users' tastes and expectations.

Users' preferences can be expressed with text in natural language or with tags. They may also be expressed under the form of a *rating*-score on a multi-point scale. This modality has become one of the most popular ways of expressing one's preferences, specifically in e-services. The success of ratings is, in parts, due to the fact that they are automatically processable. They can be transformed into numerical values (if not yet numeric) and many operations can be conducted on them such as users' or items' average rating. Due to this facility, some algorithms have been designed to transform users' opinions expressed in natural language or with tags into a value point on the rating scale [14].

At the same time, ratings only require a small amount of time to express one's preferences. They are generally perceived as an easy task, but several works have

C. Huemer and T. Setzer (Eds.): EC-Web 2011, LNBIP 85, pp. 184–195, 2011.

highlighted important drawbacks, among which inconsistencies of ratings and limited precision [9,1]. We ask if we could not find another modality that would be as easy as ratings and that would not have ratings' drawbacks.

In this paper we propose a new modality based on the following acknowledgement: in everyday life, rating items is not such a natural mechanism. Indeed, we do not rate sweaters when we want to buy one. It is more likely that we will compare them two by two, and purchase the preferred one. Based on this observation, we propose to get users' overall preferences by asking them to *compare* pairs of items in place of asking them to rate them ("I prefer x to y").

In an exploratory work [3], we had shown that comparisons could be used as input preference data of a CF system and that, in some cases, the accuracy of the recommendations was comparable to that obtained with ratings. In this paper we focus on the relevance of this new modality, taking the user's point of view into account. We specifically concentrate on the way users perceive this modality, whether they express preferences similar to those revealed when rating items, and confront the quality of the recommendations deduced from each modality. After presenting the limitations of ratings, particularly in recommender systems, we focus on two user-studies we conducted to gather users' overall preferences on both expression modalities. We subsequently address three research questions: 1) Are users in favor of this new modality for expressing their preferences? 2) Is there a mapping between users' preferences expressed with both modalities? 3) Is the accuracy of the recommendations similar when they express their preferences by comparisons of items and by rating them? In this preliminary work, we discuss possible answers to these questions and show that asking users to compare items in place of rating them is a highly promising modality, especially for CF.

2 Related Work

2.1 Expressing Preferences with Ratings

Multi-point rating scales have become one of the most common feedback modalities. A great deal of research has studied the use of ratings as input preference data, but the fundamental issue of the optimal number of points in rating scales is still unresolved [12]. Several drawbacks have been identified: inconsistency, limited precision and influence of labels. We introduce these issues hereafter.

Inconsistency. Users' ratings face the well-known intra-user variability issue, also referred to as inconsistency or noise. This inconsistency may have several explanations. First, it is difficult to quantify one's preferences and to assign a rating point. Second, the mood and the context may influence the rating we assign to an item. Third, the granularity of scales may conduct to incoherences: if a scale is too large, users may have too many choices and assign different rating values to two equally liked items, or to one item at two different times [13]. When users are asked to rate items twice, their inconsistency has been evaluated at 40% [9]. A more recent work in recommenders showed that the noise in ratings may lead to a variation of the RMSE of more than 40% [1].

Limited precision. In many rating systems, the granularity of the scale is quite small, which may limit the discrimination power of ratings and thus their precision. A user might judge two items differently but give them the same score due to the limited scale. As a consequence, small scales may lead to imprecise ratings and possibly frustrated users [9]. In addition, although users' preferences are not linear (on a five-point rating scale there is a larger difference between a 2 and a 3 than between a 4 and a 5), the scales are processed as if they were, such as in CF; it may thus impact the quality of such systems [7].

Psychometric researches measured the reliability of different scales, with respect to granularity [12]. They showed that the less accurate scales (in terms of reliability, discriminating power and users' preferences) turn out to be those with the fewest number of rating points.

Maximal scale point. Because scales are bounded, once users have given the maximal rate to an item, they cannot express that any other item is better. This may have substantial consequences, as highly appreciated items are generally those that most reflect users' preferences. Recently, a first step towards the automatic customization of scales was achieved. Cena *et. al* showed that there is not always a bijection between two scales, confirming that their granularity influences the preferences expressed [7].

Influence of the meaning associated with the value points. It has been proven that, given a scale granularity, the values of the points and the descriptive labels associated with scale points have psychological influence on users, resulting in differences in the distribution of the ratings [2].

2.2 Expressing Preferences with Comparisons

The comparisons that we propose in this paper share some similarity with four feedback mechanisms, detailed in [11]. Whilst showing users an ideal item, they propose alternatives and use users' feedback to revise the current search query. *Value elicitation* and *tweaking* are two feature-level techniques, whereas *rating-based* and *preference-based* feedback methods operate at the case (or item) level. A popular version of the latter approach is *critiquing*, as proposed and studied by Pu and Chen [8]. A critique is for instance the feedback "I would like something cheaper than this item".

Despite these approaches relying on the act of comparing items, we are convinced that they are fundamentally different from our proposed *comparisons*, both in terms of goal and data representation. These feedback strategies are often directed at helping users to find an ideal product, and modelize the tradeoffs between compared items in terms of varying features (then used to update the query). The novelty of our paper resides in the fact that we aim to model users' overall preferences: preference-based feedback, not those corresponding to the current goal of the user, and above all that we record the preference relation between items, independently of items' attributes.

3 Motivation for Comparing Items

3.1 Advantages of Comparing

In Section 2 we showed that asking users to rate items in order to express their preferences has several drawbacks. However, few alternative preference expression modalities have become as popular as ratings. Reflecting on how we behave in real-life, where we often end-up comparing two items rather than rating them, we propose to use comparisons as a new modality for expressing preferences. Thus, rather than saying "I like this item and I give it a four out of five", a user will say "I prefer j to i" ($i < j$), or "I prefer i to j"($i > j$), or "I appreciate them equally" ($i = j$).

We believe that comparing items can be more appropriate than ratings for expressing preferences, for the following reasons:

- First, we are convinced that comparing items is easier than giving them a score. By asking users to compare items, the problem of quantifying a preference (Section 2) is avoided. In addition, [6] showed that making comparisons is faster than absolute judgement (ratings). We thus hope that using comparisons will lead to a higher users' participation rate.
- Second, we believe that comparing is less inconsistent than ratings as, contrary to rating, there is no need to remember previously compared pairs to compare a new one.
- Third, the problem of limited precision (Section 2) of ratings is avoided. When comparing items, users have a local point of view, focused on the two items to be compared. The resulting comparisons, represented as a preference relation [3], is made up of an un-predefined and adaptive number of levels.

One of the drawbacks of using comparisons is the increase in the number of comparisons needed to establish a ranking of items [5]. Another disadvantage is that no quantitative information is known about "how much" the user prefers an item to another. These issues are not the focus of this paper, and ways to alleviate them are discussed in [10].

Convinced that the advantages outweigh these drawbacks, we trust that comparing items can be more appropriate than ratings for expressing preferences.

3.2 Algorithmic Predisposition of Comparisons

In our recent preliminary work [3], we proposed a formalization of CF where input data is a set of comparisons. We showed that the classical memory-based approach can be used with such data. We also conducted experiments to evaluate the adequacy and the performance associated with the use of comparisons in CF. As we did not have any input data made up of "real" comparisons at our disposal, we simulated such a dataset. We used a corpus of ratings that we converted into comparisons. The resulting comparisons had thus the same drawbacks as ratings: inconsistency and limited precision. Furthermore, the quantitative dimension of ratings was lost during the transformation into comparisons. Even so, the performance obtained was similar, and in some cases better to the one reached with ratings. We believe that these findings highlight the algorithmic predisposition of comparisons.

4 Experiments

4.1 Experiment Framework

We chose to work on the domain of motion pictures. We selected movies from the box-office, maximizing chances that users would be able to evaluate them. Our dataset was composed of 200 *films* and 150 *television series*. To run focused experiments, we built our own online website and relied on one evaluation page for each modality: *rating* or *comparing*. Both are shown in Figure 1 and displayed basic information (title of the movie, genre, year and poster). The rating page's feedback mechanism was a one to five star rating scale. The comparisons page displayed the same information but divided into two columns, A and B. Below both movies were three links that allowed users to express $a < b$, $a > b$ or $a = b$. For each movie, a large "I do not know this movie" button was available.

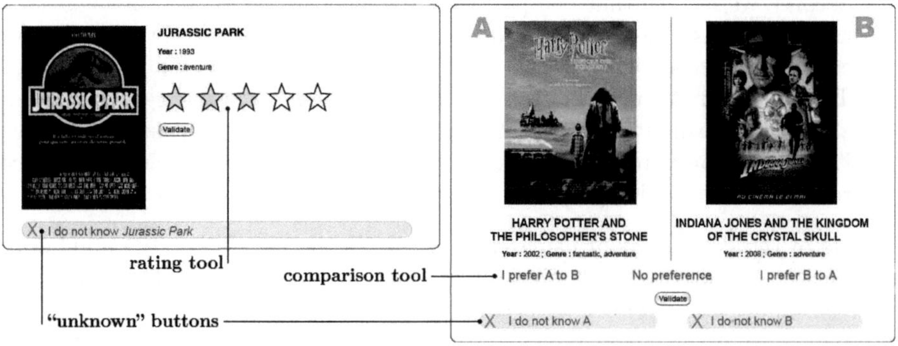

Fig. 1. The rating page (left) and comparison page (right) of the user-study

4.2 Evaluation Setup

We set up two user-studies. Experiment 1 sought to gather users' overall preferences between both expression modalities. We adopted a within-subject design: each user tried one modality (rating or comparing) on one dataset (films or tv series), before testing the opposite combination. Experiment 2 also relied on a within-subject design, but was more in-depth and aimed at understanding whether comparisons expressed the same preferences as ratings. For this reason, users first rated movies, and were then asked to compare pairs of the same movies the following day (the pairs of movies to be compared have been randomly selected within the set of rated movies). The one day gap was introduced to reduce the effects of learning and fatigue.

The general procedure in both studies was similar. Users received basic instructions, before starting a *three minute session* to either rate, or compare movies. Since a comparison concerns two items, rather than one for a rating, we decided to impose a fixed session duration. At the end of both sessions in Experiment 1, users were presented with three preference questions: Q1 Which evaluation modality did you prefer? – Q2 Which evaluation modality was the easiest to use? – Q3 Which evaluation modality was the fastest to use?

As an incentive, EUR 10.- gift vouchers were proposed in a draw to users who had completed a study. Experiment 1 collected 100 users, with 52 males and 48 females. Users were mainly young (71% in the 18-24 age group), French (77%), familiar with Internet (98% use it daily) and watched films at least once a week (50%). We therefore expect them to be comfortable with the new proposed comparison modality. Experiment 2 being more detailed, only 25 users were recruited but their demographic distribution was similar.

5 Results

In this section we will first present the findings from Experiment 1, that focus on users' acceptance of comparisons. We then study the correspondence between preferences expressed through ratings and comparisons from Experiment 2. Last we focus on the quality of recommendations made when exploiting either users' ratings or comparisons.

5.1 Are Users in Favor of Comparisons?

In Experiment 1, after all participants had experienced both the rating and comparison mechanism once, we gave them a questionnaire asking each user to vote on which modality (rating, comparison or neither) they had liked most. Figure 2 shows the distribution of the 100 users' answers. With Q1 we can observe that 53% of users preferred the comparisons, against 42% for the ratings. Q2 indicates that 56% of users found comparisons to be easier than ratings. The amount of uncertain people is here higher, reaching 11%. Finally, for Q3, more participants found that it was faster to do comparisons than to rate, at respectively 54% against 42%. A Chi-square test of independence confirms that there was no ordering effect.

Overall, these results show that users are in favor of the comparison mechanism. Under all three tested dimensions, users found that the comparing modality was better than the traditional and wide spread rating mechanism. This is very encouraging: one must not forget that users have been confronted to rating systems for many years, not only online but also in real-life, especially on a topic such as movies. This was the first time they were confronted to a comparison mechanism.

5.2 Do Users Express the Same When Comparing and Rating?

In this section, we analyze the preferences expressed by the users in Experiment 2: when they compare items two by two versus when they rate items.

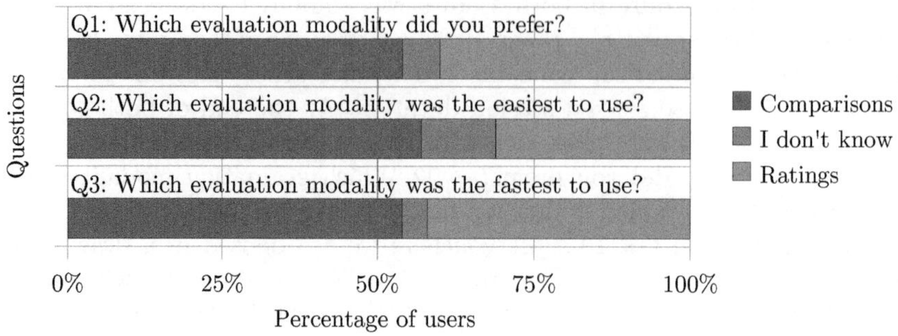

Fig. 2. Users' preferences between rating and comparison

The dataset containing the comparisons will be referred to as *CompDS* and the one containing ratings will be referred to as *RatDS*. Note that on average 33 ratings/comparisons have been collected within the three minute sessions.

A direct linking between *CompDS* and *RatDS* cannot be performed. Indeed, not only is the input data in *CompDS* made up of ordered pairs of items whereas it is single items in *RatDS*, but also the preference value is a comparison ($<$, $>$ or $=$) in *CompDS* and a rating score (from 1 to 5) in *RatDS*. Consequently we decided to transform one dataset into the format of the second. As comparisons contain no quantitative information, converting them into ratings is a challenging task. Oppositely, transforming ordered pairs of rated items into comparisons is straightforward: we chose to apply this conversion. For instance, if user u rated the item i_1 with a 5 and i_2 with a 4, this information will become the comparison $i_1 > i_2$. To allow a correspondence-computation between ratings and comparisons, not all pairs of items have been transformed into comparisons: we chose to transform only the pairs which had been compared by users in *CompDS*. The resulting corpus will be referred to as *RatCompDS*.

Table 1. Distribution of comparison values according to the preference modality

	Comparisons (*CompDS*)	Ratings (*RatCompDS*)
$i_1 < i_2$	42.4%	39.0%
$i_1 > i_2$	45.9%	38.5%
$i_1 = i_2$	11.7%	22.5%

Table 1 presents the proportion of each comparison value ($<$, $>$ or $=$), for both modalities. First, we can see that the distribution of $<$ and $>$ is homogeneous in both modalities. Second, users assign identical ratings to pairs of items in 22.5% of the cases. However this is around twice more than the percentage of cases where they consider items as equivalent (11.7%) when they compare them.

Table 2 details the correspondence between preferences expressed in *CompDS* and those in *RatCompDS*. Each line of the table represents one comparison

Table 2. Correspondence of rating preferences and comparison preferences

		Ratings (*RatCompDS*)		
		$r(i_1) < r(i_2)$	$r(i_1) > r(i_2)$	$r(i_1) = r(i_2)$
Comparisons (*CompDS*)	$i_1 < i_2$	**74.1**	6.1	*19.8*
	$i_1 > i_2$	8.9	**71.3**	*19.8*
	$i_1 = i_2$	30.1	27.2	42.7

value in *CompDS*. They show the distribution of the ratings on the corresponding pairs of items in *RatCompDS*, and sum up to 100%.

When users compare two items and judge them as *different*: $i_1 < i_2$ or $i_1 > i_2$, the corresponding ratings have the same trend in respectively 74.1% and 71.3% (on average 72.7%) of the cases. In the remaining 27.3%, 19.8% correspond to equal ratings. This means that although users judge two items as being different through a comparison, they assign them both the same rating. This can be explained by the limited precision of ratings highlighted in Section 2. For this reason, we believe that it is reasonable to consider these 19.8% as non contradictory preferences. Consequently, we can say that when users judge two items as different through comparisons, in 92.5% of the cases they assiged coherent ratings: equal ratings or ratings with the same trend.

When users compare i_1 and i_2 and judge them as *equivalent*, they give them the same ratings in only 42.7% of the cases. When focusing on the 57.3% of remaining cases, 42% correspond to pairs of adjacent ratings (that differ by only 1 point). This high value may be explained by the inconsistencies of users' ratings presented in Section 2, and by the fact that no precise meaning had been associated to each rating value in the experiments. Thus, these 42% should be considered as coherent with the comparisons. Consequently, we believe that when users compare two items as being equivalent, the ratings are coherent with these comparisons in 84.7% of the cases: they assign them similar or adjacent ratings.

As a conclusion, we feel that it is reasonable to say that, although there is no direct mapping between ratings and comparisons, they are mainly coherent.

We conducted an additional evaluation, with the aim of studying the pertinence of exploiting comparisons in the frame of CF. We raise the following question: are the respective top-n (preferred) items the same in *RatDS* and *CompDS*? For each user u, we build the preference relation that corresponds to his/her comparisons (as done in [3]). The number of ranks of these preference relations varies according to the users, from 3 to 9 levels. We then ask if the items on the top ranks in the preference relations are the preferred items in terms of ratings? Figure 3 presents the distribution of the ratings according to the first three top-rank values in the preference relation. We can see that the items on the top of the preference relations (rank 1) are mainly items with rating values of 5 and 4 (average rating: 3.99). When the rank of the items increases, the average rating value decreases. The average rating of items in rank 2 is 3.07 and the one in rank 3 is 2.60. The graph supports that items highly ranked in the preference relation extracted from comparisons, tend to be those that have been preferred by users in the sense of ratings.

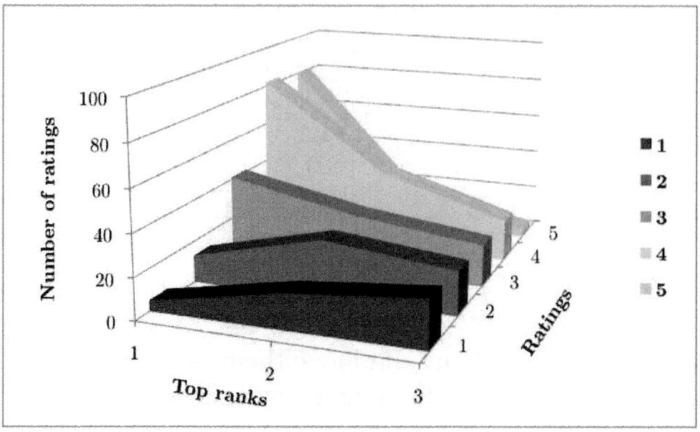

Fig. 3. Repartition of ratings in function of top ranks in preference relations

5.3 How Accurate Are the Recommendations from Both Modalities?

To obtain an initial impression of the potential of comparisons, we conducted a small-scale experiment in the frame of CF. We asked users to evaluate the quality of the recommendations generated with either of the two preference expression modalities. To build a recommendation list from ratings, we used a classical memory-based CF approach with the cosine measure as similarity between users [4], computed on users' preferences acquired from previous experiments. To build a recommendation list from comparisons, we used the above memory-based collaborative filtering, adapted to comparisons, as was already done in [3]. As we used the same recommendation algorithm in both cases, the quality of the recommendation lists are directly comparable. We built a recommendation list for only the 25 users from the second study; all the users from the first study were used to compute users' similarities.

First, we asked each user to rate the top 10 items from the recommendation list, they could rate (whether they had seen them or not). To ensure that each user can rate 10 items (and that the resulting rating lists are comparable) we presented recommendation lists of 30 ordered movies (starting from the best). Figure 4 presents, for each rating value, the average number of items that have been rated with this value, in each rated list. We can see that the average number of items which received a top rating value (5 and 4), is larger in the comparisons' lists. The ratings' lists contain more low rating values. The distribution of comparisons is centered around higher grades than for ratings.

Second, we collected users' global opinion on the recommendation lists by asking them which one they preferred. 16 users preferred the recommendations from comparisons against 9 for ratings. Without trying to read too far into these results[1], we can confidently say that our proof-of-concept worked: the

[1] Due to the small number of users, statistical tests could not be computed.

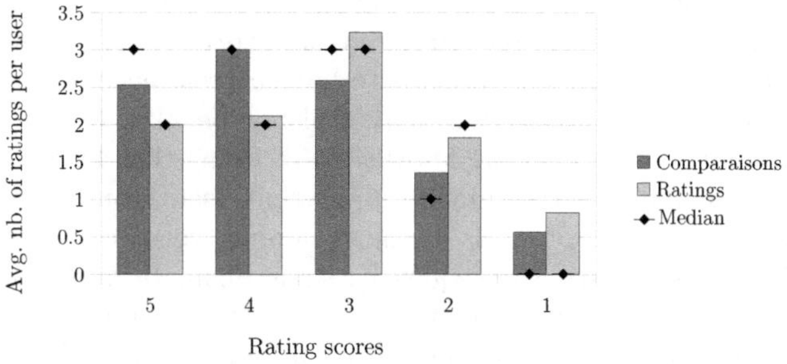

Fig. 4. Distribution of rating scores across the top-10 recommendations

comparisons appear to have generated recommendations at least as valuable to users, as a rating based approach. This finding confirms our exploratory work [3].

6 Discussion

Our results show that when focusing on pairs of items, comparisons are mainly coherent with ratings (in more than 85% of the comparisons). From a global point of view, the analysis of the preference relation versus the set of ratings also shows similar tendencies. Nevertheless, the two modalities are not equivalent and would deserve a more refined analysis. When we constructed the preference relations, we only made sure that all items were compared and connected in one single graph. Unfortunately, some relations (comparisons) are of high importance to build an accurate preference relation, whereas others can be useless. For instance, supposing we know that $i > j$, finding out that $k > j$ says little about the relation between i and k, whereas knowing that $k > i$ allows to propose that $k > i > j$ (in case we assume transitivity). Even though this issue has no consequence on the analysis of pairs of items, it influences the global perspective. Thus we believe that the comparative examination of both modalities could be refined by controlling which comparisons are presented to users [10].

The findings also reveal that the comparison modality solves the problem for choosing the optimal rating scale. Indeed, when asking users to compare items, they unconsciously build their own scale, with the granularity that fits their preferences. We observed that for some users, three levels are enough, whereas others need up to nine levels of ranking (within the three-minute timeframe). We are therefore confident that comparisons can be an excellent answer to the problem of customizing rating scales, raised in [7].

In the case of inconsistencies in comparisons, the task of de-noising preferences is facilitated. Indeed, the relation between two items can be known or deduced from several relations in the preference relation. Thus, in the case of inconsistencies in preferences, the choice of the edges to be kept is facilitated (for example by using a majority vote).

Our results showed that, although quite similar to ratings, comparisons seem to allow users to express finer preferences, especially when users' ratings were equal. However, reflecting on long-term perspectives, we do not yet envisage to solely exploit preferences acquired through comparisons. Because of the qualitative nature of comparisons, it is possible to have a preference relation, made up of several levels, where the top item may still not be liked by the user. When exploiting comparisons in CF, the knowledge of items that have actually been liked is crucial so as to not recommend items that users would not like. At the same time, as the number of levels in the preference relation grows, this quantitative problem disappears. Consequently, some absolute preferences (such as ratings), might be useful to ensure the accuracy of recommendations at first, and we envisage to hybridize both modalities in our future work.

We believe that we could exploit ratings to establish a first classification, before refining the highly rated items by using comparisons. However, we cannot envisage to ask users to express their preferences with both modalities. To solve this problem, we could collect users' implicit feedback from which we could deduce ratings, viewed as an additional information to comparisons. We could also use this deduced information to identify appreciated items and refine by asking users to compare them.

7 Conclusion

The most popular modality for expressing one's preferences is rating: on a predefined multi-point scale, we choose the point that reflects best our preference. However, although several studies have put forward drawbacks of ratings (inconsistency, limited precision, etc.), no other modality has yet supplanted ratings. We have proposed an alternative: comparisons, that asks users to compare pairs of items. To assess the pertinence of this modality, we performed two user-studies. We show that users are in favor of comparisons as they find them easier, faster and on the whole prefer them. Our results also reveal that comparisons express preferences similar to those of ratings, as ranks in preference relations seem to be coherent with ratings. To finish this inital work, we generate recommendations based on either ratings or comparisons, and show that comparisons give very promising results. Consequently, we are convinced that comparisons are a highly promising new modality for preference expression, that could possibly improve the user experience, especially in the frame of collaborative filtering.

These initial findings encourage us to explore comparisons in depth. We are studying the stability of comparisons through time *vs.* that of ratings. To cope with the problem of the large number of comparisons required, we focus on a strategy about the sequences of comparisons to be asked to users, in order to build a precise preference relation while minimizing the number of comparisons asked to users.

References

1. Amatriain, X., Pujol, J.M., Oliver, N.: I like it.. I like it not: Evaluating User Ratings Noise in Recommender Systems. In: Proc. of UMAP Conf. (2009)
2. Amoo, T., Friedman, H.: Do numeric values influence subjects' responses to rating scales? J. of International Marketing and Marketing Research 26, 41–46 (2001)

3. Brun, A., Hamad, A., Buffet, O., Boyer, A.: Towards preference relations in recommender systems. In: Workshop on Preference Learning at ECML-PKDD (2010)
4. Candillier, L., Meyer, F., Boullé, M.: Comparing state-of-the-art collaborative filtering systems. In: Proc. of 5th International Conference on Machine Learning and Data Mining in Pattern Recognition (MLMD), pp. 548–562 (2007)
5. Carterette, B., Bennett, P.: Evaluation measures for preference judgments. In: Proc. of the Annual ACM SIGIR Conference, pp. 685–686 (2008)
6. Carterette, B., Bennett, P., Chickering, D., Dumais, S.: Here or there; preference judgments for relevance. In: Proc. of ECIR, pp. 16–27 (2008)
7. Cena, F., Vernero, F., Gena, C.: Towards a customization of rating scales in adaptive systems. In: Proc. of the User Modeling, Adaptation, and Personalization (UMAP), pp. 369–374 (2010)
8. Chen, L., Pu, P.: Experiments on the preference-based organization interface in recommender systems. ACM Trans. Comput.-Hum. Interact 17, 5:1–5:33 (2010)
9. Cosley, D., Lam, S., Albert, I., Konstan, J., Riedl, J.: Is seeing believing?: how recommender system interfaces affect users' opinions. In: Proc. of the Intelligent User Interfaces (IUI) (2003)
10. Jones, N., Brun, A., Boyer, A.: Initial Perspectives From Preferences Expressed Through Comparisons. In: Int. Conf. on Human-Computer Interaction (July 2011)
11. McGinty, L., Smyth, B.: Comparison-based recommendation. In: Craw, S., Preece, A.D. (eds.) ECCBR 2002. LNCS (LNAI), vol. 2416, pp. 575–589. Springer, Heidelberg (2002)
12. Preston, C., Colman, A.: Optimal number of response categories in rating scales: reliability, validity, discriminating power, and respondent preferences. Acta Psychologica 104(1), 1–15 (2000)
13. Schafer, B., Frankowski, D., Herlocker, J., Sen, S.: Collaborative Filtering Recommender Systems. In: The Adaptive Web. Methods and Strategies of Web Personalization, pp. 291–324. Springer, Heidelberg (2007)
14. Turney, P.: Thumbs up or thumbs down? semantic orientation applied to unsupervised classification of reviews. In: Proc. of the Association for Computational Linguistics (ACL), pp. 417–424 (2002)

Understanding Recommendations by Reading the Clouds

Fatih Gedikli, Mouzhi Ge, and Dietmar Jannach

Technische Universität Dortmund,
44221 Dortmund, Germany
firstname.lastname@tu-dortmund.de

Abstract. Current research has shown the important role of explanation facilities in recommender systems based on the observation that explanations can significantly influence the user-perceived quality of such a system. In this paper we present and evaluate explanation interfaces in the form of *tag clouds*, which are a frequently used visualization and interaction technique on the Web. We report the result of a user study in which we compare the performance of two new explanation methods based on personalized and non-personalized tag clouds with a previous explanation approach. Overall, the results show that explanations based on tag clouds are not only well-accepted by the users but can also help to improve the efficiency and effectiveness of the explanation process. Furthermore, we provide first insights on the value of personalizing explanations based on the recently-proposed concept of item-specific tag preferences.

Keywords: recommender systems, collaborative filtering, explanations, tag clouds, tag preferences.

1 Introduction

The capability of a recommender system (RS) to explain the underlying reasons for its proposals to the user has increasingly gained in importance over the last years both in academia and industry. Amazon.com, for example, as one of the world's largest online retailers, allows their online users not only to view the reasons for its recommendations but also to influence the recommendation process and exclude individual past purchases from the recommendation process.

Already early research studies in the area – such as the one by Herlocker et al. [1] – have shown that the provision of explanations and transparency of the recommendation process can help to increase the user's acceptance of collaborative filtering RS. Later on, Tintarev and Masthoff [2] analyzed in greater detail the various goals that one can try to achieve with the help of an explanation facility. Among other aims, good explanations could help the user to make his or her decision more quickly, convince a customer to buy something, or develop trust in the system as a whole.

The question, however, is not only what makes a *good* explanation but also how can we automatically construct explanations which are *understandable* for

C. Huemer and T. Setzer (Eds.): EC-Web 2011, LNBIP 85, pp. 196–208, 2011.

the online user. With respect to the second aspect, Herlocker et al. for example experimented with different visual representations such as histograms of the user's neighbors' ratings. Later, Bilgic and Mooney [3] however observed that such neighborhood-style explanations are good at promoting items but make it harder for users to evaluate the true quality of a recommended item. Thus, they introduced a different, text-based explanation style ("keyword-style explanations") in order to overcome this problem which can in the long term lead to dissatisfaction with the system.

In this work we propose to use *tag clouds* as a means to explain the recommendations made by an RS because tag clouds have become a popular means in recent years to visualize and summarize the main contents, e.g., of a web page or news article. Our hypothesis is that tag clouds are more suitable than keyword-style explanations to achieve the following typical goals of an explanation capability: user satisfaction, efficiency, and effectiveness. As a whole, by achieving these goals, we aim to also increase the users' overall *trust* in the RS.

The paper is organized as follows. In Section 2, we summarize previous works in the area. Section 3 describes the different explanation interfaces, which we evaluated in a user study. Details of the study as well as the discussion of the results are finally presented in Sections 4 and 5 respectively.

2 Previous Works

The concept of explanation has been widely discussed in the research of intelligent systems, especially in knowledge-based systems. An explanation facility enables a system to provide understandable decision support and an accountable problem solving strategy. Therefore explanation is considered as one of the important and valuable features of knowledge-based systems [4]. In recent years, the concept of explanations has also been studied and adopted in the area of recommender systems. An explanation can be considered as a piece of information that is presented in a communication process to serve different goals, such as exposing the reasoning behind a recommendation [1] or enabling more advanced communication patterns between a selling agent and a buying agent [5].

To clarify the goals of providing explanations in recommender systems, Tintarev and Masthoff [2] conduct a systematic review and identify seven goals: transparency (explaining why a particular recommendation is made), scrutability (allowing interaction between user and system), trust (increasing the user's confidence in the system), effectiveness (helping the users make better decisions), persuasiveness (changing the user's buying behavior), efficiency (reducing the time used to complete a task) and satisfaction (increasing usability and enjoyment). In this paper, we propose novel explanation methods and analyze them in line with four of these goals: efficiency, effectiveness, satisfaction and trust.

Efficiency means the ability of an explanation to help decreasing the user's decision-making effort. One direct measurement is to compute the time difference of completing the same task with and without an explanation facility or across different explanation facilities. For example, in the user study of Pu and Chen [6], the authors present two different explanation interfaces to users and compared the time needed to locate a desired item in each interface. *Effectiveness* relates to whether an explanation helps users making high-quality decisions. One possible approach to measure effectiveness is to examine if the user is satisfied with his or her decision. Besides, persuasiveness can be inferred from the study of effectiveness. Vig et al. [7] present four kinds of explanations to users and let users rate how well different explanations help the users decide whether they like a recommended item. An explanation which helps user make better decisions, is considered effective. Compared with persuasiveness, Bilgic and Mooney [3] argue that effectiveness is more important than persuasiveness in the long run as greater effectiveness can help to establish trust and attract users. *Satisfaction* refers to the extent of how useful and enjoyable an explanation helps the users to assess the quality of a recommended item. In the context of recommender system, *trust* can be seen as a user's willingness to believe in the appropriateness of the recommendations and making use of the recommender system's capabilities [8]. Trust can thus be used to determine the extent of how credible and reliable the system is. Tintarev and Masthoff [2] admit the difficulty of measuring trust and suggest measuring it through user loyalty and increased sales. We believe that it is also possible to implicitly examine trust by inferring it from the positive effects of efficiency, effectiveness and satisfaction.

Additionally, note that developing high-quality explanations in recommender systems can further profit from considering different views from related research communities such as intelligent systems, human-computer interaction and information systems. In this paper, we therefore extend the works of [9] and [10] and study the state-of-the-art user interface of tag clouds. Using this interface, we aim to provide an innovative and personalized user interface to achieve higher recommender quality.

3 Explanation Interfaces

In this section we will provide an overview of the three different explanation interfaces, which were evaluated in this work: keyword style explanations (KSE), tag clouds (TC), and personalized tag clouds (PTC). KSE, which relies on automatically extracted keywords from item descriptions, is used as the baseline method because this visualization approach has performed best according to effectiveness in previous work. The new methods TC and PTC, however, make use of user-contributed tags, which are a highly popular means of organizing and retrieving content in the Web 2.0.

Keyword-Style Explanations (KSE). The KSE interface as shown in Figure 1 has performed the best in the study by Bilgic and Mooney [3]. The interface consists of a top-20 list of keywords, which are assumed to be the most important ones for the user. Note that KSE – in contrast to the other interfaces – does not make use of user-generated tags at all. Instead, it relies on keywords that are automatically extracted from the content description of each item. Internally, an item description has different "slots". Each slot represents a "bag of words",

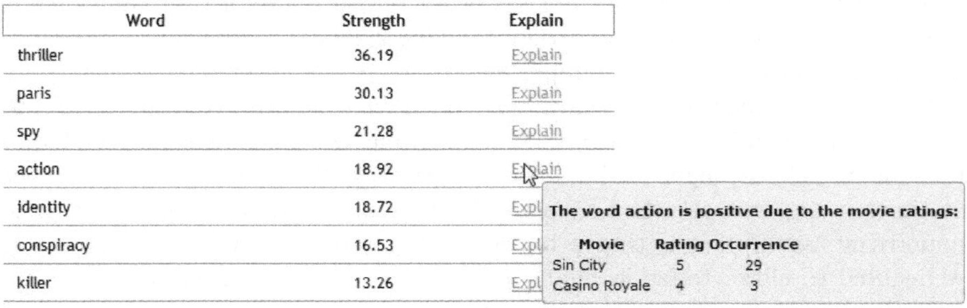

Fig. 1. Keyword style explanation (KSE)

that is, an unordered set of words together with their frequencies. Since we are considering the movie domain in our study, we organize a movie's content description using the following five slots: director, actors, genre, description and related-titles. We have collected relevant keywords about director, actors, genre and related-titles from the IMDb website and the MovieLens data set[1]. The data for the description slot was collected by crawling movie reviews in Amazon as well as synopsis information collected from Amazon, Wikipedia and moviepilot[2].

In the KSE-style approach, the importance of a keyword is calculated using the following formula: $strength(k) = t * userStrength(k)$, where t stands for the number of times the keyword k appears in slot s. The function $userStrength(k)$ expresses the target user's affinity towards a given keyword. This aspect is estimated by measuring the odd ratios for a given user, that is, how much more likely a keyword will appear in a positively rated example than in a negatively rated one. More formally: $P(k|\text{positive classification})/P(k|\text{negative classification})$. A naïve Bayesian text classifier is used for estimating the probabilities. More details about the KSE-style interface are given in [3].

Beside the list of important keywords, the KSE explanation interface provides a link ("Explain") for each keyword that opens a pop-up window containing all the movies that the user has rated which contain the respective keyword. In this pop-up window the user is provided with both the user's past rating for the movie and the number of times the keyword appears in the corresponding slot.

Note that in [3], the KSE approach performed best in the book domain with respect to effectiveness. However, the evaluation of efficiency and satisfaction was not part of their work but will be analyzed in our study.

Tag Clouds (TC). Tag clouds as shown in Figure 2 (a) have become a frequently used visualization and interaction technique on the Web. They are often incorporated in Social Web platforms such as Delicious and Flickr[3] and are used to visually present a set of words or user-generated tags. In such tag clouds, attributes of tags such as font size, weight or color can be varied to represent

[1] http://www.imdb.com, http://www.grouplens.org/node/73
[2] http://www.amazon.com, http://www.wikipedia.org, http://www.moviepilot.de
[3] http://www.del.icio.us, http://www.flickr.com

relevant properties like relevancy or frequency of a keyword or tag. Additionally, the position of the tags can be varied. Usually, however, the tags in a cloud are sorted alphabetically from the upper left corner to the lower right corner.

In our basic approach of using tag clouds as a not-yet-explored means to explain recommendations, we only varied the font size of the tags, i.e., the larger the font size, the stronger the importance of the tag. We simply used the number of times a tag was attached to a movie as a metric of its importance. The underlying assumption is that a tag which is often used by the community is well-suited to characterize its main aspects. For all other visual attributes we used the standard settings (font sizes etc.). In our future work we also want to analyze the influence of these attributes in explanation scenarios.

Figure 2 (a) shows an example for a movie explanation using the TC interface. Tags such as "Quentin Tarantino" or "violence" have been used by many people and are thus displayed in a larger font size.

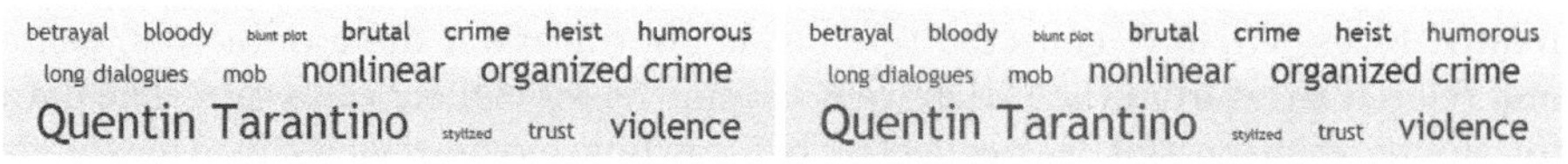

(a) Tag cloud (TC) (b) Personalized tag cloud (PTC)

Fig. 2. Tag cloud explanation interfaces

Personalized Tag Clouds (PTC). Figure 2 (b) finally shows an interface called personalized tag cloud (PTC), which unlike the TC interface is able to exploit the concept of item-specific *tag preferences* [11,12]. The idea of tag preferences is that users should be allowed to assign preferences to tags in order to express their feelings about the recommendable items in more detail. Thus users are not limited to the one single overall vote anymore. In the movie domain, tag preferences can give us valuable information about what users particularly liked/disliked about a certain movie, e.g., the actors or the plot. The PTC interface represents a first attempt to exploit such tag preferences for explanation purposes.

In contrast to the TC interface, we vary the color of the tags according to the user's preference attached to the tag. Blue-colored tags are used to highlight aspects of the movie toward which the user has a positive feeling, whereas tags with a negative connotation are shown in red. Neutral tags, for which no particular preference is known, are shown in black. Again, the font size is used to visualize the importance or quality of a tag. An example of the PTC interface for a crime movie is shown in Figure 2 (b). According to the explanation, the user is assumed to like this movie because of its director *Quentin Tarantino*, whereas *violence* and *brutality* are reasons not to watch this movie.

As explanations are usually presented for items which the user does not know yet, we have to first *predict* the user's feeling about the tags attached to a movie. For this purpose, we analyze the tag preference distribution of the target user's nearest neighbors and decide whether the target user will like, dislike or feel neutral about the item features represented by these tags. In order to predict a preference for a particular tag, the neighbors preferences for this tag are summed up and normalized to our preference scale for tags. Note that in our study users were able to give preferences to tags on a 5-point scale with half-point increments (0.5 to 5). If the normalized preference lies between $[0.5, 2.0]$ or $[3.5, 5.0]$, we will assume negative or positive connotation respectively; otherwise we will assume that the user feels neutral about the tag.

It is important to know that the interfaces KSE and PTC are personalized, whereas TC represents a non-personalized explanation interface.

4 Experimental Setup

We have conducted a between-subjects user study in which each subject was confronted with all explanation interfaces presented above. In this section, we will shortly review the experimental setup which consisted of two phases.

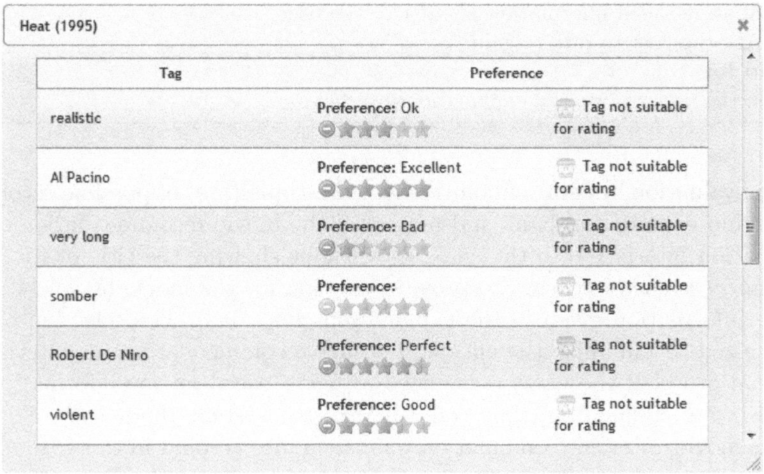

Fig. 3. Rating (tags of) the movie *Heat (1995)* on a Likert scale of 0.5 to 5

Experiment - phase 1. In the first phase of the experiment, the participants were asked to provide preference information about movies and tags to build the user profiles. The users had to rate at least 15 out of 100 movies[4]. After rating a movie, a screen was shown (Figure 3) in which users could rate up to 15 tags assigned to the movie[5]. On this screen, users could rate an arbitrary number of tags; skip tags, in case they thought that they were not suitable for a given movie; or explicitly mark tags as inappropriate for rating. Note that users were not allowed to apply their own tags as we want to ensure that we have a reasonable overlap in the used tags.

[4] We have limited the number of movies to 100 in order to be able to find nearest neighbors in the PTC approach.

[5] The tags were taken from the "Movie-Lens 10M Ratings, 100k Tags" data set (http://www.grouplens.org/node/73).

Experiment - phase 2. In the second phase, which took place a few weeks after the first session, the subjects used an RS[6] which presented them movie recommendations based on the user profile from the first phase. In addition, the different explanation interfaces were shown to the user. In the following, we will introduce our evaluation procedure which extends the procedure proposed by Bilgic and Mooney [3]:

Procedure 1. User evaluation

```
 1: R = Set of recommendations for the user.
 2: E = Set of explanation interfaces KSE, TC, PTC.
 3: for all randomly chosen (r, e) in R x E do
 4:    Present explanation using interface e for recommendation r to the user.
 5:    Ask the user to rate r and measure the time taken by the user.
 6: end for
 7: for all recommendation r in R do
 8:    Show detailed information about r to the user.
 9:    Ask the user to rate r again.
10: end for
11: Ask the user to rate the explanation interfaces.
```

The evaluation system randomly selected a tuple (r, e) of possible recommendation and explanation pairs and presented the movie recommendation r using explanation interface e to the end-user without showing the title of the movie. The user was then expected to provide a rating for the movie by solely relying on the information given in the explanation (lines 1-6). The selection order is randomized to minimize the effects of seeing recommendations or interfaces in a special order. If the users recognized a movie based on the information presented in an explanation, they could inform the system about that. No rating for this movie/interface combination was taken into account in this case to avoid biasing effects. We additionally measured the time needed by the users to submit a rating as to measure the *efficiency* of the user interface. These steps were repeated for all movie/interface combinations. Afterwards, we again presented the recommendations to the user, this time showing the complete movie title and links to the corresponding movie information pages at Wikipedia, Amazon and IMDb. We provided information about movies to reduce the time needed for completing the experiment since watching the recommended movies would be too time consuming. The users were instructed to read the detailed information about the recommended movies and then asked to rate the movies again (lines 7-10). According to [3], from the point of view of an end-user, a good explanation system can minimize the difference between ratings provided in the lines 5 (explanation rating) and 9 (actual rating). Thus we can also measure *effectiveness/persuasiveness* by calculating the rating differences. At the end of the experiment, the users were asked to give feedback on the different explanation interfaces (as to measure *satisfaction* with the system) by rating the system as

[6] We used a classical user-based collaborative filtering algorithm.

a whole on a 0.5 (lowest) to 5 (highest) rating scale (line 11). Again, the order was randomized to account for biasing effects.

5 Empirical Evaluation

5.1 Participants

We recruited 19 participants (four female) from five different countries. Most of them were students at our institution with their age ranging from 22 to 37 (average age was 28 years). Ten participants declared high interest in movies, whereas eight were only to a certain extent interested in movies. One person was not interested in movies at all.

5.2 Collected Data

The participants provided a total of 353 overall movie ratings and 5,295 tag preferences. On average, each user provided 19 movie ratings and 279 tag preferences and assigned 15 tag preferences to each rated movie. Because participants were also allowed to repeat phase 2 of our user study, we collected a total of 848 explanation ratings (on average 45 ratings per user).

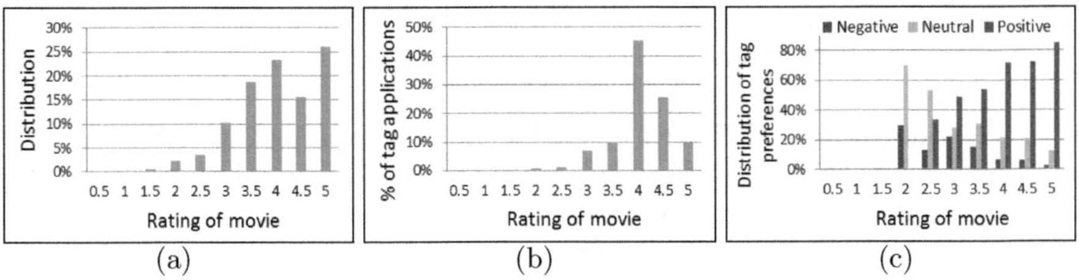

Fig. 4. Distribution of (a) movie ratings, (b) tag applications over movie ratings and (c) negative, neutral and positive tags applied to movies with different ratings

Figure 4 (a) shows the distribution of the movie ratings collected in our study. It can be seen that users preferred to rate movies they liked, i.e., a *positivity bias* is present among the participants which is in line with the findings of other researchers [13,12]. Vig et al. [12] showed that the positivity bias is also present for the taggers, that is, taggers apply more tags to movies they liked compared to movies they rated badly. This finding is also consistent with our results, as shown in Figure 4 (b). Users applied four times more tags to movies they rated with 4 or higher compared to movies to which they gave less than 4 points. Figure 4 (b) shows another interesting effect, which is only partly visible in the data of Vig et al. [12]. Users applied seven times more tags to movies rated with 4 or 4.5 points compared to movies rated with 5 points – the highest rating value – although there are more movies rated with 5 points than with 4 or 4.5

points, as shown in Figure 4 (a). We believe that this effect may be due to users' demand for justifying non-5-point ratings, i.e., users want to explain to the community *why*, in their opinion, a particular movie does not deserve a 5 point rating.

Figure 4 (c) finally shows the distribution of negative, neutral and positive tags applied to movies with different ratings[7]. As expected, a user's movie rating has a strong influence on the tag preferences assigned to a movie. The number of positive (negative) tag preferences increases (decreases) with the overall movie rating. Again, the results are comparable with those reported in [12].

5.3 Hypotheses, Results and Discussion

We tested three hypotheses. First, we hypothesized that the tag cloud interfaces TC and PTC enable users to make decisions faster (**H1**:Efficiency). We believe this as we think the visual nature of a tag cloud allows users to grasp the content information inside a cloud faster compared to KSE, which are organized in a more complex tabular structure. We also believe that users enjoy explanations from TC and PTC more than in the KSE style as we assume that tag cloud explanations are easier to interpret for the end user (**H2**:Satisfaction). We further conjecture that users make better buying decisions when their decision is based on TC or PTC rather than KSE (**H3**:Effectiveness). We believe this because we think that compared to TC or PTC, there is a higher risk of misinterpreting KSE because users always have to consider both the keyword and its corresponding numerical importance value, whereas in TC and PTC the importance is encoded in the font size of a tag.

In the following we will have a closer look at the results which are summarized in Table 1. Note that throughout this work we have used the Friedman test with the corresponding post-hoc Nemenyi test as suggested by Demšar [14] for a comparison of more than two systems.

Table 1. (a) Mean time for submitting a rating. (b) Mean response of the users to each explanation interface. (c) Mean difference of explanation ratings and actual ratings. Bold figures indicate numbers that are significantly different from the base cases (N is the sample size and α is the significance level).

		KSE	TC	PTC	N	α
(a)	Mean time [sec]	30.72	**13.53**	**10.66**	60	0.05
	Standard deviation	19.72	8.52	5.44		
(b)	Mean interface rating	1.87	**3.74**	**3.87**	19	0.05
	Standard deviation	0.90	0.65	0.62		
(c)	Mean difference	-0.46	**-0.13**	**-0.08**	283	0.05
	Standard deviation	1.00	1.01	1.03		
	Pearson correlation	0.54	0.79	0.83		

[7] For clarity reasons, we have classified the tag preferences into the tag preference groups *negative* (< 2.5 points), *neutral* ($2.5 - 3$ points) and *positive* (> 3 points).

Efficiency. To test our hypothesis of improved efficiency of tag clouds, we analyzed the time measurement data which was automatically collected in our study. Table 1 (a) shows the mean times (in seconds) for submitting a rating after seeing the corresponding explanation interface. We can see that the time needed when using the tag cloud approaches is significantly shorter than for KSE. Thus, we can conclude that the data supports hypothesis H1. The data also indicates that the PTC method helps users to make decisions slightly faster than the TC approach, but the difference was not statistically significant.

Satisfaction. Table 1 (b) shows the mean response on overall satisfaction of 19 users to each explanation interface based on a Likert scale of 0.5 to 5. It can be seen that users prefer the PTC approach over the TC presentation style and the TC style over the KSE method, which supports hypothesis H2. Again, the differences between the keyword-style explanations and the tag cloud interfaces are significant but no significant difference among the tag cloud interfaces could be found although the data indicates that users favor PTC-style explanations. One possible reason is that tag clouds are in general capable of visualizing the context in a concise manner and can thus help users reduce the time needed to understand the context which in turn increases user satisfaction.

Effectiveness / Persuasiveness. Bilgic and Mooney [3] propose to measure effectiveness by calculating the rating differences between explanation rating and actual rating, as described in Section 4. If the difference is 0, the explanation and the actual rating will match perfectly, i.e., the explanation helps the user to accurately predict the quality of an item. Otherwise, if the difference is positive (negative), users will overestimate (underestimate) the quality of an item. In this context we talk about the persuasive power of an explanation system.

Table 1 (c) shows the mean difference of explanation ratings and actual ratings. The histograms showing the mean differences are presented in Figure 5.

The mean differences of the tag cloud interfaces are close to 0 which is an indication that the interfaces are valuable for users to accurately estimate the quality of an item. Note that we have also considered the Pearson correlation between explanation and actual ratings to account for averaging effects. From the user's point of view, a good explanation interface has a mean difference value of 0, a low standard deviation, and a high correlation between both rating values.

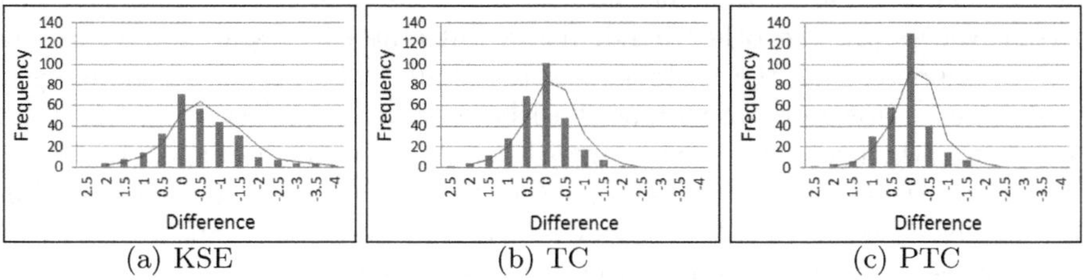

Fig. 5. Histograms showing the differences between interface and actual ratings

Users can estimate item quality most precisely with the help of the PTC interface. TC explanations are also a good estimator for item quality. The KSE interface has a significantly different value of −0.46 which means that KSE cause the user to underestimate the actual rating on average by −0.46. On a 5-point scale with half-point increments an underestimation of −0.46 on average can be considered as important. Note that in [3], KSE reached a value of 0. We think that the difference in the mean values comes from the different domains considered in our studies (movie domain vs. book domain). Overall the results support our last hypothesis H3.

Next we will discuss about the tradeoff between effectiveness and persuasiveness and the influence of persuasiveness on the user's trust in an RS.

Trust. As mentioned above, effectiveness can be measured by the rating difference before and after the consumption or inspection of a recommended item. Smaller differences are indicators of higher effectiveness. Therefore, if the rating for an item based only on the explanation is the same as the rating after the user has consumed the item, we can consider the explanation as highly effective. In the other case, the limited effectiveness will negatively impact on user satisfaction and the trust in the RS.

Consider the following case. A user rates an item with 4 (good) based only on the explanation. After consuming this item, however, the user rates the item with 2 (bad). This means that the user found this item is not as good as expected given only the explanation. In this scenario the user may consider the explanation to be not trustful. We call this effect *positive persuasiveness*, as the system successfully persuades the user to consume/buy the item. Conversely, if the user initially rates the item first with 2 and finally with 4, this means that the explanation does not correctly reflect the truth. In this case, the user may find the explanation to be inaccurate and lose the interest in using this system. We call this effect *negative persuasiveness*. Both positive and negative persuasiveness can cause the loss of trust to users.

The question remains, which form of persuasiveness is better. From a user's perspective, positive persuasiveness may leave the user with the impression that the system is cheating because the system overstates the advantages of the item. This may cause the user to completely abandon the system. However, from a business perspective, if a firm intents to promote a new product or convince the user to adapt a new version of a product, positive persuasiveness may help to increase effects of advertisement and user's familiarity to this product. Negative persuasiveness, on the other hand, has a different effect and may cause the user to suppose that the system does not really take his or her preferences into account. However, we assume it to be a rather "safe" strategy, if we are able to keep the negative persuasiveness level within a certain range. Overall, we argue that it is important to choose the direction of the persuasiveness according to different cases and goals. We can either align positive persuasiveness with the business strategy or control the negative persuasiveness at an acceptable level.

6 Summary

In this work, we have presented the results of a user study in which three explanation approaches were evaluated. We have compared keyword-style explanations, which performed best according to effectiveness in previous work, with two new explanation methods based on personalized and non-personalized tag clouds. The personalized tag cloud interface additionally makes use of the recent idea of item-specific tag preferences. We have evaluated the interfaces on the quality dimensions efficiency, satisfaction and effectiveness (persuasiveness) and discussed their impact on the user's trust in an RS.

The results show that users can make better decisions faster when using the tag cloud interfaces rather than the keyword-style explanations. In addition, users generally favored the tag cloud interfaces over keyword-style explanations. This is an interesting observation because users preferred even the non-personalized explanation interface TC over the personalized KSE interface. We assume that there are factors other than personalization such as the graphical representation, which play a crucial role for effective explanation interfaces. The results also indicate that users preferred PTC over TC. We believe that with PTC users need less time to come to an even better conclusion because the font color of a tag already visualizes a user's feeling about the tag and reduces the risk of misinterpreting a tag[8]. Although we view content and the visualization to be tightly interrelated in explanations (as done in previous works), we plan to run experiments in which we evaluate effects of content and visualization separately.

We believe that higher user satisfaction, efficiency, and effectiveness have positive impact on the users' overall trust in the RS which ensures user loyalty and long term wins. In future we want to show in a larger study that the differences between the TC and PTC approaches are significant.

Our future work includes the evaluation of further quality dimensions such as transparency; in addition, we plan to estimate a user's tag ratings automatically in order to reduce the time needed for completing the experiment. This way, we hope to be able to conduct broader studies which involve more test persons.

References

1. Herlocker, J.L., Konstan, J.A., Riedl, J.: Explaining collaborative filtering recommendations. In: CSCW 2000, New York, pp. 241–250 (2000)
2. Tintarev, N., Masthoff, J.: Effective explanations of recommendations: User-centered design. In: RecSys 2007, New York, pp. 153–156 (2007)
3. Bilgic, M., Mooney, R.J.: Explaining recommendations: Satisfaction vs. promotion. In: Beyond Personalization 2005, San Diego, pp. 13–18 (2005)
4. Berry, D.C., Broadbent, D.E.: Explanation and verbalization in a computer-assisted search task. Quart. Journ. of Experim. Psychology 39(4), 585–609 (1987)

[8] For example, consider the case where users see the tags *Bruce Willis* and *romantic movie* in a tag cloud and wonder whether they will like the performance of their action hero in a romantic movie.

5. Jannach, D., Zanker, M., Felfernig, A., Friedrich, G.: Recommender Systems - An Introduction. Cambridge University Press, Cambridge (2010)
6. Pu, P., Chen, L.: Trust building with expl. interfaces. In: IUI 2006, Sydney, pp. 93–100 (2006)
7. Vig, J., Sen, S., Riedl, J.: Tagsplanations: Explaining recommendations using tags. In: IUI 2009, Sanibel Island, Florida, pp. 47–56 (2009)
8. Cramer, H., Evers, V., Ramlal, S., Someren, M., Rutledge, L., Stash, N., Aroyo, L., Wielinga, B.: The effects of transparency on trust in and acceptance of a content-based art recommender. User Mod. and User-Adap. Inter. 18, 455–496 (2008)
9. Sen, S., Vig, J., Riedl, J.: Tagommenders: Connecting users to items through tags. In: WWW 2009, Madrid, pp. 671–680 (2009)
10. Kim, H.N., Ji, A.T., Ha, I., Jo, G.S.: Collaborative filtering based on collaborative tagging for enhancing the quality of recommendation. Electronic Commerce Research and Applications 9(1), 73–83 (2010)
11. Gedikli, F., Jannach, D.: Rating items by rating tags. In: RSWEB 2010, Barcelona, pp. 25–32 (2010)
12. Vig, J., Soukup, M., Sen, S., Riedl, J.: Tag expression: Tagging with feeling. In: UIST 2010, New York, pp. 323–332 (2010)
13. Marlin, B.M., Zemel, R.S., Roweis, S., Slaney, M.: Collaborative filtering and the missing at random assumption. In: UAI 2007, Vancouver, pp. 267–275 (2007)
14. Demšar, J.: Statistical comparisons of classifiers over multiple data sets. Journal of Machine Learning Research 7, 1–30 (2006)

Recommendation by Example in Social Annotation Systems

Jonathan Gemmell, Thomas Schimoler, Bamshad Mobasher, and Robin Burke

Center for Web Intelligence
School of Computing, DePaul University
Chicago, Illinois, USA
{jgemmell,tschimoler,mobasher,rburke}@cdm.depaul.edu

Abstract. Recommendation by example is common in contemporary Internet applications providing resources similar to a user-selected example. In this paper this task is considered as a function available within a social annotation system offering new ways to model both users and resources. Using three real-world datasets we motivate several conclusions. First, a personalized approach outperforms non-personalized approaches suggesting that users perceive the similarity between resources differently. Second, the manner in which users interact with social annotation systems vary producing datasets with variable characteristics and requiring different recommendation strategies to best satisfy their needs. Third, a hybrid recommender constructed from several component recommenders can produce superior results by exploiting multiple dimensions of the data. The hybrid remains powerful, flexible and extensible despite the underlying characteristics of the data.

Keywords: Social Annotation Systems, Resource Recommendation, Recommendation by Example, Personalization, Hybrid Recommendation.

1 Introduction

Recommendation by example is a ubiquitous function of modern Web applications. Users select a resource and the system provides an ordered list of similar resources. In the context of music a user may be listening to a song and ask the system to recommend related music. The characteristics of that resource may represent the user's intention better than textual keywords ever could. Selecting a song from the recommendation list will in turn produce a new recommendation. In this manner the user can seamlessly navigate through the resource space.

This type of recommendation is commonplace but typically it is not personalized. While recommendation by example must take into account the selected resource, we believe that the recommender engine must also take advantage of the user preferences. Two users, by way of example, may ask for more movies like the Maltese Falcon. One user may mean, "give me more hard-boiled detective movies" regardless of actor or year. Another may mean, "show me more Humphrey Bogart movies" and may not necessarily be focused on mysteries. A third may be satisfied with popular movies from the 1940s. Leveraging a user's profile the system can personalize the results in order to identify similar resources from the viewpoint of the user.

C. Huemer and T. Setzer (Eds.): EC-Web 2011, LNBIP 85, pp. 209–220, 2011.

For our experimental study we restrict our analysis to a particular type of application common in the Social Web, social annotation systems, in which users annotate online resources with arbitrary labels often called tags. The user's selection of which tags to apply to a resource provides insights about which characteristic of the resource are important to the user. Moreover if the user has applied identical tags to two different resources we can assume that the two resources are similar from the viewpoint of that user. Other users may describe those resources differently. Working under these assumptions, social annotations systems permit an experimental methodology for studying personalized recommendation by example.

In this paper several recommenders are evaluated. We use a recommender based on cosine similarity as a starting point, a simple algorithm that one might expect in a recommendation by example scenario. We further propose a linear weighted hybrid which leverages several component recommenders. The hybrid permits the flexible integration of other recommenders with the cosine similarity model. These personalized models based on collaborative filtering emphasize the user model rather than the model of the example resource.

Our results conducted on three real world datasets reveal that 1) personalization improves the performance of recommendation by example in social annotation systems, 2) the hybrid effectively exploits multiple components to produce superior results, 3) differences in the datasets require an emphasis on different components and 4) the flexibility of the proposed hybrid framework enables it to adapt to these differences.

The rest of the paper is organized as follows. In Section 2 we position our contribution to the field with regard to similar efforts. In Section 3 we formalize the notion of personalized resource recommendation by example and describe our linear-weighted hybrid in addition to the components from which it is formed. Our experimental results and evaluation follow in Section 4. Finally, we conclude the paper with a discussion of our results.

2 Related Work

The recommendation by example paradigm has long been a core component of E-commerce recommender and information retrieval systems [26,31]. Early important approaches to the problem include association rule mining [1] and content-based classification [16]. Work by Salton and Buckley [23] demonstrated the importance of user feedback in the retrieval process. Content-based filtering has been combined with collaborative filtering in several ways [2,3,20] in order to improve prediction effectiveness for personalized retrieval. More generally, hybrid recommender systems [4] have been shown to be an effective method of drawing out the best performance among several independent component algorithms. Our work here draws from this prior work in applying a hybrid recommender to the domain of social annotation systems and specifically accommodating a recommendation by example query.

There has been considerable work on the general recommendation problem in social annotation systems. Generalizable latent-variable retrieval model for annotation systems [30] can be used to determine resource relevance for queries of several forms. Tagging data was combined with classic collaborative filtering in order to further filter a user's domain of interest [27]. More recently, several techniques [12,13,17] have built upon and refined this earlier work. None of these approaches, however, deal with the possibility of resources themselves as queries.

Some work has been done in regards to resource-to-resource comparison in social annotation, although little in the way of direct recommendation. Some have considered the problem of measuring the similarity of resources (as well as tags) in a social annotation system by various means of aggregation [18]. An author-topic latent variable model has been used in order to determine web resources with identical functionality [21]. They do not, however, specifically seek to recommend resources to a particular user, but rather simply enable resource discovery utilizing the annotation data.

Our own previous work regarding annotation systems has focused on the use of tag clusters for personalized recommendation [11,29] and hybrid recommenders for both tag [6] and resource [7,8,10] recommendation. Here we extend our examination of a linear-weighted hybrid of simple algorithms for the specific problem of recommendation by example. This work further demonstrates the versatility and effective performance of this framework.

3 Recommendation by Example in Social Annotation Systems

We define resource recommendation as the production of an ordered list of resources likely to be of interest to a particular user. A special case of resource recommendation is one in which the user supplies a resource as an example. The system is required to recommend resources similar to the example. Taken as a sequence of recommendations the user can navigate from resource to resource exploring the resource space. This type of browsing is commonplace in applications recommending music, journal articles or consumer products just to name a few.

A key conjecture in this work is that personalization can be used to improve the user experience. Two users may perceive the similarity between resources differently. They may, for example, like a particular song but for different reasons. One enjoys the guitar solos. The other is influenced by the vocals. If these two users were to ask for similar songs, the recommendation engine must accommodate the differences in their taste.

In this work we limit our investigation of recommendation by example to social annotation systems, which enable users to annotate resources with tags. The collection of users, resources and tags provide a rich environment for users to explore. We call this space URT and view it as a three dimensional matrix in which an entry is 1 if u tagged r with t and is 0 otherwise.

A recommendation by example algorithm in this domain takes the form $\phi(u, r_q, r)$ where u is the user, r is potential recommendation and r_q is used by the recommender engine as an example. This function assigns a real-valued score to each potential recommendation describing its relevance to the user and the query resource. A system computing such a function can iterate over all possible resources and recommend the resources with the highest scores. The final result relieves users from the burden of information overload by providing a personalized view of the information space.

To tackle this problem we propose a linear-weighted hybrid algorithm constructed from simple components. The components vary in the information they capture. The models based on cosine similarity, for example, ignore the user profile and focuses on the example resource. The collaborative filtering algorithms focus more on the user profile. The hybrid is able to aggregate these simply models into a cohesive whole.

In general terms the hybrid is composed of recommendation components κ_1 through κ_k, whose output is combined by computing a weighted sum [4]. We assume that each component makes its own computation of the function $\phi_i(u, r_q, r)$. The output is normalized to be in the range $[0..1]$. Each component also has a weight α_i in the same range and we require that these values sum to 1. The hybrid is therefore defined as:

$$\phi(u, r_q, r) = \sum_{i=1}^{k} \alpha_i \phi_i(u, r_q, r) \tag{1}$$

To ascertain the correct α_i for each component we use a hill climbing technique, which is both simple and efficient. A subset of the data is selected as a holdout set for learning the algorithm parameters, including the α values. The α vector is initialized with random positive numbers. The recommender then operates over the holdout set, using the remaining data as training data. The accuracy of recommendations is calculated as described in Section 4.2. The vector is then randomly modified and tested again. If the accuracy is improved, the change is accepted; otherwise it is most often rejected. Occasionally a change to the α vector is accepted even when it does not improve the results in order to more fully explore the α space. Modifications continue until the vector stabilizes. Then the α vector is randomly reset and learning proceeds again.

Now we turn to the components that make up our hybrid. Many of these components rely on two-dimensional projections of the three dimensional annotation data [19]. Such projections reduce the dimensionality of the data, but sacrifice some of its informational content. For example, the relation between resources and tags can be defined as $RT(r, t)$, the number of users that have applied t to r.

$$RT(r, t) = \sum_{\forall u \in U} URT(u, r, t) \tag{2}$$

This notion strongly resembles the "bag-of-words" vector space model [24]. Similarly, we can produce a projection UT in which a user is modeled as a vector over the set of tags, where each weight, $UT(u, t)$, measures how often a user applied a particular tag across all resources. In all, there are six possible two-dimensional projections: UR, UT, RU, RT, TU, TR. In the case of UR, we have not found it useful to weight resources by the number of tags a user applies, as this is not always indicative of the user interest. Rather we define UR to be binary, indicating whether or not the user has annotated the resource.

CS_{rt} , CS_{ru} : Because users apply tags to resources, we can model resources as a vector of tags as taken from RT. This allows us to measure the cosine similarity between query resource and a potential recommendation. We call this technique CS_{rt}. However this approach is not personalized. Noticing that resources can also be described as a vector of users described by RU we can again use cosine similarity to judge the relevance of a resource to the example given by the user. We call this technique CS_{ru}.

KNN_{ur} , KNN_{ut} : These algorithms operate like the well-known user-based collaborative filtering algorithm [15,28]. We rely on a matrix of user profiles gathered from UR or UT. Depending on which projection is used we describe the component as either KNN_{ur} or KNN_{ut}. To make recommendations, we filter the potential neighbors to only those who have used the example resource r_q. We perform cosine similarity to find the k nearest neighbors and use these neighbors to recommend resources using a weighted sum based on user-user similarity. Filtering users by the query resource focuses the algorithm on the user's query but still leaves a great deal of room for resources dissimilar to the example. These approaches however are strongly personalized.

KNN_{ru} , KNN_{rt} : These algorithms are analogous to item-based collaborative filtering [5,25], which relies on discovering similarities among resources rather than among users. The projections RU (resources as vectors of users) and RT (resources as vectors of tags) are employed. This procedure ignores the query resource entirely, instead focusing on the similarity of the potential recommendations to those the user has already annotated. Again a weighted-sum is used as in common in collaborative filtering.

Each of these algorithms exploits different dimensions of the data and each has their own benefits and drawbacks. CS_{rt} focuses on the similarity between two resources but ignores the user preferences. KNN_{ru} and KNN_{rt} disregard the query resource and concentrates on the user history. Instead of attempting to integrate all dimensions of the data into a single cumbersome algorithm we rely on the hybrid to leverage the benefits of each of its component recommenders.

It should be noted that other integrative techniques have been proposed to leverage multiple dimensions of the data. In particular graph based approaches such as Adapted PageRank [14] and tensor factorization algorithms such as Pairwise Interaction Tensor Factorization [22] ($PITF$) have meet with great success in tag recommendation. However the computational requirements of Adapted Pagerank make it ill-suited for large scale deployment; a Pagerank vector must be calculated for each recommendation.

$PITF$ on the other hand offers a far better running time. Nevertheless adapting the tag recommendation algorithm to resource recommendation is not straightforward. First, $PITF$ prioritizes tags from both a user and resource model in order to make recommendations thereby reusing tags. In resource recommendation the algorithm cannot promote resources from the user profile as these are already known to the user. This requirement conflicts with the assumptions of the prioritization model; all possible recommendation are in effect treated as negative examples.

Second, tensor factorization methods, $PITF$ included, normally require an element from two of the data spaces in order to produce elements from the third. For example a user and resource can be used to produce tags. In recommendation by example the input is a user and a resource while the expected output also comes from the resource space. Furthermore in our investigation into tag-based resource recommendation [9], we found that collaborative filtering algorithms often outperform $PITF$. A fundamental advantage of the proposed linear weighted hybrid framework in comparison to other integrative models is that it can be adapted to wide variety of recommendation tasks.

4 Experimental Evaluation

In this section we describe the methods used to gather and pre-process our datasets. Our evaluation metrics and methodology are described. We then examine the results for each dataset, and finally draw some general conclusions.

4.1 Datasets

Our experiments were conducted using data from three large real-world social annotation systems. On all datasets we generate p-cores [14]. When possible we constructed 20-cores from the datasets. If the dataset was not large enough to render a 20-core, we instead constructed a 5-core.

Citeulike is a popular online tool used by researchers to manage and catalog journal articles. The site owners make their dataset freely available to download. Once a 5-core was computed, the remaining dataset contains 2,051 users, 5,376 resources, 3,343 tags and 105,873 annotations.

Amazon is America's largest online retailer. The site offers a myriad of ways for users to express opinions of the products. Recently Amazon has added social annotations to this list. After taking a 20-core of the data, it contained 498,217 annotations with 8,802 users, 10,679 resource and 5,559 tags.

LastFM users upload their music profiles, create playlists and share their musical tastes online. Users have the option to tag songs, artists or albums. The tagging data here is limited to album annotations. A p-core of 20 was drawn from the data. It contains 2,368 users, 2,350 resources, 1,141 tags and 172,177 annotations.

4.2 Methodology

While recommendation by example is an important area of study there does not exist to our knowledge social annotations datasets in which a user has explicitly stated he believes two items are similar. However in these systems a user applies tags to resources, in effect describing it in a way that is important to the user. We work under the assumption that if a user annotates two resources in the same way then these two resources are from the viewpoint of the user similar. Segmenting the results into cases in which one, two, three, four or five tags are in agreement allow us to analyze the results when there is very high probability that two resources are similar (when a user applies several similar tags to the resources) or when the probability is lower (when only a single tag is applied to both resources).

For each data set, we evenly divide it into five equal partitions. Four partitions were used as training data and the fifth was used for the learning of the parameters including the number of neighbors for the collaborative filtering approaches and the α values for the linear-weighted hybrid. That partition was then discarded and four-fold cross-validation was performed using these remaining four partitions. One partition P_h was selected as a holdout set and the remaining partitions served as training data for the recommenders.

To evaluate the recommendation by example algorithms, we iterated over all annotations in P_h. Each annotation contains a user, a resource and a set of tags applied by

Table 1. The α values for the components of the linear-weighted hybrid

	CS_{rt}	CS_{ru}	KNN_{ur}	KNN_{ut}	KNN_{ru}	KNN_{rt}
Citeulike	0.332	0.014	0.145	0.037	0.046	0.426
LastFM	0.077	0.082	0.035	0.075	0.682	0.049
Amazon	0.129	0.004	0.402	0.085	0.088	0.291

the user to the resource. We compare these tags to the tags in the user's annotations from the training data. If there is a match we generate a test case consisting of the user, the resource from the training data as the example resources and the resource from the holdout data as the target resource. The example resource and target resource may have one tag in common or several. We evaluate these cases separately looking at as many as five matching tags.

We use recall to evaluate the recommenders. It measures the percentage of items in the holdout set that appear in the recommendation set. Recall is a measure of completeness and is defined as $|R_h \cap R_r|/|R_h|$ where R_h is a set containing the target resource and R_r is the set containing the recommendations. We measure recall in the top 10 recommended items. Since each test case has only one target resource this measure is also known as *hit ratio*. The results are averaged for each user, averaged over all users, and finally averaged over all four folds.

4.3 Experimental Results

Figures 1 through 3 shows the results of our experiments. As per Section 4.2 we identify cases in which the user has annotated two resources with the same tags. Table 1 presents the learned α values of the component recommenders. The sum of these values is 1 and represents the relative contribution on the components. In the remainder of this section we discuss each dataset individually before concluding our paper with the general findings.

Citeulike. Citeulike users annotate journal articles. Its members are therefore mostly comprised of researches using the system to organize their library of related work. They often use tags drawn from their field and focus on articles within their area of expertise. The result is relatively clean datasets with strong dimensions relating tags to users and resources.

CS_{rt} does very well as one might expect. The tags applied to resources are indicative of their characteristics and using this data allows the algorithm to discover similar resources. KNN_{rt} is the second best performing component. This result is perhaps more surprising since it completely ignores the example resource. However this result is explainable by the nature of the user interactions found in Citeulike; users are focused on their area of expertise. Resources and tags in the user profile are strongly indicative of the user's interest making the user profile quite focused.

When performing item-based collaborative filtering in Citeulike it appears better to model resources as tags rather than users as shown by the relative performance of KNN_{ru} and KNN_{rt}. Likewise the cosine similarity model which describes resources

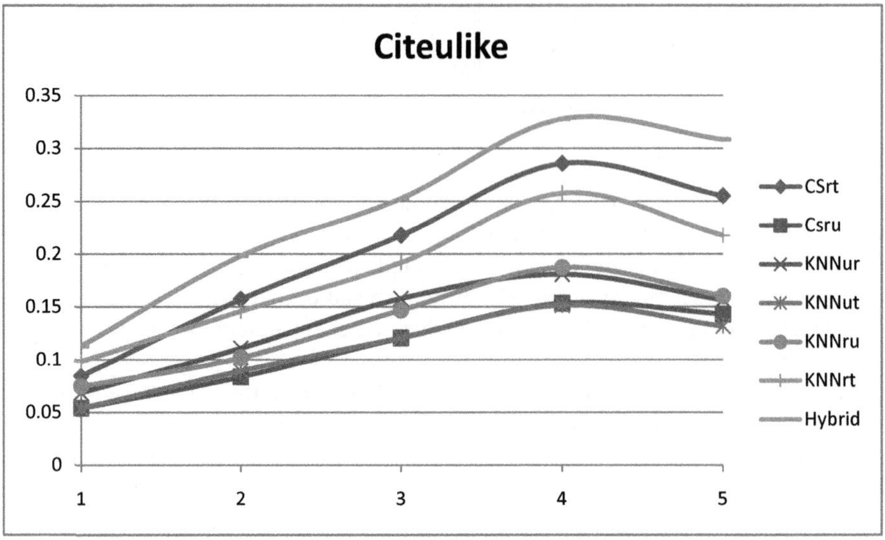

Fig. 1. Citeulike: The hit-ratio for six recommendation by examples algorithms for cases where there is an agreement of one through five tags. The hybrid is composed of all six techniques.

as tags outperform the method which models them as users. These results underscore the care which users exhibit when assigning keywords to resources, likely because they employ Citeulike to organize resources for latter retrieval.

The hybrid outperforms its constituent parts by as much as 5 percent. The α values shown in Table 1 reveal that the hybrid relies most strongly on CS_{rt} and KNN_{rt} the two strongest individual components. Yet KNN_{ur} also makes a strong showing accounting for almost 15% of the hybrid. This result shows that even though a technique may perform poorly alone, it may contribute unique information to a hybrid.

LastFM. LastFM users share their musical tastes and discover new music online. The site has evolved considerable overtime, but still allows its users to tag music (songs, artists or albums). As opposed to Citeulike its users take considerably less care when applying tags to resources. Generic tags such as 'rock' or non-descriptive tags such as 'album_i_own' are common. More often however the users interact with one another explicitly forming friendships, joining groups, comparing music tastes or browsing each other's profiles. This observation is confirmed in the relative performance of CS_{rt} and CS_{ru} as well as KNN_{ru} and KNN_{rt}. The user space is far more developed and modeling resources as users produces better results than modeling them as tags.

The collaborative approaches KNN_{ru} and KNN_{ur} which largely ignores the example resource outperforms the cosine similarity models which focuses entirely on the example. This result implies that in the music domain a user's profile is more important than the example he provides in a recommendation by example scenario.

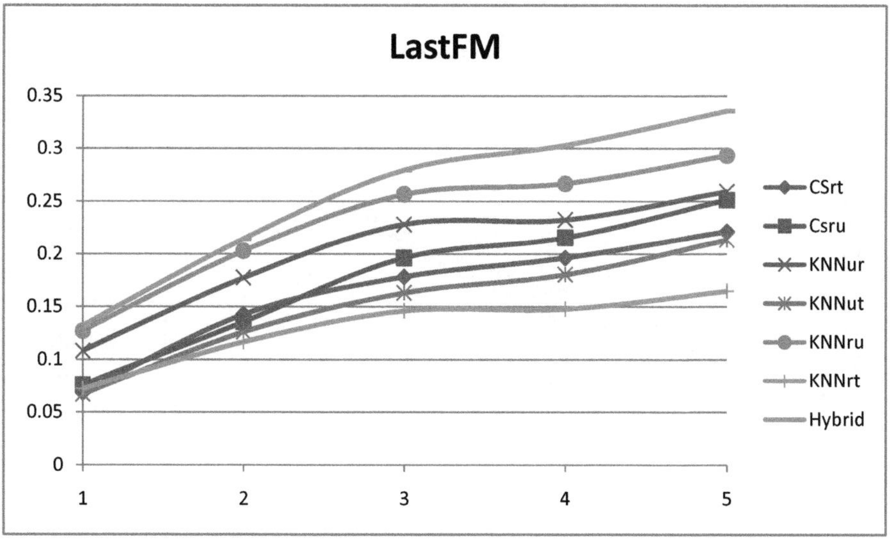

Fig. 2. LastFM: The hit-ratio for six recommendation by examples algorithms for cases where there is an agreement of one through five tags. The hybrid is composed of all six techniques.

The hybrid again outperforms its individual components again by as much as 5 percent. However, the contributions of the components differ. The hybrid is dominated by KNN_{ru} and the remaining components offer single digit contributions. In contrast to Citeulike which has several strong dimensions, LastFM's data is narrowed to the user-resource dimension. The remaining components play a small roll in the hybrid, but their complimentary information provide enough additional information to improve the performance of the hybrid.

Amazon. At the Amazon Web site customers are allowed to tag products. Often these tags are drawn from the product description such as 'HDTV'. Also the product space is easily separable – clothes and books, or mysteries and romance. Customers often focus on a few of these interests rather than annotating several disparate items. These characteristics make the Amazon data an easier target permitting as much as 70 percent hit ratio.

The simple components whether they draw on the relation between users and resources or resources and tags all perform equally well. Their equivalent performance might lead one to think that they are interchangeable. To the contrary when aggregated into a hybrid the proposed framework is able to leverage the benefits offered from each component. The individual components are exploiting different dimensions of the data.

While the hybrid outperforms its components once again we also see that it relies on different algorithms to do so. KNN_{ur} is the dominate recommender followed by KNN_{rt}. This is suggested by an understanding of how users interact with the Web site. They focus on particular domains forming a strong user-resource relation. Moreover

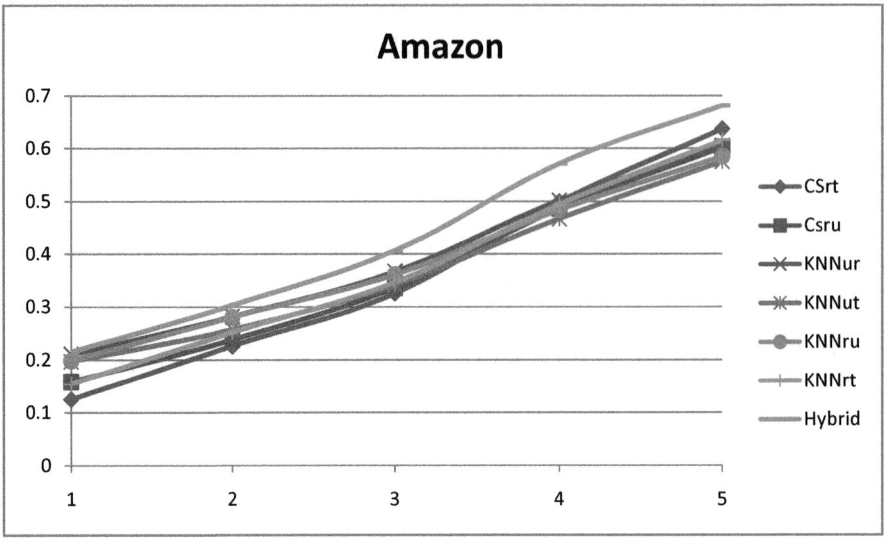

Fig. 3. Amazon: The hit-ratio for six recommendation by examples algorithms for cases where there is an agreement of one through five tags. The hybrid is composed of all six techniques.

they often use preconceived tags generated strong user-tag and resource-tag connections. These two component, leveraging different dimensions of the data, work together in order to offer meaningful advantages to the hybrids.

5 Conclusion

In this work we have investigated recommendation by example for use in social annotation systems. This type of user interaction offers a great deal of utility to users as they explore very large resource spaces. Our belief that personalization is important to satisfying the user's needs is confirmed with experimentation using three real world datasets. In order to blend the benefits of personalization with techniques focused on the example we proposed a linear-weighted hybrid. The hybrid was able to effectively exploit multiple components to produce superior results even though differences in the datasets required an emphasis on different components.

Our proposed linear-weighted hybrid offers additional advantages. It can exploit multiple dimensions of the data, while maintaining the speed and simplicity of if its parts. Second, it is extensible allowing additional components based on the underlying data. For example, systems that include ratings or allow users to generate friendship links can exploit this information by adding additional components to the hybrid. Finally, by analyzing the relative contributions of the components one can gain insights into how the components interact and reveal interesting patterns of user behavior.

Acknowledgment. This work was supported in part by a grant from the Department of Education, Graduate Assistance in the Area of National Need, P200A070536.

References

1. Agrawal, R., Imielinski, T., Swami, A.N.: Mining Association Rules between Sets of Items in Large Databases. In: Buneman, P., Jajodia, S. (eds.) Proceedings of the 1993 ACM SIGMOD International Conference on Management of Data, Washington, D.C, pp. 207–216 (1993)
2. Balabanović, M., Shoham, Y.: Fab: content-based, collaborative recommendation. Commun. ACM 40(3), 66–72 (1997)
3. Basu, C., Hirsh, H., Cohen, W.W.: Recommendation as Classification: Using Social and Content-Based Information in Recommendation. In: AAAI/IAAI, pp. 714–720 (1998)
4. Burke, R.: Hybrid recommender systems: Survey and experiments. User Modeling and User-Adapted Interaction 12(4), 331–370 (2002)
5. Deshpande, M., Karypis, G.: Item-Based Top-N Recommendation Algorithms. ACM Transactions on Information Systems 22(1), 143–177 (2004)
6. Gemmell, J., Ramezani, M., Schimoler, T., Christiansen, L., Mobasher, B.: A fast effective multi-channeled tag recommender. In: European Conference on Machine Learning and Principles and Practice of Knowledge Discovery in Databases Discovery Challenge, Bled, Slovenia (2009)
7. Gemmell, J., Schimoler, T., Mobasher, B., Burke, R.: Hybrid tag recommendation for social annotation systems. In: 19th ACM International Conference on Information and Knowledge Management, Toronto, Canada (2010)
8. Gemmell, J., Schimoler, T., Mobasher, B., Burke, R.: Resource Recommendation in Collaborative Tagging Applications. In: E-Commerce and Web Technologies, Bilbao, Spain (2010)
9. Gemmell, J., Schimoler, T., Mobasher, B., Burke, R.: Tag-based resource recommendation in social annotation applications. In: User Modeling, Adaptation and Personalization, Girona, Spain (2011)
10. Gemmell, J., Schimoler, T., Ramezani, M., Christiansen, L., Mobasher, B.: Resource Recommendation for Social Tagging: A Multi-Channel Hybrid Approach. In: Recommender Systems & the Social Web, Barcelona, Spain (2010)
11. Gemmell, J., Shepitsen, A., Mobasher, B., Burke, R.: Personalizing Navigation in Folksonomies Using Hierarchical Tag Clustering. In: 10th International Conference on Data Warehousing and Knowledge Discovery, Turin, Italy (2008)
12. Guan, Z., Wang, C., Bu, J., Chen, C., Yang, K., Cai, D., He, X.: Document recommendation in social tagging services. In: Proceedings of the 19th International Conference on World Wide Web, WWW 2010, pp. 391–400. ACM, New York (2010)
13. Guy, I., Zwerdling, N., Ronen, I., Carmel, D., Uziel, E.: Social media recommendation based on people and tags. In: Proceeding of the 33rd International ACM SIGIR Conference on Research and Development in Information Retrieval, SIGIR 2010, pp. 194–201. ACM, New York (2010)
14. Jäschke, R., Marinho, L., Hotho, A., Schmidt-Thieme, L., Stumme, G.: Tag recommendations in folksonomies. In: Kok, J.N., Koronacki, J., Lopez de Mantaras, R., Matwin, S., Mladenič, D., Skowron, A. (eds.) PKDD 2007. LNCS (LNAI), vol. 4702, pp. 506–513. Springer, Heidelberg (2007)
15. Konstan, J., Miller, B., Maltz, D., Herlocker, J., Gordon, L., Riedl, J.: GroupLens: Applying Collaborative Filtering to Usenet News. Communications of the ACM 40(3), 87 (1997)
16. Lewis, D.D., Schapire, R.E., Callan, J.P., Papka, R.: Training algorithms for linear text classifiers. In: Proceedings of the 19th Annual International ACM SIGIR Conference on Research and Development in Information Retrieval, SIGIR 1996, pp. 298–306. ACM, New York (1996)
17. Liang, H., Xu, Y., Li, Y., Nayak, R., Tao, X.: Connecting users and items with weighted tags for personalized item recommendations. In: Proceedings of the 21st ACM conference on Hypertext and Hypermedia, HT 2010, pp. 51–60. ACM, New York (2010)

18. Markines, B., Cattuto, C., Menczer, F., Benz, D., Hotho, A., Gerd, S.: Evaluating similarity measures for emergent semantics of social tagging. In: Proceedings of the 18th International Conference on World Wide Web, WWW 2009, pp. 641–650. ACM, New York (2009)
19. Mika, P.: Ontologies are us: A unified model of social networks and semantics. Web Semantics: Science, Services and Agents on the World Wide Web 5(1), 5–15 (2007)
20. Pennock, D.M., Lawrence, S., Popescul, R., Ungar, L.H.: Probabilistic Models for Unified Collaborative and Content-Based Recommendation in Sparse-Data Environments. In: Proceedings of the 17th Conference in Uncertainty in Artificial Intelligence, pp. 437–444 (2001)
21. Plangprasopchok, A., Lerman, K.: Exploiting Social Annotation for Automatic Resource Discovery. In: Proceedings of AAAI Workshop on Information Integration (April 2007)
22. Rendle, S., Schmidt-Thieme, L.: Pairwise Interaction Tensor Factorization for Personalized Tag Recommendation. In: Proceedings of the Third ACM International Conference on Web Search and Data Mining, New York (2010)
23. Salton, G., Buckley, C.: Improving retrieval performance by relevance feedback, vol. 41, pp. 288–297. Wiley, San Francisco (1990)
24. Salton, G., Wong, A., Yang, C.: A Vector Space Model for Automatic Indexing. Communications of the ACM 18(11), 613–620 (1975)
25. Sarwar, B., Karypis, G., Konstan, J., Reidl, J.: Item-Based Collaborative Filtering Recommendation Algorithms. In: 10th International Conference on World Wide Web, Hong Kong, China (2001)
26. Schafer, J.B., Konstan, J.A., Riedl, J.: E-Commerce Recommendation Applications. Data mining and knowledge discovery 5(1), 115–153 (2001)
27. Sen, S., Vig, J., Riedl, J.: Tagommenders: connecting users to items through tags. In: WWW 2009: Proceedings of the 18th International Conference on World Wide Web, pp. 671–680. ACM, New York (2009)
28. Shardanand, U., Maes, P.: Social Information Filtering: Algorithms for Automating Word of Mouth. In: SIGCHI Conference on Human Factors in Computing Systems, Denver, Colorado (1995)
29. Shepitsen, A., Gemmell, J., Mobasher, B., Burke, R.: Personalized Recommendation in Social Tagging Systems using Hierarchical Clustering. In: ACM Conference on Recommender Systems, Lausanne, Switzerland (2008)
30. Wu, X., Zhang, L., Yu, Y.: Exploring social annotations for the semantic web. In: Proceedings of the 15th International Conference on World Wide Web, Edinburgh, Scotland (2006)
31. Yang, Y., Chute, C.G.: An example-based mapping method for text categorization and retrieval. ACM Trans. Inf. Syst. 12, 252–277 (1994)

Trust-Based Selection of Partners

Maria Joana Urbano, Ana Paula Rocha, and Eugénio Oliveira

LIACC / Departamento de Engenharia Informática
Faculdade de Engenharia, Universidade do Porto
Rua Dr. Roberto Frias, 4200-465 Porto, Portugal,
{joana.urbano,arocha,eco}@fe.up.pt

Abstract. The community of multi-agent systems has been studying ways to improve the selection of partner agents for joint action. One of such approaches consists in estimating the trustworthiness of potential partners in order to decrease the risk inherent to interacting with unknown agents. In this paper, we study the effect of using trust in the process of selecting partners in electronic business. We empirically evaluate and compare different trust-based selection methods, which either use trust in a preselection phase previous to the negotiation, in the negotiation process, or in both of these stages. We here briefly introduce a computational model of trust that uses a simple machine learning mechanism to dynamically derive the expected tendencies of behavior of potential candidate partner agents. The results obtained in our comparison study allow us to point to the best trust-based selecting methods to use in specific situations.

Keywords: Computational trust, selection of partners, multi-agent systems.

1 Introduction

Trust is an important area of research in several disciplines, including sociology, psychology, philosophy, economics, distributed systems and distributed artificial intelligence. In fact, some authors considers it a public good that enables production and exchange and that is vital for the survival of the society [1].

The research area of multi-agent systems has been proposing computational trust models that help recognizing the different social behaviors of the communities in artificial societies. These models are considered essential for making more informed decisions in these societies of agents, reducing the risk associated to the information asymmetry problem in open and dynamic environments.

Some of these models provide probabilistic or heuristic-based aggregation engines that compute the trustworthiness of the agents in evaluation based on the available evidences on these agents [2,3,4]. Other models are proposed with the aim of being resistant to attacks, such as fraud, badmouthing, collusion, and other forms of deceptive behavior [5]. Still other computational models propose to incorporate in their trust reasoning important concepts imported from the

C. Huemer and T. Setzer (Eds.): EC-Web 2011, LNBIP 85, pp. 221–232, 2011.

social sciences area, such as forgiveness, prejudice, asymmetry, regret, erosion and coherence (e.g. [6][7][8][9]).

Independently of the original purpose, the majority of these proposals is based in the strong assumption that the use of computational trust mechanisms to select partners enhances the decision process and gives higher values of utility to the selecting agent. Moreover, these models are empirically evaluated in scenarios where service customers seek the best provider of services, using, in their selection process, no other differentiating factor than the estimated trustworthiness of the candidate agents.

However, there may exist specific real-world situations where the most trustworthy agent is not the one that offers the best payoff to the selecting agent. Let us consider two hypothetical examples. In the first example, firm A is a manufacturer of t-shirts and firms B and C are providers of fabric. Firm A knows, from experience, that B rarely fails a contract. In the same way, it also knows that C is less reliable, and sometimes it delays a delivery; however, firm C offers better utility (possibly derived from better quality of the product or better shipment and payment conditions) than firm B when it does not breach the contracts. In this case, the fact that B is more trustworthy than C can mean that B is more useful to A than firm C?

The second example depicts a recruitment scenario and is related to the use of trust in the selection decision as a *prefiltering* activity. In the example, firm D has one position open for Java programmers for which it has received more than three hundred applications. The firm has the possibility of preselecting the best candidates according to their trustworthiness, before pursuing to a deeper and more expensive analysis of the candidates. In this case, how many candidates shall be returned by the filtering process?

In this paper, we address the questions raised in the examples introduced above. In particular, we study the effect of using different methods based on trust for selecting partners. This study is enhanced by considering two distinct situations: in the first one, the proposals received by a buyer in a negotiation process are relatively similar and yield comparable utility to the buyer. In the second situation, the proposals are more disparate.

The remainder of this paper is structured as follows. Section 2 introduces related work. Section 3 presents the scenario and notation used in this paper and Section 4 revisits the computational trust model that serves as basis to our study. Section 5 presents the experiments and the main results of our study. Finally, Section 6 concludes the paper and presents future work.

2 Related Work

The majority of the papers in the area of computational trust assumes that trust is the only dimension to take into attention when selecting partners. Falcone and Castelfranchi [10], Kerschbaum et al. [5] and Maximilien and Singh [11] refer that trust must be used additionally to other relevant dimensions, but do not provide a practical study on the complementary use of such dimensions.

Gujral et al. [12] and Griffiths [13] propose models of partner selection based on multi-dimensional trust but do not refer the preselection phase. The work by Padovan et al. [14] develops a scenario that depicts a small value chain. The selection of partners is performed by ranking the received offers by the assessed offer price, which includes the expected value of loss based on a reputation coefficient. This work does not consider preselection.

The work by Kerschbaum et al. [5] addresses the problem of member selection in virtual organizations and considers the possibility of selection of candidate partners based on the reputation of agents, prior to the negotiation phase. The authors also consider the use of trust in the negotiation phase, both as another negotiation dimension, such as price and delivery time, or as a factor in deciding between equally well-suited candidates. However, the empirical evaluation of their trust model is focused on testing its resistance to attacks, and they do not model negotiation in their experiments.

Our work goes further than the related work in the sense that it provides an empirical study on the effect of using different trust-based selection methods – including preselection and the use of trust in the negotiation phase – on the utility of the selecting agents.

3 Scenario and Notation

The scenario used in this paper simulates an Electronic Institution (EI) through which buyer agents select the best suppliers of textile fabric using a simple one round, multi-attribute negotiation protocol. In this section, we describe this scenario and formalize its key concepts.

Every buyer registered in the EI has a business need, which is assigned randomly at setup. This need is represented by a fabric and associated values of quantity, price and delivery time.

The set of possible fabrics is given by $F = \{cotton, chiffon, voile\}$. The values of quantity, price and delivery time are assigned randomly from sets $Q = \{q \in \mathbb{N} : q \in [v_{quant,min}, v_{quant,max}]\}$, $P = \{p \in \mathbb{N} : p \in [v_{price,min}, v_{price,max}]\}$ and $D = \{d \in \mathbb{N} : d \in [v_{dtime,min}, v_{dtime,max}]\}$, respectively. The values $v_{i,min}$ and $v_{i,max}$ define the minimum and maximum values allowed for attribute i, respectively.

This way, buyers announce their needs in the form of a call for proposals (*cfp*), as defined next.

Definition 1. Call for proposals $cfp \in F \times Q \times P \times D$
A call for proposals cfp is an ordered tuple from the 4-ary Cartesian product $F \times Q \times P \times D$.

All suppliers registered in the EI are able to provide any type of fabric. When a buyer sends a *cfp* to a defined set of suppliers, each one of these suppliers generates a proposal with its own values for the quantity, price and delivery time attributes. These values are generated randomly following a uniform distribution in the range $[v_{i,p,min}, v_{i,p,max}]$, where $v_{i,p,min}$ and $v_{i,p,max}$ are defined in equations 1 and 2, respectively.

$$v_{i,p,min} = \max\ ((1-\delta) \times v_{i,cfp},\ v_{i,min})\ . \tag{1}$$

$$v_{i,p,max} = \min\ ((1+\delta) \times v_{i,cfp},\ v_{i,max})\ . \tag{2}$$

In Equation 1, $v_{i,cfp}$ is the value defined in the *cfp* for attribute i (quantity, price or delivery time), and $\delta \in [0,1]$ is a *dispersion* parameter that allows to define how distant the generated proposal is from the preferences of the buyer, as stated in the *cfp*.

After receiving the proposals from the suppliers, the buyer calculates the utility of each one of them. The utility of a proposal, μ_p, is given by the complement of the *deviation* between the client preferences specified in the *cfp*, for all the negotiable items price, quantity and delivery time, and what is offered in the received proposal (cf. Equation 3).

$$\mu_p = 1 - \frac{1}{k} \times (\sum_{i}^{k} \frac{|v_{i,cfp} - v_{i,p}|}{v_{i,max} - v_{i,min}})\ . \tag{3}$$

In Equation 3, which is adapted from [15], $v_{i,p}$ is the value of the negotiation attribute i of the current proposal in evaluation and k is the number of negotiation attributes considered.

After calculating the utilities of all received proposals, the buyer makes a decision concerning the selection of the *best* proposal. In this paper, we analyze three different approaches for the selection of the best proposal: i) proposals are sorted by their utility (as calculated in Equation 3), and the best proposal is the one that has the highest utility; ii) proposals are sorted by the trustworthiness of the proponent suppliers, and the best proposal is the one which corresponds to the highest value of trustworthiness; and iii) proposals are sorted by the weighted sum of their utility and the trustworthiness of the corresponding proponents, and the best proposal is the one that presents the highest value for this weighted sum. Methods ii) and iii) assume that, previous to the evaluation phase, the buyer estimates the trustworthiness τ of all suppliers that presented a proposal, using the computational trust algorithm presented in Section 4. In addition, method iii) defines the weighting parameter $\omega_\tau \in [0,1]$, which allows to configure the importance assigned to the trustworthiness component in this selection method (cf. Equation 4).

$$weighting\ sum:\ \omega_\tau \times \tau + (1-\omega_\tau) \times \mu_p\ . \tag{4}$$

In addition to the process described above, we must refer that the buyers have the possibility to preselect the supplier agents that will receive the *cfp's*, by filtering them by their trustworthiness. After this filtering is done, the selection of the best proposal proceeds as described before.

Finally, after the selection of the best proposal, the buyer establishes a contract with the selected supplier, stipulating that the latter must provide the

Table 1. The set of all handicaps considered in our scenario

Handicap	Description
HFab	handicap in specific fabric
HQt	handicap in high quantities
HDt	handicap in low delivery times
HFabQt	handicap in specific fabric *and* high quantities
HFabDt	handicap in specific fabric *and* low delivery times
HQtDt	handicap in high quantities *and* low delivery times

fabric at the conditions of quantity, price and delivery time described in its proposal.[1]

Suppliers can either fulfill or violate the contracts associated to their business interactions, according to their model of behavior. The sample space of outcomes is thus given by $O = \{f, v\}$, where outcome $o = f$ corresponds to a fulfillment of the contract and outcome $o = v$ corresponds to a contractual breach.

In this paper, we model the behavior of suppliers using probabilities. Every supplier that is registered in the EI has an intrinsic degree of performance reflecting the fact that it has some *handicap* in providing specific components in certain *circumstances*. Therefore, at setup, each supplier is randomly assigned a handicap following a uniform distribution over all possible handicaps considered in this paper, which are informally described in Table 1.

The outcome of the interaction between the buyer and the selected supplier is further used to update the value of the trustworthiness of this supplier.

4 The Trust Model

In this section, we briefly describe the computational trust model that serves as basis to our study. It consists of two main components. The first component is *Sinalpha* ([7]), a general aggregator that we have developed that computes the trustworthiness scores of the agents in evaluation based on the trust evidences available on these agents.

The second component of the model is *Contextual Fitness* (*CF*), a situation-aware, machine learning-based component that we have developed [16] in order to refine the trustworthiness scores computed by *Sinalpha*, taking into account the current *situation* in assessment. Equation 5 shows the formula used to compute the trustworthiness of agent ag in the specific situation s.

$$\tau(ag, s) = \tau_{sinalpha}(ag) * \tau_{CF}(ag, s) \quad (5)$$

In the equation above, $\tau_{sinalpha}(ag) \in [0, 1]$ gives the trustworthiness score as computed by *Sinalpha*, and $\tau_{CF}(ag, s) \in \{0, 1\}$ gives the value returned by the situation-aware tuner.

[1] The negotiation mechanism we present in this paper is deliberately simple, as it does not constitute the focus of this work. We assume that the conclusions derived from our study using this mechanism are still valid in the presence of other, more complex negotiation protocols.

The mode of operation of the *situation-aware* component is based on the dynamic extraction of *tendencies of failure* from the past behavior of the agent in evaluation. In order to extract these tendencies, we developed an algorithm that uses the *information gain* metric [17]. This metric is used in the ID3 algorithm [17] as a machine learning classification algorithm; however, we use it in an incremental way, by generating a new tree every time a selecting agent needs to assess the trustworthiness of agent ag in evaluation.

Before we proceed to the description of the CF algorithm, we first give the formal notion of trust evidence.

Definition 2. Trust evidence $evd \in Evd$
A trust evidence $evd \in Evd$ *is an ordered tuple from the 6-ary Cartesian product* $Evd = AG \times AG \times F \times Q \times D \times O$, *where* AG *is the set of all agents registered in the EI.*

Using this definition, we can define $Evd^{ag} \subset Evd$ as the subset of all trust evidences that are available to the selecting agent about agent ag in evaluation, such that $Evd^{ag} = AG \times AG^{*} \times F \times Q \times D \times O$, where $AG^{*} = \{ag\}$.

The CF algorithm is illustrated in Algorithm 1.

Algorithm 1. The algorithm of the situation-aware component

1: **function** CF (s, Evd^{ag}) returns a value in $\{0, 1\}$
2: $\quad s$: context of current situation
3: $\quad Evd^{ag}$: set of trust evidences on agent ag
4: $tree^{ag} \leftarrow$ generateTree (Evd^{ag})
5: **for each** negative rule nr_i in $tree^{ag}$ **do**
6: $\quad t_{neg} \leftarrow$ extract negative tendency from rule nr_i
7: $\quad$ **if** there is a match between t_{neg} and s **then**
8: $\quad\quad$ **return** 0
9: **return** 1

Observing Algorithm 1, we verify that it first generates a classification tree from the set of evidences Evd^{ag}, using the evidence outcome as class attribute (line 4). This tree classifies the elements of Evd^{ag} in different classes, corresponding to the elements of the set O of all possible evidence outcomes. Then, for each branch in the tree corresponding to *negative* classes (line 5), a tendency of failure t_{neg} is extracted (line 6). If this tendency matches situation s in assessment (line 7), this means that the agent has a *tendency to fail* in situations similar to the current one, and the algorithm returns the value 0 (line 8). Otherwise, it returns the value 1 (line 9).

Being an incremental process, the algorithm allows for the extracted tendencies of behavior of the evaluated target to change dynamically with the size of the historical data on the agent, being, this way, very responsive to the changes of behavior of the agents in assessment. Another good property of this algorithm is that it is able to extract negative tendencies of behavior since the first evidences available, achieving good performances with very small datasets.

5 Experiments

We ran a set of experiments in order to analyze the effect of using trust on the selection phase of automatic negotiation processes. Most of the papers on computational trust show the benefits of using trust in the selection of partners, but these are described exclusively in terms of the number of successful transactions. In these experiments, we compared different selection methods, including those that do not use trust, those that use trust in a preselection phase previous to the negotiation, those that use trust in the negotiation process and, finally, those that use trust in a preselection phase *and* in the negotiation process.

5.1 Testbed and Methodology

All experiments described in this paper were performed using the Repast simulation tool [18] and the scenario described in Section 3.

We ran six different experiments, according to the selection methods in evaluation. Table 2 presents these experiments.

As can be observed in Table 2, we tested two different filtering approaches (experiments 2, 3, 5 and 6): the first one preselected 10% of the most trustworthy suppliers registered in the EI, and the second one preselected 50% of this population. In experiments 1 and 4, no trust-based preselection was performed and all suppliers were allowed to proceed to the negotiation phase.

In all experiments, we used 20 buyer agents and 50 supplier agents. Every supplier had a 95% chance to succeed in case it did not present a handicap in the situation embedded in the *cfp*. This probability dropped to 5% when its handicap matched the cfp's situation.

Each experiment was composed of 30 *episodes*, and at every episode each buyer started a new negotiation cycle by issuing a new *cfp*. At the first episode of each experiment, the repository of trust evidences was cleaned, which means that the trustworthiness of all suppliers was set to zero. Finally, we ran every experiment 20 times. At every new run, the buyer agents changed their preferential values regarding their business needs, by randomly picking up new values from sets F, Q, D and P.

In order to enhance our study on the effect of using trust in selection processes, we considered two different values for the dispersion parameter δ: 0.2 and 1.0 (cf. equations 1 and 2). As mentioned in Section 3, parameter δ is used to

Table 2. Different types of experiments, based on the places where trust was used

#	Selection Method	Preselection	Negotiation
1	No Trust	—	—
2	Trust in preselection (10%)	√	—
3	Trust in preselection (50%)	√	—
4	Trust in negotiation	—	√
5	Trust in preselection (10%) and in negotiation	√	√
6	Trust in preselection (50%) and in negotiation	√	√

configure how distant the proposals generated by the suppliers are from the conditions specified in the received *cfp*. In these experiments, the value 0.2 was used to configure small deviations, which means that all the proposals received by the buyer agent were close to its preferential values for current interaction; in opposition, the value of 1.0 allowed for a greater dispersion in the utility of the proposals received by the buyer agent.

5.2 Evaluation Metrics

In order to evaluate and compare each one of the selection methods considered in the experiments, we used six different performance metrics. The first metric was the *utility of the interaction* (μ_t), given in Equation 6. We averaged this utility over all buyers and all episodes.

$$\mu_t = \begin{cases} \mu_p, \text{ if } o = f \ , \\ 0, \text{ if } o = v \ . \end{cases} \tag{6}$$

The second metric was the *number of positive outcomes* (o^+) obtained by all buyer agents in an episode, averaged over all episodes. The third metric was the *number of different suppliers* (Δ_{sup}) selected by all buyers in one episode, averaged over all episodes. The fourth and the fifth metrics measured the *trustworthiness of the supplier* and the *utility of the proposal* selected by a buyer in one episode (τ_s and μ_s, respectively), averaged over all buyers and all episodes. Finally, the sixth metric was the *number of unfitted choices* (ζ) performed by a buyer, averaged over all buyers and all episodes. This latter metric is related to the *CF* component of our computational trust model. It concerns the choice of a supplier that the buyer knows has an handicap in the current business conditions.

5.3 Results

In this section, we start by presenting the results obtained for a dispersion value (δ) of 0.2, and then we present the values obtained for $\delta = 1.0$.

Experiments with $\delta = 0.2$. The first part of the experiments was performed using $\delta = 0.2$. We first measured the average utility of the proposals *received* by a buyer in one episode and averaged it over all buyers and all episodes. The value we obtained for this average was 0.93, with a standard deviation of 0.03. These values were obtained consistently for all the selection methods tested. Their meaning is that the suppliers offered proposals with approximated utility and close to the buyers' preferences.

Table 3 presents the results obtained in this first set of experiments for the metrics described in Section 5.2.

In experiments 4.x, 5.x and 6.x, the utility of the interaction (μ_t) is a weighted sum of the trustworthiness of the supplier and the utility of its proposal. In the experiments, we used two different values for the weight of the trust component, $\omega_\tau = 0.1$ and $\omega_\tau = 0.5$ (cf. Equation 4).

Table 3. Results obtained with $\delta = 0.2$

#	Selection Method	μ_t	o^+	Δ_{sup}	τ_s	μ_s	ζ
1	No Trust	0.69	0.70	0.84	0.17	0.98	0.21
2	Trust in preselection (10%)	0.82	0.85	0.35	0.80	0.96	0.00
3	Trust in preselection (50%)	0.79	0.81	0.75	0.41	0.98	0.01
4.1	Trust in negotiation ($\omega_\tau = 0.1$)	0.82	0.87	0.23	0.83	0.95	0.00
4.2	Trust in negotiation ($\omega_\tau = 0.5$)	0.79	0.85	0.11	0.90	0.93	0.00
5.1	Trust in presel. (10%) & in neg. ($\omega_\tau = 0.1$)	0.83	0.88	0.18	0.88	0.95	0.00
5.2	Trust in presel. (10%) & in neg. ($\omega_\tau = 0.5$)	0.82	0.88	0.11	0.90	0.93	0.00
6.1	Trust in presel. (50%) & in neg. ($\omega_\tau = 0.1$)	0.83	0.87	0.22	0.85	0.95	0.00
6.2	Trust in presel. (50%) & in neg. ($\omega_\tau = 0.5$)	0.83	0.89	0.11	0.91	0.93	0.00

From the results presented in Table 3, we verify that the selection method that did not rely on trust got worse results for the metric utility of the interaction ($\mu_t = 0.69$), as it would be expected. This method selected the suppliers by the utility of their proposals, which allowed for the selection of proposals with very high values of utility ($\mu_s = 0.98$) and for a high degree of exploration of new partners ($\Delta_{sup} = 0.84$). However, the trustworthiness of the selected suppliers was in average very low ($\tau_s = 0.17$), and a relevant number of unfitted choices was done ($\zeta = 0.21$). In consequence, the number of positive outcomes was relatively low ($o^+ = 0.70$).

The results presented in Table 3 also show that the mixed use of trust, both in preselection and in the negotiation phase (experiments 5.x and 6.x), got the best results in terms of the utility of interaction ($\mu_t \approx 0.83$), for all combinations of the degree of filtering (10% and 50%) and ω_τ. In this case, we verified that although reinforcing the trust component in the negotiation phase ($\omega_\tau = 0.5$) allowed for higher values of the trustworthiness of the selected suppliers (τ_s), relaxing this value ($\omega_\tau = 0.1$) allowed for higher values of the utility of the selected proposals (μ_s). Also, the difference between filtering the 10% or the 50% more trustworthy agents was not relevant for $\delta = 0.2$.

Finally, we observed that both the use of standalone, stricter preselection (10%) and the use of trust in negotiation with $\omega = 0.1$ allowed for similar good results of μ_t (0.82), and approximated values of o^+, τ_s and μ_s. The use of standalone, more relaxed preselection (50%) and the use of trust in negotiation with $\omega = 0.5$ got lower values of μ_t (0.79), with the first method exploring more the utility of the proposals ($\mu_s = 0.98$) in detriment to the trustworthiness of suppliers ($\tau_s = 0.41$), and the latter having an opposite behavior ($\mu_s = 0.93$ and $\tau_s = 0.90$).

Experiments with $\delta = 1.0$. In the second part of the experiments, we wanted to evaluate the effect of each one of the selection methods when the dispersion in the utilities provided by different suppliers was bigger. For that, we configured δ to have value 1.0. In this case, the measured value for the average utility of the received proposals was 0.73, with a standard deviation of 0.11, showing a higher variance in the proposals made by the suppliers.

Table 4. Results obtained with $\delta = 1.0$

#	Selection Method	μ_t	o^+	Δ_{sup}	τ_s	μ_s	ζ
1	No Trust	0.66	0.71	0.83	0.17	0.93	0.21
2	Trust in preselection (10%)	0.73	0.87	0.36	0.80	0.84	0.00
3	Trust in preselection (50%)	0.73	0.80	0.76	0.41	0.92	0.02
4.1	Trust in negotiation ($\omega_\mathcal{T} = 0.1$)	0.75	0.83	0.63	0.58	0.91	0.00
4.2	Trust in negotiation ($\omega_\mathcal{T} = 0.5$)	0.67	0.88	0.14	0.88	0.77	0.00
5.1	Trust in presel. (10%) & in neg ($\omega_\mathcal{T} = 0.1$)	0.73	0.87	0.32	0.83	0.85	0.00
5.2	Trust in presel. (10%) & in neg ($\omega_\mathcal{T} = 0.5$)	0.66	0.86	0.13	0.89	0.77	0.00
6.1	Trust in presel. (50%) & in neg ($\omega_\mathcal{T} = 0.1$)	0.77	0.85	0.59	0.64	0.90	0.00
6.2	Trust in presel. (50%) & in neg ($\omega_\mathcal{T} = 0.5$)	0.66	0.86	0.14	0.89	0.77	0.00

Table 4 presents the results obtained in this second set of experiments for the metrics described before.

The results obtained and presented in Table 4 show relevant differences from the results obtained with $\delta = 0.2$. In fact, the combined use of trust in preselection and in negotiation did not achieve the same good performance as observed with $\delta = 0.2$, for $\omega_\mathcal{T} = 0.5$. As illustrated in Table 4, in experiments 5.2 and 6.2, the buyers kept selecting the same trustworthy agents again and again ($\Delta_{sup} \approx 0.14$), showing a rather parochial behavior. This had the cost of decreasing the utility of the selected proposals ($\mu_s = 0.77$) in a significant manner, with just a slight improvement in the trustworthiness of the selected suppliers ($\tau_s = 0.89$). In a general case, we can observe in Table 4 that all trust methods that used trust in negotiation with a strong weight for the trust component ($\omega_\mathcal{T} = 0.5$) got as little value for μ_t as the selection approach that did not use trust at all. In the same way, approaches using more restricted preselection (10%) exhibited significantly lower values of μ_t than their counterparts using $\delta = 0.2$.

The results obtained also show that the combined use of a more relaxed filtering of suppliers (50%) and a lower weight of the trust component ($\omega_\mathcal{T} = 0.1$) had again achieved the best result for the average utility of interaction ($\mu_t = 0.77$). This approach allowed for a better equilibrium between the trustworthiness of the selected suppliers and the utility of the selected proposals.

5.4 Interpretation of Results

The results obtained and presented in the sections above allow us to conclude that parochialism in partner selection is acceptable when the proposals in evaluation are not too disparate ($\delta = 0.2$). In this case, selection methods strongly supported on trust reveal to be good choices, as they are able to select more reliable partners without the expense of loosing utility.

However, we have shown that when the standard deviation of the utility of the received proposals is about 11% of the mean, the excessive use of trust is not acceptable, as parochialism prevents buyers from exploring partners that offer deals with higher utilities. In both the situations that we have studied, a method that preselects half of the population of candidate suppliers and then moderately uses trust in negotiation revealed to be a better choice (experiments 6.1 in tables 3 and 4).

6 Conclusions

Recently, different agent-based trust models have been proposed as support mechanisms to the selection of partners. These proposals are based on the hard assumption that trust enhances the selection process, but no studies were presented on the role of trust in the presence of other selection differentiation factors.

In this paper, we empirically evaluated and compared different selection methods based on trust. We concluded that methods that strongly rely on trust are not adequate when the proposals in evaluation are disparate. The best solution seems to be the trust-based preselection of about half of the candidate partners, followed by a selection process where the weight of the trust component must be adjusted to the estimated dispersion of the proposals' utilities.

As future work, we intend to explore other prefiltering options and different other combinations of the parameters configured in the experiments. We also intend to explore other computational trust models in our study.

Acknowledgments. This research is funded by FCT (Fundação para a Ciência e a Tecnologia) project PTDC/EIA-EIA/104420/2008. The first author enjoys a PhD grant with reference SFRH/BD/39070/2007 from FCT.

References

1. Dasgupta, P.: Trust as a Commodity. In: Gambetta, D. (ed.) Trust: Making and Breaking Cooperative Relations, Department of Sociology, University of Oxford, pp. 49–72 (2000)
2. Jøsang, A., Ismail, R.: The Beta Reputation System. In: Proceedings of the 15th Bled Electronic Commerce Conference (2002)
3. Huynh, T.D., Jennings, N.R., Shadbolt, N.R.: An integrated trust and reputation model for open multi-agent systems. Autonomous Agents and Multi-Agent Systems 13, 119–154 (2006)
4. Yu, B., Singh, M.P.: An Evidential Model of Distributed Reputation Management. In: Proceedings of the First International Joint Conference on Autonomous Agents and Multiagent Systems: part 1., AAMAS 2002, pp. 294–301(2002)
5. Kerschbaum, F., Haller, J., Karabulut, Y., Robinson, P.: Pathtrust: A trust-based reputation service for virtual organization formation. In: Stølen, K., Winsborough, W.H., Martinelli, F., Massacci, F. (eds.) iTrust 2006. LNCS, vol. 3986, pp. 193–205. Springer, Heidelberg (2006)
6. Marsh, S., Briggs, P.: Examining Trust, Forgiveness and Regret as Computational Concepts. In: Golbeck, J. (ed.) Computing with Social Trust. Human-Computer Interaction Series, pp. 9–43. Springer, London (2009)
7. Urbano, J., Rocha, A.P., Oliveira, E.: Computing confidence values: Does trust dynamics matter? In: Lopes, L.S., Lau, N., Mariano, P., Rocha, L.M. (eds.) EPIA 2009. LNCS, vol. 5816, pp. 520–531. Springer, Heidelberg (2009)

8. Melaye, D., Demazeau, Y.: Bayesian dynamic trust model. In: Multi-Agent Systems and Applications Iv, Proceedings, vol. 3690, pp. 480–489 (2005)
9. Joseph, S., Sierra, C., Schorlemmer, M., Dellunde, P.: Deductive coherence and norm adoption. Logic Journal of the IGPL 18, 118–156 (2010)
10. Castelfranchi, C., Falcone, R., Pezzulo, G.: Trust in information sources as a source for trust: a fuzzy approach. In: Procs. of the Second International Joint Conference on Autonomous Agents and Multiagent Systems, AAMAS 2003, pp. 89–96 (2003)
11. Maximilien, E.M., Singh, M.P.: Agent-based trust model involving multiple qualities. In: Proceedings of the Fourth International Joint Conference on Autonomous Agents and Multiagent Systems (July 2005)
12. Gujral, N., DeAngelis, D., Fullam, K.K., Barber, K.S.: Modeling multi-dimensional trust. In: Procs. of The Workshop on Trust in Agent Societies at AAMAS 2006, pp. 35–41 (2006)
13. Griffiths, N.: Task delegation using experience-based multi-dimensional trust. In: Proceedings of the Fourth International Joint Conference on Autonomous Agents and Multiagent Systems, AAMAS 2005, New York, NY, USA, pp. 489–496 (2005)
14. Padovan, B., Sackmann, S., Eymann, T., Pippow, I.: A prototype for an agent-based secure electronic marketplace including reputation-tracking mechanisms. Int. J. Electron. Commerce 6, 93–113 (2002)
15. Rocha, A.P., Oliveira, E.: An electronic market architecture for the formation of virtual enterprises. In: Proceedings of the IFIP TC5 WG5.3 / PRODNET Working Conference on Infrastructures for Virtual Enterprises: Networking Industrial Enterprises, pp. 421–432. Kluwer, B.V., Deventer, The Netherlands (1999)
16. Urbano, J., Rocha, A.P., Oliveira, E.: Trustworthiness tendency incremental extraction using information gain. In: Proceedings of the 2010 IEEE/WIC/ACM International Conference on Web Intelligence and Intelligent Agent Technology, WI-IAT 2010, vol. 2, pp. 411–414. IEEE Computer Society, Los Alamitos (2010)
17. Quinlan, J.R.: Induction of Decision Trees. Mach. Learn. 1, 81–106 (1986)
18. North, M., Howe, T., Collier, N., Vos, J.: A declarative model assembly infrastructure for verification and validation. In: Takahashi, S., Sallach, D.L., Rouchier, J. (eds.) Advancing Social Simulation: The First World Congress. Springer, Heidelberg (2007)

A High-Level Agent Interaction Protocol Based on a Communication Ontology

Roman Popp and David Raneburger

Institute of Computertechnology,
Vienna University of Technology,
Gusshausstrasse 27-29, A–1040 Vienna, Austria
{popp,raneburger}@ict.tuwien.ac.at

Abstract. Electronic commerce (eCommerce) environments have been emerging together with the Internet for the last decades. This led to a heterogeneous eCommerce landscape, resulting in interoperability problems between interacting agents. Interaction protocols like FIPA-ACL support the definition of the exchanged *messages* format and therefore, improve the interoperability. However, they do not support the specification of the exchanged *data* format, or how this data shall be processed. This leads to further interoperability problems. We propose the use of an interaction ontology — the Communication Ontology — as an agent interaction protocol. A Communication Ontology combines a domain ontology, a discourse ontology and an action ontology to specify the flow of interaction as well as the exchanged data format and messages and how they shall be processed. The combination of these three ontologies into one ontology improves the interoperability between the interacting agents and supports quick adaptations that become necessary, due to quickly evolving markets and rapid technological advances.

Keywords: Communication Ontology, Agent Interaction Protocol, Message Processing.

1 Introduction

Rapid technological advances and quickly evolving markets led to a heterogeneous eCommerce environment in the Internet. Therefore, the interoperability between agents that interact in such an environment is still an issue [1,2,3].

Interaction protocols (e.g., Agent Communication Languages [4]) provide the basis for interoperability, as they support the format definition of the exchanged messages. Further interoperability problems occur however, if the agents use different domain ontologies. Approaches to solve this problem are either the use of a common domain ontology [5] or a defined mapping between different domain ontologies [6]. Domain ontologies however, do not specify which operations shall be performed on the exchanged data. This complicates agent interaction, because there is no way for an agent to request the performance of a certain operation on the exchanged data from its interaction partner. This may lead

C. Huemer and T. Setzer (Eds.): EC-Web 2011, LNBIP 85, pp. 233–245, 2011.

to interoperability problems as an agent cannot know if its interaction partner processes the exchanged data as expected. Such operations may even require the completion of other operations upfront. Therefore, such operation must be executed in a predefined order. This order defines the expected behavior of the agent. To prevent agents from deviating from their expected behavior it is important to provide a means to specify the flow of interaction on a higher level than the request-response pairs supported by interaction protocols like FIPA-ACL[1]. Such high-level specifications precisely define the interaction between two agents and therefore, avoid the related interoperability problems.

We propose an interaction ontology to solve the interoperability problems presented above. This interaction ontology is called *Communication Ontology* and supports the specification of operations and the flow of interaction additionally to the exchanged messages and their content (i.e., exchanged data).

The Communication Ontology combines three ontologies, the Discourse Ontology, the Domain Ontology and the Action Notification Ontology. The Discourse Ontology is based on human speech theories, namely Speech Act Theory [7], Rhetorical Structural Theory (RST) [8] and Conversation Analyses [9], and captures the interaction between two agents. While Speech Act Theory and Conversation Analyses can be seen as a common basis for many agent communication languages, the use of RST is new in this area. We adapt concepts from RST to capture the flow interaction between two agents. The Domain Ontology captures the application domain and the Action Notification Ontology specifies the semantics of the content of the messages (i.e., Communicative Acts) that are exchanged. The content of a Communicative Act consists of domain objects and operations that shall be performed on them.

We use our Communication Ontology to capture discourses. A discourse defines the interaction between two agents that is required to reach a specific goal. An agent can support from 1 to n discourses, which it uses to meet its design objectives. Using discourses makes building agents with complex design objectives more affordable, because the agent's designer does not have to deal with preconditions of operations in the agent itself. Instead, the designer can select discourses (e.g., from a Communication Ontology repository) according to their goals and use them to meet the given design objective for the agent.

Compared to standard Agent Communication Languages like FIPA-ACL, Communication Ontologies provide more elaborate means to specify discourses. Furthermore, a discourse does not only specify the exchanged messages but also their semantics (i.e., how they shall be processed by the interacting agents). This means that the Communication Ontology provides a precise functional interface definition for the interacting agents and therefore, improves their interoperability. While interacting, the agents use the same Communication Ontology and thus the same Domain Ontology.

The reminder of this paper is organized in the following manner. First we provide an overview of state-of-the-art approaches for agent interaction protocols

[1] At the time of the writing the FIPA-ACL definition can be found at: `http://www.fipa.org/repository/aclspecs.html`

and improved agent interoperability. Subsequently we present background information on the previously published Discourse Ontology in order to make this paper self contained. In the next chapter we present the Domain and the Action Notification Ontology, followed by the Communication Ontology, which links these ontologies. We show that the Communication Ontology specifies the functional interface of the agents involved in the interaction before we draw the conclusions from our research.

2 State of the Art and Related Work

Most agent interaction protocols are based on the Knowledge Query and Manipulation Language (KQML) or FIPA-ACL [4]. KQML is a language and protocol for communication among software agents and knowledge-based systems. FIPA-ACL is an agent communication language based on Speech Act Theory. KQML and FIPA-ACL focus on the messages that are exchanged between two agents and not on their interaction on a higher level than request-response or question-answer. Compared to KQML we do not only support the manipulation and query of data, but provide more elaborate means to model the interaction between two agents. Just like FIPA-ACL, we use Speech Act Theory to define the exchanged messages, but we additionally adapt concepts from Rhetorical Structure Theory (RST) to define the flow of the messages. In particular, we use relations derived form RST to relate typical interaction patterns like request-response. These relations allow to model the interactive aspects of the discourse (i.e., the flow of Communicative Acts) between two agents.

Moore proposes an approach for flexible automated electronic communication [10], based on Speech Act Theory. This approach however, rather defines a set of common actions that can be interpreted by the agents than a complete interaction ontology.

Wang and Hongshuai propose an OWL based Communication Ontology in Distributed Multi-Agent Systems (MAS) to facilitate agent communication in [11]. Their approach aims at integrating semantic web standards such as OWL in MAS. Singh introduces Social Semantics for Agent Communication Languages to improve agent interoperability in MAS [12]. In contrast to these approaches we do not aim for MAS. Our Communication Ontology supports the interaction definition between exactly two agents. However, each agent may use more than one Communication Ontology at one point in time and may thus interact with more than one agent concurrently.

Bermúdez introduces Communicative Acts and the need for an action and a domain ontology [13]. With respect to this approach we provide the same kind of ontologies, but we additionally provide an upper ontology in order to make it easily adaptable for new domains and the corresponding applications.

The Universal Business Language (UBL) [5] specifies a scheme to unify domain ontologies for business documents. A similar approach for a unified B2B e-trading construction marketplace is presented in [14]. An XML-Framework for agent-based e-Commerce, which aims to support the data interchange between several companies, is introduced in [15]. An ontology that maps data between different ontologies to improve agent interoperability is used in [6]. In contrast to these approaches we have a different scope. The focus of our approach is to improve agent interoperability through a common high-level interaction protocol, our Communication Ontology, rather than unifying the ontology that represents the application domain.

3 Background

We developed our Discourse Ontology for automated UI generation [16,17,18]. In the context of automated UI generation we call it Discourse Model, because we apply concepts from model-driven software development. This section provides information on the Discourse Ontology in order ease the understanding of the Communication Ontology and to make this paper self-contained.

Our Discourse Ontology is based on three human language theories. We use *Communicative Acts*, derived from **Speech Act Theory** [7], to model the basic units of communication (i.e., the messages that are exchanged by the agents). **Conversation Analysis** [9] describes the relationship between such Communicative Acts and offers two concepts that we adopted for our approach. The first concept are *Adjacency Pairs*. An Adjacency Pair models typical turn-takings during a conversation (e.g., request-response or question-answer). This means that it links an opening Communicative Act (e.g., a *Question* or *Request*) and one or more closing Communicative Acts (e.g., the *Answer* to a Question or the *Accept/Reject* to a Request). The second concept that we adopted from Conversation Analysis is *Inserted Sequences*. An Inserted Sequence is an additional discourse, which an agent can start in case it does not have enough information to respond to a request. Such Inserted Sequences are embedded in Adjacency Pairs and model the interaction that is needed to get the required information. **Rhetorical Structure Theory** (RST) [8] focuses on the function of text and is widely used for automated generation of natural language. We use RST relations to relate Adjacency Pairs or sub-discourses. A sub-discourse in this context is a sub-part of a discourse that contains itself relations and Adjacency Pairs. The relations are used to model the flow of interaction and lead to a tree structure of the discourse. Examples for such relations are an *Alternative* or *Joint* relation, which can both have 1 to n children. A Joint means that all its child branches need to be finished before the relation itself is finished, whereas an Alternative means that only 1 child branch needs to be finished. In our approach we enriched the relations adopted from RST with relations that simply specify the flow of events and have no additional semantics in the sense of RST. An example for such a relation is the *IfUntil* relation. An IfUntil relation supports the specification of conditions, which are used to decide whether the corresponding sub branch is finished or not. The formal definition of the procedural semantics of each relation is given as a statechart (see [17] for further details).

Figure 1 introduces the discourse for a simple Flight Booking scenario between a *Customer* agent and an *Airline* agent. The black framed discourse in the upper left edge shows the Adjacency Pair that models the request from the

Customer agent to buy a ticket. The yellow and green rounded boxes represent the exchanged Communicative Acts. Their fill color represents the associated agent that utters the Communicative Act, green for Customer agent and yellow for the Airline agent. The Adjacency Pair that relates the opening (i.e., the Request sent by the Customer agent) and closing (i.e., the Accept and Reject sent by the Airline agent) Communicative Acts is represented as a diamond. In the course of interaction an Inserted Sequence is started by the Airline agent to collect the data needed to book a flight. The symbol for an Inserted Sequence is the small icon that consists of three cubes and three dots. The Inserted Sequence in Figure 1 starts the discourse shown in the same figure.

The left side of Figure 1 shows the questions for the departure and the destination airport and the flight date. The Adjacency Pairs of the departure and the destination airport are connected with a Joint relation. This indicates that they are available at the same point in time and can be answered in an arbitrary order. A further Joint relation is used to connect this Joint with the OpenQuestion Adjacency Pair for the flight date. It would be possible to add a third nucleus branch to the airport Joint relation, but the relation between destination and departure airport is stronger than to the date. We use the hierarchy to express the strength of the relation. This information provides rendering hints for the automated UI generation from a discourse [16]. The Tree branch of an IfUntil relation is executed until the corresponding condition is fulfilled. In our running example this condition checks if the Airline agent is able to provide a flight with the given departure and destination airport at the given date. If the condition is true the Then branch of the IfUntil relation is executed. The Then branch in Figure 1 allows the Customer agent to select one of the flights provided by the Airline agent. After the Customer agent has selected a flight the first branch of the Sequence relation is finished and the second branch is executed. This branch contains the questions for the credit card and the passenger data. The root node of this discourse is an Alternative relation, that relates the discourse subtree for the data collection described so far with an Informing Communicative Act of the Customer agent. This allows the Customer agent to cancel the buying process at any point in time during the execution of the discourse.

4 High-Level Agent Interaction Protocol

The core idea of this work is to use the presented Discourse Ontology as interaction protocol between two agents. In order to solve the interoperability problems presented in Section 1, we additionally introduce a Domain Ontology and an Action Notification Ontology. We combine these three ontologies into our Communication Ontology to support the precise definition of the interaction between two agents.

Using our Communication Ontology as communication protocol has two strong points that improve agent interoperability compared to other communication protocols based on Communicative Acts. The first strong point is that our Communication Ontology does not only define the messages that are exchanged (i.e.,

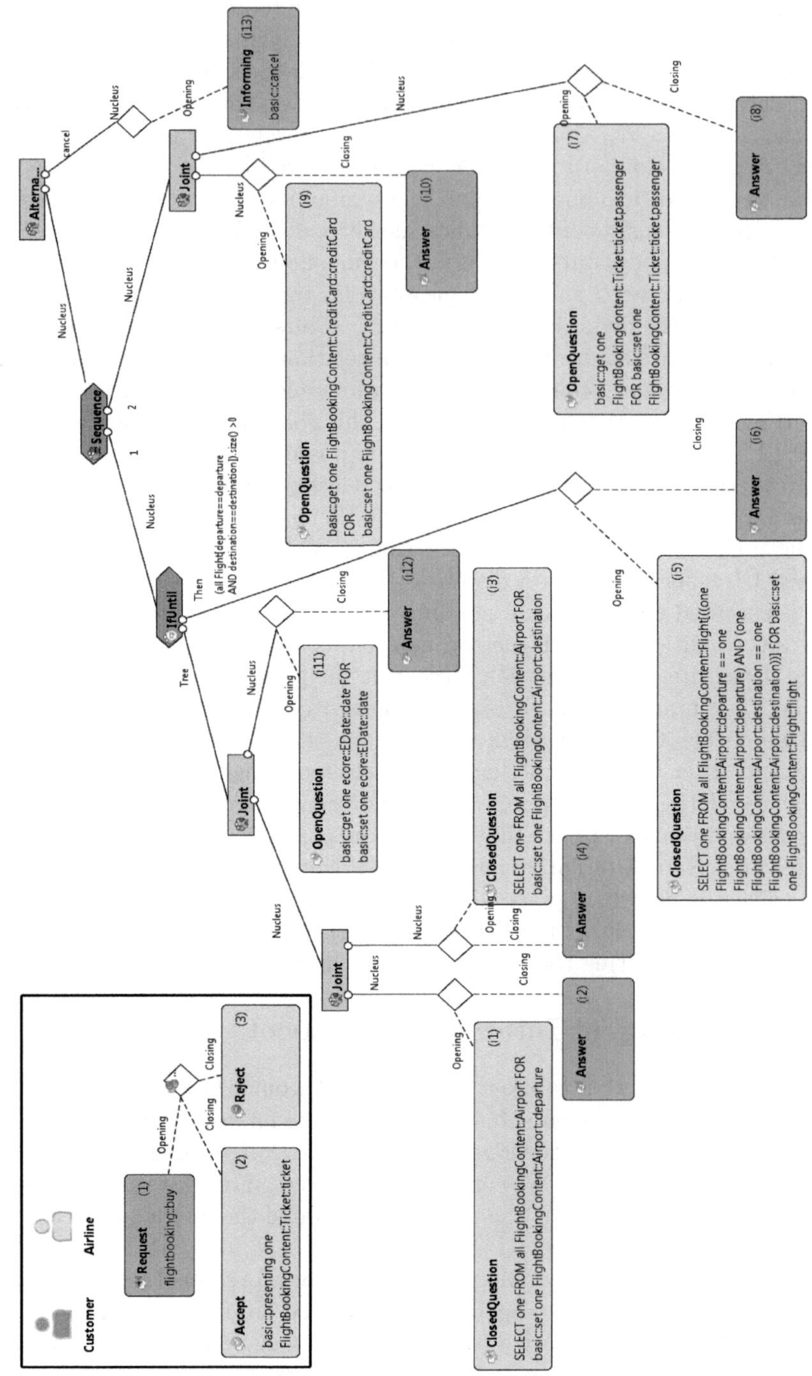

Fig. 1. Flight Booking Discourse

the Communicative Acts), but also the relations between the Adjacency Pairs that relate them. These relations are a formal definition of the sequence of the messages and therefore, support an unambiguous definition of the interaction itself. A second strong point of our approach is the possibility to precisely define the content of each Communicative Act using the Domain and the Action Notification Ontology. The *Domain Ontology* captures the application domain and defines the structure of the content objects of the Communicative Acts. The *Action Notification Ontology* captures the operations that can be performed on the domain objects. Both strong points prevent unexpected agent behavior.

The remainder of this section describes the Domain, the Action Notification and the Discourse in detail, before we present the Communication Ontology that combines them.

4.1 Domain Ontology

The *Domain Ontology* defines all objects that are relevant in the interaction between the two communicating agents. The agents exchange and store individuals of Domain Ontology concepts during runtime.

Figure 2 shows an excerpt of the Flight Booking Domain Ontology. This excerpt defines the concept *Airport* with the properties *name* and *airportcode* and the concept *Flight* with the properties *number* and *date*. The relations between the concepts specify that each *Flight* has 1 *departure* and 1 *destination* airport. The Customer and the Airline agents exchange and process individuals of these concepts during runtime.

4.2 Action Notification Ontology

The Action Notification Ontology specifies which operations can be performed on domain objects during the course of interaction. Operations can either be Actions or Notifications. *Actions* specify requests to an agent (e.g., *get* or *set* of a variable), whereas *Notifications* are used to inform an agent (e.g., *presenting* information). An example for a simple action is the *select* Action. A select signifies that an agent shall select one or more objects out of a list of objects. As a basis for most applications we defined a set of common Actions and Notifications like *get*, *set*, *select* and *presenting*, in a *basic* Action Notification Ontology. Figure 3 shows an excerpt of this *basic* ontology.

Most probably this basic set of Actions and Notifications needs to be extended for different application domains. For example, we added the *buy* action for our Flight Booking example.

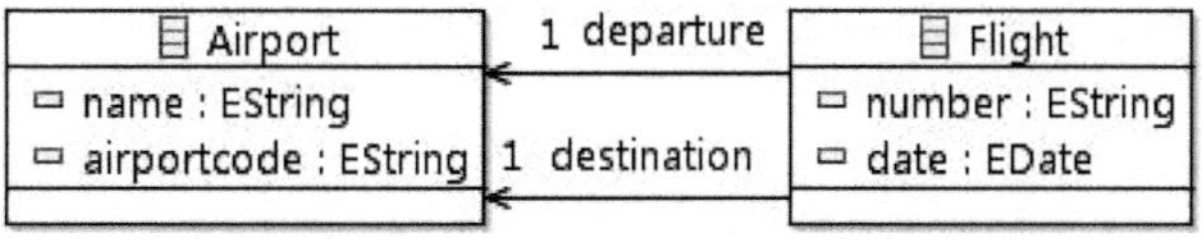

Fig. 2. Excerpt of the Flight Booking Domain of Discourse Ontology

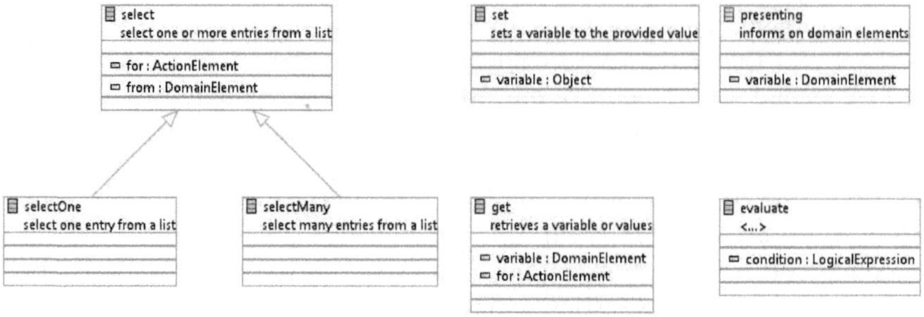

Fig. 3. Excerpt of the *Basic* Action Notification Ontology

To support quick and easy adaptability of the Action Notification Ontology we provide an upper ontology with the concepts shown in Figure 4. The *Element* concept is a common superclass for the *Action* and the *Notification* concepts, because both can have *Attributes* and *Parameters*. Attributes and Parameters can be used to parametrize Actions and Notifications. The difference between Attributes and Parameters is that Attributes specify variables only, and Parameters specify a variable and the corresponding value. This difference can be illustrated with two Actions from our *basic* Action Notification Ontology. The *get* Action requires the specification of two Attributes. The first Attribute is called *variable* and specifies the variable that shall be fetched. The additionally required *for* Attribute specifies the Action or Notification that shall be performed on the variable. A *set* Action in contrast requires the specification of a Parameter, because it needs to specify which variable should be set and the corresponding value. An example for a Notification with a Parameter is the *presenting* Notification. We use the *presenting* Notification in our Flight Booking example to inform the Customer agent about the purchased ticket.

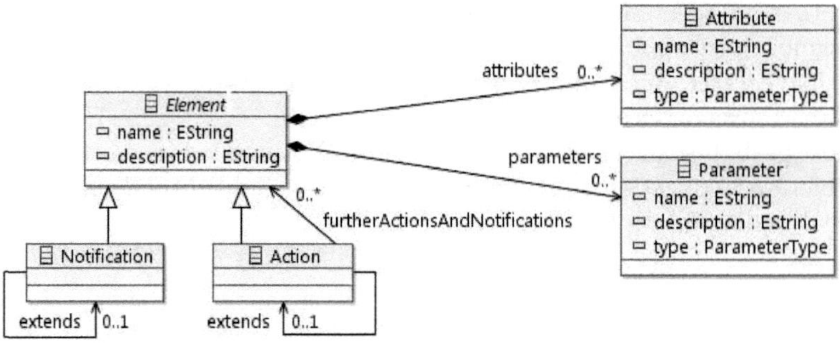

Fig. 4. The Action Notification Ontology

4.3 Discourse Ontology

The Discourse Ontology specifies the flow of events (i.e., Communicative Acts) during the interaction (for details see Section 3). However, there is one characteristic that needs to be considered if discourses (i.e., individuals of the Discourse Ontology) are applied in the domain of eCommerce. It is necessary that the Agent A (i.e., the service requester) starts the conversation, so that Agent B (i.e., the service provider) knows the requester. Therefore, the main part of running example is embedded as Inserted Sequence in the black framed Adjacency Pair shown in the upper left edge of Figure 1.

4.4 Communication Ontology

The Communication Ontology combines the Discourse, the Domain and the Action Notification Ontology, and supports the explicit definition of a *propositional content* for each Communicative Act. The propositional content refers to objects defined in the Domain Ontology and operations defined in the Action Notification Ontology. In case of Communicative Acts that represent requests for information (e.g., *OpenQuestions* or *ClosedQuestions*), however, the content of the *Answer* does not have to be specified explicitly, because it is implicitly defined through the content of the question.

Individuals of the Action Notification Ontology represent the abstract syntax specification for the propositional content. Let us illustrate the corresponding concrete syntax and the implicit definition of the *Answer* with the *ClosedQuestion* Communicative Act i1 (i.e., the question for selecting a departure airport) in our Flight Booking example. The Communicative Act type ClosedQuestion implies that the corresponding agent needs to provide a list of values from which the interaction partner can select one or more entries as answer. The propositional content of Communicative Act i1 is specified as ***SELECT one FROM all FlightBookingContent::Airport FOR basic::set one FlightBookingContent::Airport::departure***. The first part of this specification, the *SELECT one* refers to the *SelectOne* action defined in the basic Action Notification Ontology (see Figure 3). The SelectOne Action requires the specification of a *from* Parameter and a *for* Attribute. The second part of the content specification starts with *FROM*, which indicates that this part specifies the from Parameter. The from Parameter is specified as *all FlightBookingContent::Airport*. This means that all individuals of the class *Airport*, specified in the *FlightBookingContent* Domain Ontology, shall be provided. Subsequently the *for* attribute of the SelectOne Action is specified as indicated by the key word *FOR*. This for Attribute is specified as *basic::set one FlightBookingContenet::Airport::departure*. Its first part refers to the *set* Action of the basic Action Notification Ontology. This set Action has one Parameter, *variable*, which is specified as a variable of the type *Airport* with the name *departure* from the *FlightBookingContent* Domain Ontology. We did not specify the content of the *Answer* Communicative Act i2 explicitly, because it is implicitly specified by the from Parameter of the corresponding *ClosedQuestion*'s *select* Action.

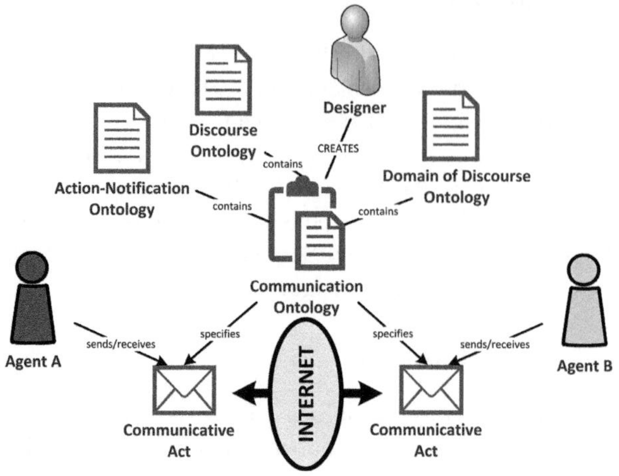

Fig. 5. The Communication Ontology as Interaction Protocol

Apart from the propositional content specification of Communicative Acts, the Action Notification Ontology supports the definition of actions that evaluate conditions specified in a discourse. An example for such a condition is the repeat condition of the IfUntil relation in Figure 1. This condition specifies that the then branch can only be executed after a departure and a destination airport have been selected. The Action *evaluate* in Figure 3 defines such an Action with one Attribute, the logical expression that shall be evaluated.

So far we presented how the Communication Ontology is used to define the interaction between two agents at design time. This interaction specification together with the precise definition of the propositional content supports runtime interpretation and thus the use of Communication Ontologies as interaction protocol (see Figure 5). The upper part of the Figure 5 depicts that the designer creates a Communication Ontology through the combination of the Discourse, the Domain and the Action Notification Ontology. The Communication Ontology does not only specify the Communicative Acts, but also the interaction between Agent A and Agent B. This interaction is performed through the exchange of Communicative Acts between the two agents via the Internet at runtime. We provide a platform, the *Unified Communication Platform*, which each agent uses to interpret its Communication Ontologies during runtime. The Unified Communication Platform assures that each agent interprets the Communication Ontologies in the same way. Thus, it improves the agent interoperability by assuring that the interaction follows the defined discourses.

5 Functional Interface Definition

The propositional content of a Communicative Act refers to the Action Notification and the Domain Ontology. The Actions and Notifications specify how the messages have to be processed by the corresponding agent. This definition of

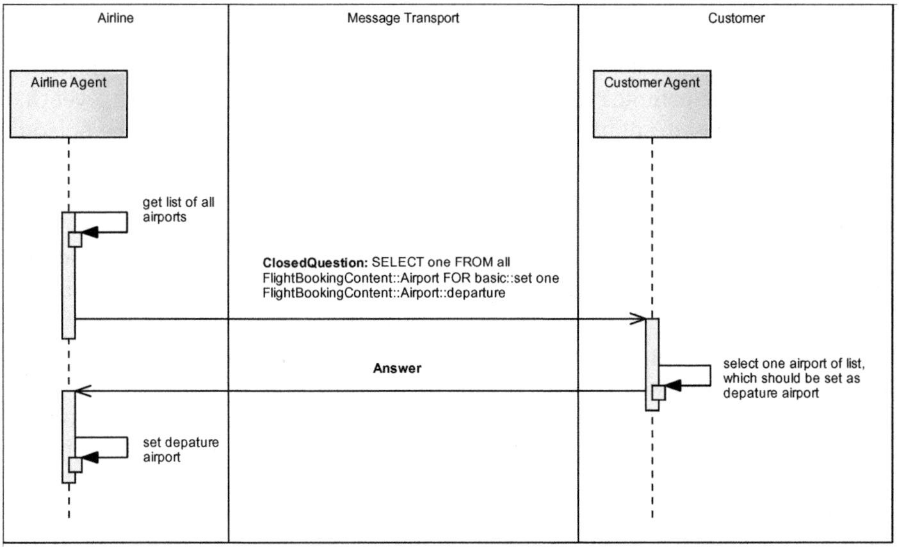

Fig. 6. The Use of the Functional Interface during Runtime

tasks that have to be performed by an agent are, de facto, a *functional interface definition.* The propositional content is part of a Communicative Act, which is directly assigned to an agent. Thus, the functional interface of each agent is defined through the propositional content of the assigned Communicative Acts.

Let us illustrate this functional interface definition using the leftmost Adjacency Pair in our Flight Booking example once more. This Adjacency Pair models the selection of the departure airport and relates the ClosedQuestion i1 and the corresponding Answer i2. Figure 6 shows in detail which functional requirements are specified through the propositional content of ClosedQuestion i1. A UML Sequence Diagram is used to illustrate their sequence. This sequence corresponds to the runtime interpretation of the Adjacency Pair that models the selection of the departure airport. Before the Airline agent is able the send the ClosedQuestion i1 it needs to acquire a list of all available airports. Subsequently, it sends Communicative Act i1 over the Internet to the Customer agent. Now the Customer agent has to select the departure airport out of the received list. Consequently, the Customer agent sends the selected airport back to the Airline agent, using the Answer Communicative Act i2. The content of the Answer does not have to be specified explicitly, because it is already specified by the content of the ClosedQuestion. After the Airline agent received the answer, it has to set the departure airport variable. All these requests to the functionality of the agents are defined through the Action Notification Ontology and are part of the agents' functional interface definition. The Unified Communication Platform does not consider the semantics for the definition of the agents' functional interface. It evaluates only the Parameters and Attributes of the elements and is therefore able to handle all Action Notification Ontologies.

6 Conclusion

In this paper we introduced a Communication Ontology that supports the precise definition of more complex interaction between two agents on a higher level than the typical request-response pair. Our Communication Ontology does not only support the definition of the exchanged messages, but also the specification of the operations that an agent shall perform. Both characteristics prevent unexpected agent behavior and improve their interoperability.

We used our Communication Ontology to realize a shopping scenario that involved robot trolleys, a cash desk and human users [19]. All actors in this shopping scenario can be interpreted as agents interacting in a supermarket environment. The application that we created to implement this scenario used discourses (i.e., individuals of the Communication Ontology) to specify the interaction between the user and the trolley or the cash desk, as well as the interaction between two trolleys or a trolley and the cash desk. These discourses were successfully used as interaction protocol for the communication between the trolley agents, the cash desk agent and the user agent (via a multi modal user interface). This scenario proofs that our Communication ontology can be used as a Communication Protocol between different actors or agents.

Though more research will be necessary we claim that our Communication Ontology is a first step towards better interoperability between agents in heterogeneous environments like the current eCommerce landscape.

References

1. Camarinha-Matos, L.M.: Virtual organizations in manufacturing: Trends and challenges. In: 12th Int. Conf. On Flexible Automation and Intelligent Manufacturing, Dresden, Germany, July 15-17 (2002)
2. Bravo, M., Velazquez, J.: Measuring heterogeneity between web-based agent communication protocols. In: Chung, S., Herrero, P. (eds.) OTM-WS 2008. LNCS, vol. 5333, pp. 656–665. Springer, Heidelberg (2008) 10.1007/978-3-540-88875-8_89
3. Bogg, P., Beydoun, G., Low, G.: Problem-solving methods in agent-oriented software engineering. In: Song, W.W.W., Xu, S., Wan, C., Zhong, Y., Wojtkowski, W., Wojtkowski, G., Linger, H. (eds.) Information Systems Development, pp. 243–254. Springer, New York (2011) 10.1007/978-1-4419-7355-9_21
4. Labrou, Y.: Mutli-agents systems and applications, pp. 74–97. Springer-Verlag New York, Inc., New York (2001)
5. Grimley, M., Cournane, M.: Universal business language (ubl) 2.0 naming and design rules (Decemeber 2009), `http://docs.oasis-open.org/ubl/prd2-UBL-2.0-NDR/prd2-UBL-2.0-NDR.xml`
6. Koppensteiner, G., Merdan, M., Lepuschitz, W., List, E., Vittori, L.: Ontology-oriented framework for virtual enterprises - accomplished within the project: Future network-based semantic technologies (funset-science). In: KEOD, pp. 300–307 (2009)
7. Searle, J.R.: Speech Acts: An Essay in the Philosophy of Language. Cambridge University Press, Cambridge (1969)
8. Mann, W.C., Thompson, S.: Rhetorical Structure Theory: Toward a functional theory of text organization. Text 8(3), 243–281 (1988)

9. Luff, P., Frohlich, D., Gilbert, N.: Computers and Conversation. Academic Press, London (January 1990)
10. Moore, S.A.: A foundation for flexible automated electronic communication. Info. Sys. Research 12, 34–62 (2001)
11. Wang, L., Hongshuai, Z.: Ontology for communication in distributed multi-agent system. In: International Symposium on Distributed Computing and Applications to Business, Engineering and Science, vol. 0, pp. 588–592 (2010)
12. Singh, M.: A social semantics for agent communication languages. In: Dignum, F.P.M., Greaves, M. (eds.) Issues in Agent Communication. LNCS, vol. 1916, pp. 31–45. Springer, Heidelberg (2000) 10.1007/10722777_3
13. Bermúdez, J., Goñi, A., Illarramendi, A., Bagüés, M.I.: Interoperation among agent-based information systems through a communication acts ontology. Inf. Syst., 1121–1144 (December 2007)
14. Li, H., Cao, J., Castro-Lacouture, D., Skibniewski, M.: A framework for developing a unified b2b e-trading construction marketplace. Automation in Construction 12(2), 201–211 (2003)
15. Glushko, R.J., Tenenbaum, J.M., Meltzer, B.: An xml framework for agent-based e-commerce. Commun. ACM 42, 106–114 (1999)
16. Falb, J., Kavaldjian, S., Popp, R., Raneburger, D., Arnautovic, E., Kaindl, H.: Fully automatic user interface generation from discourse models. In: Proceedings of the 13th International Conference on Intelligent User Interfaces (IUI 2009), pp. 475–476. ACM Press, New York (2009)
17. Popp, R., Falb, J., Arnautovic, E., Kaindl, H., Kavaldjian, S., Ertl, D., Horacek, H., Bogdan, C.: Automatic generation of the behavior of a user interface from a high-level discourse model. In: Proceedings of the 42nd Annual Hawaii International Conference on System Sciences (HICSS-42). IEEE Computer Society Press, Piscataway (2009)
18. Raneburger, D., Popp, R., Kavaldjian, S., Kaindl, H., Falb, J.: Optimized GUI generation for small screens. In: Hussmann, H., Meixner, G., Zuehlke, D. (eds.) Model-Driven Development of Advanced User Interfaces. Studies in Computational Intelligence, vol. 340, pp. 107–122. Springer, Berlin (2011)
19. Kaindl, H., Popp, R., Raneburger, D., Ertl, D., Falb, J., Szep, A., Bogdan, C.: Robot-supported cooperative work: A shared-shopping scenario. In: Hawaii International Conference on System Sciences, vol. 0, pp. 1–10 (2011)

When Trust Is Not Enough

John Debenham[1] and Carles Sierra[2]

[1] QCIS, UTS, Broadway, NSW 2007, Australia
debenham@it.uts.edu.au
[2] Institut d'Investigació en Intel·ligència Artificial - IIIA,
Spanish Scientific Research Council, CSIC
08193 Bellaterra, Catalonia, Spain
sierra@iiia.csic.es

Abstract. The degree of *trust* that an agent has for another is the strength of the agent's belief that the other will enact its commitments without variation. A strong sense of trust may be sufficient justification for one agent to sign a contract with another when all that matters is the possibility of variation between commitment and enactment. In non-trivial contracts the agents' information is typically asymmetric with each agent knowing more about its ability to vary its actions within its contractual constraints than the other. To enable an agent to deal with the asymmetry of information we propose two models. First, a *relationship model* that describes what one agent knows about another, *including* the belief that it has in the reliability of that information. Second an integrity model where *integrity* is the strength of an agent's belief that the other will not take advantage of its information asymmetries when enacting its commitments.

1 Introduction

The term *trust* is used in the sense of "certainty based on past experience", and is commonly used particularly as the strength of belief that an agent has in another's desire to enact its commitments without variation. The literature on trust is enormous. The seminal paper [1] describes two approaches to trust: first, as a belief that another agent will do what it says it will, or will reciprocate for common good, and second, as constraints on the behaviour of agents to conform to trustworthy behaviour. Trust is used here in line with the first approach where trust is something that is learned and evolves, although this does not mean that we view the second as less important [2]. *Reputation* is the opinion (more technically, a social evaluation) of a group about something — in a social environment. Reputation [3] feeds into trust. [4] presents a comprehensive categorisation of trust research: policy-based, reputation-based, and trust in information resources. [5] presents an interesting taxonomy of trust models in terms of nine types of trust models. [6] describes a powerful model that integrates interaction and role-based trust with witness and certified reputation.

Information asymmetry between contractually-bound agents has been studied extensively, and reached prominence with the award of the 2001 Nobel Prize in Economics to George Akerlof, Michael Spence, and Joseph E. Stiglitz "for their analyses of markets with asymmetric information." Contract theory tackles information asymmetry by

C. Huemer and T. Setzer (Eds.): EC-Web 2011, LNBIP 85, pp. 246–257, 2011.

invoking the unrealistic concept of a *complete contract* that specifies the consequences of every possible state of the world [7]. In real situations, agents accept that contracts are incomplete and rely on their contractual partner to 'do the right thing'. In other words, an agent relies on them to act with integrity, where *integrity* is the strength of belief that the other will *not* take advantage of its information asymmetries when enacting his commitments. An agent will be (economically) motivated to act with integrity when it prefers to develop an on-going (business) relationship with another agent rather than taking full advantage of each opportunity as it occurs. An agent who exhibits this latter behaviour may need to continually seek new trading partners if past partners are not motivated to trade again. It is proposed that the development of a sense of integrity comes hand-in-hand with the development of (business) relationships. In particular, the estimation of integrity is predicated on the existence of a model of relationships.

This paper is concerned with tools to manage variations in agent behaviour that may take advantage of information asymmetries whilst being trustworthy, i.e. within its contractual commitments. Two tools are proposed. First, relationships described in Section 2, and an associated relationship model described in Section 3. Second, an integrity model described in Section 4. Section 5 concludes.

2 'Relationships' between Agents

There is evidence from psychological studies that humans seek a *balance* in their negotiation relationships. The classical view [8] is that people perceive resource allocations as being distributively fair (i.e. well balanced) if they are proportional to inputs or contributions (i.e. equitable). However, more recent studies [9,10] show that humans follow a richer set of norms of distributive justice depending on their *intimacy* level: equity, equality, and need. *Equity* being the allocation proportional to the effort (e.g. the profit of a company goes to the stock holders proportional to their investment), *equality* being the allocation in equal amounts (e.g. two friends eat the same amount of a cake cooked by one of them), and *need* being the allocation proportional to the need for the resource (e.g. in case of food scarcity, a mother gives all food to her baby).

We believe that the perception of balance in dialogues (in negotiation or otherwise) is grounded on social relationships, and that every dimension of an interaction between humans can be correlated to the social closeness, or *intimacy*, between the parties involved. The more intimacy the more the need norm is used, and the less intimacy the more the equity norm is used. This might be part of our social evolution. There is ample evidence that when human societies evolved from a hunter-gatherer structure[1] to a shelter-based one[2] the probability of survival increased when food was scarce.

In this context, we can clearly see that, for instance, families exchange not only goods but also information and knowledge based on need, and that few families would consider their relationships as being unbalanced, and thus unfair, when there is a strong

[1] In its purest form, individuals in these societies collect food and consume it when and where it is found. This is a pure equity sharing of the resources, the gain is proportional to the effort.

[2] In these societies there are family units, around a shelter, that represent the basic food sharing structure. Usually, food is accumulated at the shelter for future use. Then the food intake depends more on the need of the members.

asymmetry in the exchanges (a mother explaining everything to her children, or buying toys, and then does not expect reciprocity). In the case of partners there is some evidence [11] that the allocations of goods and burdens (i.e. positive and negative utilities) are perceived as fair, or in balance, based on equity for burdens and equality for goods.

The perceived balance in a negotiation dialogue allows negotiators to infer information about their opponent, about its stance, and to compare their relationships with all negotiators. For instance, if we perceive that every time we request information it is provided, and that no significant questions are returned, or no complaints about not receiving information are given, then that probably means that our opponent perceives our social relationship to be very close. Alternatively, we can detect what issues are causing a burden to our opponent by observing an imbalance in their information or utilitarian utterances on that issue.

A *relationship* between two agents is somehow encapsulated in their *history* that is a complete record of their interactions. This potentially large amount of information is usually summarised by agents into various models. For example, the majority of agents construct a world model and a trust model. This paper is concerned with two models that are designed to assist an agent to deal with pervasive information asymmetry founded on the observation that each agent knows more about its own commitments and its intended enactments than any other agent. These two models are a relationship model described in Section 3 and an integrity model described in Section 4.

This Section describes the LOGIC illocutionary framework for classifying argumentative interactions. This framework was first described in [12] where it was used to help agents to prepare for a negotiation in the *prelude stage* of an interaction[3]. This paper generalises that framework and uses it to define one of the two dimensions of the relationship model described in Section 3, the second dimension is provided by the structure of the ontology[4]. The five LOGIC categories for information are quite general:

- Legitimacy contains *information* that may be part of, relevant to or in justification of contracts that have been signed.
- Options contains information about *contracts* that an agent may be prepared to sign.
- Goals contains information about the *objectives* of the agents.
- Independence contains information about the agent's *outside options* — i.e. the set of agents that are capable of satisfying each of the agent's needs.
- Commitments contains information about the *commitments* that an agent has.

and are used here to categorise all incoming communication that feeds into the agent's relationship model. As we will see this categorisation is not a one-to-one mapping and some illocutions fall into multiple categories. These categories are designed to provide a model of the agents' information that is relevant to their relationships, and are

[3] The five stages of an interaction dialogue are described in Section 4.

[4] All that we require of the ontology is that it has a partial order $\leq$ defined by the is-a hierarchy, and a distance measure between concepts such as: $\delta(c_1, c_2) = e^{-\kappa_1 l} \cdot \frac{e^{\kappa_2 h} - e^{-\kappa_2 h}}{e^{\kappa_2 h} + e^{-\kappa_2 h}}$ which is described in [13] where l is the shortest path between the concepts, h is the depth of the deepest concept subsuming both concepts, and κ_1 and κ_2 are parameters scaling the contribution of shortest path length and depth respectively.

not intended to be a universal categorising framework for all utterances. The LOGIC framework for managing communication is illustrated in Figure 1. A simplified formal model relates the LOGIC framework to the BDI model:

- $L = \{B(\alpha, \varphi)\}$, that is a set of *beliefs*.
- $O = \{\text{Plan}(\langle\alpha_1, \text{Do}(p_1)\rangle, \ldots, \langle\alpha_n, \text{Do}(p_n)\rangle\}$, that is a set of *joint plans*.
- $G = \{D(\alpha, \varphi)\}$, that is a set of *desires*.
- $I = \{\text{Can}(\alpha, Do(p))\}$, that is a set of *capabilities*.
- $C = \{I(\alpha, \text{Do}(p))\} \cup \{\text{Commit}(\alpha, \text{Do}(p))\}$, that is a set of *commitments* and *intentions*.

This paper is written from the point of view of an agent α is in a *multiagent system* with a finite number of other agents $\mathcal{B} = \{\beta_1, \beta_2, \ldots\}$, and a finite number of *information providing agents* $\Theta = \{\theta_1, \theta_2, \ldots\}$ that provide the *context* for all events in the system — Θ^t denotes the state of these agents at time t. α observes the actions of another agent β in the context Θ^t. The only thing that α 'knows for certain' is its *history* of past communication that is retains in the repository $\mathcal{H}^t_\alpha$. Each *utterance* in the history contains: an illocutionary statement, the sending agent, the receiving agent, the time that the utterance was sent or received.

Observations are of little value unless they can be verified. α may not posses a comprehensive range of reliable sensory input devices. Sensory inadequacy is dealt with invoking an *institution agent*, ξ, that truthfully, accurately and promptly reports what it sees. So if β commits to delivering twelve sardines at 6:00pm, or states that "it will rain tomorrow" and is committed to the truth of that prediction, then α will eventually be in a position to verify those commitments when ξ advises what actually occurs. ξ is simply a convenient abstraction to deal with the problem of sensory inadequacy of software agents. As we will see below, agent α qualifies all utterances received, including offers, information, arguments, with an epistemic probability representing α's belief in their veracity. ξ is the only agent that α believes is always truthful.

All communication is recorded in α's history $\mathcal{H}^t_\alpha$ that in time may contain a large amount of data. The majority of agent architectures include models that summarise the contents of $\mathcal{H}^t$; for example, a *world model* and a *trust model*. In this paper we describe two models, a *relationship model* and an *integrity model* that are specifically designed to assist an agent to manage information asymmetries. To build the relationship model we will use the LOGIC framework to categorise the information in utterances received. That is, α requires a categorising function $v : U \rightarrow \mathcal{P}(\{\text{L,O,G,I,C}\})$ where U is the set of utterances. The power set, $\mathcal{P}(\{\text{L,O,G,I,C}\}$, is required as some utterances belong to multiple categories. For example, "I will not pay more for wine than the price that John charges" is categorised as both Option and Independence.

3 The Relationship Model $\mathcal{R}^t_{\alpha\beta}$

All of α's models are summaries of its history $\mathcal{H}^t_\alpha$. The *relationship model* that α has of β consists of four component models. First, α's *intimacy model* of β's private information describes *how much* α knows about β, $I^t_{\alpha\beta}$. Second, α's *reliability model* of *how reliable* is the information summarised in $I^t_{\alpha\beta}$, $R^t_{\alpha\beta}$. Third, α's *reflection model* of β's model of α's private information, $J^t_{\alpha\beta}$. Fourth, a *balance model*, $B^t_{\alpha\beta}$, that measures the difference in the rate of growth of $I^t_{\alpha\beta}$ and $J^t_{\alpha\beta}$.

The remainder of this section details how these four models are calculated. This is achieved by extracting data from the process used to update the agent's world model $\mathcal{M}^t$ — if an agent maintains the currency of their world model then the marginal cost of building these four models is low. The description given employs the machinery to update the world model in our information-based agents [14]. However it can be adapted to the machinery used by any agent that represents uncertainty in its world model using probability distributions, in which case $\mathcal{M}^t = \{X_i\}_i$ where X_i are random variables. In addition to the world model and the models described in this paper an agent may construct other models such as a *trust model* and an *honour model* [15].

The idea of intimacy and balance is that intimacy summarises the degree of closeness, and *balance* is degree of fairness. Informally, *intimacy* measures how much one agent knows about another agent's private information, and *balance* measures the extent to which information revelation between the agents is 'fair'. The *intimacy* and *balance* models are structured using the LOGIC illocutionary framework and the ontology $\mathcal{O}$[5]. For example, the communication $\text{Accept}(\beta, \alpha, \delta)$ meaning that agent β accepts agent α's previously offered deal δ is classified as an Option, and $\text{Inform}(\beta, \alpha, \textit{info})$ meaning that agent β informs α about *info* and commits to the truth of it is classified as Legitimacy. The *balance model* of α's relationship with β, $B^t_{\alpha\beta}$, is the element by element numeric difference of $\frac{d}{dt} I^t_{\alpha\beta}$ and $\frac{d}{dt} J^t_{\alpha\beta}$ across the structure $\{\text{L,O,G,I,C}\} \times \mathcal{O}$.

3.1 The Components $I^t_{\alpha\beta}$, $R^t_{\alpha\beta}$ and $J^t_{\alpha\beta}$

The *intimacy* of α's relationship with β, $I^t_{\alpha\beta}$, is the amount that α knows about β's private information and is represented as real numeric values over $\{\text{L,O,G,I,C}\} \times \mathcal{O}$. Suppose α receives utterance u from β and that the LOGIC category $f \in v(u)$, where v is the categorising function described above. For any concept $c \in \mathcal{O}$, define $\Delta(u, c) = \max_{c' \in u} \delta(c', c)$ where δ is a semantic distance function such as that described in Footnote 4. Denote the value of $I^t_{\alpha\beta}$ in position $(f, c) \in \{\text{L,O,G,I,C}\} \times \mathcal{O}$ by $I^t_{\alpha\beta(f,c)}$ then:

$$I^t_{\alpha\beta(f,c)} = \rho \times I^{t-1}_{\alpha\beta(f,c)} + (1 - \rho) \times \mathbb{I}^t(u) \times \Delta(u, c) \tag{1}$$

for any c, where ρ is the discount rate, and $\mathbb{I}^t(u)$ is Shannon information gain as given by Equation 7. α's estimate of β's intimacy on α, $J^t_{\alpha\beta}$, is constructed similarly by assuming that β's reasoning apparatus mirrors α's.

The reliability model for utterance u is updated subsequent to the receipt of u when the institution agent ξ advises α that u' was observed instead of u that was expected. Denote the value of $R^t_{\alpha\beta}$ in position (f, c) by $R^t_{\alpha\beta(f,c)}$ then:

$$R^t_{\alpha\beta(f,c)} = \rho \times R^{t-1}_{\alpha\beta(f,c)} + (1 - \rho) \times \mathbb{R}^t(u)|u' \times \Delta(u, c) \tag{2}$$

for any c, where ρ is the discount rate, and $\mathbb{R}^t(u)|u'$ is given by Equation 9.

[5] Only a subset of the ontology is required. The idea is simply to capture "How much has Carles told me about wine", or "how much do it know about his commitments (possibly with other agents) concerning cheese".

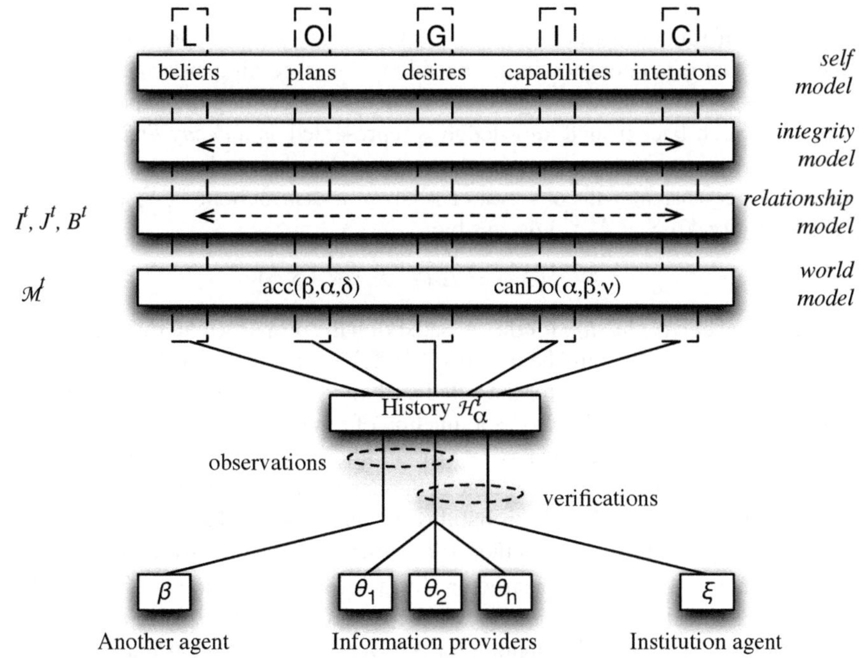

Fig. 1. The LOGIC framework for categorising information in an agent's relationship model

Utterances are represented in the world model $\mathcal{M}^t_\alpha$ as probability distributions, (X_i), in first-order probabilistic logic $\mathcal{L}$. For example, in a simple multi-issue contract negotiation α may estimate $\mathbb{P}^t(\text{acc}(\beta, \alpha, \delta))$, the probability that β would accept contract δ, by observing β's responses. The distribution $\mathbb{P}^t(\text{acc}(\beta, \alpha, \delta)) \in \mathcal{M}^t_\alpha$ is classified as an Option in LOGIC. Using shorthand notation, if β sends the message $\text{Offer}(\delta_1)$ then α may derive the constraint: $K^{\text{acc}(\beta,\alpha,\delta)}(\text{Offer}(\delta_1)) = \{\mathbb{P}^t(\text{acc}(\beta, \alpha, \delta_1)) = 1\}$, and if this is a counter offer to a former offer of α's, δ_0, then: $K^{\text{acc}(\beta,\alpha,\delta)}(\text{Offer}(\delta_1)) = \{\mathbb{P}^t(\text{acc}(\beta, \alpha, \delta_0)) = 0\}$. In the not-atypical special case of multi-issue bargaining where the agents' preferences over the individual issues *only* are known and are complementary to each other's, maximum entropy reasoning can be applied to estimate the probability that any multi-issue δ will be acceptable to β by enumerating the possible worlds that represent β's "limit of acceptability" [14]. As another example, the predicate $\text{canDo}(\alpha, \beta, \nu)$ meaning β is able to satisfy α's need ν — this predicate is classified as Independence in LOGIC.

Updating $\mathcal{M}^t_\alpha$ is complicated the need to take the integrity of utterances received into account — it would certainly be foolish for α to believe that every utterance received from β was correct — whereas all utterances received from the institution agent ξ *are* assumed to be correct. The procedure for doing this, and for attaching an *a priori* belief to utterances (see Equation 10), is summarised in Section 3.3.

3.2 Estimating the information in an utterance: $\mathbb{I}^t(u)$

$\mathcal{M}^t_\alpha$ is a set of random variables, $\mathcal{M}^t = \{X_i, \ldots, X_n\}$ each representing an aspect of the world that α is interested in. In the absence of in-coming messages the integrity of $\mathcal{M}^t$ decays. α may have background knowledge concerning the expected integrity as $t \to \infty$. Such background knowledge is represented as a *decay limit distribution*. One possibility is to assume that the decay limit distribution has maximum entropy whilst being consistent with observations. Given a distribution, $\mathbb{P}(X_i)$, and a decay limit distribution $\mathbb{D}(X_i)$, $\mathbb{P}(X_i)$ decays by:

$$\mathbb{P}^{t+1}(X_i) = \Delta_i(\mathbb{D}(X_i), \mathbb{P}^t(X_i)) \tag{3}$$

where Δ_i is the *decay function* for the X_i satisfying the property that $\lim_{t\to\infty} \mathbb{P}^t(X_i) = \mathbb{D}(X_i)$. For example, Δ_i could be linear: $\mathbb{P}^{t+1}(X_i) = (1-\nu_i) \times \mathbb{D}(X_i) + \nu_i \times \mathbb{P}^t(X_i)$, where $\nu_i < 1$ is the decay rate for the i'th distribution. Either the decay function or the decay limit distribution could also be a function of time: Δ^t_i and $\mathbb{D}^t(X_i)$.

The following procedure updates $\mathcal{M}^t$ for all utterances $u \in U$. Suppose that α receives a message u from agent β at time t. Suppose that this message states "If I were you then something is so" with probability z, and suppose that α attaches an epistemic belief $\mathbb{R}^t_{\alpha\beta}(u)$ to u — a method for estimating $\mathbb{R}^t(u)$ is given below. Each of α's active plans, s, contains constructors for a set of distributions $\{X_i\} \in \mathcal{M}^t$ together with associated *update functions*[6], $K_s(\cdot)$, such that $K^{X_i}_s(u)$ is a set of linear constraints on the posterior distribution for X_i. Denote the prior distribution $\mathbb{P}^t(X_i)$ by $\boldsymbol{p}$, and let $\boldsymbol{p}_{(u)}$ be the distribution with minimum relative entropy[7] with respect to $\boldsymbol{p}$: $\boldsymbol{p}_{(u)} = \arg\min_{\boldsymbol{r}} \sum_j r_j \log \frac{r_j}{p_j}$ that satisfies the constraints $K^{X_i}_s(u)$. Then let $\boldsymbol{q}_{(u)}$ be the distribution:

$$\boldsymbol{q}_{(u)} = \mathbb{R}^t_{\alpha\beta}(u) \times \boldsymbol{p}_{(u)} + (1 - \mathbb{R}^t_{\alpha\beta}(u)) \times \boldsymbol{p} \tag{4}$$

and then let:

$$\mathbb{P}^t(X_{i(u)}) = \begin{cases} \boldsymbol{q}_{(u)} & \text{if } \boldsymbol{q}_{(u)} \text{ is "more interesting" than } \boldsymbol{p} \\ \boldsymbol{p} & \text{otherwise} \end{cases} \tag{5}$$

A general measure of whether $\boldsymbol{q}_{(u)}$ is *more interesting* than $\boldsymbol{p}$ is: $\mathbb{K}(\boldsymbol{q}_{(u)} \| \mathbb{D}(X_i)) > \mathbb{K}(\boldsymbol{p} \| \mathbb{D}(X_i))$, where $\mathbb{K}(\boldsymbol{x} \| \boldsymbol{y}) = \sum_j x_j \ln \frac{x_j}{y_j}$ is the Kullback-Leibler distance between two probability distributions $\boldsymbol{x}$ and $\boldsymbol{y}$.

Finally merging Equation 5 and Equation 3 we obtain the method for updating a distribution X_i on receipt of a message u:

$$\mathbb{P}^{t+1}(X_i) = \Delta_i(\mathbb{D}(X_i), \mathbb{P}^t(X_{i(u)})) \tag{6}$$

---

[6] A sample update function for the distribution $\mathbb{P}^t(acc(\beta, \alpha, \delta))$ is given above.

[7] Given a probability distribution $\boldsymbol{q}$, the *minimum relative entropy distribution* $\boldsymbol{p} = (p_1, \ldots, p_I)$ subject to a set of n linear constraints $\boldsymbol{g} = \{g_j(\boldsymbol{p}) = \boldsymbol{a_j} \cdot \boldsymbol{p} - c_j = 0\}, j = 1, \ldots, n$ (that must include the constraint $\sum_i p_i - 1 = 0$) is: $\boldsymbol{p} = \arg\min_{\boldsymbol{r}} \sum_j r_j \log \frac{r_j}{q_j}$. This may be calculated by introducing Lagrange multipliers $\boldsymbol{\lambda}$: $L(\boldsymbol{p}, \boldsymbol{\lambda}) = \sum_j p_j \log \frac{p_j}{q_j} + \boldsymbol{\lambda} \cdot \boldsymbol{g}$. Minimising L, $\{\frac{\partial L}{\partial \lambda_j} = g_j(\boldsymbol{p}) = 0\}, j = 1, \ldots, n$ is the set of given constraints $\boldsymbol{g}$, and a solution to $\frac{\partial L}{\partial p_i} = 0, i = 1, \ldots, I$ leads eventually to $\boldsymbol{p}$. Entropy-based inference is a form of Bayesian inference that is convenient when the data is sparse [16] and encapsulates common-sense reasoning [17].

This procedure deals with integrity decay, and with two probabilities: first, the probability z in the utterance u, and second the belief $\mathbb{R}^t_{\alpha\beta}(u)$ that α attached to u. the Shannon information gain in X_i is:

$$\mathbb{I}^t X_i = \mathbb{H}^t(X_i) - \mathbb{H}^{t-1}(X_i)$$

and if the distributions in $\mathcal{M}^t$ are independent then the Shannon information gain for $\mathcal{M}^t$ following the receipt of utterance u is:

$$\mathbb{I}^t(u) = \sum_{X_i} \mathbb{I}^t X_i \tag{7}$$

3.3 Estimating the Reliability of an Utterance: $\mathbb{R}^t(u)$

$\mathbb{R}^t_{\alpha\beta}(u)$ is an epistemic probability that takes account of α's personal caution. An empirical estimate of $\mathbb{R}^t_{\alpha\beta}(u)$ may be obtained by measuring the 'difference' between commitment and observation. Suppose that u is received from agent β at time t and is verified by the institution agent, ξ, as u' at some later time t'. Denote the prior $\mathbb{P}^t(X_i)$ by $\boldsymbol{p}$. Let $\boldsymbol{p}_{(u)}$ be the posterior minimum relative entropy distribution subject to the constraints $K_s^{X_i}(u)$, and let $\boldsymbol{p}_{(u')}$ be that distribution subject to $K_s^{X_i}(u')$. We now estimate what $\mathbb{R}^t_{\alpha\beta}(u)$ should have been in the light of knowing *now*, at time t', that u should have been u'.

The idea of Equation 4, is that $\mathbb{R}^t_{\alpha\beta}(u)$ should be such that, *on average* across $\mathcal{M}^t$, $\boldsymbol{q}_{(u)}$ will predict $\boldsymbol{p}_{(u')}$ — no matter whether or not u was used to update the distribution for X_i, as determined by the condition in Equation 5 at time u. The *observed reliability* for u and distribution X_i, $\mathbb{R}X_i{}^t(u)|u'$, on the basis of the verification of u with u', is the value of k that minimises:

$$\mathbb{R}X_i{}^t(u)|u' = \arg\min_k \mathbb{K}(k \cdot \boldsymbol{p}_{(u)} + (1-k) \cdot \boldsymbol{p} \parallel \boldsymbol{p}_{(u')})$$

where $\mathbb{K}$ is the Kullback-Leibler distance. The predicted *information* in u with respect to X_i is:

$$\mathbb{I}X_i{}^t(u) = \mathbb{H}^t(X_i) - \mathbb{H}^t(X_{i(u)}) \tag{8}$$

that is the reduction in uncertainty in X_i where $\mathbb{H}(\cdot)$ is Shannon entropy. Equation 8 takes account of the value of $\mathbb{R}X_i{}^t(u)$.

If $\mathbf{X}(u)$ is the set of distributions in $\mathcal{M}^t$ that u affects, then the *observed reliability* of β on the basis of the verification of u with u' is:

$$\mathbb{R}^t(u)|u' = \frac{1}{|\mathbf{X}(u)|} \sum_i \mathbb{R}X_i{}^t(u)|u' \tag{9}$$

For any concept $c \in \mathcal{O}$, $\mathbb{R}^t(c)$ is α's estimate of the reliability of information from β concerning c. In the absence of incoming communications the integrity of this estimate will decay in time by: $\mathbb{R}^t(c) = \chi \times \mathbb{R}^{t-1}(c)$ for decay constant $\chi < 1$ and close to 1. On receipt of communication u concerning c that is subsequently verified as u':

$$\mathbb{R}^t(c) = \mu \times \mathbb{R}^{t-1}(c) + (1-\mu) \times \mathbb{R}^t(u)|u' \tag{10}$$

where μ is the learning rate, that estimates the reliability of β's advice on any concept c. This completes the estimation of $\mathbb{I}^t(u)$ and $\mathbb{R}^t(u)$.

4 The Integrity Model $\mathcal{I}^t_{\alpha\beta}$

Agents interact through various forms of dialogues. This paper is concerned with *commitment dialogues* that contain at least one commitment, where a *commitment* may be to the truth of a statement or may be a contractual commitment. We assume that all commitment dialogues take place in some or all of the following five stages:

1. the *prelude* during which agents prepare for the interaction
2. the *negotiation* that may lead to
3. *signing* a contract
4. the *enactment* of the commitments in the contract
5. the *appraisal* of the complete interaction process that is made when the goods or services acquired by enactment of the contract have been consumed

The term *trust* is commonly used to refer to the enactment of commitments [4], and is evaluated at the completion of the enactment step in a commitment dialogue. 'Integrity' is distinct from trust, and is concerned with the appraisal of the dialogue including the behaviour of partner agents in commitment dialogues. For example, when ordering a bottle of wine, the merchant is *trustworthy* if the bottle is delivered as contractually specified, and the merchant will have acted with *integrity* if the wine is in good condition when it is consumed — possibly at a considerably later time.

The *integrity* of agent β is the strength of α's belief that β will enact its contractual commitments so as to take account of α's interests rather than executing the contract selfishly 'to the letter'. For example, "I haven't got the strawberries you ordered because yesterday's hail storm is likely to have bruised the fruit". Integrity is measured on a finite, fuzzy scale containing values such as 'perfect' and 'terrible'. For some dialogues the appraisal stage may take place a considerable time after the enactment stage; for example, "Carles advised me to buy the Mercedes and I after three years I am still delighted with it" that implicitly rates the quality of Carles' advice. This time delay is the reason that some business relationships necessarily take time to develop.

The integrity model is required to do the following. Given a particular need ν and the prevailing contextual information Θ^t, $\mathcal{I}^t_{\alpha\beta}$ aims to estimate the integrity of each agent in satisfying ν on the basis of the past commitment dialogues recorded in $\mathcal{H}^t_\alpha$. From the set of commitment dialogues in $\mathcal{H}^t_\alpha$ with agent β, we first form $\mathcal{C}^t_{\alpha\beta}$ that contains: an abstraction of the need that triggered the dialogue, the prevailing contextual information and the resulting evaluation of the dialogue. The abstraction of the need ν is to a chosen level using the $\leq$ relation in the ontology — see Footnote 4. For example, $\mathcal{H}^t_\alpha$ may contain a dialogue involving buying potatoes from β in which case $\mathcal{C}^t_{\alpha\beta}$ could contain a record involving 'root vegetables' together with the contextual information that prevailed at that time, and the evaluation.

$\mathcal{I}^t_{\alpha\beta}$ aims to form beliefs on the evaluation of future commitment dialogues with agent β based on $\mathcal{C}^t_{\alpha\beta}$ by treating the evaluations as values of the dependent variable. This can be interpreted as a pattern mining exercise from the information in $\mathcal{C}^t_{\alpha\beta}$ to find the 'best' hypothesis that describes $\mathcal{C}^t_{\alpha\beta}$. One neat way to perform this induction is the *minimum description length principle* [18] that is founded on the minimisation of the cost of communicating a body of knowledge from one agent to another that thus has a fundamental affinity with distributed autonomous systems:

$$\mathcal{I}^t_{\alpha\beta} \triangleq \arg\min_M(\mathbb{L}(M) + \mathbb{L}(\mathcal{C}^t_{\alpha\beta} \mid M)) \tag{11}$$

where $\mathbb{L}(M)$ is the length of the shortest encoding of M, and $\mathbb{L}(\mathcal{C}^t_{\alpha\beta} \mid M)$ is the length of the shortest encoding of $\mathcal{C}^t_{\alpha\beta}$ given M. This definition is as neat as it is computationally expensive — it divides $\mathcal{C}^t_{\alpha\beta}$ into that which may be generalised and that which may not.

The definition of $\mathcal{I}^t_{\alpha\beta}$ in Equation 11 appears problematic for three reasons. First, if M can be any Turing computable model the definition is not computable, second there should be a language for representing M, and third the meaning of 'the length of the shortest encoding' is not clear. The second and third reason have been resolved [18]. The first, computability problem can be solved by restricting the models to some specific class. If the models are restricted to Bayesian decision graphs over finite spaces then Equation 11 is computable [19].

The model does not take time into account. In some applications old observations may be poorer indicators that recent ones, but this is not always so. To allow for varying strength of observations with time we construct instead $\mathcal{C}^{*t}_{\alpha\beta}$ that is the same as $\mathcal{C}^t_{\alpha\beta}$ except each appraisal, x, is replaced by a random variable X over appraisal space. These probability distributions are constructed by: $\lambda \times X + (1 - \lambda) \times D_X$ where D_X is the *decay limit distribution*[8] for X — and X is a distribution with a '1' indicating the position of the appraisal and 0's elsewhere. This fine-grained approach gives control over the integrity decay of each observation.

Despite its elegance, Equation 11 is computationally expensive and we now describe methods for evaluating integrity for given ν and Θ^t for various β's. We represent the relationship between need ν, context Θ^t and appraisal a using conditional probabilities, $\mathbb{P}^{t'}_{\alpha\beta}(a|\nu, \Theta^t)$. If ν is a need, Θ^t the context that prevailed at the time t commitments were made, and a the resulting subsequent appraisal performed at time t' then $\mathbb{P}^{t'}_{\alpha\beta}(a|\nu, \Theta^t)$ is the probability that a will be observed at time t' given that β had been selected to service need ν in context Θ^t at time t.

Any attempt to estimate $\mathbb{P}^{t'}_{\alpha\beta}(a|\nu, \Theta^t)$ has to deal with the unbounded variation in context Θ^t. We assume that there is a finite set of 'essentially different' contexts Γ and then estimate $\mathbb{P}^t_{\alpha\beta}(a|\nu, \gamma)$ for $\gamma \in \Gamma$. Suppose that $\mathbb{P}^t_{\alpha\beta}(a_i|\nu, \gamma)$ is observed where $a_i \in A$ the finite appraisal space. Then α attaches an epistemic strength $d \in [0, 1]$ to this observation that is the probability that the same appraisal would be observed if the process was repeated for the same ν and γ. Then $\mathbb{P}^{t+1}_{\alpha\beta}(a|\nu, \gamma)$ is the distribution with minimum relative entropy to the prior $\mathbb{P}^t_{\alpha\beta}(a|\nu, \gamma)$ subject to the constraint that $\mathbb{P}^{t+1}_{\alpha\beta}(a_i|\nu, \gamma) = d$.

In general it is desirable that observations should effect integrity estimates that are semantically close. This is achieved by appealing to a semantic similarity function, δ, such as that described in Footnote 4, if observation $\mathbb{P}^t_{\alpha\beta}(a_i|\nu', \gamma')$ is made with strength

[8] If the decay limit distribution is unknown we use a maximum entropy distribution.

d' then the posterior for $\mathbb{P}^{t+1}_{\alpha\beta}(a|\nu,\gamma)$ is the distribution with minimum relative entropy to the prior $\mathbb{P}^{t}_{\alpha\beta}(a|\nu,\gamma)$ subject to the constraint that:

$$\mathbb{P}^{t+1}_{\alpha\beta}(a_i|\nu,\gamma) = \frac{b_i \times d''}{((1-b_i)\times(1-d''))+(b_i \times d'')}, \text{ only if } d'' > 0.5$$

where $d'' = d' \times \delta(\nu,\nu') \times \delta(\gamma,\gamma')$ discounts the effect of d' using δ, and the condition $d'' > 0.5$ limits the update region to ν and γ that are semantically close to ν' and γ' — this method assumes that the observations are independent. Then in the absence of new observations $\mathbb{P}^{t}_{\alpha\beta}(a|\nu,\gamma)$ decays by Equation 3.

The estimate for $\mathbb{P}^{t}_{\alpha\beta}(a|\nu,\gamma)$ in the previous paragraph enables α to predict, or guess, the appraisal that will be observed if α selects β to satisfy need ν in context γ. It may be convenient to have a numeric score for β's expected integrity given particular circumstances. One way to do this is to construct an 'ideal' distribution $\mathbb{P}^{t}_{I}(a|\nu,\gamma)$ and to define integrity as the relative entropy between this ideal distribution and the estimated distribution:

$$G(\alpha,\beta,\nu,\gamma) = 1 - \sum_{a} \mathbb{P}^{t}_{I}(a|\nu,\gamma)\log\frac{\mathbb{P}^{t}_{I}(a|\nu,\gamma)}{\mathbb{P}^{t}_{\alpha\beta}(a|\nu,\gamma)}$$

A simpler way is to used a metricated, totally ordered appraisal space and to define integrity as expectation: $G(\alpha,\beta,\nu,\gamma) = \sum_i a_i \times \mathbb{P}^{t}_{\alpha\beta}(a_i|\nu,\gamma)$.

5 Discussion

This paper addresses the problem of dealing with information asymmetry that includes the observation that each agent knows more about its own commitments, and its intended enactments, than any other agent. Further agents may, and often do, deliberately conceal information to take strategic advantage. An agent can act in a perfectly trustworthy way, in the sense described above, whilst taking full advantage of the asymmetry of its information: "Well I did precisely what you asked me to do".

We have proposed two approaches to deal with information asymmetry. The first builds on the observation that in complex situations human agents prefer to interact with those with whom there is some depth of relationship to dealing with strangers. A relationship model has been described that measures the amount of private information that one agent knows about another, the reliability of that information and the balance in their information exchanges. Calculating these models is not simple, but substantially reuses those that update the agent's world model, and so the marginal cost of building the relationship model is small. The second approach models integrity that measures overall satisfaction with an interaction; it is updated at the appraisal stage that may be a considerable time after contract enactment.

Future work will focus on trialling the relationship model and the integrity model in a simulated marketplace. There can be no guarantee that an agent will act with integrity no matter how strong its relationships. So our goal will be to develop institutional incentives for agents to act with integrity based on published reputation measures, and then to show that the models described in this paper may be used to protect against unscrupulous exploitation of asymmetric information.

References

1. Ramchurn, S., Huynh, T., Jennings, N.: Trust in multi-agent systems. The Knowledge Engineering Review 19, 1–25 (2004)
2. Arcos, J.L., Esteva, M., Noriega, P., Rodríguez, J.A., Sierra, C.: Environment engineering for multiagent systems. Journal on Engineering Applications of Artificial Intelligence 18 (2005)
3. Sabater, J., Sierra, C.: Review on computational trust and reputation models. Artificial Intelligence Review 24, 33–60 (2005)
4. Artz, D., Gil, Y.: A survey of trust in computer science and the semantic web. Web Semantics: Science, Services and Agents on the World Wide Web 5, 58–71 (2007)
5. Viljanen, L.: Towards an ontology of trust. In: Katsikas, S., Løpez, J., Pernum, G. (eds.) Trust, Privacy and Security in Digital Business TrustBus 2005, pp. 175–184. Springer, Heidelberg (2005)
6. Huynh, T., Jennings, N., Shadbolt, N.: An integrated trust and reputation model for open multi-agent systems. Autonomous Agents and Multi-Agent Systems 13, 119–154 (2006)
7. Bolton, P., Dewatripont, M.: Contract Theory. MIT Press, Cambridge (2005)
8. Adams, J.S.: Inequity in social exchange. In: Berkowitz, L. (ed.) Advances in Experimental Social Psychology, vol. 2. Academic Press, New York (1965)
9. Sondak, H., Neale, M.A., Pinkley, R.: The negotiated allocations of benefits and burdens: The impact of outcome valence, contribution, and relationship. Organizational Behaviour and Human Decision Processes, 249–260 (1995)
10. Valley, K.L., Neale, M.A., Mannix, E.A.: Friends, lovers, colleagues, strangers: The effects of relationships on the process and outcome of negotiations. In: Bies, R., Lewicki, R., Sheppard, B. (eds.) Research in Negotiation in Organizations, vol. 5, pp. 65–94. JAI Press (1995)
11. Bazerman, M.H., Loewenstein, G.F., White, S.B.: Reversal of preference in allocation decisions: judging an alternative versus choosing among alternatives. Administration Science Quarterly, 220–240 (1992)
12. Sierra, C., Debenham, J.: The LOGIC Negotiation Model. In: Proceedings Sixth International Conference on Autonomous Agents and Multi Agent Systems AAMAS 2007, Honolulu, Hawai'i, pp. 1026–1033 (2007)
13. Li, Y., Bandar, Z.A., McLean, D.: An approach for measuring semantic similarity between words using multiple information sources. IEEE Transactions on Knowledge and Data Engineering 15, 871–882 (2003)
14. Sierra, C., Debenham, J.: Information-based agency. In: Proceedings of Twentieth International Joint Conference on Artificial Intelligence, IJCAI 2007, Hyderabad, India, pp. 1513–1518 (2007)
15. Sierra, C., Debenham, J.: Trust and honour in information-based agency. In: Stone, P., Weiss, G. (eds.) Proceedings Fifth International Conference on Autonomous Agents and Multi Agent Systems, AAMAS 2006, pp. 1225–1232. ACM Press, Hakodate (2006)
16. Cheeseman, P., Stutz, J.: On The Relationship between Bayesian and Maximum Entropy Inference. In: Bayesian Inference and Maximum Entropy Methods in Science and Engineering, American Institute of Physics, Melville, NY, USA, pp. 445–461 (2004)
17. Paris, J.: Common sense and maximum entropy. Synthese 117, 75–93 (1999)
18. Grünwald, P.D.: The Minimum Description Length Principle. MIT Press, Cambridge (2007)
19. Suzuki, J.: Learning bayesian belief networks based on the MDL principle: An efficient algorithm using the branch and bound technique. IEICE Transactions on Information and Systems E81-D, 356–367 (1998)

LocalRank - Neighborhood-Based, Fast Computation of Tag Recommendations

Marius Kubatz, Fatih Gedikli*, and Dietmar Jannach

Technische Universität Dortmund,
44221 Dortmund, Germany
firstname.lastname@tu-dortmund.de

Abstract. On many modern Web platforms users can annotate the available online resources with freely-chosen tags. This Social Tagging data can then be used for information organization or retrieval purposes. Tag recommenders in that context are designed to help the online user in the tagging process and suggest appropriate tags for resources with the purpose to increase the tagging quality. In recent years, different algorithms have been proposed to generate tag recommendations given the ternary relationships between users, resources, and tags. Many of these algorithms however suffer from scalability and performance problems, including the popular *FolkRank* algorithm. In this work, we propose a neighborhood-based tag recommendation algorithm called *LocalRank*, which in contrast to previous graph-based algorithms only considers a small part of the user-resource-tag graph. An analysis of the algorithm on a popular social bookmarking data set reveals that the recommendation accuracy is on a par with or slightly better than FolkRank while at the same time recommendations can be generated instantaneously using a compact in-memory representation.

Keywords: recommender systems, collaborative filtering, social tagging.

1 Introduction

More and more Social Web platforms such as Delicious or Flickr but also e-commerce sites such as Amazon allow their users to annotate the online resources with freely-chosen tags[1]. In recent years, these community-created *folksonomies* have emerged as a valuable tool for content organization or retrieval in the participatory web. In contrast, for example, to formal Semantic Web ontologies, Social Tagging represents a more light-weight approach, which does not rely on a pre-defined set of concepts and terms that can be used for annotation. The advantage of Social Tagging lies in the fact that no special knowledge is required by the users. On the other hand, the value of the community-provided tags can be limited because no consistent vocabulary may exist as users have their own

* Contact author.

[1] http://delicious.org, http://flickr.com, http://www.amazon.com

C. Huemer and T. Setzer (Eds.): EC-Web 2011, LNBIP 85, pp. 258–269, 2011.

style and preferences which tags they use and which aspects of the resource they annotate. A picture of a car could for instance be annotated with tags such diverse as "red", "cool", or "mine"[1]. In [2], for example, Sen et al. reported that only 21% of the tags in the MovieLens system[2] had adequate quality to be displayed to the user.

One way to counteract this effect is to provide the user with a list of tag recommendations to choose from. When the users are provided with a set of tag suggestions, the goal is that the annotation vocabulary as a whole becomes more homogenous across users and that in addition the tagging volume increases, see [3]. In recent years, several approaches to building such *tag recommenders* have been proposed. The state-of-the-art *FolkRank* algorithm [4], for example, represents one early graph-based recommendation approach which was inspired by Google's PageRank [5] and which is still used as a baseline for comparison in the development of new tag recommender approaches today. Later on, different other tag recommendation algorithms have been proposed that rely on techniques such as tensor factorization and latent semantic analysis [6,7], follow a probabilistic approach [8,9,10] or use hybridization strategies [11]. Some approaches also even go beyond recommendation, and try to automatically generate and attach personalized tags for Web pages [12].

Beside improving the predictive accuracy, the question of scalability and the time needed for computing the recommendations is a major issue for the different approaches. Rendle et al. [6,7] for example conclude that FolkRank does not scale to larger problem sizes and report much shorter running time figures for their own tensor factorization approach. A clustering approach is developed in [13] to allow for "real-time" recommendation.

In this work, we also focus on the issue of scalability of tag recommendation to larger data sets. We therefore propose a graph- and neighborhood-based tag recommendation approach, which is not only capable of generating tag recommendations very quickly also for larger data sets, but which can also be efficiently updated when new data arrives. At the same time, we show that despite its simplicity, the accuracy of our method is comparable to that of FolkRank on the commonly-used Delicious data set.

2 FolkRank and LocalRank

2.1 Folksonomies and FolkRank

The LocalRank algorithm proposed in this paper is based on the ideas of FolkRank, which we will shortly discuss in the following section. Hotho et al. [4] define a folksonomy as a tuple $\mathbb{F} := (U, T, R, Y, \prec)$ where

- U, T , and R are finite sets, whose elements are called users, tags, and resources,
- Y is a ternary relation between them, i. e., $Y \subseteq U \times T \times R$, called tag assignments, and

[2] http://www.movielens.org

– $\prec$ is a user-specific subtag/supertag-relation, i.e., $\prec \subseteq U \times T \times T$, called subtag/ supertag relation. Note that in our work $\prec$ is an empty set[3].

The main idea of Google's PageRank algorithm is that pages are important when linked by other important pages. Therefore, PageRank views the web as a graph and uses a weight spreading algorithm to calculate the importance of the pages. FolkRank adopts this idea and assumes that a resource is important if it is tagged with important tags from important users. As a first step, a given folksonomy $\mathbb{F} = (U, T, R, Y)$ is converted into an undirected tripartite graph $\mathbb{G}_\mathbb{F}$, where the set of nodes $V = U \dot\cup T \dot\cup R$ and the set of edges E and their weights is determined by the elements of Y.

Note that $\mathbb{G}_\mathbb{F}$ is different from the directed unipartite web graph. Hotho et al. therefore propose the Folksonomy-Adapted PageRank (FA-PR) algorithm to compute a ranking of the elements and which also takes the weights of the edges into account[4]. Since $\mathbb{G}_\mathbb{F}$ is undirected, a part of the weight spread over an edge will flow back in each iteration.

Formally, the weight spreading function is $\overrightarrow{w} = dA\overrightarrow{w} + (1-d)\overrightarrow{p}$, where A is the row-stochastic version of the adjacency matrix of $\mathbb{G}_\mathbb{F}$, $\overrightarrow{w}$ is the vector containing the rank values for the elements of V, $\overrightarrow{p}$ a preference vector whose elements sum up to 1 and d a factor determining the influence of $\overrightarrow{p}$. When a non-personalized ranking of the elements of $\mathbb{G}_\mathbb{F}$ is to be computed, d can be set to 1. When the goal is to personalize the ranking (or support topic-specific rankings), more weight can be given to elements in $\overrightarrow{p}$ which correspond to the user preferences or a given topic. Similar to PageRank, Folksonomy-Adapted PageRank works by iteratively computing $\overrightarrow{w}$ until convergence is achieved.

The FolkRank algorithm finally computes $\overrightarrow{w}$ two times – one time including the user preferences and one time without them – and compares the differences between the rankings of the two $\overrightarrow{w}$ vectors. The "winners" of the inclusion of the preference vector therefore get higher rank values. Recommending tags for a given resource or user can be accomplished by taking the n elements with the highest rank values.

Overall, FolkRank has shown to lead to highly accurate results and even the more recent algorithms mentioned above are only slightly more accurate than FolkRank on some evaluation data sets. However, one of the major issues of FolkRank are the steep computational costs involved in the computation of recommendations. Note that while the non-personalized ranks can be computed in an offline phase, this is not manageable for the personalized ranking. For analysis purposes, we use the original Java implementation provided by the developers of FolkRank[5] and evaluated it on three Delicious data sets at different density. Computing a single recommendation list for this data set consisting of about 36,000 thousand users, 70,000 bookmarks, 21,000 tags, and 7,000,000 assignments required about 20 seconds on a typical desktop PC (AMD Athlon

[3] For this reason we will simply denote a folksonomy as a quadruple $\mathbb{F} := (U, T, R, Y)$.

[4] Note that FolkRank is not limited to the calculation of weights for the tags but can also be used to compute weights of users and resources.

[5] `http://www.kde.cs.uni-kassel.de/code`

II Dual Core, 2.9Ghz, 8GB Ram) when the maximal number of iterations is set to 10. When pre-computing the unbiased ranks, the running time is reduced to about 10 seconds on average. Note that, given that FolkRank always propagates the weights through the whole network, the non-personalized weights have to be re-computed (or at least updated on a regular basis) when new tag assignments are added to the system.

2.2 LocalRank

In order to address the issues of scalability and updates, we propose LocalRank, a new tag recommendation algorithm which in contrast to FolkRank computes the rank weights only based on the local "neighborhood" of a given user and resource. Instead of considering all elements in the folksonomy, LocalRank focuses on the *relevant* ones only. Given a folksonomy $\mathbb{F} = (U, T, R, Y)$, its representation as $\mathbb{G}_{\mathbb{F}}$, a user $u \in U$ and a resource $r \in R$, we first compute the following sets of relevant elements.

- $Y_u \subseteq Y$ is the set of all (u, t, r)-assignments of Y where u is the given user.
- Analogously, $Y_r \subseteq Y$ is the set of all (u, t, r)-assignments of Y where r is the given resource.
- The set of user-relevant tags T_u is defined to be the set of all tags appearing in the (u, t, r)-assignments of Y_u.
- The resource-relevant tags T_r are analogously defined as the set of tags from the assignments in Y_r.
- The overall set of relevant tags to be ranked by the algorithm is $T_u \cup T_r$.

Figure 1 visualizes the local neighborhood of a user and a resource as two subgraphs of $\mathbb{G}_{\mathbb{F}}$, constructed using the sets Y_u and Y_r. The side aspect is that the sets can be represented efficiently as a compact data structure in memory. Note that the two subgraphs can also be connected in $T_u \cap T_r$.

The rank computation in LocalRank takes into account how often a certain tag was used by a user and how often a tag was attached to a resource. A similar approach was presented as *most popular tags by user* and *most popular tags by resource* in [14]. Although the efficiency of the combination of these approaches – known as *most popular ρ-mix* – is comparable to our approach, the accuracy

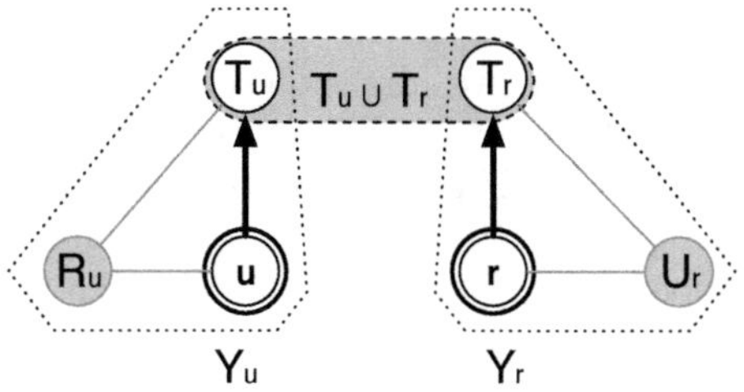

Fig. 1. Neighborhood of relevant tags for a given user-resource query

results, however, are worse than those of FolkRank. Note that in our approach, the popularity information is used as a factor in the rank computation of each tag in $T_u \cup T_r$. The (non-local) information how often other users have tagged other resources with these tags, however, is not exploited in LocalRank.

Rank computation and weight propagation in LocalRank is done similar to FolkRank but without iterations. The arrows in Figure 1 indicate the direction of the propagation of user and resource weights (see below) towards the tags.

In the FolkRank implementation the weight of a node v depends on the total number of nodes $|V|$ in the folksonomy and is set to $w = 1/|V|$. The frequency of the node's occurrence in Y is denoted as $|Y_v|$ and is defined as the number of (u, t, r)-assignments in Y, in which v appears. Overall, in FolkRank, the amount of weight spread by a node v to all its adjacent nodes is $w/|Y_v|$.

LocalRank, in contrast, approximates the weights for a given u and r with $w = 1/N$, where N is the total number of their neighbors in $\mathbb{G}_\mathbb{F}$. The amount of weight that is spread by the user and resource is calculated as $w/|Y_u|$ and $w/|Y_r|$ respectively.

In $\mathbb{G}_\mathbb{F}$, both algorithms calculate the weight gained by a node x by multiplying the spread weight $w/|Y_v|$ with the weight of the edge (v, x) which is equal to $|Y_{v,x}|$. While FolkRank repeatedly computes the weight gained by x for each (v, x) pair of nodes, LocalRank computes it once for each tag t in $T_u \cup T_r$.

The rank of each $t \in T_u$ is calculated as follows:

$$rank(t) = |Y_{u,t}| \times \frac{1/N}{|Y_u|} \tag{1}$$

The rank of tags in T_r is calculated similarly:

$$rank(t) = |Y_{r,t}| \times \frac{1/N}{|Y_r|} \tag{2}$$

Intuitively, we finally assume that tags that appear in both sets ($t \in T_u \cap T_r$) are on principle more important than the others and should receive a higher weight. Therefore we sum up the individual rank weights obtained from the two calculations.

LocalRank propagates the weight of the given user and resource nodes to all their adjacent tags. Therefore, it computes rankings for user and resource relevant tags and returns a list of tags and their ranks. The recommendation of tags can then be done by picking the top n elements with the highest rank values.

Note that in our evaluation we also experimented with a variation of the calculation scheme in which we introduced a weight factor to balance the importance of the different tag sets. The intuition behind this idea was that tags in T_r are generally more important than those in T_u because they already describe the resource. Elements of T_u capture the popularity of a tag with the particular user and should have less importance as they are not necessarily meaningful to the resource. A similar approach to balancing the influence of user and resource related tags was presented in [14]. The experiments however showed that the introduction of such a weight factor did not help to further improve the results.

Table 1. Data sets used in experiments

	p-core 1	p-core 5	p-core 10
Users	71,756	48,471	36,486
Tags	454,587	47,984	21,930
Resources	3,322,519	169,960	70,412
Y-assign.	17,802,069	8,963,895	7,157,654

3 Evaluation

3.1 Data Sets

In order to evaluate our approach both with respect to accuracy and run-time behavior, we ran tests on different versions of the Delicious data set, which is also used by many other researchers in the area of data mining and tag recommendation.

Delicious is a "social bookmarking tool", where users can manage collections of their personal web bookmarks, describe them using keywords (tags) and share them with other users. For our experiments, we used a data set of users, bookmarks and tags provided on courtesy of the DAI-Labor[6], which in its raw version contains more then 400 million tags applied to over 130 million bookmarks by nearly 1 million users.

In order to compare our work with previous work, we first extracted a smaller subset of manageable size from the large data set which included only the tag assignments posted between July 27 and July 30, 2005. By recursively adding tag assignments posted prior to July 27 for all users and resources present in the subset, a "core folksonomy" was constructed (as was also done in [15]). After this initial extraction step, we also applied p-core preprocessing to the data set. This preprocessing step guarantees that each user, resource, and tag occurs in at least k posts. That way, infrequent elements are removed from the folksonomy, thus reducing potential sources of noise in the data. At the same time, the *density* of the data is increased. Varying the p-core level therefore helps us to analyze the predictive accuracy of our methods at different density levels. In summary, experiments have been run on the three p-core levels 1, 5, and 10. As suggested in literature we removed for the p-core 5 and p-core 10 data sets all posts that had more than 30 tags, as they usually are spam.

3.2 Evaluation Procedure

We use the *LeavePostOut* evaluation procedure described in [15], a variant of leave-one-out hold-out estimation.

For all preprocessed folksonomies, we first created a subset $\tilde{U}$ consisting of 10% randomly chosen users from U (the test set). For each user in $\tilde{U}$, we pick one of the user's posts randomly. A post p is a tuple $(u, r, tags(u, r))$, where

[6] `http://www.dai-labor.de/en/irml/datasets/delicious`

$tags(u, r) := \{t \in T \mid (u, t, r) \in Y\}$ is the set of tags associated with the post. The task of the tag recommender consists of predicting a set of tags $\tilde{T}(u, r)$ for p based on the folksonomy $\mathbb{F} \setminus \{p\}$.

The predictive accuracy is determined using the usual information retrieval metrics *precision* and *recall*:

$$precision(\tilde{T}(u, r)) = \frac{|tags(u, r) \cap \tilde{T}(u, r)|}{|\tilde{T}(u, r)|} \tag{3}$$

$$recall(\tilde{T}(u, r)) = \frac{|tags(u, r) \cap \tilde{T}(u, r)|}{|tags(u, r)|} \tag{4}$$

The F1 metric, finally, is computed as the harmonic mean of precision and recall. The size of $\tilde{T}(u, r)$, that is, the length of the recommendation list, influences precision and recall. Longer recommendation lists naturally lead to higher recall values and lower precision. In the experiments, we therefore varied the length of the recommendation lists n from 1 to 20[7].

We used the following other parameters in our experiments. For FolkRank, we used the parameters suggested in [15] and set the weight parameter d to 0.7. The parameter ϵ is used in FolkRank as an indicator of reaching convergence. This means that no further iterations were made and the results were returned when the sum of all weight changes was less than 10^{-6}. As suggested in [15] we set the maximum number of iterations to 10 as an alternative stop condition.

3.3 Accuracy Results

Figures 2 to 4 show the accuracy results for the different p-core levels. On the left hand side of the figures, we plot precision and recall values for the different recommendation list lengths. At the right hand side, the values of the F1 measure are shown for recommendation lists of varying length.

Regarding the F1 measure, no strong differences between FolkRank and our LocalRank metric can be observed for all data sets. On the p-core 1 data set, LocalRank is slightly better on the overall F1 measure. A closer look reveals that LocalRank achieves higher precision and recall values for list lengths of $n > 11$. LocalRank also leads to slightly better values than FolkRank with respect to both measures for the p-core 5 data set (Figure 3) and for list lengths $n < 8$. The results for the p-core 10 data set are nearly identical for all evaluated recommendation list lengths, see Figure 4.

We conducted a sign test to analyze whether the observed differences are statistically significant [16]. For the p-core 5 and p-core 10 data sets, no significant differences regarding the obtained F1 measure for the two algorithms could be observed for all list lengths. For the largest and most realistic p-core 1 data set, however, LocalRank's F1 values are significantly higher ($p < .05$) for list lengths

[7] Note that for the p-core level 1 folksonomy and also for the p-core level 5 folksonomy, the average number of tags per resource is below 20 (3 for p-core 1, 17 for p-core 5), which means that a precision of 100% cannot be achieved.

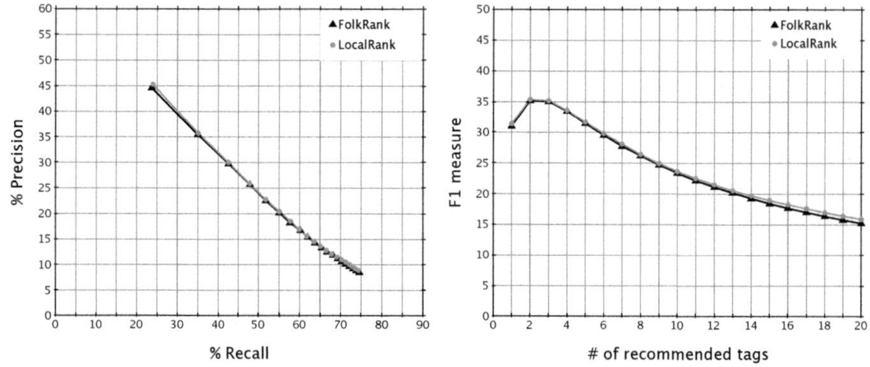

Fig. 2. Results for the p-core level 1 data set

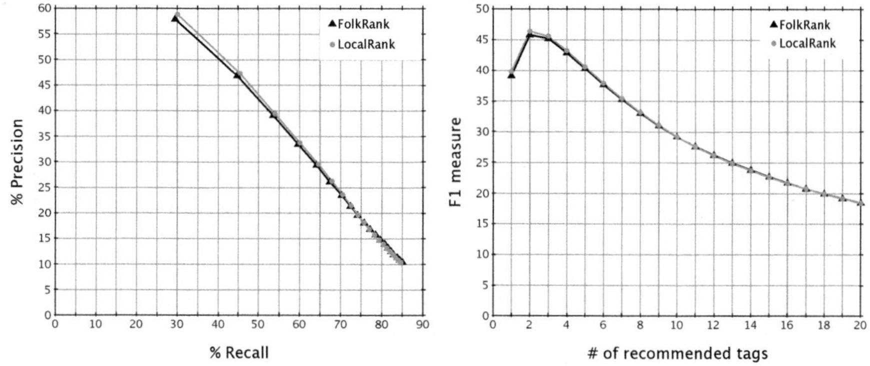

Fig. 3. Results for the p-core level 5 data set

greater than 11. Overall, we therefore conclude that LocalRank is mostly on a par with FolkRank with respect to predictive accuracy on the Delicious data set at the examined p-core levels and even outperforms FolkRank in certain situations on low-density data sets.

We are aware that in very recent works new algorithms have been proposed which outperform FolkRank's predictive accuracy on certain data sets, collected for example from BibSonomy[8]. Gemmel et al. in [11] for example evaluate their hybrid approach on a p-core 20 data set collected from Delicious and observed an improvement over FolkRank. This more recent and very dense data set (p-core 20), which also involved manual selection of users and tags was however not available to us, so that a direct comparison was not possible. Rendle et al. in [17] compare their tensor factorization approach with FolkRank on a very small BibSonomy data set and could show that for longer top-n recommendation lists, their approach is slightly better on the F1 measure. Overall, we view FolkRank therefore still as one of the state-of-the-art techniques for tag recommendation

[8] `http://www.bibsonomy.org`

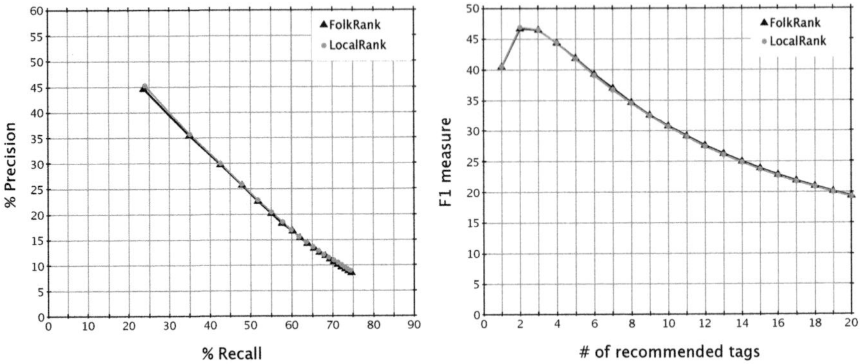

Fig. 4. Results for the p-core level 10 data set

and use it as a baseline for comparison because most current literature refers to it as a baseline. The availability of the source code is also a reason to chose FolkRank in order to ensure a fair comparison between algorithms.

3.4 Run-Time Efficiency Results

As mentioned above, because of FolkRank's approach to propagate weights over the full folksonomy for each query, the algorithm suffers from scalability problems which are mentioned also in [6] and [11].

Time measurements. Table 2 shows the average time needed for generating one recommendation list for the different p-core levels of the Delicious data sets. Note that with the Java-based version of the original FolkRank implementation from [4], more than 20 seconds are required for generating one single recommendation list using the above-described hardware configuration. As described in Section 2.1, FolkRank computes the rank vector $\overrightarrow{w}$ using the Folksonomy-Adapted PageRank (FA-PR) two times: with and without the preference vector. The first two columns of Table 2 show the computation time needed for these two phases. When we assume that the folksonomy does not change, the non-biased preference weights can be computed in advance and do not have to be re-computed for each recommendation. When relying on this re-use the computation time for FolkRank can be cut by about 50%.

Implementation and memory requirements. Similar to the implementation of FolkRank, our implementation of LocalRank is memory-based, that is, all the

Table 2. Running times for recommendations in milliseconds

	FA-PR w. preferences	FA-PR w/o preferences	FolkRank total	LocalRank
p-core 1	18,774	20,336	39,110	< 1
p-core 5	15,320	16,959	32,279	< 1
p-core 10	9,390	10,466	19,856	< 1

required data is kept in memory. Actually, the time needed for the calculation of a recommendation list is on average constantly below one millisecond and does not increase when the size of the folksonomy increases. Beside the lower computational complexity of the neighborhood-based LocalRank algorithm itself, the more or less constant access time is made possible through a compact in-memory representation of the data and a pre-processing step at startup. In the pre-processing step, simple statistics such as $|Y_u|$, $|Y_r|$ and the number of neighbors for each user and resource are pre-computed. In addition, two adjacency lists are constructed that represent the graph structure and are required for the weight propagation step: one stores the information which user posted which tags, the other one contains information about the tags attached to each resource. Once the pre-processing step is performed, the generation of recommendation lists at run-time is based on simple arithmetical operations based on the data which are organized in lookup tables. Note that when new data comes in, the lookup tables can be very quickly updated because only local changes in the "neighborhood" of the newly added elements have to be made.

The required overhead in terms of additionally required memory is limited. For the simple counting statistics (e.g., number of assignments per tag) 4 integer arrays with a total size of $2*|U|+2*|R|$ are required. Two further hash maps are used to store the weights $|Y_{u,t}|$ and $|Y_{r,t}|$ of existing user/tag and resource/tag combinations in $|Y|$. Finally, the two adjacency lists are of length $|U|$ and $|R|$, where each list entry points to its assigned tags, the total number of which is $|T|$. Overall this means that $|Y|$ pointers to elements of T are required.

Comparison with other approaches. Based on our compact in-memory representation, even the p-core 1 data set can be kept in memory. Note that for example in the work by Gemmel et al. [11] "due to memory and time constraints" only a 10% fraction of a given Delicious data set was used. This data set was by the way the largest one in their evaluation and with 700,000 tag assignments, which is more than twenty times smaller than the p-core 1 data set used in our experiments. Note that for even larger data sets, one additional implementation option for LocalRank would be to store the most memory-intensive adjacency lists on disk in a (NoSQL) database. Typical database lookups with the given hardware configuration and data volumes usually take a few milliseconds per query. A prototypical implementation of a disk-based recommender for very large folksonomies is part of our current work.

Another work which reports prediction run times is [6]. Here, Rendle et al. compare the run times of their tensor factorization approach with FolkRank. After a linear time learning phase, their algorithm makes predictions only based on the learned model. The needed prediction time depends only on the relatively small number of factorization dimensions for users, resources, and tags as well as the number of tags $|T|$. A characteristic of their method is that it achieves better accuracy results when the model contains more dimensions (64 and 128) but is not accurate as FolkRank when the number of dimensions is lower (e.g., 8 or 16). In their paper, a graphical illustration with no exact number of running times is given. Running times range from nearly zero for the low-dimensional case up to about 10 or 15 milliseconds for the 64-factor model. Unfortunately, no numbers are given for the most accurate 128-dimensional model. While their implementation based on Object-Pascal very clearly outperforms their C++ implementation of FolkRank, the data sets taken from BibSonomy and last.fm[9] used in their evaluation are comparably small (2,500 and 75,000 assignments). The number of assignments in $|Y|$ used in their experiments is less than a 1% of our data sets. Unfortunately, also no information about the time needed to train the model (in particular for the higher-dimensional case) is given. Overall, while some accuracy improvements over our LocalRank method can be achieved using the approach described in [6] when a high-dimensional model is learned, it remains partially unclear how their approach scales to larger problem sizes both with respect to training time and prediction time.

In [13], a clustering-based, probabilistic approach for "real-time tag recommendation" is proposed and evaluated on data sets derived from Delicious and CiteULike[10]. The approach is based on a two-stage framework consisting of a learning phase and an online tag recommendation phase. The authors report running times of about a bit more than 1 second that are required to determine suitable tags for a given document on a server machine with 3GHz. Compared to our evaluation, their data set obtained from Delicious is very small (218,088 tags) when compared to the 17 million tags used in our p-core 1 data set. Unfortunately, the authors of [13] do not compare the accuracy of their approach with the one of FolkRank but with a relatively simple method based on vector similarity.

4 Summary and Outlook

In this paper we proposed LocalRank, a runtime-efficient tag recommendation algorithm, which despite its simplicity is capable of generating highly-accurate tag recommendations in real-time and even slightly outperforms FolkRank on the Delicious p-core level 1 data set. Compared to other approaches, LocalRank is not only quicker but also allows us to process larger data sets. Finally, from a practical perspective, our algorithm is also very easy to implement.

Our future work includes the analysis of the algorithm on further data sets in order to determine whether it is sufficient also for other Social Tagging platforms to consider only the neighborhood of a given user-resource recommendation query. From an algorithmic perspective, we are currently working on an algorithm variant in which the "depth" of the weight-spreading process can be increased, for example to the second or third level, without increasing the prediction times too much.

Beyond that, we plan to develop a disk-based implementation of the algorithm, e.g., based on a database system, in order to analyze how massive tagging data can be processed in an efficient and scalable manner.

[9] `http://www.last.fm`

[10] `http://www.citeulike.org`

References

1. Jannach, D., Zanker, M., Felfernig, A., Friedrich, G.: Recommender Systems - An Introduction. Cambridge University Press, Cambridge (2010)
2. Sen, S., Harper, F.M., LaPitz, A., Riedl, J.: The quest for quality tags. In: Proc. ACM GROUP 2007, Sanibel Island, Florida, USA, pp. 361–370 (2007)
3. Begelman, G., Keller, P., Smadja, F.: Automated tag clustering: Improving search and exploration in the tag space. In: Proc. Collaborative Web Tagging Workshop at WWW 2006, Edinburgh, Scotland (2006)
4. Hotho, A., Jäschke, R., Schmitz, C., Stumme, G.: Information retrieval in folksonomies: Search and ranking. In: Sure, Y., Domingue, J. (eds.) ESWC 2006. LNCS, vol. 4011, pp. 411–426. Springer, Heidelberg (2006)
5. Brin, S., Page, L.: The anatomy of a large-scale hypertextual web search engine. Computer Networks 30(1-7), 107–117 (1998)
6. Rendle, S., Balby Marinho, L., Nanopoulos, A., Lars, S.T.: Learning optimal ranking with tensor factorization for tag recommendation. In: Proc. ACM SIGKDD 2009, Paris, France, pp. 727–736 (2009)
7. Symeonidis, P., Nanopoulos, A., Manolopoulos, Y.: A unified framework for providing recommendations in social tagging systems based on ternary semantic analysis. IEEE Trans. Knowl. Data. En. 22, 179–192 (2010)
8. Krestel, R., Fankhauser, P., Nejdl, W.: Latent dirichlet allocation for tag recommendation. In: Proc. ACM RecSys 2009, New York, USA, pp. 61–68 (2009)
9. Hu, M., Lim, E.P., Jiang, J.: A probabilistic approach to personalized tag recommendation. In: Proc. IEEE SocialCom 2010, Minneapolis, MN, USA, pp. 33–40 (2010)
10. Bundschus, M., Yu, S., Tresp, V., Rettinger, A., Dejori, M., Kriegel, H.P.: Hierarchical bayesian models for collaborative tagging systems. In: Proc. IEEE ICDM 2009, pp. 728–733 (2009)
11. Gemmell, J., Schimoler, T., Mobasher, B., Burke, R.: Hybrid tag recommendation for social annotation systems. In: Proc. ACM CIKM, Toronto, pp. 829–838 (2010)
12. Chirita, P.A., Costache, S., Nejdl, W., Handschuh, S.: P-tag: Large scale automatic generation of personalized annotation tags for the web. In: Proc. WWW 2007, Banff, Alberta, Canada, pp. 845–854 (2007)
13. Song, Y., Zhuang, Z., Li, H., Zhao, Q., Li, J., Lee, W.C., Giles, C.L.: Real-time automatic tag recommendation. In: Proc. SIGIR 2008, Singapore, pp. 515–522 (2008)
14. Jäschke, R., Marinho, L., Hotho, A., Lars, S.T., Gerd, S.: Tag recommendations in social bookmarking systems. AI Commun. 21, 231–247 (2008)
15. Jäschke, R., Marinho, L.B., Hotho, A., Schmidt-Thieme, L., Stumme, G.: Tag recommendations in folksonomies. In: Kok, J.N., Koronacki, J., Lopez de Mantaras, R., Matwin, S., Mladenič, D., Skowron, A. (eds.) PKDD 2007. LNCS (LNAI), vol. 4702, pp. 506–514. Springer, Heidelberg (2007)
16. Demšar, J.: Statistical comparisons of classifiers over multiple data sets. Journal of Machine Learning Research 7, 1–30 (2006)
17. Rendle, S., Lars, S.T.: Pairwise interaction tensor factorization for personalized tag recommendation. In: Proc. ACM WSDM 2010, New York, USA, pp. 81–90 (2010)

Random Indexing and Negative User Preferences for Enhancing Content-Based Recommender Systems*

Cataldo Musto, Giovanni Semeraro, Pasquale Lops, and Marco de Gemmis

Department of Computer Science
University of Bari "Aldo Moro", Italy
{cataldomusto,semeraro,lops,degemmis}@di.uniba.it

Abstract. The vector space model (VSM) emerged for almost three decades as one of the most effective approaches in the area of Information Retrieval (IR), thanks to its good compromise between expressivity, effectiveness and simplicity. Although Information Retrieval and Information Filtering (IF) undoubtedly represent two related research areas, the use of VSM in Information Filtering is much less analyzed, especially for content-based recommender systems.

The goal of this work is twofold: first, we investigate the impact of VSM in the area of content-based recommender systems; second, since VSM suffer from well-known problems, such as its high dimensionality and the inability to manage information coming from negative user preferences, we propose techniques able to effectively tackle these drawbacks. Specifically we exploited Random Indexing for dimensionality reduction and the negation operator implemented in the Semantic Vectors open source package to model negative user preferences. Results of an experimental evaluation performed on these enhanced vector space models (eVSM) and the potential applications of these approaches confirm the effectiveness of the model and lead us to further investigate these techniques.

Keywords: Content-based Recommender Systems, Dimensionality Reduction, Personalization, Vector Space Models.

1 Introduction

The recent phenomenon of Web 2.0 and the consequent explosion of Social Web platforms contributed to the enormous growth of the available information and underlined the need for systems able to effectively manage this surplus of data. In this scenario, tools helping users in finding what they really need, such as Information Filtering systems [1], are rapidly emerging. These systems usually work in three steps:

* This research was partially funded by MIUR (Ministero dell'Universita' e della Ricerca) under the contract Legge 593/2000, DM 19410 MBLab "Laboratorio di Bioinformatica per la biodiversita' molecolare" (2007-2010).

C. Huemer and T. Setzer (Eds.): EC-Web 2011, LNBIP 85, pp. 270–281, 2011.

1. *Training Step:* the system acquires information about a target user (what she knows, what she likes, the task to be accomplished, demographical or contextual informations and so on). This step could be accomplished in an explicit or implicit way, that is to say, by asking users to explicitly express her preferences or by analyzing her behavior.
2. *User Modeling:* the information previously extracted are modeled and stored, according to the filtering model implemented in the system.
3. *Filtering:* finally, the system filters the information flow by exploiting the user profile. The goal of this step is to find the most relevant items for a target user, usually ranked according to a relevance criterion.

In recent years IR and IF followed two separated research paths, although the strong analogies between them have already been underlined by Belkin and Croft in 1992 [2]. Indeed, even if the goal is slightly different, both content-based recommendation and retrieval processes are carried out by processing a set of items represented as textual documents. In the first case the system performs a progressive filtering of the information not relevant for a target user in a space of items, while in the second one the system tries to retrieve the most relevant documents from the entire corpus w.r.t. the user informative need. Furthermore, the concept of 'query' (describing short-term user needs) is replaced in IF by the concept of 'user profile', that describes long-term user preferences and represents the input that triggers the whole recommendation process. Finally, typical IR-based weighting techniques (such as TF/IDF [3]) and measures (such as the Cosine Similarity [4]) can be easily applied in IF, for example to assign weights to the terms stored in a content-based user profile and to perform similarity calculations between items and a user profile. Anyway, despite these analogies, the impact of IR-based models in the area of IF has not yet been properly investigated.

In the area of Information Retrieval the Vector Space Model (VSM) emerged as one of the most effective state-of-the-art approaches, thanks to its good compromise between expressivity, effectiveness and simplicity. However, VSM suffers from at least three important problems: first, the approach is not incremental. This means that even the addition of a new item to the corpus requires that the whole vector space has to be generated again from scratch. This is a problem especially felt for real-world data, because the generation of high-dimensional vector spaces is a very complex and computationally expensive task. Furthermore, VSM cannot manage the information coming from negative user preferences. This is a well-known drawback, that can be ignored for IR systems (because the query usually contains only information about user informative needs), but not for the IF ones because as proved by many contributions in the area of text categorization (e.g., naive Bayes [5], SVM [6], etc.), both positive and negative preferences have to be modeled. Finally, VSM is not able to manage neither the latent semantics of each document nor the position of the terms that occur in it. For example, given a document and a permutation of its terms, their representation in the VSM is absolutely the same, although the conveyed information could be different. The main contribution of this work is to exploit the overlapping between IR and IF research areas to evaluate the impact of IR-based models in the area of IF by comparing their performance with respect to other content-based filtering models. Furthermore, we introduced two 'enhanced vectors space models' (eVSM) that exploit techniques able to overcome classical VSM problems by ensuring good efficiency, scalability and the ability of managing both latent semantics of documents and negative user preferences in a more effective way. Specifically, in this work we have used Random Indexing, an incremental technique for dimensionality reduction, and a negation operator based on quantum mechanics implemented in the Semantic Vectors [7] open source package to model negative user preferences.

The paper is organized as follows: related work are described in Section 2. Section 3 introduces the techniques we exploited in this work, such as Random Indexing, while in section 4 we focus the attention on the description of both filtering models. Results emerged from the experimental evaluation are described in Section 5. Finally, future directions are sketched in Section 6.

2 Related Work

Vector Space Model, introduced by Salton et al. [8] in 1975, is considered as one of the most effective retrieval models in the IR research community. Raghavan [9] gives a good overview of Vector Space model issues in the area of IR. The use of VSM as content-based filtering model [10] has been previously investigated by Cohen and Hirsh [11]and Nouali and Blache [12]. Berry et al. [13] pointed out the need for dimensionality reduction techniques as a mean to improve the effectiveness and the scalability of VSMs. LSA [14] and PLSI [15] are two of the most well-known techniques that perform this step, but their computational complexity is of hindrance to implement these approaches in real-world applications. In these scenarios effective techniques for dimensionality reduction such as Random Indexing [16], emerged. The effectiveness of this approach has already been demonstrated in [17] with an application for image and text data. Recently the research about semantic vector space models gained more and more attention: the survey by Turney and Pantel [18] about the use of VSM for semantic processing of text analyzed the main issues and the first packages developed in this area, such as S-Space[1] and Semantic Vectors (SV)[2]. The SV package was implemented by Widdows [7]: it implements a Random Indexing algorithm and defines a negation operator based on quantum mechanics [19]. Some initial investigations about the effectiveness of the Semantic Vectors for retrieval and filtering tasks are reported in [20] and [21].

3 eVSM for Content-Based Recommender Systems

In this section we will describe the techniques exploited for building enhanced vector space models. In our opinion, a VSM can be defined *enhanced* if:

---

[1] `http://code.google.com/p/airhead-research/`

[2] `http://code.google.com/p/semanticvectors/`

1. The whole vector space is built in an *incremental way*;
2. The model is able to catch the *semantics* of documents;
3. The model is able to manage the information coming from *negative evidences*.

In our approach we tackled the first two issues through the introduction of Random Indexing, while the last one is managed by exploiting Semantic Vectors. In this section we will give a complete overview of both the theoretical basis of the Random Indexing approach and the main features implemented in the Semantic Vectors open source package.

Hereafter we could refer to the *items to be filtered* and to the *user profiles* as *documents*. Indeed, in a content-based filtering model the terms are considered synonyms because we assume that items to be filtered are described by means of some textual content. For example, in a movie recommendation scenario we can assume that an item (movie) will be represented by its title, cast, plot and so on.

3.1 Random Indexing

Random Indexing is an efficient, scalable and incremental technique for dimensionality reduction. Following this approach, we can represent terms and documents as points in a vector space with a considerable reduction of the features that describe them. To sum up, through this model we can obtain results comparable to other well-known methods (such as Singular Value Decomposition), but with a tremendous savings of computational resources.

This approach belongs to the class of the so-called *distributional models*. These models state that the meaning of a word can be inferred by analyzing its use (that is to say, its *distribution*) within a corpus of textual data. According to the *distributional hypothesis* "words that occur in the same contexts tend to have similar meanings". For example, we can state that the terms *wine* and *beer* have similar meanings because they often co-occurs with the same words (e.g. *drink*) The goal of Random Indexing is to shift the classical VSM representation based on a n-dimensional term-document matrix towards a more compact and flexible k-dimensional term-context matrix (see figure 1).

This dimensionality reduction is obtained by multiplying the original term-document matrix with a matrix R built in a random way. Formally, given a corpus of n terms and m documents represented in the original matrix A, the reduced k-dimensional matrix B is obtained as follows:

$$A^{n,m} * R^{m,k} = B^{n,k} \tag{1}$$

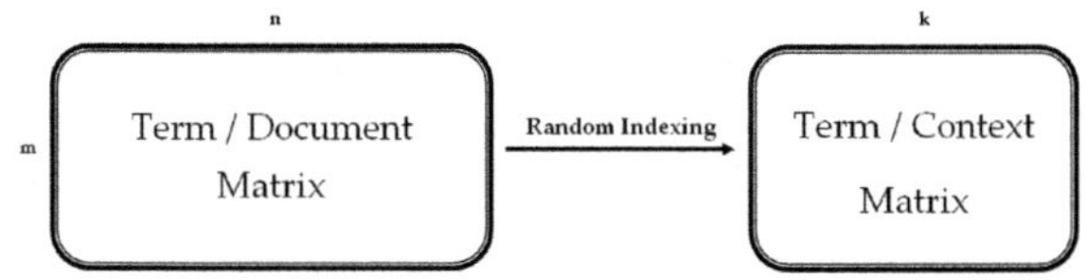

Fig. 1. Dimensionality reduction process through Random Indexing

So, the key concept behind the building of the *random* matrix is the definition of the concept of "context". Given a word, we could think at the *context* as a piece of text, variable in size, which surrounds that word. Following the famous Wittgenstein sentence *"meaning is its use"*, in Random Indexing the context is exploited to infer the meaning of the word by analyzing the meaning of the other words that more often co-occur within its own context.

In general, the "meaning" of a term (its position in the Vector Space) is obtained by following these steps:

1. *A context vector* is assigned to each term. This vector has a fixed dimension (k) and it can contain only values in $\{-1, 0, 1\}$. Values are distributed in a random way, but the number of non-zero elements is much smaller.
2. The Vector Space representation of a *term* (denoted by $\boldsymbol{t}$) is obtained by summing the context vectors of all the terms it co-occurs with.
3. The Vector Space representation of a *document* (denoted by $\boldsymbol{d}$) is obtained by summing the context vectors of all its terms.
4. The Vector Space representation of a *user profile* for a user u (denoted by $\boldsymbol{p}_u$) is obtained by combining the context vectors of all the *terms* that occur in the documents liked in the past by the user u. The unique difference between the filtering models proposed in this work is the way previously liked documents are combined.

Given a set of documents, by following this approach we can build a low-dimensional Vector Space that guarantees scalability, effectiveness and a better semantic modeling of the documents since each term is no longer represented in an atomic way, as in the classical keyword-based methods, but its position in the space depends on the terms it co-occurs with. The main advantage behind Random Indexing (whose theoretical reliability has been proved by the studies about near-orthogonality by Hecht-Nilsen [22]) is that in this low-dimensional space, as stated by Johnson and Lindestrauss in their lemma [23], the distance between points is preserved (Figure 2) so it is possible to perform calculations and compute similarity between items represented in the vector space with a minimum loss of accuracy balanced by the enormous gain in efficiency.

3.2 Semantic Vectors

Through Random Indexing we can build low-dimensional vector spaces that maintain the original expressivity of the model. However, they still inherit a classic problem of VSM: the information coming from negative evidences is not managed in any way and does not contribute to the position that the item assumes in the vector space. In content-based recommender systems, especially for building user profiles, this is an important aspect because negative user preferences have to be modeled, too. In order to tackle this problem we exploited the Semantic Vectors (SV) open-source package, a set of libraries that implements a Random Indexing approach and extends it by introducing a negation operator based on quantum mechanics. In SV the negation operator is used mainly to define queries that contain negative terms, such as *A not B*, for retrieval tasks.

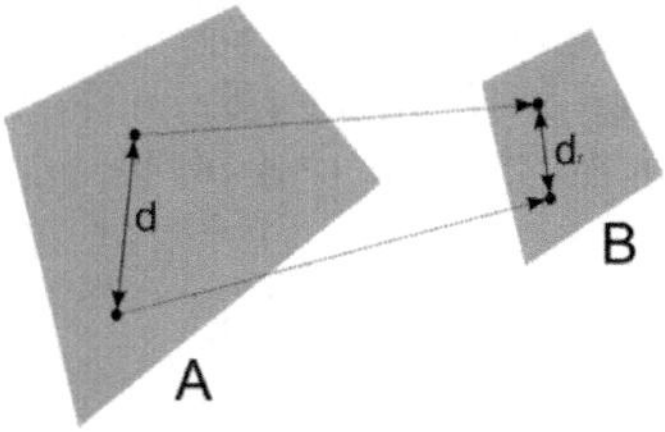

Fig. 2. A visual explanation of the Johnson-Linderstrauss lemma

From a theoretical point of view, this kind of query represents the projection of the vector A on the subspace orthogonal to those generated by the vector B. Intuitively, in our recommendation models we will define two vectors: the first for modeling positive preferences and the second modeling negative ones. The negation operator will be used to identify the subspace that will contain the items as close as possible to the positive preference vector and as far as possible to negative one. In the next section we will analyze thoroughly this aspect.

4 Recommendation Models

The recommendation approaches proposed in this work try to prove that the exploitation of the classical IR-based measures can be useful for filtering items represented as points in an *enhanced vector space*. The main idea behind our models is to build a vector space for each user, where both user profile and items to be filtered are represented through the techniques described in the previous section. Next, by exploiting the classical similarity measures between vectors (such as the classical *cosine similarity*) it is possible to efficiently obtain the set of the most relevant items for the target user, that is to say, the points in the space that are nearest to her profile.

In this work we proposed four different recommendation models, all based on Random Indexing and Semantic Vectors. The main difference between the approaches lies in the way the evidences about both positive and negative user preferences are combined in order to model the user profile in the vector space.

4.1 Random Indexing-Based Model

This approach is based on the assumption that the information coming from the items a user liked in the past can be a reliable source of information to build accurate user profiles. Therefore, let $d_1..d_n \in D$ be a set of already rated items, and $r(u, d_i)$ $(i = 1..n)$ the rating given by the user u to the item d_i. We can describe the set of positive items for user u, denoted by I_u, as follows:

$$I_u = \{d \in D | r(u, d) \geq \beta\} \tag{2}$$

Thus, given a threshold β, the profile of a user consists of the set of the terms occurring in the documents she liked in the past. As stated above, the *Random*

Indexing is exploited to build the user profile in an incremental way, that is to say by simply summing all the *document vectors* for each document in I_u. Let $|I_u|$ be the cardinality of the set I_u and let $\boldsymbol{d}_i$ be the vector space representation of the document d_i, we can define the user profile $\boldsymbol{p}_u$ as follows:

$$\boldsymbol{p}_u = \sum_{i=1}^{|I_u|} \boldsymbol{d}_i \tag{3}$$

That is undoubtedly the simplest Random Indexing-based filtering model that could be defined. In the experimental evaluation we will refer to this model as **RI**.

4.2 Weighted Random Indexing-Based Model

The main drawback of the RI method is that the user profile $\boldsymbol{p}_u$ is built without taking into account the ratings provided by the target user for the items she liked. In other terms, it is *independent* from the rates provided by the target user (provided that they are above or below the threshold β). The second model, called *Weighted Random Indexing-based (**W-RI**)*, enriches the previous one by simply associating to each *document vector*, before combining it, a weight equal to the rating provided by the user for it. More formally:

$$\boldsymbol{p}_u = \sum_{i=1}^{|I_u|} \boldsymbol{d}_i * r(u, d_i) \tag{4}$$

In this way the model will increase the weight of the items liked by the user.

4.3 Semantic Vectors-Based Model

The main idea behind Semantic Vectors-based model (**SV**) is to exploit the negation operator to represent in the user profile both positive and negative preferences, as in the classical text classification approaches (e.g. Naïve Bayes, Support Vector Machines and so on). We can think at this model as an extension of the previously described RI model. Unlike RI, in which a single user profile $\boldsymbol{p}_u$ is built, in SV filtering model two user profile vectors, one for positive preferences and one for negative ones, are inferred. The set of positive items I_u^+ and the positive user profile vector $\boldsymbol{p}_{+u}$ are identical to the set of positive items I_u and the user profile $\boldsymbol{p}_u$ in RI, while the set of negative items, denoted by I_u^-, is defined as follows:

$$I_u^- = \{d \in D | r(u, d_i) < \beta\} \tag{5}$$

The negative user profile vector, denoted by $\boldsymbol{p}_{-u}$, is built by summing the vector space representations of the items in I_u^-. Formally:

$$\boldsymbol{p}_{-u} = \sum_{i=1}^{|I_u^-|} \boldsymbol{d}_i \tag{6}$$

Thus, given the profile vectors $\boldsymbol{p}_{+u}$ and $\boldsymbol{p}_{-u}$ we can use Semantic Vectors to instantiate the vector $\boldsymbol{p}_{+u}$ *NOT* $\boldsymbol{p}_{-u}$, that is exploited to find the items represented in the vector space that contain as much as possible features that occur in the documents in I_u^+ and as less as possible features from I_u^-.

4.4 Weighted Semantic Vectors-Based Model

As RI, the SV model has its weighted counterpart, called **W-SV**. This model shares the same idea of the W-RI model and the same weighting schema described in 4.2, with the unique difference that in the negative profile I_u^- the items with a lower rate are given higher weights in order to exclude as much as possible the features disliked by the target user. More formally, the set I_u^+ and I_u^- are built by following the same formula introduced in the previous section, while the vectors $\boldsymbol{p}_{+u}$ and $\boldsymbol{p}_{-u}$ are inferred in this way:

$$\boldsymbol{p}_{+u} = \sum_{i=1}^{|I_u^+|} \boldsymbol{d}_i * r(u, d_i) \tag{7}$$

$$\boldsymbol{p}_{-u} = \sum_{i=1}^{|I_u^-|} \boldsymbol{d}_i * (MAX - r(u, d_i)) \tag{8}$$

where MAX is the highest rating that can be assigned to a document.

5 Experimental Evaluation

The goal of the experimental evaluation was to measure the effectiveness of RI and SV models, as well as of their weighted variants W-RI and W-SV, in term of predictive accuracy and goodness of the proposed ranking. The experimental session has been carried out on a subset of the 100k MovieLens dataset[3], containing 40,717 ratings provided by 613 different users on 520 movies. Since content-based information were crawled from the English version of Wikipedia, we excluded from the original MovieLens dataset the movies without a Wikipedia entry. In Table 1 contains some statistics about the dataset: the original term-document matrix contained 7.351 rows (*features*) and 520 columns (*items*) on average. Since the dimension of each *context vectors* was set to 200, after Random Indexing the size of the matrix was reduced by 62% (from 520 to 200 columns).

User profiles were learned by analyzing the ratings stored in the MovieLens dataset. Each rating was expressed as a numerical vote on a 5-point Likert scale, ranging from 1=strongly dislike to 5=strongly like. All the ratings above 2 were considered as positive, while the ratings under this threshold were considered as negative. The session was organized through a 5-fold cross validation: for each fold and for each user we built a vector space for the user profile and the items to be filtered. By exploiting a simple cosine similarity measure we ranked

[3] `http://www.grouplens.org/node/73`

Table 1. Content-based MovieLens dataset statistics. The average number of features was calculated by counting the features occurring on average in the documents rated by each user.

Items	520	Ratings	40,717
Ratings (avg. per user)	66.44	Positive ratings	83.8%
Features	24,975	Features (avg. per user)	7,351

the items, assuming the nearest ones as the most relevant. The metric used to evaluate the effectiveness of the approaches was the *Average Precision@n*, where n was set to 1, 3, 5 and 10. We preferred the Average Precision@n instead of the simple Precision@n because it takes into account also the position of the correctly classified items.

Specifically, in our experimental evaluation we tried to give an answer to three questions:

1. Does the weighting scheme improve the predictive accuracy of the recommendation models?
2. Does the negation operator improve the predictive accuracy of the recommendation models?
3. How do the recommendation models perform w.r.t. other content-based filtering approaches?

As shown in Figure 3 the weighting scheme, even in this naive form, improves the predictive accuracy of the system for all the metrics. The improvement is greater for the AV-P@1 and AV-P@3. This is a good outcome because in this kind of task it is crucial to put *good* items at the top of the recommendation list.

Figure 4 shows that also the introduction of the negation operator is able to improve the predictive accuracy of the system in all metrics. In this case we can note a lower improvement for the W-SV model. This could suggest to introduce different weighting techniques for the negative component of the user profile.

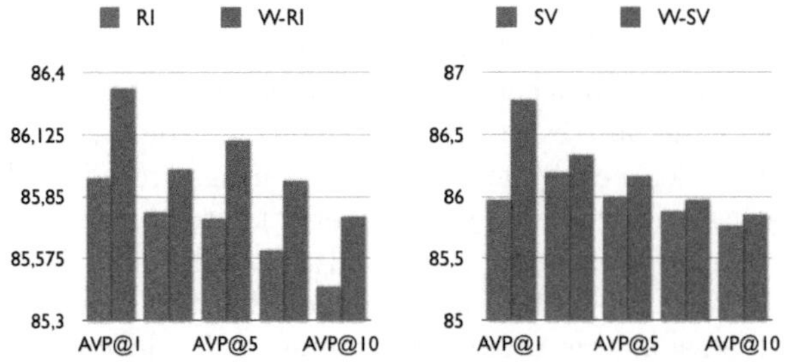

Fig. 3. Analysis of the impact of the weighting schema by comparing RI vs. W-RI and SV vs. W-SV

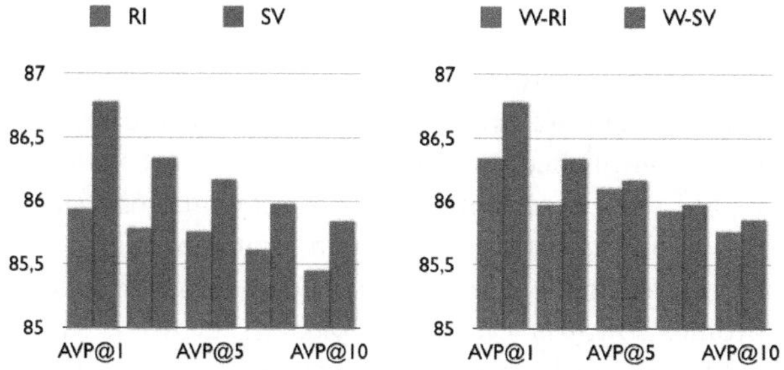

Fig. 4. Analysis of the impact of the negation operator by comparing RI vs. SV and W-RI vs. W-SV

Table 2. Average Precision

Metric	RI	W-RI	SV	**W-SV**	*TF/IDF*	*Bayes*
AV-P @1	85,93	86,33	85,97	**86,78**	*86,27*	*86,39*
AV-P @3	85,78	85,97	86,19	**86,33**	*85,85*	*85,97*
AV-P @5	85,75	86,10	85,99	**86,16**	*86,70*	*85,83*
AV-P @10	85,45	85,76	85,76	**85,85**	*85,58*	*85,75*

Finally, in Table 2 the results obtained by our recommendation models are compared w.r.t. a naive Bayes filtering algorithm (described in [24]) and a classical VSM based on the complete term/document matrix without any dimensionality reduction. As shown in Table 2, the *W-SV* model gained the best results, with an increase of the Average Precision between 0.1% and 0.4% w.r.t. the bayesian classifier and around 0.5% w.r.t. the original VSM. Finally, none of the experiments obtained a statistically significant difference between the values of Average Precision. This outcome has been certainly influenced by the extreme imbalance of the dataset (over 80% of positive ratings) and should be verified again through deeper experimental evaluations.

6 Conclusions and Future Directions

In this work we introduced the first results emerged from an initial investigation on the impact of enhanced VSM, such as Random Indexing-based and Semantic Vectors-based ones, on Content-based Recommender Systems. The main outcome of the experimental evaluation is that, even in this first prototype and even with a naive weighting scheme, the filtering model shows an accuracy comparable to that obtained by other content-based filtering techniques such as the Bayesian classifier. Furthermore, the introduction of a negation operator, a totally novel aspect for VSM, lets us manage also the information about the disliked items and their features. The results obtained with the W-SV model represents a promising starting point for further investigations in this area. In the future we will introduce other weighting schemas and we will compare the results with those obtained by other algorithms capable of managing negative user feedbacks (e.g. Rocchio). Another important aspect to be investigated is the impact of Natural Language Processing techniques on the model. We will try to analyze the impact of single lexical categories on the accuracy of filtering tools. This task will be accomplished by comparing the effectiveness of the system with user profiles built by exploiting only a single category (for example, only names, only verbs or only entities). Finally, a promising future direction could be represented by the exploitation of Linked Data in order to shift the classical keyword-based profiles towards a more complex structure in which relationships are explicitly coded and can be used for recommendation tasks.

References

1. Hanani, U., Shapira, B., Shoval, P.: Information filtering: Overview of issues, research and systems. User Model. User-Adapt. Interact. 11(3), 203–259 (2001)
2. Belkin, N., Croft, B.: Information filtering and information retrieval. Comm. ACM 35(12), 29–37 (1992)
3. Baeza-Yates, R., Ribeiro-Neto, B.: Modern Information Retrieval. Addison-Wesley, Reading (1999)
4. Tan, P.-N., Steinbach, M., Kumar, V.: Introduction to Data Mining. Pearson Education (2006)
5. Kim, S.-B., Han, K.-S., Rim, H.-C., Myaeng, S.-H.: Some effective techniques for naive bayes text classification. IEEE Trans. Knowl. Data Eng. 18(11), 1457–1466 (2006)
6. Joachims, T.: Text categorization with support vector machines: learning with many relevant features. In: Nédellec, C., Rouveirol, C. (eds.) ECML 1998. LNCS, vol. 1398, Springer, Heidelberg (1998)
7. Widdows, D.: Orthogonal negation in vector spaces for modelling word-meanings and document retrieval. In: ACL 2003, pp. 136–143 (2003)
8. Salton, G., Wong, A., Yang, C.S.: A vector space model for automatic indexing. Commun. ACM 18(11), 613–620 (1975)
9. Raghavan, V.V., Wong, S.K.M.: A critical analysis of vector space model for information retrieval. Journal of the American Society for Information Science 37(5), 279–287 (1986)
10. Lops, P., de Gemmis, M., Semeraro, G.: Content-based recommender systems: State of the art and trends. In: Ricci, F., Rokach, L., Shapira, B., Kantor, P.B. (eds.) Recomender Systems Handbook, pp. 73–105. Springer, Heidelberg (2011)
11. Cohen, W.W., Hirsh, H.: Joins that generalize: Text classification using WHIRL. In: KDD 1998, pp. 169–173 (1998)
12. Nouali, O., Blache, P.: A semantic vector space and features-based approach for automatic information filtering. Expert Syst. Appl. 26(2), 171–179 (2004)
13. Berry, M.W., Drmac, Z., Jessup, E.R.: Matrices, Vector Spaces and Information Retrieval. SIAM Review 41(2), 335–362 (1999)
14. Deerwester, S., Dumais, S.T., Furnas, G.W., Landauer, T.K., Harshman, R.: Indexing by latent semantic analysis. JASIS 41(6), 391–407 (1990)
15. Hofmann, T.: Probabilistic latent semantic indexing. In: Proceedings of the 22nd Annual International SIGIR Conference (1999)
16. Sahlgren, M.: An introduction to random indexing. In: Methods and Applications of Semantic Indexing Workshop, TKE 2005 (2005)

17. Bingham, E., Mannila, H.: Random projection in dimensionality reduction: applications to image and text data. In: KDD 2001, pp. 245–250. ACM, New York (2001)
18. Turney, P.D., Pantel, P.: From frequency to meaning: Vector space models of semantics. J. Artif. Intell. Res (JAIR) 37, 141–188 (2010)
19. van Rijsbergen, C.J.: The Geometry of Information Retrieval. Cambridge University Press, Cambridge (2004)
20. Basile, P., Caputo, A., Semeraro, G.: Semantic vectors: an information retrieval scenario. In: Melucci, M., Mizzaro, S., Pasi, G. (eds.) IIR 2010 - Proceedings of the First Italian Information Retrieval Workshop, Padua, Italy, January 27-28, pp. 1–5 (2010)
21. Musto, C.: Enhanced vector space models for content-based recommender systems. In: Proceedings of the Fourth ACM Conference on Recommender Systems, Ser. RecSys 2010, pp. 361–364. ACM, New York (2010), http://doi.acm.org/10.1145/1864708.1864791
22. Hecht-Nielsen, R.: Context vectors: general purpose approximate meaning representations self-organized from raw data. In: Computational Intelligence: Imitating Life, pp. 43–56. IEEE Press, Los Alamitos (1994)
23. Johnson, W., Lindenstauss, J.: Extensions of lipschitz maps into a hilbert space. Contemporary Mathematics (1984)
24. Lops, P., de Gemmis, M., Semeraro, G., Musto, C., Narducci, F., Bux, M.: A semantic content-based recommender system integrating folksonomies for personalized access. In: Castellano, G., Jain, L.C., Fanelli, A.M. (eds.) Web Personalization in Intelligent Environments. Studies in Computational Intelligence, vol. 229, pp. 27–47. Springer, Heidelberg (2009)

Using User Personalized Ontological Profile to Infer Semantic Knowledge for Personalized Recommendation

Ahmad Hawalah and Maria Fasli

School of Computer Science and Electronic Engineering
University of Essex
Colchester, UK
{ayhawa,mfasli}@essex.ac.uk

Abstract. A key feature in developing an effective web personalization system is to build and model a dynamic user profiles. In this paper, we propose a novel method to construct user personalized ontological profiles based on each user's interests and view. We also propose an Enhanced Spreading Activation Technique (ESAT) to infer and recommend new items to a user based on each user's personalized ontological profile. Using the MovieLens dataset, we show that our approach achieves the highest prediction accuracy, and outperforms other recommendation approaches that were proposed in the literature.

Keywords: recommender system, ontological user profile, user modeling, spreading activation.

1 Introduction

Since the information volume in the Internet is growing drastically, there is a more need for personalization and recommender systems. The main aim of such systems is to provide users with tailored contents based on each user needs and preferences. Many recommender systems have been proposed in the literature to recommend contents based on each user's interests [1, 2, 3, 4, 5]. However, during the last few years, ontology has been widely used with recommender systems. Many studies in the literature proposed using a domain or reference ontology to model user profiles and hence provide more effective personalization and recommendation [6, 7, 8]. Typically, most of these studies create an instance of a domain ontology and assign it to each user (i.e. called ontological user profiles). However, this technique of constructing ontological user profiles has many limitations. The first limitation is that the ontological profiles are constructed as instances of a reference ontology. Therefore, all users would have the same profile ontology but with different interest weights associated to the interested concepts. The main problem of such profile construction is that any reference ontology is usually designed by ontology engineers based on their understanding of the ontology's domain. Such representation of a reference ontology does not necessarily reflects each user's view on the domain. Moreover, each user may have different view of how a number of concepts might be related and linked to each other. This view is typically formed based on each user's personal experience and preferences. Therefore, it would be infeasible to assign the same instance of ontology to all users.

C. Huemer and T. Setzer (Eds.): EC-Web 2011, LNBIP 85, pp. 282–295, 2011.

Another important limitation of current approaches in personalization is that most of the users profiling approaches rely just on the structure and relations of a reference ontology which are explicitly identified to provide personalization. These approaches are incapable to infer and exploit hidden semantic relations between interested concepts in user profiles. This lack of inference would defiantly impact on the recommendation that is provided to users, and hence the overall performance.

Therefore, in this paper, we propose a new mechanism to construct a *Personalized Ontological Profile (POP)* which is formed based on each user's interests and view. In this personalized ontological profile, the hidden knowledge and relationships between concepts is exploited. The discovered knowledge is then utilized to provide a personalized ontological representation that is capable to automatically reason and adapt itself to the changes in a user's behaviour implicitly without the need of any intervention from the user. Based on the constructed POP, a novel mechanism that is called an *Enhanced Spreading Activation Technique (ESAT)* to infer and recommend new items to a user is proposed. In this mechanism some of the limitations of current Spreading Activation techniques are addressed and overcome. Finally, we validate our approaches on using a Movie dataset.

2 Previous Work

Many studies in the field of personalization have suggested diverse tools and techniques to infer, extend and recommend new items and services that users might be interested in. Collaborative and content-based filtering are two widely developed and applied techniques to provide recommendation to users in the literature [1,2,3,4,5]. In collaborative filtering, the main assumption is that similar users are likely to be interested in similar items. The main mechanism in this approach is to compare each user's interests with other users' interest histories to find the most similar users (i.e. neighbours). These historical interests of neighbours are then used to provide recommendation to a user. Many studies have applied this approach to provide personalized experience. Mobasher, Jin and Zhou [1] for example, have investigated utilizing item semantic information for computing similarities in order to provide more accurate recommendation. However, collaborative filtering has been argued to have some limitation when handling for example cold-start and first-start situations [1].

On the other hand, content-based filtering provides recommendations based on a user's previous interactions and interests. The main goal of this approach is to capture user interests (implicitly or explicitly) and provide more items or services similar to the captured interests. One popular technique that is used in content-based filtering is the Spreading Activation mechanism. Many studies have employed this mechanism to explore user ontological profiles in order to infer and recommend items and services that a user might be interested in [2, 3, 5]. Blanco-Fernández et al. [2] for instance, suggested exploiting the semantic information of user interests and applying spreading activation mechanism in order to overcome the overspecialization problem in recommendation. A semantic reasoning mechanism over ontologies was proposed to find semantically related items to users' actual interests. Liang et al. [3] also proposed a semantic-expansion approach based on the spreading activation. User interests, which are extracted from a user reading history, are presented in this study as keyword vectors.

Liang et al. suggested using a semantic-expansion method based on the spreading activation technique to construct a semantic-expansion network. This network contains all the new extended concepts which would be recommended to a user.

3 Personalized Ontological Profile (POP)

In this section we propose a new approach to construct a personalized ontological profile (hereinafter POP) for each user. This approach includes three phases: (1) capturing user interests, (2) building the POP, (3) grouping related concepts together.

Capturing users' interests and preferences in the first phase is the key element in any personalization system. These interests and preferences could be collected explicitly by asking each user about what preference they like [9], or implicitly from click-history data [10], semantic web browsing [8, 11] or log files [12]. In both ways, a list of interests with weights would be available which represents each user's interests and preferences. In this paper, we assume that the interests and their weights are already available. However, we make no assumption about how these interests are collected as our approach is fixable to model and adapt to any type.

Once user interests are available, the second phase which is building the POP is initialized. The main goal of this phase is to first exploit the hidden semantic relationships between all the user interests and then to combine all related interests into groups. For the first point, we borrow the method of the lowest common ancestor that was proposed by Aho et al. [13]. The main idea behind this method is to link interested concepts under the lowest common ancestor. However, one limitation of this method is relying on just hierarchal concepts. As we use ontology in this paper, we extend this approach to include any hierarchal and non-hierarchal concepts. Moreover, we consider more complex ontologies where concepts might have more than one hierarchal parent. In order to deal with each of these challenges, we introduce six semantic relations which might occur between any two concepts:

- Direct Parent-Child relation (Direct P-C): when one concept is a direct hierarchal parent of the other concept (e.g. Romance → Titanic in Fig. 1).
- Indirect Parent-Child relation (Indirect P-C): two concepts are Indirect P-C related when these two concepts are not Direct P-C related and one of them is a super-concept of the other. (e.g. Romance → James Cameron in Fig. 1).
- Direct Shared-Parent relation (Direct S-P): two concepts are Direct S-P when these two concepts share the same direct parent (e.g. adventure and action in Fig. 1 share the same parent Movie Genre).
- Indirect Shared-Parent relation (Indirect S-P): two concepts are Indirect S-P when these two concepts share the same parent in any level, but not the direct parent (e.g. The Da Vinci Code and Avatar are Indirect S-P in Movie Genre in Fig. 1).
- Direct Shared-Child relation (Direct S-C): two concepts are Direct S-C when these two concepts share the same direct sub-concept or property (e.g. Cast away and Forrest Gump both played by Tom Hanks in Fig. 1).
- Indirect Shared-Child relation (Indirect S-C): when two concepts share the same sub-concept or property in any level but not the direct sub-concept or property (e.g. Mystery and Forrest Gump in Tom Hanks in Fig. 1).

All of the above relation types are important when building user POP and grouping related concepts together. In order to group two or more concepts together, it is important to explore whether these concepts share at least one common characteristic or not. Generally, the philosophy of this idea is to reason users' interests and try to find hidden semantic relations among them. In general, people in real life for example, can classify any related person to them based on this person's situation and characteristic. For example, if two people are brothers, then their relationship can be described as a family. If two people are students in the same classroom, then we can address them as classmates. However, in some cases people might share more than one characteristic. For example two students might be brothers and at the same time attend the same classroom. In this case, these two people would be both family and classmates, and hence their relations would be stronger than if they share just one characteristic. In this paper, we attempt to apply this concept when constructing user ontological profile. When a user shows some interest in some concepts, we firstly process each concept and try to see how this concept can be added to the user ontology with regards to the relations with other existed concepts. For each new concept, two different scenarios are proposed.

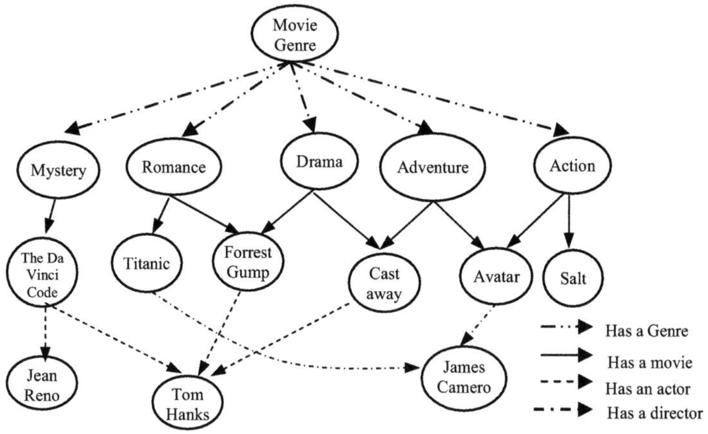

Fig. 1. A fragment of a movie ontology

General group (G-Group): A general group is basically created to group a set of concepts that do not share a specific characteristic (i.e. two people being brother) but rather share a general characteristic (i.e. two people are human being). With respect to ontological user profiles a general group is created when the lowest common ancestor of a new concept and other concepts in the profile is Indirect S-P. As a result we group such concepts and create a general group. For example, if a user profile contains two interesting movies *The Da Vinci Code* and *Avatar*, then these two movies would be in a general group as there is no common specific characteristics other than that both concepts are movies (see figure 2.1).

Specific group (S-Group): A specific group is created when two or more concepts share the same direct related parents (Direct S-P), or if the new concept is a Direct or Indirect P-C related to an existed concept. However, if one of the existed concepts is already in a general group, then this concept would be disjoined and a new S-group that contains both this concept and the new one would be created. To illustrate, in figure 2.2 a user shows an interest in a new movie Titanic. As the movie Titanic and Forrest Gump have the same lowest common ancestor *Romance*, the Forrest Gum is disjoined from the G-Group (see figure 2.1) and a new S-Group is created which includes Titanic and Forrest Gump. However, S-group can also be created if two or more concepts are Direct or Indirect S-C related. Furthermore, a concept might be a member of more than one S-Group as for example two movies might be in one S-group if they were played by the same actor, or directed by the same director. For illustration, in figure 2.3 a new movie Cast Away is added to the user profile. As we firstly search for other concepts with respect to the lowest common ancestor, we found that a movie Forrest Gump and Cast Away have two characteristics in common. The first is that both movies are under the Drama Genre, and at the same time they both played by Tom Hanks. As a result, two S-groups are created a group that includes all Drama Movies, and a group that includes all movies that were played by Tom Hanks.

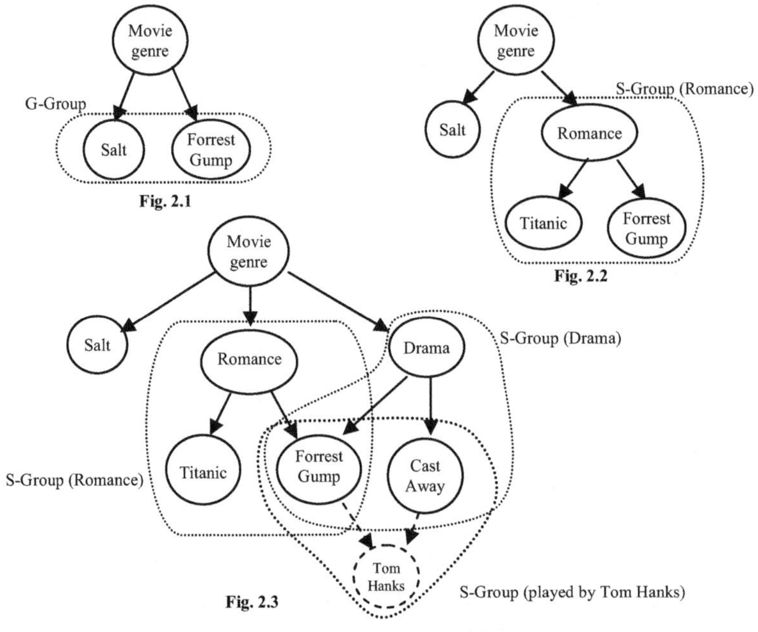

Fig. 2. General and specific groups

The above proposed approach allows us to explore and infer more relationships between concepts and interests. For example, from figure 2.3, our approach can infer that a user might be a fan of Tom Hanks based on his interest on Cast Away and Forest Gump movies even if this user did not explicitly provide this information. Moreover, the way of structuring and constructing ontological user profiles provides two significant features. The first feature is to personalize a user ontological profile based on each user's perspective and preferences. This particular feature would be very important in large ontologies that contain complex and rich relations and where concepts might be classified under more than one super-concept. The second feature of the proposed approach is grouping concepts that share the same characteristic together. This feature allows us to understand not just what a user is interested in, but also why he might be interested in such concepts. Furthermore, when a set of related concepts appeared together at the same time in a user profile, they should be considered as more significant than if they appeared isolated. For example if a user is interested in The Da Vinci Code, Cast away and Forrest Gump movies, then we can infer that a user might have a stronger interest in movies played by Tom Hanks than other actors. So it would be feasible to recommend more movies played by Tom Hanks to this particular user. In the next section, this particular issue is addressed by firstly compute the strength of each group. Then for each group, we enhance the importance of all the concepts in this group based on its strength.

4 Computing the Group Strength

In this section we introduce a novel approach to compute a group strength based on the assumption that a set of related concepts appeared together at the same time would be more important than if they appeared isolated. However in order to address this assumption, different aspects should be considered. As a group in a user profile contains a set of concepts, the first and the most important aspect is to measure how these concepts are related to each other with respect to the reference ontology. Because ontologies provide highly expressive ground for describing concepts and a rich variety of interrelations among them, it is important to utilize a mechanism that is able to deal with such complicity. Therefore, in the next section we propose a new method to measure the semantic relatedness between two concepts in an ontology.

4.1 Computing Semantic Relatedness between Two Concepts

The main goal of this method is to find semantic relatedness between concepts taking into the consideration (1) the ontology's unique structure, (2) different types of relations including hierarchal and non-hierarchal (semantic) relations between concepts and (3) different properties that are tied to both the structure of an ontology and its relations. The first property that we consider is the depth of a concept. In this property, we assume that concepts deep in an ontology are more closely related than concepts higher in the ontology. The second property is the distance between two concepts. In this property, we assume that closer concepts are more related than far ones. The third property is the maximum depth of a concept. In addition, the concept's maximum depth is basically the maximum depth of its most specific leaf concept (sub-concept). For example, in figure 1, the maximum depth of a concept Drama is 4, because the most specific sub-concept under Drama is Tom Hanks (i.e. the root concept is considered as in depth 1).

Taking all the above aspects into the consideration, we propose a novel Semantic Relatedness Measure (SRM) that measures the relatedness between any two concepts in an ontology. In this method, the relation between two concepts which corresponds to any of the proposed relations in section 3 is measured as follows:

Stage 1: as each relation type in an ontology has different meaning, we assign a different weight to each relation. This weight w should reflect the membership degree between two direct concepts $w(c_i, c_j)$. For example, in figure 1, there are four different relations namely: *Has a genre*, *Has a movie*, *Has an actor* and *Has a director*. All of these types should be assigned weights that reflect their importance which not necessarily be the same.

Stage 2: computing semantic relatedness for Direct Parent-Child relation (Direct P-C). For any two concepts that share the same direct super-concept, we compute the semantic relatedness as follows:

$$Rel_{Direct\ P-C}\ (c_i, c_j) = \frac{w(c_i, c_j) \times c_{j\_level}}{c_{j\_max\ depth}} \quad (1)$$

Where: c_i is the super-concept of cj and cj is a sub-concept of c_i. $w(c_i, cj)$ is the weight of the relation between c_i and cj and it is identified using stage one. $cj_{\_level}$ is the hierarchal level of cj. $cj_{\ max\ depth}$ is the maximum depth of the concept cj.

Stage 3: computing semantic relatedness for Indirect Parent-Child relation (Indirect P-C). The semantic relatedness for Indirect P-C related concepts is computed as follows:

$$Rel_{\text{Indirect}\ P-C}\ (c_i, c_j) = \frac{\sum \text{DR}\,(c_i \rightarrow c_j) \times c_{i\_level}}{c_{j\_level} \times \sum |(c_i \rightarrow c_j)|} \quad (2)$$

Where $\sum \mathbf{DR}\,(c_i \rightarrow c_j)$ is the sum of the semantic relatedness weights between c_i and c_j. If a c_i is not directly related to c_j e.g. $c_i \rightarrow c_x \rightarrow c_j$ then the $\sum \mathbf{DR}\,(c_i \rightarrow c_j)$ = DR(c_i , c_x) + DR (c_x , c_j). $\sum |(\mathrm{c_i} \rightarrow \mathrm{c_j})|$ is the number of relations between c_i and c_j , c_{i_level} is the total number of concepts between the root and concept c_i, and it is given as follows:

$$c_{i\_level} = \sum |(root \rightarrow c_i)| \quad (3)$$

c_{j_level} is the total number of concepts between the root and the super-concept c_i and the number of concepts between c_i and c_j, and it is computed as follows:

$$c_{j\_level} = \sum |(root \rightarrow c_i)| + |(c_i \rightarrow c_j)| \quad (4)$$

Stage 4: computing semantic relatedness for Direct Shared-Parent relation (Direct S-P), Indirect Shared-Parent relation (Indirect S-P), Direct Shared-Child relation (Direct S-C) and Indirect Shared-Child relation (Indirect S-C). In order to compute the relatedness between concepts belong to any of these relations, we first compute the relatedness between each concept c_i and c_j and the common concept c_{common} using formula (1) or (2). Formula (1) is used when a concept and the common concept are Direct P-C, while the formula (2) is used when these concepts are Indirect P-C related. Then, we use the formula (5) to find the semantic relatedness of any Direct or Indirect S-P or S-C relations:

$$Rel\ (c_i, c_j) = Rel(c_{common}, c_i) * Rel(c_{common}, c_j) \quad (5)$$

Where c_{common} is the direct common concept that is shared by two concepts c_i and c_j. The final semantic relatedness between two concepts is a positive weight between [0,1]. After measuring the semantic relatedness for concepts in an ontology, we move to the second important aspect which is computing the strength of a group.

4.2 Computing the Group Strength

After measuring the semantic relatedness between concepts, we move to the second important aspect which should be considered when computing the strength of a group. As a group contains a set of members, the strength of this group should be based on the strength of the relations between its members. In other words, a group gains its strength from the relations among its members. Furthermore, not only the relation weights impact on the group strength, but also the number of members in such a group. That is, the more number of members in a group, the stronger the group gets. In order to address all of these assumptions; we first compute the semantic relatedness for all concepts in a group as we stated earlier, and then compute the average of all relation weights in a group using the next formula:

$$SR.average = \frac{\sum_{c \in G}^{n}(semantic\ relatedness\ (c_i, c_j))}{|total\ number\ relations|} \tag{6}$$

It should be noticed that all the relations including those between each two concepts and between concepts and the shared characteristic are considered when computing the average. For example, if we want to compute the average weight of the S-group (romance) in figure 2.3, we sum the semantic relatedness weights for (Romance, Titanic), (Romance, Forest Gump), (Titanic, Forest Gump) and then divide the total by the total number of relations which is three. Once the average is computed, we propose the next formula to compute the group strength taking into the account all the assumptions presented earlier.

$$Group\ strength = \alpha . \left(1 - \left(\frac{1 - SR.average}{\sqrt{2}_{((1-SR.average))+|\ relations|}} \right) \right) \tag{7}$$

Once we computed the strength of a group, the significance of its members can then be enhanced based on the computed group strength. The weight for each relation between two concepts in a group is adjusted based on the group strength. As each relation might have different weight, we propose the next formula to compute the new weight for each relation based on both the actual relation's weight and the group strength.

$$New\_RW(c_i, c_j) = \left(Old_{RW(c_i,c_j)} + Group\ strenght\right) - \left(Old_{RW(c_i,c_j)} * Group\ strenght\right) \tag{8}$$

Where New_RW is the new adjusted relation's weight, $Old_{RW(c_i,c_j)}$ is the old relation's weight and Group strength is the strength of the group that include both ci and cj.

Finally, by applying this formula to adjust all the relation weights between members in a group two advantageous are observed. The first is that we addressed the assumption that if a set of related concepts appeared together at the same time would be more important than if they appeared isolated. The next advantage is to adapt the relations' weights based on user interests and the relations between these interests.

Once the personalized ontological profile (POP) which might contains a number of groups is constructed, we can then extend user interests by inferring more concepts that a user might be interested in. In the next section, the widely used Spreading Activation technique is introduced to exploit personalized ontological profiles and infer more concepts to a user.

5 Enhanced Spreading Activation Technique (ESAT)

Spreading Activation (SA) technique is a computational mechanism to explore information in a network and then infer useful knowledge. SA technique consists of two components a semantic network and a SA mechanism. The semantic network contains nodes and relations between these nodes. Each node in the network has a weight and called an activation value which represents its importance. Similarly, the relations that link two nodes in the network also have weights that represent how nodes are related to each other. The second component of the SA technique is the SA mechanism which works as follows: (1) initial set of activation nodes are identified. (2) The activation value for each node is spread to all nodes that are linked to it. (3) The activation value of each new direct-related node is computed based on the input value from the referred node and the weight of the relation joining the two nodes. Therefore, the stronger the relation between the referred node and direct-related node, the larger activation value is assigned to the related node. (4) The SA process is repeated until a termination condition is met. The termination condition could be either reaching the end of the network, or reaching pre-defined maximum activated or processed nodes. (5) Finally, nodes with the highest activation values are selected.

However, this typical SA mechanism suffers from three essential limitations that restrain the process of inferring and extending user interests. These problems are (1) SA technique considers just the main structure of a network (in our case a reference ontology), but not the structure of user ontological profiles. (2) SA technique considers just direct relations between nodes, but not the semantic relations that might not be identified explicitly. As a result the SA technique is incapable to infer and exploit the hidden knowledge in a complex ontolgoies. (3) Typical SA technique use just pre-defined weights for relations between nodes. However, these weights which represent how two nodes are related to each other are usually static and might not represent users' preferences. In other words, a user might see that two particular nodes are closely related, while another user might consider the same two concepts as not related at all. In order to address all of these problems, we propose a novel SA mechanism called Enhanced Spreading Activation Technique (ESAT). As in the previous section we introduced a new approach to construct a personalized ontological profile based on each user's preferences and interests, we utilize users' personalized profiles and a reference ontology to provide more effective SA mechanism. In addition, by using users' personalized ontological profile we overcome the first limitation as a user ontological profile is basically constructed and formed with respect to each user's interests and preferences. The second limitation is also overcome as our proposed reasoning mechanism is able to infer and exploit hidden knowledge in the user profile. Finally, the third limitation is also addressed as we firstly used the Semantic Relatedness approach in section 4.1 that measures the relatedness between any two concepts based on the ontology's unique structure and the hidden semantic knowledge. Secondly, taking advantage of the grouping mechanism that was introduced in section 4.2 which is used to adapt and adjust the relation weights between concepts in a group. Therefore, the limitation three is addressed as relation weights are adaptable based on users' preferences. Finally, we introduce our ESAT algorithm which explains how the ESAT works as follows:

Algorithm 1. Enhanced Spreading Activation Technique (ESAT)

```
POP={IC_1, ..., IC_i} interested concept in personalized ontological user profile with interest score.
IW(IC_i), interest weight (the activation value).
GR_i , group in POP.
GS(GR_i), group strength of a group i.
AC = activator concept;
AV=0;
Initialize activatorQueue;
Initialize inferredConceptsQueue;
foreach IC_i ∈ POP do
    activatorQueue.Clear;
    IC_i.AV = IW(IC_i);
    activatorQueue.Add (IC_i);
    While activatorQueue.Count > 0 do
        AC_s= activatorQueue[0];
        activatorQueue.Remove (AC_s);
        if PassRestrictions (AC_s) do
            DirectRelatedConcepts = GetDirectRelatedConcepts(AC_s);
            foreach C_i in DirectRelatedConcepts do
                if IC_i and C_i in one GR do //if both these concepts in one group in POP
                    RW(IC_i, C_i) = (RW(IC_i, C_i) + (GR.strenght)) − (RW(IC_i, C_i) * (GR.strenght))
                end
                C_i.AV = (( RW(AC_s, C_i) * AC_s.AV ) + (RW(IC_i,C_i) * IW(IC_i))) / 2;
                activatorQueue.Add (C_i);
                if inferredConceptsQueue.Contains (C_i) do
                    C_i.AV += C_i.AV;
                    inferredConceptsQueue.Update (C_i);
                else
                    inferredConceptsQueue.Add (C_i);
                end
            end
        end
    end
end
Suggest top N items from the inferredConceptsQueue.
```

6 Experiment

In this section we look at whether our proposed approach of constructing the personalized ontological profiles (POP) and the ESAT are effective to firstly learn and adapt to users' interests and then to infer more concepts that might be of interest to them. In order to evaluate our system it is important to have two components: a reference ontology and a set of user interests. For this purpose, we use the data provided by the MovieLens data set[1] which consists of ratings of 940 real users on

[1] http://www.grouplens.org/node/73

1682 movies on a 1-5 rating scale. These movies are categorized based on the Internet Movie Database (IMDb[2]) which contains a total of 25 different categories. As there is no standard or common movie ontology, we first create a movie reference ontology based on the data extracted from the MovieLens dataset and the IMDb. This ontology contains two main classes: movie's genre and movie's name. For each movie, four properties are provided: actors, directors, country and year of release. Movies' names were extracted from the MovieLens dataset that contains 1682 movies, while other information was extracted from the IMDb by using a wrapper.

Users' personalized ontological profiles are then built from the MovieLens ratings. We firstly, select users with more than 60 ratings. For each user, 50 ratings are stored in a learning dataset, while the remaining ratings are stored in a test dataset. Then a number of ratings from the learning dataset are randomly selected and processed by our system in order to create a personalized ontological profile for each user. The spreading activation mechanism then processes the interests in each user profile and suggests 10 movies with the highest activation values. Finally, we compare the activation value for each suggested movie against the user's actual rating for the same movie in the test dataset. This experiment is repeated 6 times to test how our system would perform when our system constructs and learns a user profile using different N movie ratings (5, 10, 20, 30, 40 and 50) from the learning dataset. Finally, in order to measure the accuracy of the recommendations, the Mean Absolute Error (MAE) is used to compute the deviation between the predictions and actual user ratings. That is, having a set of actual user ratings ***a*** and predicted value ***p*** for ***n*** number of movies, the MAE is measured as:

$$\text{MAE} = \frac{\sum_{i=1}^{n} |a-p|}{n} \tag{9}$$

However, as the user ratings is between 1 and 5, and the predications made by our system are from 0 and above, we normalized all values to be from 0 to 1, and hence the MAE would be from 0 to 1.

6.1 Experiment1: Identifying α Value

In the first experiment we examined the impact of the parameter α in equation (7) on the performance of our approach by repeating the experiment when $\alpha \in \{0.1, 0.2 \ldots 1\}$. Next table demonstrates the average MAE for each α value.

Table 1. Average MAE of our approach using different α values

α	0.1	0.2	0.3	0.4	0.5	0.6	0.7	0.8	0.9	1
Average MAE	0.1556	0.1542	0.1525	0.1515	0.1523	0.1541	0.1565	0.1594	0.1625	0.1648

The optimal MAE is achieved when $\alpha = 0.4$. In the next experiment, we use this α value to recommend new movies to users and estimate the prediction ratings made by our approach.

[2] `http://www.imdb.com/`

6.2 Experiment 2: Prediction Accuracy

In this experiment, our proposed approach is used to recommend top 10 movies and predict their ratings. In order to evaluate our approach, we compare the performance of our approach against four different recommendation approaches. The first approach is using the ESAT without constructing personalize ontological profiles (POP), but with simple profiles construction. The second approach is popularity approach where recommendation is provided based on the popularity of each movie. This popularity is computed from all the users' ratings in the learning dataset. The third approach is a content-based recommendation approach. For this type we select the approach that was suggested by Liang et al. [3] which uses Spreading Activation technique to provide recommendations. We select this particular study as it is the most similar study to our work. The final approach is the item-based collaborative filtering recommendation approach as in [1]. Next figure shows the MAE which was computed across all these five approaches when using 5, 10, 20, 30 ,40 and 50 movie ratings in the user profile learning.

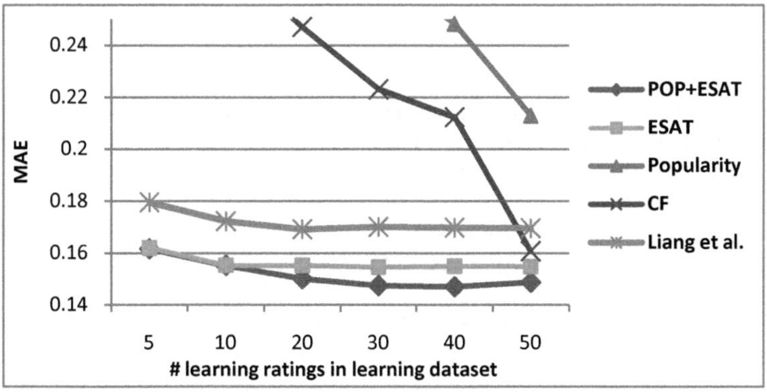

Fig. 3. MAE for five approaches using different N ratings

Figure 3 clearly shows the weakness of both CF and popularity approaches when a few number of ratings are available in the learning dataset. However, when 50 movie ratings are available for each user profile in the CF to learn from, the prediction accuracy improved substantially. However, with regards to our approach, figure 3 clearly demonstrates that using both POP and ESAT outperformed all other approaches. Moreover, as more number of ratings is available in the learning dataset, the better performance is achieved. However, when user profiles have just 5 or 10 movies, the results show that grouping related concepts together is not important as applying the ESAT with and without POP achieved similar results. However, when user profiles have more than 10 movies, our approach of using POP and ESAT started to provide better predictions. This shows that our approach is able to find hidden semantic knowledge and provide more accurate recommendations.

7 Conclusion and Future Work

In this paper, we presented an approach for constructing user personalized ontological profile (POP). The main feature of this approach is the ability to exploit the hidden semantic relations between user interests and to combine the related interest into groups (general or specific). A novel method was also proposed to compute the semantic relatedness between two concepts in an ontology. The weights of semantic relatedness between concepts in each group in the POP were then used to compute the strength of each group and adjust the relation weights between interested concepts in this group accordingly. In order to recommend new items to a user, an Enhanced Spreading Activation Technique was proposed (ESAT) that uses the semantic relatedness approach to build a semantic network. In this technique, we addressed and overcome different limitations that usually appear in spreading activation techniques. Our experiments showed that our approach achieved higher performance than other recommendation approaches. In the future work, we plan to investigate how the negative feedback might be considered to improve the overall performance of our approach.

References

1. Mobasher, B., Jin, X., Zhou, Y.: Semantically Enhanced Collaborative Filtering on the Web. In: Berendt, B., Hotho, A., Mladenič, D., van Someren, M., Spiliopoulou, M., Stumme, G. (eds.) EWMF 2003. LNCS (LNAI), vol. 3209, pp. 57–76. Springer, Heidelberg (2004)
2. Blanco-Fernández, Y., López-Nores, M., Pazos-Arias, J.: Adapting Spreading Activation Techniques towards a New Approach to Content-Based Recommender Systems. IIMSS 6, 1–11 (2010)
3. Liang, T.P., Yang, Y., Chen, D., Ku, Y.C.: A semantic-expansion approach to personalized knowledge recommendation. Decision Support Systems 45, 401–412 (2007)
4. Sieg, A., Mobasher, B., Burke, R.: Improving the effectiveness of collaborative recommendation with ontology-based user profiles. In: Proc. of Intl. WIHFR, pp. 39–46 (2010)
5. Gao, Q., Yan, J., Liu, M.: A Semantic Approach to Recommendation System Based on User Ontology and Spreading Activation Model. In: IFIP, pp. 488–492 (2008)
6. Challam, V., Gauch, S., Chandramouli, A.: Contextual Search Using Ontology-Based User Profiles. In: Proceedings of RIAO 2007, Pittsburgh, USA (2007)
7. Jiang, X., Tan, A.: Learning and inferencing in user ontology for personalized Semantic Web search. Information Sciences: an International Journal 179 (2009)
8. Liang, T.P., Lai, H.-J.: Discovering user interests from Web browsing behavior. In: International Conference on Systems Sciences, pp. 203–212 (2002)
9. Paramythis, A., König, F., Schwendtner, C., van Velsen, L.: Using Thematic Ontologies for User- and Group-Based Adaptive Personalization in Web Searching. In: Detyniecki, M., Leiner, U., Nürnberger, A. (eds.) AMR 2008. LNCS, vol. 5811, pp. 18–27. Springer, Heidelberg (2010)
10. Li, L., Yang, Z., Wang, B., Kitsuregawa, M.: Dynamic Adaptation Strategies for Long-Term and Short-Term User Profile to Personalize Search. In: APWeb, pp. 228–240 (2007)

11. Sumalatha, M.R., Vaidehi, V., Kannan, A., Anandhi, S.: Information Retrieval using Semantic Web Browser-Personalized and Categorical Web Search. In: ICSCN 2007, pp. 238–243 (2007)
12. Mohammed, N.U., Duong, T.H., Jo, G.S.: Contextual Information Search Based on Ontological User Profile. In: Pan, J.-S., Chen, S.-M., Nguyen, N.T. (eds.) ICCCI 2010. LNCS, vol. 6422, pp. 490–500. Springer, Heidelberg (2010)
13. Aho, A., Hopcroft, J., Ullman, J.: On Finding Lowest Common Ancestors in Trees. SIAM J. Comput., 115–132 (1976)

Beyond Similarity-Based Recommenders: Preference Relaxation and Product Awareness

Maciej Dabrowski[1] and Thomas Acton[2]

[1] Digital Enterprise Research Institute Galway
National University of Ireland Galway, Ireland
maciej.dabrowski@deri.org
[2] Business Information Systems Group
J.E. Cairnes School of Business & Economics
National University of Ireland Galway, Ireland
thomas.acton@nuigalway.ie

Abstract. Product awareness is an important aspect of online shopping decisions. Contemporary product catalogs aim at improving customers' decisions through products search and filtration. Form-based tools that are offered filter out products that do not fully match stated requirements, leading to lower product awareness and thus affecting overall decision quality. This research proposes preference relaxation as an alternative to existing similarity-based product recommendation agents used in such context. Building on previous work, we discuss two variants of a novel method for preference relaxation, so called Soft-Boundary Preference Relaxation with Addition and with Replacement, and evaluate their effect on product awareness in a user experiment with 87 participants. Our results indicate that the preference relaxation methods, in particular the Soft-Boundary Preference Relaxation with Replacement, can be successfully used to improve customers' product awareness in online catalogues.

Keywords: Recommender Systems, Preference Relaxation, eCommerce, Decision Making.

1 Introduction

Consumers seeking a suitable product online, such as a car to buy or an apartment to rent , often need to choose from a considerable number of options. To address this issue e-commerce sites offer functionality to search or filter products, usually by asking a user to fill a form to provide preferences for a desired product. The process of searching online product catalogues to locate the product(s) that best match consumers product needs is often referred to as preference-based search [1], and often demands iterative refinement of consumers preferences to arrive to product lists of a manageable size. Product search requires effort and can be very frustrating [2], and so aiding consumers in preference formation is one of the key concerns in online shops.

C. Huemer and T. Setzer (Eds.): EC-Web 2011, LNBIP 85, pp. 296–307, 2011.

Numerous studies propose the use of recommendations or suggestions to improve consumer decision-making [3,4]. The preference-based search tools referred to as recommendation agents (RAs) [5] are organized using the following categories: content and/or collaborative recommender systems, utility-based tools, and preference relaxation methods. The great majority of existing preference relaxation techniques are applied to avoid cases where no products match specified requirements (so called failing queries [6]). The existing tools supporting customers in online product search fail to fulfill the five objectives for preference-based search tools that impact overall performance of recommendation agents: (a) maximization of choice quality, (b) minimization of choice effort, (c) maximization of product awareness, (d) compensatory processing to enable identification of best offers that do not fully fit stated requirements, (e) relaxation of over-specified preferences - to avoid empty product search result lists (i.e. failing queries).

This paper discusses the limitations of existing recommendation agents and argues that the use of preference relaxation in product search, not only in cases of failing queries, is a valuable approach for the identification of product suggestions from the perspective of the five requirements mentioned above. In particular, the classical approach to preference relaxation [7], referred here as the Standard Preference Relaxation (see Section 3.2) may increase consumers decision-making performance when applied to all, not only failing, product search queries. Nevertheless, the major disadvantage of the Standard Preference Relaxation method is related to possible negative effect on decision effort. In order to address this drawback, this research proposes a novel Soft-Boundary Preference Relaxation method in two variants (with Addition and with Replacement) and examines its impact on consumers decision-making performance in a user experiment focused on the effects of the methods on product awareness.

The contributions of this work include the evaluation of the use of preference relaxation in product search in a comparative study of Logical Filtering, Standard Preference Relaxation, and Soft-Boundary Preference Relaxation. The experiments described in this paper extend the previous studies of the preference relaxation methods presented here, which involved a series of simulations based on a leave-one-out approach [8]. In this work we focus on the impact of the discussed methods on product awareness indicated by diversity of consideration sets (i.e. items seriously considered for purchase) formed by customers shopping for products, and by the share of accepted suggestions they seriously consider for purchase. We report the results of a between-subjects experiment that involved 87 participants and show that the Soft-Boundary Preference Relaxation method outperforms Logical Filtering and Standard Preference Relaxation.

The remainder of the paper is structured as follows. First, we give an overview of the problem under study. Further, we define the preference relaxation methods studied in this work in Section 3 and define a set of research hypotheses in Section 4. The evaluation methodology, the experimental results, and the discussion of findings are detailed in the Section 5. Finally, we conclude the paper with an overview of the contributions in Section 6.

2 Background

A number of studies studies propose the use recommendations to improve consumer decision-making performance [1,4]. Among many approaches (see [9] for a detailed review), similarity-based recommenders are one of the most popular methods for identification of product suggestions. On the other hand, recent studies [10] indicate that recommendation agents (RA) [5] should provide a consumer with a set of product choices that contains offers not only similar to their stated preferences (i.e. relevant) but also diverse, to improve product awareness. Indeed, according to the Look-ahead principle [1],"suggestions should not be optimal under the current preference model, but should provide high likelihood of optimality when an additional preference is stated". Diverse sets of suggested products aid customers in formation of more accurate preference models [1] and cater for dynamism in user preferences - a problem recognized in recommender systems research [11].

Many existing shopping websites offer product search mechanisms, typically based on a form-filling approach [1] where customers state their desired product characteristics or preferred ranges of attribute values (e.g. acceptable price). The assumption that the decision maker can accurately state which levels within an attribute are acceptable versus unacceptable is a fundamental to a self-explicated approach [12]. Further, product search and filtering mechanism offered online adhere to a conjunctive approach in which all the alternatives that possess at least one attribute with unacceptable values are rejected from further consideration. However, Klein [13] found that decision makers often fail to reject alternatives with attribute levels which they themselves had previously described as unacceptable, and found that significant numbers of participants can choose an alternative described with at least one attribute level they initially indicated as "completely unacceptable", which indicates that the conjunctive approach is not suitable for shopping scenarios. Indeed, the rigidity of typical preference elicitation (filtering) mechanisms is a well established problem [14] that can not only affect decision quality but also lead to elimination of all available products from consideration. In such cases, preference relaxation [7], often implemented based on similarity [6], is used to identify product suggestions that do not fully fit the requirements stated by a customer. However, if such suggestions are identified solely based on similarity and/or diversity, they may not be valuable to customers and thus impact quality of their decisions. Preference relaxation mechanisms may assist in alleviating such problems. Further, a decision aid supporting preference relaxation can be seamlessly integrated with the existing online shopping websites to improve consumer decisions.

Our research differs from these approaches in a number of ways. First, we primarily focus on reduction of type I error by extending the preferences provided by a consumer (which, however, can lead to discovering alternatives that may lead to providing preference on additional attributes). Second, we propose the Soft-Boundary Preference Relaxation method (see the next section) that augments the similarity-based approaches to product recommendations with the

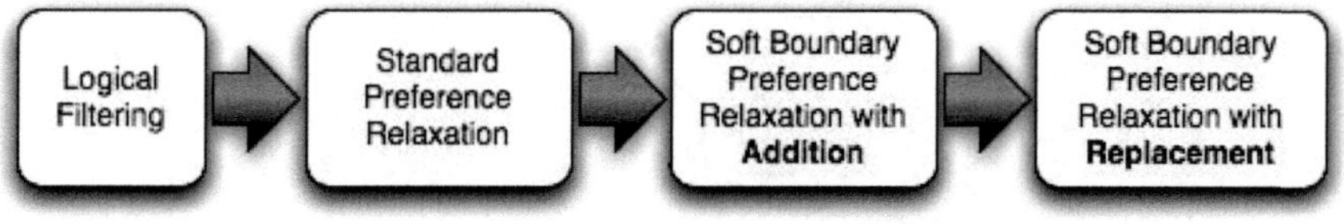

Fig. 1. Summary of preference relaxation methods

focus on higher quality of suggestions. We argue that the preference relaxation methods discussed here can positively impact product awareness and lead to improvement in decision-making performance of online store customers.

3 Preference Relaxation Methods

Consider a customer who intends to buy a used car priced between 7000 and 8000 with reasonable mileage (25k to 75k km). Would he or she be willing to pay slightly more (8100) for a car with mileage lower than expected (11000 km)? The ability to locate offers with such characteristics which, albeit require compromise, may provide consumers with a better awareness of possible choices they find valuable.

This section provides a comprehensive overview of the preference relaxation methods (see Figure 1) evaluated in this paper.

3.1 Logical Product Filtering

To avoid information overload, common techniques such as filtration are used to limit the number of products presented to customers to only those items that fully match the criteria they stated. In the above example, a customer using such a product search tool, and who provided preferences on price (7000 to 8000) and mileage (25k to 75k km) would be presented with only those offers that fully satisfy all the stated criteria, that is, are both within the price and mileage range. This approach is often referred to as product filtration using hard-constraints or logical filtering [7] and has a number of limitations acknowledge in the literature.

3.2 Standard Preference Relaxation

When no products that fully satisfy stated customers requirements are available in a store, preference relaxation mechanism can be employed to relax over-specified product requirements and inform customers about available options that partially fit their needs. For example, it there are no offers in the 7000 to 8000 price range, the preference can be relaxed to retrieve product suggestions that satisfy a less strict requirement (e.g. 6750 to 8250). However, the extent of relaxation is not a trivial task. In contrast to other studies [6,7], this work investigates the application of the Standard Preference Relaxation (SR) to all product search queries

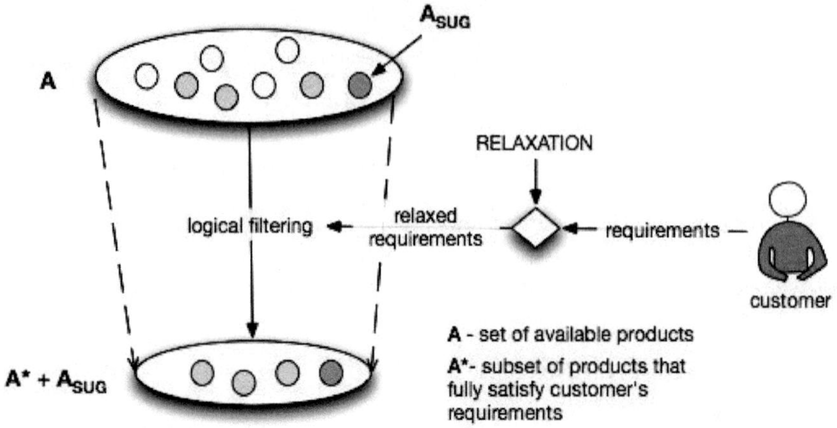

Fig. 2. Summary of preference relaxation methods

3.3 Soft-Boundary Preference Relaxation

The number of product suggestions identified by the standard method (SR) can be very high. Therefore, in contrast to common similarity-based approaches [7], the methods proposed in this article suggest the use of concepts from the Decision Theory (e.g. Pareto-optimality and utility [15]) to identify a small number of optimal product suggestions that are not necessarily the most similar to customers requirements. Thus, the Soft-Boundary Preference Relaxation (SBR) methods minimize the additional effort related to the inclusion of additional, suggested offers in the result set, maximize the quality and diversity of the recommendations while taking into account the degree to which they satisfy customers needs through similarity. In the SBR with Addition variant, the identified suggestions are added to the result set. To further minimize additional decision effort, we propose the SBR with Replacement, where the products of low value to customer (identified with an algorithm that uses the concept of Edge Sets [8] to soften the preference bounds) are replaced with the high quality suggestions. Please refer to [8] for details on the methods and algorithms described in this section.

4 Hypotheses

Commensurate with the results of the previous studies [8] that employed simulations based on a *Leave-one-out* [16] method to provide initial comparison the preference relaxation methods discussed here, we expected both Standard Preference Relaxation (SR) and Soft-Boundary Preference Relaxation (SBR) methods to positively influence customers product awareness. Vahidov and Ji argued that customers make more satisfactory decisions when provided with product suggestions that educate them about available product options and that positively influence their product awareness [17]. Tools that support online product search should therefore increase product awareness through recommendation of quality offers that may not fully satisfy stated pro-duct requirements. Such tools, also referred to as compensatory recommendation agents [18], minimize elimination of valuable alternatives and increase the diversity of products considered by customers. Indeed, many studies highlight that recommendation agents should allow consideration of a diverse set of products. Therefore, the use of preference relaxation should allow customers to evaluate valuable alternatives that would have been filtered out otherwise and lead to more diverse consideration sets. On the other hand, product suggestions should be acceptable to customers. Viappiani and Falting [19] proposed the look-ahead principle and argued that product suggestions should be optimal after probable adjustments of customers preferences, not according to the current preference model. Although some methods [20,7] produce very diverse sets of recommendations, customers are very likely to reject suggestions that are too dissimilar to their current product requirements [6]. Therefore, a recommendation agent should seek to provide customers with product suggestions that they are willing to accept. We expected that the preference relaxation methods examined in this study provide quality suggestions that would be accepted by customers. This expectation regarding the Standard Preference Relaxation and the Soft-Boundary Preference Relaxation methods was formalized with the following hypotheses:

H1: Standard Preference Relaxation (SR) increases product awareness.
H2: Soft-Boundary Preference Relaxation (SBR) with Addition increases product awareness.
H3: Soft-Boundary Preference Relaxation (SBR) with Replacement increases product awareness.

5 Evaluation

5.1 Datasets

Two datasets described in detail in this section were used in the user study.

Digital cameras. Following existing research in Recommender Systems [9,5], the first dataset used in our experiment consisted of 1813 digital cameras extracted from Amazon.com[1] web store available in the "Point & Shoot Digital Cameras" category. The products were extracted using Java software and Web Services API provided by Amazon . Information on a number of attributes was collected for each product: brand, model, price, zoom, screen size, resolution, and weight. Furthermore, customer rating on each product was also extracted. The above attributes were manually classified into cost-type and benefit-type categories.

Used car advertisements. The second dataset consisted of 2650 used car advertisements collected from the most popular website in Ireland (`http://carzone.ie/`,

[1] `http://amazon.com/`

a member of Autotrader media group). Additional attributes for used cars in the set not present in advertisements, such as reliability, were automatically generated using standard information retrieval methods based on product reviews collected from car review websites (e.g. whatcar.com). Generated attributes were classified as benefit-type and given scores ranging from 0 to 5 to resemble star ratings (e.g. 5 points for maintenanceCost describes the relatively lowest maintenance cost).

5.2 Method

Our experiment involved three steps: a tutorial that demonstrated the use of shopping website used in the experiments, a practice task that allowed participants to familiarize themselves with the system, and a main task. This section describes the steps of the user experiment in detail.

First, the system explained the purpose of the study and the experimental procedure to participants. Next, the pre-task questionnaire was deployed to assess participants familiarity with the task used in the experiment. Further the demonstration of software used in the shopping task was given, followed by the practice task which followed the same procedure as the main task and with similar complexity, however in a different domain (digital camera selection). Upon completion of the practice task subjects were asked to complete the main task that involved used car selection, following suggestion by Pereira [21]. The experimental procedure was evaluated with think aloud sessions.

5.3 Indicators

In our study a number of indicators were used to evaluate the four methods: non-relaxing (NR), standard relaxation (SR), Soft Boundary Preference Relaxation with addition (SBR_{ADD}), and with replacement (SBR_{REP}). In this work, we focus on the indicators of product awareness outlined below.

Product awareness is considered an important aspect of preference-based product search. Recommendation agents that provide customers with a diverse set of product suggestions educate them about available alternatives and allow adjustments of product requirements used in filtration, to find products that better satisfy customers needs [17,22]. The research on recommender systems [10,17] provides evidence that increased diversity of considered products leads to higher customer decision satisfaction [23]. On the other hand, product suggestions provided by recommendation agents satisfy only some requirements stated by a customer, therefore increase product awareness [24,25]. Many recommendation methods provide customers with products that educate them about available alternatives, thus help in improving the accuracy of their stated preferences (i.e. better fit to actual product needs) and assist in selection of more satisfactory products [19]. Therefore, this study employs the diversity of products seriously considered for purchase, and the share of recommended product suggestions in the final consideration set as indicators of consumers product awareness:

(a) Diversity of products in the consideration set
(b) Share of product suggestions in the final consideration set

Table 1. Mean diversity of consideration sets

Group	N	Mean	SD	Shapiro-WIlk's p
NR	22	.081	.035	.548
SR	20	.073	.042	.512
SBR_{ADD}	24	.082	.037	.262
SBR_{REP}	22	.115	.047	.830

5.4 Results

This section presents the experimental results for both objective performance indicators outlined in Section 5.3. Each subsection presents the relevant statistical analysis and describes the impact of the results on the research hypotheses.

Diversity of Products in Consideration Set. A one-way between the groups analysis of variance test was conducted to explore the effects of preference relaxation on the diversity of consideration sets. Analyses were performed for sets containing at least two alternatives.

First, the Shapiro-Wilk's test was conducted to assure the normality assumption. The results (see Table 1) indicate that mean values for diversity of final consideration sets followed a normal distribution ($p = .548$, $p = .512$, $p = .262$, and $p = .830$ respectively). Furthermore, Levene's test indicated no significant differences in variances among the groups ($F = 1.216$, $p = .309$).

The results of one-way ANOVA (see Table 2) show statistically significant differences [$F(3, 84) = 4.627$, $p = .005$] in diversity among the groups (see Table 2). The effect size measured with Eta Squared was large (Eta Squared = .142). Post-hoc analysis using Tukey's HSD test indicated that the mean diversity of the final consideration set of the SBR_{REP} group was significant in comparison to NR ($p = .030$), SR ($p = .006$), and SBR_{ADD} ($p = .032$). As no other differences were statistically significant, the results indicate rejection of hypothesis H1 for the this factor. On the other hand, Soft-Boundary Relaxation with Replacement led to higher diversity in consideration sets, thus providing support for the hypothesis H3 and rejection of the hypothesis H2 for this factor.

Share of Accepted Suggestions in Final Consideration Set. Non-parametric tests were conducted to evaluate differences among those groups that presented product suggestions together with search results. Thus three groups

Table 2. Results of one-way ANOVA for diversity

	Sum of Squares	df	Mean Square	F	Sig.	Eta Squared
Between Groups	.022	3	.007	4.627	.005	.142
Within Groups	.135	84	.002			
Total	.157	87				

Table 3. Average share of suggestions (non-dominated) in final consideration set

Group	Mean	Median	Shapiro-WIlk's p
SR	43.2%	46.4%	.013
SBR_{ADD}	47.7%	49.2%	.002
SBR_{REP}	51.9%	60.0%	.006

(Standard Relaxation, Soft-Boundary Relaxation with Addition, and Soft-Boundary Relaxation with Replacement) were compared based on the share of high-quality (non-dominated) suggestions in final consideration sets. First, the Shapiro-Wilk's test was performed to check the normality of distribution assumption. The results (see Table 3) indicated that share of non-dominated suggestions in the final consideration set did not follow a normal distribution (p = .013, p = .002, and p = .006 respectively).

Analysis using a Kruskal-Wallis test revealed that there was no significant difference ($\chi^2(2,74) = .768$, p = .692) between the Standard Relaxation and both Soft-Boundary Relaxation methods. Although the median share for the Soft-Boundary Preference Relaxation with Addition (Median = .492) and Soft-Boundary Relaxation with replacement (Median = .600) were higher than in case of Standard Relaxation, the differences were not statistically significant. The total share of suggestions in the final consideration set was also examined.

First, the Shapiro-Wilk's test was performed to check the normality assumption. The results (see Table 4) indicated that the total share of suggestions in the final consideration set did not follow a normal distribution (p = .000, p = .002, and p = .006 respec-tively). Analysis using a Kruskal-Wallis test revealed that there was a significant difference ($\chi^2(2,73) = 11.041$, p = .004) between the Standard Relaxation and both Soft-Boundary Relaxation methods. The median share for the Soft-Boundary Preference Relaxation with Addition (Median = .492) and Soft-Boundary Relaxation with replacement (Median = .600) were significantly lower than in case of the Standard Relaxation method (Median = 1.000). Participants using preference relaxation methods were likely to accept the suggestions proposed by the recommendation agent. Although the Standard Relaxation method resulted in a higher share of accepted suggestions in the consideration set only a subset of these suggestions (50%) were of high quality. Overall, Soft-Boundary Preference Relaxation led to higher share of non-dominated suggestions in final consideration sets. The results suggest that preference relaxation methods provide customers with high quality suggestions that are acceptable by customers and increase their product awareness, thus providing support for hypotheses H2 and H3.

5.5 Discussion

Our study highlights the benefits of applying preference relaxation approaches to product search to improve customers' product awareness. First, we showed that preference relaxation may improve the all described preference relaxation methods lead to higher product awareness through products suggestions accepted by

Table 4. Share of accepted suggestions in final consideration sets

Group	Mean	Median	Shapiro-WIlk's p
SR	81.2%	100.0%	.000
SBR_{ADD}	47.7%	49.2%	.002
SBR_{REP}	51.9%	60.0%	.006

Table 5. Summary of hypotheses

Hypothesis	**Diversity**	**Share of suggestions**	**Overall**
H1: Standard Preference Relaxation (SR) positively impacts product awareness	Rejected	Supported	Partially Supported
H2: Soft-Boundary Preference Relaxation with Addition increases product awareness	Rejected	Supported	Partially Supported
H3: Soft-Boundary Preference Relaxation with Replacement increases product awareness	Supported	Supported	Supported

customers. Indeed, our study showed that median share of high quality suggestions in final consideration sets was high. Roughly every second product considered by subjects for purchase was suggested by the relaxation mechanism. In particular, 46.6% for Standard Preference Relaxation, 49.2% and 60.0% for Soft-Boundary Preference Relaxation with Addition and with Replacement respectively. Consideration of there (recommended) products, which would have otherwise been not viewed by customers, demonstrates that preference relaxation methods successfully increased product awareness.

On the other hand, the second indicator of product awareness, that is, diversity of products in the final consideration set produced mixed results. For the Standard Preference Relaxation and the Soft-Boundary Preference Relaxation with Addition the results indicated no statistically significant differences between the diversity of consideration sets. Nevertheless, the results indicated significantly higher (with $p < .01$) diversity of considered products. This results may be attributed to the fact that subjects using the SR method dealt with much larger result sets (due to inclusion of many product suggestions) what caused information overload and led to application of choice heuristics. The analysis of overall share of accepted recommendations in final consideration sets seems to confirm this hypothesis as in case of SR method about 81% of products selected for detailed consideration were suggestions identified by the method (see Table 4).

6 Conclusions

This paper investigated the impact of preference relaxation on decision performance with focus on product awareness. We argued that during the process of filtering of the initial, very large set of products, consumers eliminate alternatives they could later consider, by providing inaccurate preferences for attributes and attribute values. In this paper we introduced and evaluated a model for a decision support tool based on preference relaxation that can limit the effects of the dynamic preferences of consumers addressing the limitations of existing methods. Moreover, we discussed the results of our experiments that show positive effects of Soft-Boundary Preference Relaxation on consumers' product awareness (see Table 5). The e-commerce application of our method to the existing form-based interfaces is straightforward and highly beneficial to providers of online shopping services as diverse result sets that lead to more consumer satisfaction and potentially higher customer retention [17].

References

1. Viappiani, P., Pu, P., Faltings, B.: Preference-based search with adaptive recommendations. AI Communications 21(2-3), 155–175 (2008)
2. Hagen, P.R., Manning, H., Paul, Y.: Must search stink? Technical report (June 2000)
3. Pu, P., Chen, L., Kumar, P.: Evaluating product search and recommender systems for e-commerce environments 8, 1–27 (June 2008)
4. Bridge, D., Ricci, F.: Supporting product selection with query editing recommendations. In: Proceedings of the 2007 ACM Conference on Recommender Systems. ACM, New York (2007)
5. Resnick, P., Varian, H.R.: Recommender systems. Communications of the ACM 40(3), 56–58 (1997)
6. McSherry, D.: Retrieval failure and recovery in recommender systems. In: 15th Artificial Intelligence and Cognitive Science Conference (AICS 2004), Castlebar, Ireland, pp. 319–338. Springer, Heidelberg (2004)
7. Mirzadeh, N., Ricci, F.: Cooperative query rewriting for decision making support and recommender systems. Applied Artificial Intelligence 21(10), 895–932 (2007)
8. Dabrowski, M., Acton, T.: Comparing techniques for preference relaxation: a decision theory perspective. In: 11th International Conference on Electronic Commerce and Web Technologies, EC-Web 2010 (2010)
9. Adomavicius, G., Tuzhilin, A.: Toward the next generation of recommender systems: A survey of the state-of-the-art and possible extensions. IEEE Transactions on Knowledge and Data Engineering 17(6), 734–749 (2005)
10. Smyth, B., McClave, P.: Similarity vs. diversity. In: Proceedings of the 4th International Conference on Case-Based Reasoning: Case-Based Reasoning Research and Development. Springer, Heidelberg (2001)
11. Cao, H., Chen, E., Yang, J., Xiong, H.: Enhancing recommender systems under volatile userinterest drifts. In: CIKM 2009: Proceeding of the 18th ACM Conference on Information and Knowledge Management, pp. 1257–1266. ACM, New York (2009), doi:10.1145/1645953.1646112
12. Klenosky, D.B., Perkins, W.S.: Deriving attribute utilities from consideration sets: An alternative to self-explicated utilities. Advances in Consumer Research 19(1), 657–663 (1992)
13. Klein, N.M.: Assessing unacceptable attribute levels in conjoint-analysis. Advances in Consumer Research 14, 154–158 (1987)

14. Chaudhuri, S.: Generalization and a framework for query modification. In: Proceedings: 6th International Conference on Data Engineering, pp. 138–145. IEEE Computer Soc Press, Los Alamitos (1990)
15. Keeney, R., Raiffa, H.: Decisions with Multiple Objectives: Preferences and Value Tradeoffs. Cambridge University Press, Cambridge (1993)
16. Burke, R.: Interactive critiquing forcatalog navigation in e-commerce. Artificial Intelligence Review 18(3-4), 245–267 (2002)
17. Vahidov, R., Ji, F.: A diversity-based method for infrequent purchase decision support in e-commerce. Electronic Commerce Research and Applications 4(2), 143 (2005)
18. Xiao, B., Benbasat, I.: E-commerce product recommendation agents: Use, characteristics, and impact. MIS Quarterly 31(1), 137–209 (2007)
19. Viappiani, P., Faltings, B.: Implementing example-based tools for preference-based search. In: Proceedings of the 6th International Conference on Web Engineering. ACM, New York (2006)
20. Stahl, A.: Approximation of utility functions by learning similarity measures. In: Logic versus Approximation. LNCS, pp. 150–172. Springer, Heidelberg (2004)
21. Pereira, R.E.: Optimizing human-computer interaction for the electronic commerce environment. Journal of Electronic Commerce 1(1), 23–44 (2000)
22. Mcginty, L., Smyth, B.: On the role of diversity in conversational recommender systems. In: Proceedings of the Fifth International Conference on Case-Based Reasoning, pp. 276–290. Springer, Heidelberg (2003)
23. McSherry, D.: Similarity and compromise. In: Ashley, K.D., Bridge, D.G. (eds.) ICCBR 2003. LNCS, vol. 2689, pp. 291–305. Springer, Heidelberg (2003)
24. Fan, W., Gordon, M.D., Pathak, P.: Effective profiling of consumer information retrieval needs: a unified framework and empirical comparison. Decision Support Systems 40(2), 213–233 (2005)
25. Pu, P., Viappiani, P., Faltings, B.: Increasing user decision accuracy using suggestions. In: Proceedings of the SIGCHI Conference on Human Factors in Computing Systems. ACM, New York (2006)

Author Index